RADICALISM IN AMERICA

Other Books by the Same Author

LEFT, RIGHT AND CENTER

THE COUNTERFEIT REVOLUTION

A WORLD IN REVOLUTION

THE CRISIS OF AMERICAN LABOR

WORKING MEN

AFRICA—AWAKENING GIANT

A COUNTRY IS BORN

THE FUTILE CRUSADE—ANTI-COMMUNISM
AS AMERICAN CREDO

RADICALISM
IN AMERICA

SIDNEY LENS

Illustrations supplied by Kean Archives, Philadelphia

THOMAS Y. CROWELL COMPANY
New York, Established 1834

To the impractical dreamers
who make history
While the practical ones
revive the jungle

ACKNOWLEDGMENTS

I AM DEEPLY GRATEFUL to Dr. Harry W. Laidler, director emeritus of the League for Industrial Democracy and one of America's foremost students of social movements, for reading this book in manuscript and giving me the benefit of his insights; to Dr. Harry Elmer Barnes, an equally renowned scholar and historian, who has fulfilled a similar function; to Professor Staughton Lynd of Yale, an associate in various ventures, who has taken time out from a grueling schedule to give this book his careful scrutiny. I, of course, am solely responsible for any errors that may remain despite their best efforts. I also am indebted to the Newberry Library in Chicago, which kindly made its facilities available to me, and above all to my effervescent wife, Shirley, who carries my burdens on her well-fortified shoulders.

CONTENTS

ILLUSTRATIONS

ILLUSTRATIONS

The seed ye sow, another reaps;
The wealth ye find, another keeps.

—PERCY BYSSHE SHELLEY

CHAPTER I

THE RADICAL AS HISTORY

THE ROLE of the radical throughout the ages has been as an antidote to privilege. Whatever his failings and ineptitudes, he has tried to repair the balance between those who have too much and those who have too little. In dozens of different ways, under innumerable philosophical flags, he has led, planned, or participated in social upheavals to uproot unjust societies and replace them with equitable ones. Where reactionaries (what we now mistakenly call the "radical" Right) would preserve and strengthen those institutions which uphold privilege, the radicals would extirpate them. Where the byword for the reactionary is self-interest, for the radical it is equality—either full equality in which all things are held in common, or, short of that, equality of opportunity. To level the material differences between men, to replace hate with love, division with unity, war with peace—these have been the goals of the radical. Whether they have been achieved, indeed whether they can be achieved, is another matter. But the radical's dream has sustained mankind since time immemorial, giving it hope and vision, purpose and meaning. It is the dream which has made nations great when they shared it, stagnant when they forgot it, and decadent when they lost it.

The radical has been a motor force of history. He has galvanized the "injured and oppressed" to remove roadblocks placed in the path of progress by the "rich and well born." If he does not always get credit for this role, it is because current radicals are usually bitterly castigated by the organs of the status quo which they challenge, while radicals of the past are made respectable by tradition. "Respectable" people, both here and in England, for instance, considered Samuel Adams a wild and dangerous revolutionary in 1775; today, of course, he is viewed as a respected founder of the Republic. "Dangerous revolutionaries" who came later and were similarly berated in their lifetimes, such as Frances Wright or "Big Bill" Haywood, are now viewed with indulgence by a society that no longer has anything to fear from them. But if the radical's part in history has been blurred, it is indisputable that he has been a vital and necessary part of it. Though his utopia has never been achieved, it has never been entirely sidetracked either. This has been particularly true of the United States.

Without the radical the United States would not have been born, for it was he who sparked the American Revolution and propelled it to victory. Without him the thirteen colonies might have remained disunited and enervated, like the twenty Latin-American republics. Certainly there would have been no *United* States, stretching from ocean to ocean. The territory that became ours through the Louisiana Purchase might have formed the base of a French empire in the Western Hemisphere and most of Latin America might have fallen prey to traditional British imperialism, as in India or Nigeria. Texas, California, New Mexico, and the lands in the West would have been the poaching grounds of other nations—Mexico, Russia, England, France—but not the United States.

Without the radical, post-Revolutionary America might also have aborted. Would the right to vote have been won so early? Free public schools? The Homestead Act? The abolition of slavery? The welfare measures of the twentieth century? The shortened work week? The relatively high living standards? The miracles of industrial advance? It is impossible to chronicle the story of the United States without noting the radical's contribution to it. Never has the radical achieved anything approximating total victory—not even in the Revolution—but he has usually been able to modify restrictive institutions. Though his ultimate dream of the ideal society has not reached fruition, he sowed innumerable reforms which the reformer later reaped. In these victories lay both his fulfillment and his frustration.

The radical's impact on the United States has taken many different forms in different periods, but, remarkably, has displayed broadly similar goals and often similar tactics.

Until early in the nineteenth century the radical fought in the main for a subversive concept called democracy; subsequently it was a subversive concept called socialism. But whether it was the radicalism of Nathaniel Bacon or that of Eugene V. Debs, the leitmotiv throughout has been to make men equal in fact as in theory. In Bacon's or Jefferson's time the road to equality seemed to lie in winning a patch of land for the common man and seeing to it that the patches were near equal. In Debs's time the road to equality seemed to lie in ownership by all men in common of the factories, railroads, and other means of production. Different milieus breed different means, even where the end object is the same. Yet there are common features throughout the saga.

Two centuries before Martin Luther King used the nobility of nonviolence as a protest against racial discrimination, Negro slaves submitted to torture and death rather than work for their slaveowners. Where Norman Thomas espoused cradle-to-the-grave welfare measures to close the gap between rich and poor, Frances Wright called for free public boarding schools to achieve equality between the children of the wealthy and the children of the downtrodden. The radical's goals, based on a variety of ideologies, or, frequently, on undisciplined blind fury, has been ever the same—to correct the balance between privilege and underprivilege.

In the colonial era, the radical strove to prevent the colonies from becoming, like Europe, a closed society.

During the Revolution, the radical sought not only independence from Britain but a host of reforms, including universal suffrage, that would protect the average man from *native* aristocrats.

For a half century after the Revolution, radicals tried to gain objectives implicit in the revolutionary struggle, such as free schools, free land, abolition of imprisonment for debt, so as to prevent a new institutionalization of privilege.

Overlapping this period and climaxed by the Civil War was the effort by another radical segment to emancipate millions of black men held in bondage.

More central to our story, as the industrial revolution took root, radicals turned to collectivist solutions—utopian communities, producers' cooperatives, but above all, beginning with mid-century and for a century thereafter, to Marxian socialism.

Now in the post-World War II period, with America embroiled in the problems of war and peace, civil rights, alienation, and cyberna-

[3]

tion, an undefined new Left is emerging, whose views cannot yet be catalogued and whose potentials are not yet certain, but which is nonetheless still seeking equality, freedom, justice, peace.

The strain of radicalism runs deep in the saga of the United States. It is neither legend nor footnote, but an integral part of American history. Without it, indeed, there is no American history.

CHAPTER II

COLONIAL REBELS

THE REBEL SPIRIT grew in early America as naturally as seed in good soil. It was not that the immigrants were radicals by persuasion. Except for a few, such as Roger Williams, most were motivated by mundane considerations. Captain John Smith and the band of 120 men who founded Jamestown in 1607 came to make their fortune. They were seeking not a new social order but, as Smith wrote, to "dig gold, wash gold, refine gold, load gold"—just as the Spanish had been doing, at much profit, in Latin America. When they could find no gold, they reconciled themselves to working the land. But what lay uppermost in their thoughts was improvement in their material plight. A couplet used in 1630 to entice men to the colonies expressed the prevailing hopes:

> *In England land scarce and labour plenty,*
> *In Virginia land free and labour scarce.*

There were some dissenters who sought freedom to practice religious "heresies," such as the Puritans who would "purify" the Established Church, or the Pilgrims who would separate from it. But even they had no intention of subverting the British system or undermining the crown. The majority of early Americans were average Englishmen imbued with old-world biases. The idea of government by consent of the governed clashed fiercely with their inbred notion that you had to obey your king whether he was good or bad. The term "democracy" they deemed subversive. God had never ordained, said the Puritan John Cotton in 1638, that democracy be considered "a fit government either for church or commonwealth."

If the "people be governor," he asked, "who shall be governed?" The only forms of rule "clearly approved and directed in scripture" were monarchy and aristocracy. To preach that all men, including servants and Indians, were equal was a blasphemy, subject to dire consequences. Quakers who made such statements in Boston or Salem might have an ear cut off or a tongue bored through.

The Puritans, at first, lived by these aristocratic principles. Though they had fled to the Western Hemisphere to escape the tyranny of the Established Church of England, they established a tyranny of their own. Their church and state were united in a restrictive theocracy. In their colony a man could not vote unless he belonged to the official church, and he could not belong to the official church unless approved by the clergy—an approval that was withheld from five out of six applicants. Whether he belonged, however, he was required to abide by its strictures, on penalty of banishment, imprisonment, and in some cases even execution if he did not. In their economic life the Puritan leaders were stodgy bourgeois for whom, in the words of one writer, "Interest is their Faith, Money their God and large Possessions the only Heaven they covet." Their meeting houses and churches reflected this belief in class hierarchy. The rich sat in the better pews, the poor in the lesser ones.

Yet even the Puritans had to modify their ways under the pressure of exigency. Since there was no Established Church here for them to "purify," they had to set up an independent one of their own. And because the colony grew too large, they had to decree *representative* government, even though they excluded those who did not own property from voting. Gradually, too, they had to deprive the clergy of its lay powers.

Whatever the original disposition of the colonists, circumstance prodded them all too often toward radical ideas and radical acts. Consider the Pilgrims who embraced democracy almost by accident. The 102 hardy souls who set sail on the *Mayflower* in September 1620 had made an arrangement with the Virginia Company to settle in its territory, north of Jamestown. But as cross winds and fierce storms drove their vessel northward, far from its original destination, they were faced with a problem. If they landed, as they must, elsewhere than Virginia, what form of government should they introduce? Some of the younger zealots suggested they use their "liberty" to recognize no foreign government—in other words, declare independence. The Mayflower Compact, drafted by the less headstrong and signed by all forty-one adult males, did not go that far, but it spoke of majority rule and promised "just and equal laws"—concepts which were then anathema in semifeudal England.

Once they unpacked in Plymouth, the Pilgrims had to make another decision: What kind of economic system should they adopt? Despite their religious dissent, they were not radical either in economic or political doctrine. Compared to the Anabaptists, Levellers, or Quakers they were in fact tame as punch. Yet they formulated a "common stock" plan that was nothing short of communistic. Under its terms the members of the community were to labor together for seven years, sharing from the common stock "their meat, drink, apparel, and all provisions." At the end of this period every adult, regardless of sex or ancestry, was to receive an equal share of the common capital and profits, including "the houses, lands, goods and chattels." The common stock plan did not work as conceived, and had to be abandoned rather early. But it is noteworthy how conditions jogged Americans in unforeseen directions.

The rebel spirit, it must be conceded, did not arise here completely untutored. The immigrants came from a society much more fluid than the rest of Europe. The old order in Britain had been under attack since the Peasants' Revolt of 1381. Though it was still a tight society—as late as 1775 only 160,000 of its nine million people enjoyed the right to vote—it was much looser than that of its neighbors on the Continent. Where France and Spain permitted only Catholics to leave for the New World, and in small number, Britain permitted emigration not only by members of its own state church but Puritans, separatists, and even Christian Communists. Spain transported its feudal baggage intact to the Western Hemisphere; Britain's was already rent. Thus the men who fled its borders had already been exposed to dangerous ideas before they embarked. Any small opportunity was likely to bring those ideas into play once more. Separated from the restraints of the mother country by a great ocean, living in sparsely settled communities, those opportunities were not infrequent.

The small Confederation of Portsmouth and Newport, for instance, declared in 1641 that "the government which this body politic doth attend unto . . . is a Democratic or Popular government;

that is to say, it is in the power of the body of freemen orderly assembled or the major part of them, to make or constitute just laws by which they will be regulated." Had these citizens made such a declaration in England, they would have been branded traitors and hauled off to prison. But in the isolation of America men did what came naturally.

The radical impulse, however, was not solely a matter of heritage. It fed on that ancient division between the "many" and the "few," which has always been the handmaiden of radicalism. As Curtis P. Nettels notes in his book *The Roots of American Civilization*, "the conflict between privileged and non-privileged . . . forms the central theme of colonial history." The "many" came here from England (or Africa) in boats driven by sail, 90 by 26 feet, weighing only 300 tons. A trip might take as little as eight to ten weeks, but sometimes as much as a half year, if the winds were unfavorable. A passenger on one of these longer voyages records that of the original 150 aboard "more than 100 perished." To sustain life "we had to eat rats and mice. We paid from 8 pence to 2 shillings for a mouse, 4 pence for a quart of water." Approximately half of those who emigrated were "indentured servants," white slaves who sold themselves in bondage for varying periods, usually four to seven years, in return for passage to the New World. Two thirds of the inhabitants of early Virginia were indentured, many of them vagrants and former prisoners. It is estimated that at any given time in the colonial period 10 to 15 percent of the population were of this class. On arriving in America, the white slave would be marched to the magistrate's office to take an oath of allegiance to the king, then marched back to be auctioned off for ten to twenty pounds, depending on his skills. If a master could not sell a servant immediately, he would turn him over to a "soul driver" who drove him through the country in chains, looking for a buyer. It was not a pretty business.

Most white slaves came here voluntarily, but not a few, especially children, were kidnaped on the streets of Europe and shipped here against their will. Thirty-five thousand were British convicts whose death sentences were commuted (three hundred crimes were then punishable by death) on condition they accept limited servitude in Virginia, Maryland, or Georgia. So many felons were sent to Virginia that its House of Burgesses in 1670 enacted legislation to contain the practice. In addition, of course, scores of thousands of black men were kidnaped from the interior of Africa and brought here for lifelong service. At the time of the Revolution, one out of six Americans was a Negro.

Contrary to belief, the white slave was often treated worse than the Negro. V. F. Calverton quotes a letter written in colonial days which has this interesting sentence: "Negroes being a property for life, the death of slaves in the prime of youth or strength is a material loss to the proprietor; they are, therefore, almost in every instance, under more comfortable circumstances than the miserable European, over whom the rigid planter exercises an inflexible severity." The only advantage enjoyed by the redemptioner vis-à-vis the black slave was that he eventually won his release and frequently a patch of land. But while that placed him a few notches ahead of his former status in England, it did not end his travail. It merely made him a small farmer—or an artisan—subject to a new set of aggrievements. If we add the small farmers and artisans who had paid their own way across the ocean, these were the elements responsible for an astonishing number of armed revolts, as well as ceaseless leftist pressures.

The objects of this hostility were the "few"—the elite of Britain whose heavy hand reached out to shackle them from afar, as well as the new oligarchies that formed all too readily on colonial soil. For the British aristocrats and traders, the colonies were a lemon to be squeezed—through credits, trade, sale of land—and they were not chary about squeezing it. "For what purpose," asked the Marquis of Carmathen, "were they [the colonists] suffered to go to that country unless the profits of their labor should return to their masters here?" The profitability of relations is attested to by the fact that in the three quarters of a century before the Revolution, England had a favorable balance of trade amounting to twenty million pounds, a sizable sum those days. The British Board of Trade vetoed more than five hundred laws passed by colonial legislatures so as to guarantee Britain against American competition.

The wealthy elements in America were hardly less acquisitive than their counterparts in Britain. Governor John Winthrop of Massachusetts staked out for himself a comfortable holding of eighteen hundred acres, and his subalterns were not far behind. Through political manipulation three Virginia families, the Carters, Beverleys, and Pages, eventually acquired a domain of almost three million acres. "Everywhere," writes Gustavus Myers, "but especially so in New York and Virginia, the landed proprietors became richer and more arrogant, while poverty, even in new country with extraordinary resources, took root and continued to grow." The owner of a manor in Suffolk County, New York, wore embroidered belts costing £110 each, and on his clothes 104 embroidered silver buttons. When walking, he carried a heavy silver-headed cane; when riding, he rode on a fancy velvet saddle, always attended by twelve Negro slaves ready to meet any whim. Robert Carter of Virginia owned sixty thousand acres and was master of six hundred slaves. Colonel Samuel Allen, when he was appointed governor of New Hampshire in 1692, decreed that the whole province was his personal property and threatened to evict, as common trespassers, settlers who refused to pay him rent. His tenure was described by the Earl of Bellomont as "much more valuable than ten of the biggest estates in England and I will rate those ten estates at £300,000 a piece, one with another, which is three millions."

By contrast, the farm laborer toiled sixteen hours a day for two or two and a half shillings, and the shoemaker and blacksmith for only slightly more. When Governor Winthrop was apprised of the fact that carpenters were earning as much as three shillings a day and common laborers two shillings sixpence, he rectified matters by having the courts decree lower scales.

Wages in the colonies admittedly were 30 to 40 percent higher than in Britain, and there were opportunities to secure land, where at home there were not. Yet the lot of the newcomer was no paradise. Not a few immigrants who had sold themselves into servitude "went mad," according to historian Wilfred S. Binkely, "when once they recognized the opportunity for a good living [was] not at once within their grasp." By 1660 poverty was so widespread in Boston that the city built an almshouse. The overseer was instructed to "set the poor to work" on such jobs as "carding, knitting, spinning, dressing hemp or flax, picking oakum," so that they would "not eat the bread of sloth and idleness, and be a burden on the public." Soon all major colonial towns had one or more poorhouses, and many required each family to take in impoverished citizens for a specified number of weeks annually. Prostitutes and beggars plied the streets, and many who received public aid had to wear a badge signifying their lower status.

II

In this galaxy of poverty and wealth, it was not the British overseas who first gave offense to would-be radicals, but the native despots, in particular the Puritans. The Puritan way of life, whatever its cultural virtues, was a deceitful and hypocritical one. The men of the Bible commonwealth did not shrink from mass killings of Pequot and Narraganset Indians, the capture and shipment of Indians to Barbados as slaves, or the swindling of their lands. Their obsession with sin was as remarkable as it was narrow minded. Men were whipped for failing to attend church, and lovers put on trial for sitting together on the Sabbath. A ship captain who kissed his wife on the street after returning from a long voyage, was fined. To disagree with Puritan theocracy was the ultimate in crimes. Thus John Winthrop, one of the colony's governors, reports that the servant, Philip Ratlif, "was censured to be whipped, lose his ears, and be banished from the plantation," because he used "most foul scandalous invectives against our churches and government." Quakers and Baptists were whipped, imprisoned, branded on their bodies, at times even hanged for their nonconformist views. Some were banished from the colony, fourteen in 1630 alone.

It was against this background that a young preacher, Roger Williams, arrived in Boston in 1631. Son of a merchant tailor, seemingly an orthodox Puritan in the old country, Williams became the implacable enemy of the theocratic order and the foremost revolutionary of his time. His enemies called him a "firebrand"; his friends said he was "divinely mad." He was probably a little of both.

Shocked by Puritan practices, Williams went to live with the Pilgrims in Plymouth for a while, but returned in 1634 to wage a campaign of denunciation against the oligarchy, which led to his banishment. He castigated the "bloody doctrine of persecution for the cause of conscience." He called the Puritan clergy "false hirelings," their churches "ulcered and gangrened," and their members "unregenerates." More than theological differences were involved in such charges. If the state could ostracize a man for his religious views and deprive him of the right to vote, he was thereby hampered in earning a living and in all other matters. Characteristically, Williams was the first man to insist the land belonged to the Indians, not to the white men, and that the king's patent gave the colonists no right to seize that land or pay a dishonest price for it. The king for him was an alien, with no more authority to give away other people's property than anyone else. Mild as this may sound to cosmopolitan ears three and a half centuries later, it was a shocking concept then. No other Englishman had ever stated such heresies. Indeed, Williams antedated Voltaire and Rousseau in expressing such views by a full century.

At issue between Williams and the Puritans was the right of the individual as against the theocratic state. He called for repeal of all laws for compulsory church attendance, as well as religious qualifications for voting. He questioned the magistrates' right to punish anyone for breaching the Sabbath. In the opinion of Puritan church leaders such beliefs were bound to lead to "heresy, apostasy, or tyranny," and had to be punished. In October 1635 the rebel preacher was tried by the General Court and ordered to "depart out of this jurisdiction within six weeks." Illness prevented the enforcement of this edict until the following spring, but meantime Williams continued his infamies. The Puritans decided therefore to ship him back to England where he would unquestionably be tried for treason—for denying the king's title to American land—and at best would have both his ears cut off, at worst face hanging. Warned of this threat, Williams and five friends fled to the wilderness where they lived in severe winter cold for fourteen weeks. Ultimately they were given refuge by the Narraganset Indians, from whom Williams purchased a piece of land on which he established the town of Providence. In accordance with his principles, he paid fair value to the Indians. That summer he was joined by other malcontents from the Bay Colony. Two years later Anne Hutchinson, another religious rebel banished for sedition and contempt, founded Portsmouth. The town of Newport came into being in 1639, and the three small centers merged into what was eventually formalized as the colony of Rhode Island.

Rhode Island, dubbed "Rogues Island" and threatened with invasion by Massachusetts, was the most democratic society of its time. Religious freedom—called voluntaryism by Williams—was absolute. Not only Quakers and Anabaptists fled there for safety but Jews and "witches." The form of government was "democratical, that is to say, a Government held by the free and voluntary consent of all, or the greater part of the free inhabitants." Officers were elected annually and subject to removal. Imprisonment for debt, one of the evils that was to plague America into the nineteenth century, was abolished, and the penal code generally revamped in the direction of humane treatment. Relations with the Indian remained friendly and scrupulously fair. The plight of the white slave was greatly mitigated, his period of servitude reduced.

For his time Roger Williams was as radical a figure as Eugene V. Debs two centuries later. Though he did not abolish private property, as other religious leftists did, and he failed to grant full equality to women, he was in the seventeenth century the embodiment of what was later to become known as the American ideal—religious liberty, individualism, political freedom.

In the wide expanse, with communications as poor as they were in early America, it is understandable that Williams' philosophy did not become universal. Even so, there were among his contemporaries not a few who leaned in the same direction. There was the Reverend Thomas Hooker, who established Connecticut on almost similar lines. "The foundation of authority," said Hooker, "is laid in the free consent of the people." There were Anne Hutchinson, John Wheelwright, William Coddington, Samuel Gorton. There were the Quakers, who believed that "all men are Christs," and who practiced the doctrine of nonviolence toward other men. There were the Huterites, the Moravians, the Mennonites, who established communistic colonies. There were the Anabaptists, who condemned the ecclesiastical state, and others. Historians may dispute how much influence such forces exerted on the evolution of the United States, but it is clear that whether their impact was small or large, they helped prevent the re-formation in America of the rigidly closed society that was Europe.

III

The religious radicals, important as they were in American annals, were essentially doctrinaires whose actions fitted preconceived ideas. Though their preachings of equality threatened the dominant classes, the economic portent of their philosophy was obscured by religious phraseology. This was not the case with the lay rebels who occupied the center of the stage in ensuing decades. For them, freedom of conscience was important, but subordinate to more mundane demands. Contrary to the popular image, there was hardly a decade of the colonial period, sometimes hardly a year, without uprisings and insurgencies.

The most dramatic revolt of the seventeenth century was Bacon's Rebellion in 1676. "Without exaggeration," writes V. F. Calverton, it was "the beginning of the struggle that was to dominate the history of this country." It was the first revolt of the common people—small farmers, impoverished freemen, even some white indentures—against the authority of a royal governor and his privileged class. It came within an inch of permanently toppling the regime of Sir William Berkeley—and perhaps, if Bacon had not died, it would have led to a revolt against British rule itself.

Nathaniel Bacon, a young man of twenty-eight, distantly related to the British philosopher Francis Bacon, had arrived in Virginia not long after being graduated from Cambridge. He was a tall man, slender, black-haired, reticent, and melancholy; he had the characteristics of one who immediately excited either loyal friendship or unbounded hostility. He spoke in pithy phrases, with little subtlety. He lacked the philosophical ability of a Jefferson and he was clearly no diplomat or politician. He cannot be called a utopian, but he had an unremitting faith in the common man, whom he was willing to lead not only against the governor but the king himself.

This was all the more remarkable because Bacon was a man of the upper class. Rich, "fashionably married," he built a grand mansion along the James River, which he called his "castle." But though he was an aristocrat by birth, he was a friend of the underdog by disposition. What he saw in the colony disturbed him: "The poverty of the country is such that all the power and sway is got into the hands of the rich, who by extortious advantages, having the common people in their debt, have always curbed and oppressed them in all manner of ways." In a famous exchange with Berkeley, Bacon expounded a philosophy which, while not erudite, was weighted on the side of the common man. In simple and blunt terms, he condemned the parsons who backed the king against the people; he rebuked the officials who exploited the great mass, and denounced the aristocratic elements who had gained vast estates through favoritism and fraud. He concluded categorically that it was his mission to change all this, by force if necessary.

The trouble in the backwoods of Virginia was both economic and political. It began with the Navigation Acts of 1660, which gave Britain a monopoly over the rich tobacco crop. In the following years the price of tobacco fell from threepence a pound to a half-penny, but when the farmers tried to sell their tobacco to other colonies, instead of to Britain, a tax of one penny a pound was levied on such trade, making it prohibitive. Simultaneously British merchants completed the squeeze by raising the price of finished goods. As the farmers went into debt, they were harried further by exorbitant interest rates. And, if these man-made woes were not enough, they had to contend with a hurricane in 1667 that left thousands homeless and destroyed much of the crop, and an epidemic in 1672–73 which killed off half the cattle.

During all this travail a small clique around Governor Berkeley formed a powerful political machine. The governor and his cronies grabbed the choicest lands, exempted themselves from taxation, held the best public jobs, and lived in a luxury comparable to that of the aristocrats of London. Much of their wealth came from a lucrative trade with the Indians, with whom they exchanged trinkets, liquor, and firearms for fur. From 1660 to 1674 Berkeley permitted no elections for the House of Burgesses, which became a rubber stamp for his depredations. Sheriffs appointed by Berkeley levied fees as they pleased. New taxes were imposed with painful regularity for projects, such as the building of forts for defense against Indians, which were seldom completed. An act of 1670 took away the right to vote from all those who did not own land. Only a spark, therefore, was needed for rebellion.

It came as a result of relations with the Indians. Trouble on this front was as old as the colony, since the Virginians—by their own admission as noted in an act passed in 1662—were guilty of "violent intrusions" into lands they had agreed were to remain Indian. Understandably, the Indians initiated attacks in reprisal. The sporadic warfare made farming difficult and in some cases impossible. Without physical security, the backwoods farmer was in serious trouble. But when he appealed to Berkeley for defense, he was met with procrastination and inactivity. The governor, though he was not a friend of the red man per se, found it useful to retain the western border of the colony as close to the seaboard as possible. Thus he could maintain easier control over his constituents while keeping the cost of furs—which he and his friends bought from the Indian—as cheap as possible. He did not want to push the Indian farther west. In the face of Berkeley's temporization, therefore, Bacon, elected to the House of Burgesses by this time, decided to take matters in his own hands. His expedition against the Indian achieved security, and in the process brought matters to a head with Berkeley as well. The governor declared Bacon a "rebel," but when he marched into Jamestown at the head of more than five hundred armed rebels on June 23, 1676, he was given a hero's welcome and assumed control of the colony.

In the brief interval that Bacon ruled, he restored a host of popular prerogatives. Restrictions on the right of freemen to vote for the burgesses were abolished. Democracy was restored to the church by granting free citizens the right to elect the vestries. Sheriffs, in the future, were to be chosen for one year only. The army was purged of many aristocratic privileges and soldiers permitted to select their own officers. Taxes were levied on the families of government ministers, who had previously been exempt.

Nor did he stop there. Evidence indicates that Bacon became fascinated with the dream of a broader colonial uprising. He conferred with John Culpeper, who later guided a similar revolt in Albemarle (North Carolina), and he foresaw a pact between Virginia, Albemarle, and Maryland to gain independence from British rule. In this—if the fragmentary material on the subject is conclusive—he anticipated Patrick Henry and Samuel Adams by a full century.

The rebellion, however, could not be sustained. On September 18 Bacon was able to drive Berkeley and six hundred poorly armed men out of the capital, but exactly one month later he died suddenly of a fever. Without his leadership the insurgency collapsed, Berkeley came back to power, and the British sent a thousand troops to "restore order." Thirty-seven of Bacon's followers were executed. One of them, Anthony Arnold, gave the royal judges a political exposition that represented the general viewpoint of the Baconians. "Kings," he said, "have no rights but what they got by conquest and the sword, and he who can by force of the sword deprive them thereof has as good and just a title to them as the king himself. If the king should deny to do me right I would think no more of it to sheath my sword in his heart or bowels than of my mortal enemies."

The same year the infection from Bacon's Rebellion spilled over to both Maryland and Albemarle (North Carolina). William Davyes and John Pate massed a group of sixty men in Calvert County, Maryland, to denounce taxation and franchise policies, as well as to inform the Catholic proprietor that they had no intention of swearing a loyalty oath. The gathering was broken up as an act of treason and its two leaders hanged. The storm, however, could not be stilled. New revolts broke out in 1681 and again in 1689, with somewhat more success. In Albemarle, George Durant and John Culpeper disputed the right of the proprietor's agent to collect quitrent—a tax in lieu of rents formerly paid to feudal lords—and certain tobacco imposts. Their resistance was sufficient to have the agent recalled and to win the release of Durant from jail. But in North Carolina, as in Maryland and Virginia, no permanent changes were made in the colonial structure.

The next radical offensive, in 1689, gained its momentum from events overseas. The people of Britain in the Glorious Revolution of 1688 had forced King James II to abdicate. Parliament was again in the saddle and hopes ran high for social change. As the news filtered back to the colonies, after March 1689, it inspired a series of complementary revolts in New England, New York, Maryland, and North Carolina. In Boston there was a minor uprising, with little bloodshed, in which Governor Andros and some of his advisers were arrested. As a result, all of the New England colonies won back some of the autonomy they had enjoyed in the past.

In New York the situation turned more serious. There a German merchant, Captain Jacob Leisler, mounted a rebellion that lasted for more than a year. The authoritarian government of New York dominated by the landlords and merchants—Bayard, Van Cortlandt, and Schuyler—was roundly hated by the small tradesmen, farmers, fishermen, and workers. From 1674 on there had been disturbances by mechanics demanding better arrangements with their employers. Finally in 1689, encouraged by the uprising in London, Leisler marched into the streets, seized the Fort of New York, and unceremoniously uprooted the proprietary government. Joined by militia, who mutinied against British troops, he was able to consolidate his hold over most of the colony from 1689 to early in 1691. His enemies said that Leisler's motives were personal, to avoid payment of customs duties, but he was immensely popular with the masses, so much so that the change in regime took place without a drop of blood. "It was never known in the Memory of Man," one of his supporters stated, "that ever a Revolution or change of Government was more regular."

Once in power, Leisler began to overhaul the rancid colonial structure toward democracy. Free men gained the right to vote, the legislature was elected—for the first time—certain trade and land monopolies were dissolved, the tax system reformed, and a committee of safety set up for democratic defense. Though he swore fealty to Protestant King William, however, the king appointed a governor to supersede him and sent in troops to regain control. Leisler and his son-in-law were arrested, presumably to be held until the crown could make a final decision on their fate. But the governor, Colonel Henry Sloughter, who fiercely disliked the rebels, signed their death warrant anyway. Leisler was hanged and most of his work undone, but it is worth noting that a few years later the British Parliament posthumously removed the "attainder for treason" against Leisler's name. The New York Assembly paid an indemnity of £2,700 to his heirs.

Looking back, it is evident that the seventeenth-century turbulence did little to alter the colonial system per se or end injustices, but it did prevent a tightening of the social fabric. It was a damper on those who would have made America a carbon copy of Tory England—or reactionary Europe. The same purpose was served in the eighteenth century by a less dramatic but an equally insistent wave of revolts, blending finally with the Revolution. Those in New York spanned most of the century, beginning with 1711, and they sometimes took place annually.

The grievances were monotonously the same in colony after colony—tight money, high rents, corruption, heavy taxes, the excessive political power of the rich. In New York four families—the Van Cortlandts, Philipses, Livingstons, and Van Rensselaers—had accumulated through favoritism, speculation, and graft a domain of 1,600,000 acres by 1697. They were virtually small emperors, like the dukes and counts of Europe. Their tenants, on the other hand, had little chance of ever owning a piece of land for themselves. Writhing under the burden of rents and discriminatory taxes, unable to gain relief in the controlled courts, they took to repeated agrarian disturbance. In the armed uprising of Hudson River Valley farmers in 1766, the landlords had to call in British troops, since the home militia proved unreliable. Eighty rebels were arrested, pilloried, fined. One of their leaders, William Prendergast, was sentenced to be hanged, but no one could be found to act as executioner. To avoid further riots the governor had him pardoned.

Throughout the 1740's and up to 1754, New Jersey farmers, especially in the eastern portion of the state, were similarly engaged in frequent insurgency. They defied court orders, broke up auction sales of defaulted farms, and attacked the prisons to rescue farmers incarcerated for debt. The militia called in to subdue the farmers in 1740 mutinied rather than shoot their neighbors. In one of their proclamations the farmers expressed goals that were clearly socialistic: "No man," they said, "is naturally entitled to a greater proportion of the earth than another. . . . [Land] was made for the equal use of all."

One of the most prolonged resistances was the one of North Carolina Regulators in the 1760's and early 1770's. It was directed against government chicanery. Officials in five Piedmont counties regarded their offices as an investment. In an audit of sheriffs' accounts in 1769 it was found that the law enforcers were delinquent to the tune of £64,000. The unfortunate taxpayer was bilked ceaselessly by unscrupulous collectors who charged more than legally due. Defaulted farms were sold by the insiders to friends at deflated prices and then resold at extortionate profits. If a farmer sought the aid of a court, this is what he might encounter, according to one contemporary report: "For entering the judgement on the court docket and issuing the execution—the work of one long minute— the justice of the peace demands forty-one shillings and five pence. Unable to pay the fee, the unfortunate debtor is confronted with the alternative of a distraint or twenty-seven days work on the justice's plantation. But even after he has worked out his debt to the justice, the poor man's account is not settled. . . . There is the damned lawyer's mouth to stop. . . . You empowered him to confess that you owed five pounds, and you must pay him thirty shillings for that or else go to work nineteen days for that pickpocket . . . ; and when that is done you must work as many days for the sheriff for his trouble and then you can go home to see your living wrecked and tore to pieces to satisfy your merchant." It was no wonder that the Regulators resisted for years until, in 1771, Governor Tryon was able, at the Battle of Alamance, to disperse them. Seven were hanged, many jailed, and others fled westward to establish the first permanent settlement in Tennessee.

That the farmer, who constituted a majority of the population in colonial times, rose so often and so militantly indicates how turbulent was this era. As a matter of fact, not even at the height of the Greenback and Populist movements a century later was the rural population so desperate and certainly not so violent.

IV

Interwoven with the radical protest of the farmer, backwoodsman, and tenant was that of the slave, Negro and white. This segment of the population was undoubtedly the most hapless and hopeless of all. Yet, as Calverton notes, "the whole structure of American society in those days was based on slavery." White men were sold in Europe for periods of bondage in America as if they were butcher's meat; and black men were captured in Africa with no more regard for their welfare than if they were inanimate commodities. Both were crammed into boats like cattle, with the resulting 20 to 50 percent death rate written off as simple depreciation. London companies made deceptive promises to attract emigrants, such as houses, gardens, orchards, fine clothes, jewels. But when they arrived, they sometimes found themselves "marched to their daily work in squads and companies under officers and the severest penalties were prescribed for a breach of discipline or neglect of duty." Conditions of the bondmen were so bad that a law passed by Virginia in 1662 to mitigate the situation noted "the barbarous usage of some servants by cruel masters" was such a "scandal and infamy" that it inhibited others from coming to the colony. It is no wonder that the chronicles of the times are filled with acts of resistance, individual or organized.

Consider the plight of Tony, a Negro slave who in 1656 belonged to Symon Overzee of Maryland. One morning, in his misery, Tony ran away. With the help of bloodhounds his master recaptured him, but when his wounds had healed he escaped once more. Again he was apprehended but this time he adopted the policy of nonviolent resistance. Tony simply sat down and refused to work. Though illiterate, he resisted to his death the indignity of slavery. Overzee tied him by the wrists in an upright position and beat him unmercifully, but Tony refused to yield. Thereupon the master poured hot lard over his chattel and ended his misery. A court freed Overzee on the ground that Tony was "incorrigible," as indeed he was.

In the same state, three years before Tony's misadventure, six white indentured servants also refused to do their chores in a complaint over poor food. They were brought to court and sentenced to thirty lashes each. Only when they begged forgiveness and promised to behave thereafter was the sentence remitted.

It was out of such individual malaise that organized revolt swelled. There seems to have been at least forty conspiracies and revolts by Negro slaves up to the time of the Revolution. During the seventeenth century Negro bondage was still a minor affair. Virginia in 1649 possessed only three hundred Negroes and in 1670 only two thousand, about 5 percent of the population. The black man was not yet a profitable investment since the only crop which used much labor was tobacco and that was planted by white indentures. Yet the slave did not accept his lot with total resignation. It is recorded, for instance, that in September 1663 an informer on the plantation of John Smith in Gloucester County, Virginia, betrayed to his master a large conspiracy of Negro slaves and white indentures. The number of rebels executed is not known, but the informer was rewarded with his freedom and five thousand pounds of tobacco.

By 1715, with the introduction of rice and indigo, the Negro population of Virginia, the Carolinas, and Maryland reached one third of the total—some 46,000 out of 123,000. Uprisings then became more frequent. Early on the morning of April 8, 1712, a group of Negro slaves in New York City set fire to a house and, armed with guns, knives, and clubs, waited for white inhabitants to cluster around it. They killed nine and severely wounded seven. Soon the area was ringed with soldiers and within twenty-four hours the malcontents were captured. Six slaves avoided their fate by committing suicide, twenty-one were hanged, burned, or broken on the wheel.

A more serious revolt took place twenty miles west of Charleston, South Carolina, in September 1739. The governor of Spanish Florida had promised American slaves their freedom if they would escape to his territory. Lured by this offer, a goodly number of Negroes overpowered and killed two guards of a magazine, armed themselves, and moved westward toward the Edisto River. On the way, with colors flying and drums beating, they shouted for liberty and enrolled more recruits. They burned and ravaged everything in their path, as if in scorched-earth warfare. One eyewitness declared that the "country about was full of flames." Thirty white men were killed, though one slaveowner, known as "a good man and kind to his slaves," was spared. In the ensuing hours and days an armed posse overtook the rebels, slaughtered thirty-four, and captured forty others. They were hanged or gibbeted alive. Ten Negroes were never accounted for; presumably they reached their haven in Florida.

A year or so later, in the same city, another plot was uncovered, involving two hundred Negroes. This time 150 of the men were rounded up when they gathered for a planning conference. Fifty were hanged, at the rate of ten a day.

The white slave, by all odds, should have been more tractable because his term of service was limited. At the end of his period of bondage loomed a rainbow of freedom and perhaps a patch of land. But the tens of thousands of white men, who for the most part had voluntarily sold themselves into slavery, were as eager as the Negro slave to finish with their tribulations. Their food was poor; housing inadequate. The white indentured servant was often lashed, branded, chained; salt was rubbed into his wounds, and in not a few instances he was flogged to death. Attempts at escape were frequent. Advertisements in the newspapers recorded many such a flight—such as the one in the *Pennsylvania Gazette,* which asked the return of James Dick, a thirty-year-old Scotsman with an iron collar on him ("this being the eighth time he ran away"), and for whom a reward of three dollars was offered.

Every now and then matters went beyond individual action. The servants fomented rebellion. In 1661, by way of example, two harassed white slaves, Isaac Friend and William Clutton, sought to organize an armed uprising in York County, Virginia. Their plan, daring as it was hopeless, was to enroll forty hardy men, arm them, and then seek other recruits "who would be for liberty and freed from bondage." Friend and Clutton agreed to "kill those that made any opposition" and to fight on until they would "either be free or die for it." As might be expected, they died for it.

The Boston *Chronicle* of September 26, 1768, reported the revolt of two hundred immigrants who seized a schooner and tried in vain to capture other vessels. They hoped to make their way to the freedom of Havana, but troops were brought out and the rebellion quelled.

V

From this brief recitation it is obvious that the inhabitants of colonial America were not silent bystanders to abuse and discrimination, nor were their conditions idyllic. Not merely the British but a native aristocracy plunged them constantly to despair, and raised them to revolt. Had it not been for these courageous and continuing acts of protest, American society might have become so totally closed by 1775 that the Revolution would have been impossible. By challenging rigid class domination, the rebels sowed the seed which the Founding Fathers harvested.

CHAPTER III

THE REVOLUTION

During the colonial period Americans considered themselves good Englishmen, pledged to crown and country. Even as John Coode led a few hundred men to topple the government of Maryland, he conceded "the Right of King William and Queen Mary to the Province of Maryland and all the English Dominions." The quarrel of most rebels was with the native elite, the native landowner, the native sheriff and magistrate. Britain, they knew, would aid the privileged classes in America in a crisis. But the radicals did not consider Britain as the *main* enemy, nor formulate their aspirations in terms of "independence." Their revolts were localized.

The reasons for this are a matter of minor controversy. Some historians have attributed it to what they call Britain's policy of "salutary neglect." Rather than a conscious policy, however, it may simply have been ineffective and loose administration. Whatever the explanation, Britain passed many laws and decrees circumscribing colonial commerce and manufacture, but they were enforced with amazing lethargy. "Enumerated" commodities, such as sugar, tobacco, wool, rice, copper ore, iron, and lumber, were supposed to be shipped from America to England exclusively, and re-exported from there by British merchants. But Americans disregarded the law with obstinate frequency. Imports from foreign lands were also required to pass through British ports, there to be reshipped to the colonies. But wiley New England traders simply took to smuggling.

Smuggling was not very difficult. The coast line was so long a good sea captain could avoid being intercepted by a British customs sloop. Thomas Hancock, who made a vast fortune after 1736 in smuggling, issued instructions to his captains to "closely observe, when you come on our coasts not to speak with any vessels." For extra precaution he urged them not to permit any communication between the sailors and their wives when the ship had arrived "at our lighthouse." If worst came to worst, the customs official—except in rare instances—could be induced to look sideways, for an adequate bribe. The extent of bribery is unknown but it was clearly widespread. Ruse also served the smugglers in good stead. Hancock, for instance, would surround Dutch tea—on which taxes were due—with a few chests of tea from England, so as to allay suspicion. Or he would send a ship with a legal load to a port in the West Indies, then have it sail secretly for South America to take on contraband for the voyage back.

The profits from smuggling were enormous. By way of example, a New England merchant could buy molasses from French possessions for from 25 to 40 percent less than from the British. Illicit commerce was so lucrative that in 1763, 97 percent of the fifteen thousand hogsheads of molasses imported into Massachusetts was smuggled. John Hancock, one of the signatories of the Declaration of Independence and a leader of the Revolution, was so successful in adding to the wealth left him by his uncle Thomas that he himself was called the "Prince of Smugglers." His fortune was considered the largest in New England. Nine tenths of the merchants in the colonies and one quarter of the signers of the Declaration of Independence engaged in this practice on one occasion or another. It was so widespread indeed that no stigma was attached to it, and merchants placed obviously smuggled wares in their shops with little fear of reprisal. Colonial courts as a rule refused to convict customs tax evaders. In 1678 a British official, sent in to investigate smuggling, seized many ships. Of the first nine cases he prosecuted, the verdict by colonial juries was not guilty in eight. So successful were the smugglers that from 1733 to 1763 it cost the British £7,600 annually in administrative expenses to collect £1,900 revenue.

The colonists became experts in evading British strictures. Colonial governments, for instance, were ordered by Britain to "discourage all manufacture and to give accurate accounts of any indications of the same." Yet colonial blacksmiths shaped iron bars into axheads, shovels, bolts, and scythes. Tin-plate artisans, working in factories with as many as twenty employees, produced kettles, coffeepots, lanterns, and Dutch ovens. Despite the caveat against the manufacture of yarn, hats, and leather goods, the colonists were making and selling finished products in increasing amounts. Britain did not exactly close its eyes, but it did not implement its laws with any vigor.

Thus the sputtering revolts of the first hundred and fifty years were antirich—American rich—rather than anti-British. Inevitably, however, the two strains of resentment were bound to be drawn together. More and more colonists were becoming competitors of England. Colonial population had grown from 114,000 in 1670 to three million a century later. The New England fleet, plying the world's waterways, numbered two thousand vessels, in addition to fishing craft. Both were economic rivals of the British. An English writer complained in 1774 that the colonies "make many things and export several manufactures, to the exclusion of English manufactures of the same kind." A time came, therefore, for a showdown, and—simultaneously—for American rebels to broaden activity from isolated revolt to unitary revolution.

The Seven Years' War (1756–63), though it gave Britain the satisfaction of defeating France for the fourth time in a century, saddled it with debts and drew it to the conclusion that it must intervene firmly in colonial affairs. The colonies, described by Lord Cornbury, governor of New York, as "twigs belonging to the main tree," must now be taught that they were "entirely dependent upon and subservient to England." They would have to pay a fair share of imperial taxes. They would have to stop their smuggling. In rapid succession, therefore, British prime ministers imposed a dozen new restrictions by law or edict—the Sugar Act (1764), the Currency Act (1764), the Stamp Act (1765), the Townshend Acts (1767), the Tea Act (1773), the Intolerable Acts (1774). To put "teeth" in these measures, the British dispatched an army of ten thousand men and, to add insult to injury, required the colonies to feed and house them. The navy was instructed to stop smuggling, and given the power—with writs of assistance—to board any ship, search any warehouse or private home, purely on its own suspicion, without court order. Those accused were to be tried in admiralty courts without jury. To make sure the colonists were not too widely dispersed for effective control, a royal proclamation prohibited settlement beyond the Appalachians and restricted fur trading to those whom the crown would grant a license.

The result of these and other measures was an escalation of hostility. Good Englishmen became bad Englishmen, and though the idea of independence did not cross their minds at once, it gradually sank in.

II

"Every revolution," according to Ralph Waldo Emerson, "was first a thought in one man's mind." The American Revolution was hatched in many heads, but the one that foresaw it most clearly and planned it most persistently belonged to Samuel Adams of Boston. The upheaval of the 1760's and 1770's brought to the fore great orators like Patrick Henry, philosophers like Thomas Jefferson, military tacticians like George Washington, pamphleteers like Thomas Paine, diplomats like Benjamin Franklin. But Sam Adams was without question its leading strategist and organizer. A dozen years before the climactic moment of Lexington and Concord, it was already clear to him the only answer for the colonies was independence, and he marked a steady course in that direction.

Sam Adams was an unlikely candidate to mastermind a revolution. He was, to begin with, rather old. When the Seven Years' War ended—and the chain of events leading to revolt began—Adams was already forty-one. His cousin John, who was to become President of the United States, was thirteen years his junior, Thomas Paine was fifteen years younger, Jefferson was a mere youth of twenty, and Alexander Hamilton was only six years old. Nor did he look the part. He was a bulky man, his clothes disreputably threadbare. His hair had grayed early, and he was afflicted with a palsy which made his hands shake and on occasion caused quavers in his voice—not the imposing figure expected to organize street mobs.

His father, Deacon Sam Adams, was an affluent merchant who owned a wharf and a brewery on Purchase Street. Adams, therefore, could begin his career at Harvard College (class of 1740) in stylish luxury, taking his meals privately rather than with the ordinary students. Even the father's business misfortunes cannot be said to have seriously affected his son. Adams the elder was a leader of the Land

Bank party, composed—in the words of its aristocratic enemies—of the "Mobility." The Land Bank was an inflationary scheme to pump £50,000 of paper currency into the economy, on real-estate collateral, to relieve small property owners and debtors. When Thomas Hutchinson—a descendant of that religious rebel who helped found Rhode Island, Anne Hutchinson—appealed to the British Parliament to stop the Land Bank and preserve "sound money," it collapsed, and the deacon lost much of his fortune. Young Sam, thereupon, had to adjust to a less exalted way of life, waiting on tables to work his way through college.

But though—then and later—he hated Hutchinson with an abiding fury, it was not because of his wealth. Years later Sam Adams enlisted the richest man in New England, John Hancock, on behalf of the patriot cause. What Adams actually opposed was aristocratic authority and conservatism, choosing instead to place his trust in the common man—"who must, under God, finally save us." As a student, he read profusely of the radical writings of John Locke and Samuel Pufendorf. His master's thesis asked the interesting and semisubversive question, "Whether it be lawful to resist the Supreme Magistrate if the Commonwealth cannot otherwise be preserved."

From the time he left Harvard until he emerged as a revolutionary strategist, Sam Adams seems to have been a monumental failure. He was put to work at a merchant's countinghouse, but was severed when the merchant complained that the would-be businessman was more interested in politics than business. His father loaned Sam a thousand pounds to go into business for himself, but Sam promptly loaned the money to a friend, who just as promptly lost it. The deacon, distraught over his son's ineptitude with money, took him into the brewery firm, but when the old man died, Sam, proving his ineptitude further, let it run down to nothing. He had no passion for anything but politics—specifically politics that served the underprivileged. As the elected tax collector for Boston, he listened to poor folk tell him about their troubles and he promptly forgot about their taxes. When his accounts were found to be short fifteen hundred pounds, he had to call on John Hancock to bail him out of his difficulties. Poor constituents, however, approved his laxity so much they re-elected him for a second term.

Whatever his failings in the world of finance, Adams had a deep-going appreciation for people. When an admirer gave his wife a slave to help her with the housework, he immediately freed the Negro woman. There was no political import to this—slavery was not an issue with the twenty thousand people of colonial Boston. It was solely in accord with his principled concern for the dignity of man. He lived frugally—even when he had money—and as biographer John C. Miller notes, he was a "kind-hearted, easy-going man who listened sympathetically to hard-luck stories and never pressed his debtors once convinced it would be a hardship for them to pay." He enjoyed drinking his pot of ale before a good fire in a tavern, talking endlessly with mechanics and shipyard workers. The tavern was for him a "nursery of revolution," where he met with the Caucus Club or the Sons of Liberty and formulated plans against the British or the local Tories. The latter dubbed him "Sam the Publican."

What Sam the Publican wanted most was to rescue the common man from the rule of the commercial and money-making classes. For a while he flirted with a religious revival movement called the Great Awakening. For a single year he published an anti-Tory weekly. Later he was James Otis' right-hand man and leading agitator in the Massachusetts Country Party. When he found the Massachusetts legislature firmly in the hands of the upper class, he turned to the humble people, went into the streets and mustered the votes to win control of the town meeting of Boston. He was, in a sense, the first big city boss. Had the times been different he might have remained a local politician, and his revolt might have simmered out fighting the Thomas Hutchinsons, rather than the British. But the full-scale intervention of the British in colonial affairs, and the confluence of interest between native and English Tories, lifted the battle to a higher pinnacle.

It was here that Adams excelled, for he knew how to combine traditional political tactics—such as running for office—with unorthodox ones, outside the pale of "normal" politics. Samuel Adams engaged in legal and extralegal activity simultaneously. He wrote petitions to the crown and made fiery speeches in governmental chambers. But his main reliance was on mass action—demonstrations, boycotts, "tea parties." He worked within the established order, but at the same time built a *dual* apparatus of government—Committees of Correspondence, Committees of Safety, the Continental Congress; and a dual militia, the "minutemen." Above all, he had a sure sense of timing. Step by step, combining propaganda, riots, and boycotts, he carried the weak and hesitant to a point where there was no other recourse but revolution.

The first windfall for Sam Adams' machinations was the Stamp Act, which was to go into effect November 1, 1765. Until then the grievances of the colonists were regional. The southern plantation colonies despaired because they were so heavily in debt. What they received from Britain for their tobacco, indigo, and other products never seemed to match what they owed in loans and imports. Thomas Jefferson estimated at the time of the Revolution that Virginians alone owed more than two million pounds to British creditors—twenty times more than the money then in circulation. Debts passed from father to son to grandson. The northern colonies felt harassed over trade. The artisans were aggrieved over limitations on manufacture; the backwoodsmen, over land restrictions; small farmers were hostile for a variety of reasons. The Stamp Act, however, since it fell on everyone, joined these grievances into a common cause. Everyone was hurt by it. Everyone would have to buy the hated stamps to affix to wills, newspapers, deeds, mortgages, licenses, dice, pamphlets, calendars. "What a blessing has the Stamp Act . . . proved," cried Adams. It could not have come at a better time, since America was then in a depression. Wartime prosperity had been followed by a fall in prices. Many merchants had to shut their doors and a banker in Massachusetts had failed for the large sum of £170,000. Everywhere there was unemployment and privation.

Adams and his friends had only to fan the flames. For their purpose there already existed a host of groups, devoted to agitation and political activity, which were willing to engage in semilegal and illegal activity. Most of them adopted the name Sons of Liberty (with an auxiliary called the Daughters of Liberty). The Liberty Boys took form first in Connecticut, then spread to Massachusetts, New York, and all but one or two other colonies. In Boston they evolved from the Caucus Club, in which Adams was the key figure; in Charleston, South Carolina, from the Firemen's Association; in Baltimore, from the Ancient and Honorable Mechanical Company; in Philadelphia, from the Heart-and-Hand Fire Company. These were the forces, as John C. Miller comments, that "led the colonies into revolution." "The whole continent," wrote George Bancroft, "rang with the cheering name of the Sons of Liberty." Their songs reflected their fervor:

> Come Rally Sons of Liberty
>   Come All with hearts United
> Our Motto is "We Dare be Free"
>   Not Easily affrighted!
> Oppression's Band we must subdue,
>   Now is the Time, or never;
> Let each Man prove this motto True
>   And Slavery from him sever.

Among the leaders of the Sons of Liberty in Boston in addition to Adams were John Hancock, Paul Revere, a silversmith, Thomas Boylston, keeper of a gaming house, Newman Greenough, a sailmaker, Joseph Eayres, a carpenter, Benjamin Church, a doctor. The Sons used secret passwords and wore a unique medal. Suspended from the neck, it had a liberty pole with the words "Sons of Liberty" on the one side and the liberty tree on the other. They could call out thousands of people at short notice, and in the words of Paul Revere's biographer, Esther Forbes, could establish "a mob rule in Boston which was stronger than any law courts."

Before the act could be implemented, the Sons of Liberty organized a wave of demonstrations and riots. They attacked the home of the stamp collector in Boston and forced him to resign his post. A building near the water front, to serve as stamp headquarters, was destroyed. The mansion of acting Governor Thomas Hutchinson was sacked, and he himself forced to flee for his life. Writing to the Board of Trade in London, Hutchinson reported bitterly that "the real authority of the Government is at an end; some of the principal ringleaders in the late riots, walk the streets with impunity; no Officers dare attack them; no Attorney General prosecute them; and no judges sit upon them." The militia, called out to suppress the riots, refused to obey orders.

Stamps were destroyed and collectors driven from their jobs everywhere. Two thousand men mobilized in New York to prevent stamps from being delivered. Placards warned that the "first Man that either distributes or makes use of Stampt Paper" should "take care of his House, Person and Effects." Lieutenant Governor Colden was told that if his troops fired on the people he would "die a matír to [his] own villainy and be hanged . . . as a memento to all wicked governors." After a while Colden agreed to turn over the "detestable paper" to the militiamen, who burned it. In many places stamp distributors were beaten and hung in effigy. Admiralty courts, which prosecuted violators, were broken into, their files destroyed. Crowds marched through the streets shouting, "Liberty, property, and no stamps."

Not all the opposition was pleased with such outbreaks. "The mob," commented Gouverneur Morris sometime later, "begins to think and reason. . . . Poor reptiles! . . . They bask in the sunshine, and ere noon they will bite, depend upon it. The gentry begin to fear this." John Dickinson believed it was sufficient to send petitions to Parliament, to write pamphlets and articles; England would eventually come around. Even Benjamin Franklin thought at first that with time Britain would yield. He had several of his relatives appointed as stamp distributors. It was Adams' genius that he could hold the moderates and radicals together. He knew when to push hard and when to hold still, when to use caustic terms and when to use soothing ones. But while he maneuvered carefully, Adams was convinced that his main reliance must be on the radicals—the Sons of Liberty, the leftists like Isaac Sears, Alexander McDougall, Christopher Gadsen, Patrick Henry, Charles Thomson ("the Sam Adams of Philadelphia")—who gave the movement its *élan*.

To coordinate activity with such allies in the various colonies, Samuel Adams formed Committees of Correspondence. Originally most of the colonies had established correspondence committees to keep contact with agents in London. Adams' committees, however, had a different function and were indeed the embryo of revolutionary power. By corresponding with radicals in other towns they highlighted common problems and formulated common strategy for colonies that normally had no direct contacts with each other. Furthermore, they circumvented the regular machinery of government and became an apparatus of their own.

III

The Stamp Act was repealed in March 1766, four months after it was made operative. The colonists had won a great victory. For a fleeting moment it seemed there was to be "no taxation without representation." Colonial merchants, worried by the demonstrations, breathed easier. Bells were rung, toasts drunk to the king, loyalty pledged to Britain. It was an uneasy truce, however. Soon Charles Townshend, chancellor of the exchequer, imposed new taxes—on glass, lead, painters' supplies, paper, and tea. They were not particularly heavy; they were expected to raise a mere forty thousand pounds a year. But they were combined with rigorous enforcement —there was the rub.

The Sons of Liberty again went into action. Those who informed against smuggling were dragged through the streets and tarred and feathered. A British revenue ship which took two American vessels in tow at Newport was boarded by a mob and burned to a crisp. When British officers in Philadelphia seized wine on which no duty had been paid, another mob attacked them and retrieved the merchandise. A collector who tried to enforce the law against John Hancock's sloop *Liberty* was tossed into the cabin and held there while rioters unloaded the ship. The colonies once again resorted to a boycott of British goods. Trade in New York fell from £482,000 to £74,000 in a single year. Merchants who refused to abide by the boycott were themselves boycotted. A poster directed against "William Jackson, an importer at the Brazen Head," read: "It is desired that the Sons and Daughters of Liberty would not buy any one thing of him, for in so doing they will bring Disgrace upon themselves and their Posterity, for ever and ever, Amen."

While the battles raged on the streets, Adams used more sophisticated methods to drive a wedge between colonial legislatures and the crown. In 1768 Adams drafted a "circular letter" to be sent by the Massachusetts House of Representatives to other legislatures. It was humble in tone, expressing "firm confidence in the King, our common head and father," but its intent was clearly to repudiate the father's authority. The colonists, it said, were not free if they were ruled by governors or judges appointed by London. They could not be represented by the British Parliament, for it was too far away.

As might be expected, the governor of Massachusetts ordered the letter withdrawn, and when the House refused, he dissolved it. A similar fate befell the assemblies of Maryland, Georgia, and South Carolina.

The arena of battle tended to swing like a pendulum between legislatures and the streets. The presence of royal troops often raised tempers beyond the boiling point. In New York Liberty Boys would put up a liberty pole only to have it cut down by the soldiers. Then a mob would gather to defend their pole. Finally in January 1770, in the Battle of the Golden Hill between Sons of Liberty and redcoats, one man was killed, several wounded. A few months later in Boston young people threw snowballs and stones at British troops. The redcoats started shooting; five citizens lost their lives, six were wounded. Feeling ran so high over this Boston Massacre that the troops had to be removed to an island—they were derisively nicknamed "Sam Adams' regiments," in honor of his efforts to win this removal. Riots and street demonstrations could not, obviously, expel Britain from the colonies, but these tactics consolidated the general public and put the British and their local friends on the defensive. When Alexander McDougall was arrested for publishing a leaflet addressed "To the Betrayed Inhabitants of the City and Colony of New York," no witnesses dared come forth to testify against him.

In 1772, when the crown put the governor of Massachusetts and the superior judges on the British payroll, an act designed to tighten London domination, Adams revived his Committee of Correspondence—which had languished for a while—to inform other towns of this "outrage." In a passionate speech before a Boston town meeting he charged that judges paid by Britain helped "the iron hand of tyranny to ravish our laws." Within two months there were eighty Massachusetts towns with similar committees discussing taxation without representation, the unconstitutional exercise of power by the king's officers, standing armies, and the like. Pennsylvania newspapers published reports of the proceedings of the Boston committee. In mid-March 1773 a group of young radicals in the Virginia House of Burgesses, led by Thomas Jefferson, Patrick Henry, and Richard Henry Lee, also set up a Committee of Correspondence, assuring contact between the two most important colonies in America. General Thomas Gage informed England that the committees —by then universal—were "assuming to themselves more power and authority than any body of men ever did, looking upon Government as at an end, and making rules and orders for the regulation of the people of the country."

The next opportunity for widening the schism with Britain came with the passage of the Tea Act of 1773. The East India Company,

Britain's largest firm, was near bankruptcy. Its warehouses were filled with seventeen million pounds of tea, while Americans bought tea smuggled in from the Dutch colonies. Since the smuggled product did not have to be transhipped from England or go through so many middlemen, its price was lower. Britain decided, therefore, to eliminate the intermediary steps and allow the East India Company to sell directly—at about 50 percent the Dutch price. One would think this would have won universal acclaim. But merchants were angry because their warehouses were filled with the higher-priced Dutch commodity; the public at large was fearful that once England had gained a monopoly of the market, it would "set them up at what price they please." And if this technique were to spread to other spheres of commerce, Americans would become, as one Pennsylvania writer put it, nothing more then "hewers of wood and drawers of water to them." The logic may have been faulty, but if Sam Adams was waiting for a miracle, this was it.

In all the ports great meetings were held. The cry was raised again: No taxation without representation. When the first three ships of the East India Company arrived in December, Adams and the Sons of Liberty were ready. A mass meeting of eight thousand in the Old South Meeting House demanded that the wares be shipped back. The governor ordered the crowd, largest ever to assemble in Boston, to disperse. Within minutes a large group of Sam Adams' followers, disguised as Indians, boarded the ships and dumped $75,000 worth of tea into the ocean. What happened in Boston was duplicated in Charleston, where tea was removed from the ships and placed in damp cellars to rot, in New York, Annapolis, and elsewhere.

There was now no turning back. Britain either had to enforce its position as ruler, or agree to independence. The measures it took—dubbed the "intolerable acts"—were so repressive they played into Adams' hand. The port of Boston was closed; its customhouse moved to Salem. Armed gunboats policed the docks. Town meetings were prohibited. The Massachusetts charter was amended so that the king, rather than the assembly, chose its council. Rioters, accused of murder, would henceforth be sent to England for trial, instead of being tried at home. There was to be no more nonsense; as a sign of its determination, the crown appointed General Thomas Gage, British army chief in America, as governor.

For their part, the revolutionaries responded by completing an independent power of their own. The first order of business was to forge a military apparatus. Typically, at a town meeting in Marblehead, Massachusetts, a resolution was passed: "Whereas a great part of the inhabitants of this town may soon be called forth, to assist in defending the Charter and the Constitution of the Province, as well as the rights and liberties of all America . . . it is necessary that they should be properly disciplined, and instructed in the art of war." Militias sprang up in every town, just as in Marblehead, dedicated not only to defend themselves but "all America." They were a natural outgrowth from the Sons of Liberty and similar organizations, often with the same leadership. They elected their officers and operated on the democratic principles for which they were fighting. It is certain that without the militia, the Revolution could not have succeeded. Eventually George Washington formed a Continental army and men like Baron von Steuben trained them in modern warfare. But the militia was the backbone of the war, fighting Tories behind the lines, rising to challenge the British in areas where Washington had no regular forces. The British, for instance, might take a port city like Savannah, but militiamen would spring up to fight guerrilla skirmishes until Washington's main force could come to its aid.

The Revolutionary War began, actually, in an attack on the militia. On the night of April 18–19, 1775, General Thomas Gage thought he could end the rebellion in one quick stroke: first, by arresting two key leaders, Samuel Adams and John Hancock, who were sleeping at the home of the Reverend Jonas Clark at Lexington; and second, by capturing a stockpile of munitions that belonged to the militia in Concord. Adams and Hancock escaped across Clark's fields, warned by the indomitable Paul Revere; and the militiamen, though they lost some ammunition, took a heavy toll of the redcoats. Throughout, Britain found itself fighting not merely an army but a people.

Side by side with the militia, the revolutionaries fashioned a political arm—the Continental Congress and the Committees of Safety. Both were a natural continuation of the Committees of Correspondence, just as the militia was a continuation of the Liberty Boys. Soon after the "intolerable acts" were passed by Parliament, the Bostonians ordered their Committee of Correspondence to communicate with other towns and colonies. The letter, drawn up by Adams, and delivered far and wide by the Liberty Boys, declared "this attack, while made immediately upon us, is doubtless designed for every other colony who will not surrender their sacred rights and liberties into the hands of an infamous ministry." Moderates tried to restrain Adams, but as General Gage reported, they were "outvoted by a great majority of the lower class." The Boston leader did not get his way entirely, particularly as regards his proposal for a boycott of British goods, but out of the tumult and maneuvers, one legislature after another appointed delegates to a Continental Congress. Where legislatures had been dissolved—in six colonies—they were chosen by rump committees or by the Sons of Liberty. On September 5, 1774, this historic congress met in Philadelphia, with fifty-six delegates present from twelve colonies (only Georgia was absent).

IV

Samuel Adams' strategy had reached fruition. The Continental Congress, though it affirmed "allegiance to his Majesty," was already an independent government. It knit together separate colonies into an association, and established in each town, city, and county, committees "to observe the conduct of all persons touching this Association." Under such names as the Committee of Safety, Committee of Sixty, Town Committee, Committee of Inspection, they apprehended and tried men friendly to Britain. As one writer described their activities in New York: "Loyalists were arrested for arming to support the British; for harboring or associating with Tories; recruiting soldiers; refusing to muster; writing or speaking against the American cause; rejecting continental money; drinking the King's health. . . . Hundreds were arrested and soon all the jails were overflowing." The committees confiscated land, imposed fines. A loyalist in Baltimore, James Christie, was made to pay five hundred pounds sterling to the revolutionary convention and nine shillings a day to each of five soldiers who "guarded" his home. Loyalists were tarred and feathered; their property seized. In New Jersey alone five hundred Tory estates were taken over and sold in smaller packages to other citizens. The Fairfax estate in Virginia, six million acres; the Philipse estate in New York, three hundred square miles; the domain of Sir William Pepperell in Maine, stretching along thirty miles of coast, were all seized by Committees of Safety.

For the following eight years the American revolutionaries were at war. But it was not just a war between nations. Had it been only that, the Americans would certainly have been defeated. Britain had nine million people; the thirteen colonies, only three million. Britain had the greatest navy ever assembled; the colonies, no navy at all. Britain had one of the best armies in Europe—at worst second only to that of France; the Americans, a ragged band of minutemen and regulars, who often deserted to tend to their crops. Britain was rich; the colonies far less endowed. If it had been solely a military engagement, the Americans could not have held out until they were joined—through Franklin's brilliant diplomacy—by France and Spain. But it was a revolution—an "idea whose time had come"—which excited its followers to enthusiasm, sacrifice, and dedication.

Arms alone could not decide it; it fed on ceaseless propaganda and agitation. Long before hostilities, the redheaded Patrick Henry had risen in the Virginia House to issue his memorable warning: "Caesar had his Brutus; Charles the First, his Cromwell; and George the Third may profit by their example." As other members shouted "Treason!" he flung back the phrase that every schoolboy remembers, "If this be treason, make the most of it." Words such as these inspired the rebels. The radicals fought with guns, surely, but more with ideas. Fighting usually covered areas in which only 2 percent of the population lived, but the ideas blanketed the whole country.

In the year after Lexington and Concord, Thomas Paine, a recently arrived immigrant of thirty-nine, published his little book *Common Sense*. In three months it had sold 120,000 copies; eventually a half million. Washington ordered his officers to read it to their troops. A king, said Paine, "is a political superfluity." "O ye that love mankind! Ye that dare oppose not only tyranny, but the tyrant, stand forth! Every spot of the old world is overrun with oppression. Freedom hath been hunted round the globe. Asia and Africa have long expelled her. Europe regards her like a stranger, and England hath given her warning to depart. O! receive the fugitive and prepare in time an asylum for mankind." His words rang with fervor: "We have it in our power to begin the world over again. . . . The birthday of a new world is at hand. . . ." When the American army was forced to retreat in what appeared like a rout across New Jersey, he wrote *The Crisis:* "These are the times that try men's souls. The summer soldier and the sunshine patriot, will, in this crisis, shrink from the service of his country; but he that

[39]

stands *now*, deserves the love and thanks of man and woman. Tyranny, like hell, is not easily conquered; yet we have this consolation with us, that the harder the conflict, the more glorious the triumph. . . ."

Another "piece of paper" played a more lasting role—Jefferson's Declaration of Independence: "We hold these truths to be self-evident, that all men are created equal, that they are endowed by their Creator with certain unalienable Rights, that among these are Life, Liberty, and the pursuit of Happiness. That to secure these rights, Governments are instituted among Men, deriving their just powers from the consent of the governed. That whenever any form of Government becomes destructive of these ends, it is the Right of the People to alter or to abolish it, and to institute new Government. . . ."

Another document, less well known, was written by George Mason of Gunston Hall, Virginia. Its importance was for the future, but it gave Americans some idea of what they were fighting for. It outlined the basic tenets of the Revolution. Called the Virginia Bill of Rights, it bore striking resemblance to the Bill of Rights later incorporated into the Constitution. It included free elections, prohibitions against "writs of assistance" and excessive bail, trial by jury, freedom of religion and press, and the rights of property, happiness, and safety. These prerogatives were to become standard in a revolutionary America but they were still considered treasonous in most of the world.

V

On April 11, 1783, Congress formally ended the "War of the Revolution." After nineteen years of strife, conflict, and fighting—since the Sugar Act—the tension was over. In the next half year all troops were discharged. General Washington presented a bill of $64,315 for his expenses during seven years of war, and retired from "the great theatre of action."

The Revolution changed America drastically. It united thirteen divided colonies into a single nation. "The distinction between Virginians, Pennsylvanians, New Yorkers and New Englanders are no more," cried Patrick Henry. "I am not a Virginian, but an American." Monarchy was jettisoned in favor of a republic. A number of states wrote into their constitution provisions against hereditary officeholders. The property qualification for voting had been abolished entirely in Pennsylvania, Delaware, North Carolina, Georgia, and Vermont. Elsewhere the amount of property needed to vote was reduced. A bill of rights was included in state constitutions. Eight states passed laws permitting Catholics the right to hold elected office, and four granted it as well to Jews. Residues of feudalism, such as quitrent, entail, and primogeniture, were abolished. (The law of entail provided that a family could not sell its land or even give it away. That was restrictive, particularly if a family wanted to engage in trade or manufacture rather than farming. The law of primogeniture required that when a man died without leaving a will, all his land went to the eldest son. Thus estates were often kept larger than practicable, and younger sons or daughters left with nothing, while some of the land remained unused.) After a while, a large territory in the west was opened for the farmer. Commerce and manufacture were encouraged. Men began to talk of abolishing slavery and setting up free schools. The penal system was improved and the number of crimes punishable by death reduced. The United States, Lafayette predicted, "will become the sure asylum of virtue, honesty, equality, and a peaceful liberty."

The American Revolution, like all revolutions, however, had been made by two classes of people. There were the poor—typified by the Sons and Daughters of Liberty—who had vague dreams not only of independence but equality. And there were the wealthier men, who were determined that the fruits of the Revolution should accrue to them. The two had made a revolution together, but there was some question, even as the guns stopped booming, whether the alliance could be sustained.

CHAPTER IV

END OF THE BEGINNING

THE RALLYING CRY of the American Revolution, galvanizing the revolutionaries into action, had been "equality." "All men are created equal," Jefferson wrote in the Declaration of Independence. But the dust of battle had hardly settled when it was obvious that aristocratic, even monarchistic, tendencies were latent in the ranks.

In the spring of 1782 a group of officers led by Colonel Lewis Nicola urged Washington to overthrow the republic, set up a monarchy, and install himself as king. The commander in chief was shocked: "Be assured, Sir," he replied, "no occurrence in the course of the war has given me more painful sensations, than your information of there being such ideas existing in the army." Gouverneur Morris, though he conceded that such an idea ran against the "taste and temper of the people," wrote to General Nathaniel Greene: "I have no hope that our union can subsist except in the form of an absolute monarchy. . . ." In March 1783 a committee of officers, dissatisfied with the workings of Congress, warned "that in any political event, the army has the alternative"—a clear threat of military dictatorship. Prominent men who had fought with Washington, such as Alexander Hamilton, were deeply convinced democracy was not a suitable form of government.

At the other pole were masses of people who felt their Revolution was being betrayed. Some, such as Captain Daniel Shays, were to take arms against the revolutionary regime itself. "Their creed," wrote General Knox, "is that the property of the United States has been protected from the confiscation of Britain by the joint exertions of all, and therefore ought to be the common property of all." Leveling spirits were widespread. The Pennsylvania constitution spoke of the need to "discourage" large property holdings "vested in a few individuals," and Maryland was so outraged by the speculations of one of its delegates to Congress that it forbade merchants to become members. Benjamin Franklin suggested liberty could be achieved only by limiting the amount of property owned by any man to what was needed to support himself and his family. Jefferson suggested that the poor be exempt from taxes while the affluent pay in "geometrical progression," so as to assure greater equality. A Virginia newspaper went so far as to urge that trade be taken "out of the hands of individuals and . . . be carried on for the benefit of the public by persons authorized by the legislature under stated but liberal salaries"—in other words, nationalization of the mercantile industry.

The divergent views represented divergent economic interests. Some had grown rich during the war by—as Washington put it— "speculation, peculation, engrossing, forestalling with all their concomitants." Others had lost everything they had. Elijah Fisher, a released prisoner of war, records in his doleful diary how, having "lost all last winter, and now that I could not get into any business and no home," he had been forced to beg for food as he made his way back to his native town. While farmers were at the front many of their farms were foreclosed for unpaid debts. Historian J. B. McMaster writes of Vermont: "One half of the community was totally bankrupt, the other half plunged in the depths of poverty." If a New Hampshire law for jailing debtors had been strictly enforced "two thirds of the community would have been in prison." The wages of laborers had fallen to fifty cents a day. There were so many lawsuits against the impoverished in Massachusetts that the *Boston Gazette* of June 5, 1786, commented ruefully that debtors were being "squeezed and oppressed, to maintain a few lawyers . . . who grow rich on the ruins of their neighbors."

The country was flooded with Continental dollars, which citizens had taken in good faith for commodities sold to the government, but which had depreciated by now to ten or twelve cents on the dollar. Many veterans had received land in return for their service, but there were innumerable others unappeased. The federal land law of 1785 was weighted against the lower class. It put up for sale government holdings in sections of 640 acres. Though the cost was only $1 an acre, $640 was outside the reach of the common man. The door was thus opened to speculators and land companies who made fabulous profits by buying large holdings and cutting them up for resale at inflated prices. The Ordinance of 1787 was even more flagrant in its favors to the affluent. The Ohio Associates, a company of "distinguished citizens," was permitted to purchase a million and a half acres for one million dollars—in Continentals. Continentals were then selling for twelve cents to the dollar. Congressmen, with stock in the Scioto Associates, a firm set up especially for their purpose, secured an even larger grant on similar terms. Four million acres were gobbled up by North Carolina speculators. Land that belonged to the people collectively was drained away by land companies for speculation.

The five years from 1783 to 1788 were—as historians called them—"critical years." Not only did the nation lack a central government to regulate commerce, resolve quarrels over boundary lines, and levy taxes, but internal strife between debtors and creditors threatened security. When the depression reached its high point in 1785–86, hardship became extreme. Crops rotted on the ground while farmers, with no money at hand, engaged in barter to supply their needs. Everywhere they demanded that the governments print paper money with which they could pay their obligations. They pleaded for a moratorium on debts or the right at least to pay them in cattle, lumber, or grain. In seven states the regimes heeded such calls and granted relief. In Rhode Island the debtors captured the legislature and passed laws under which loans could be paid in virtually worthless money. A would-be poet wrote:

> *Bankrupts their creditors with rage pursue;*
> *No stop, no mercy from the debtor crew.*

But in some states, where the debtor failed to win either a moratorium or cheap money, hostility spilled over to violence. Several hundred men armed with muskets, staves, and swords invaded Exeter, New Hampshire, where the General Court was sitting, to demand the issuance of paper money and relief from taxes. The courthouse in Rutland, Vermont, was surrounded by hundreds of men "in the saddle," led by Colonel Thomas Lee, a war veteran. After a few clashes with troops, they were disbanded.

The most serious outbreak of the "critical years" occurred in Massachusetts after the House of Representatives voted 86 to 19 against the issuance of paper money. It took six months to suppress. In many respects it was reminiscent of the Revolution itself, with its dual political and military bodies. The upheaval began with a town meeting in Worcester, which vigorously protested the "sound money" doctrine of the legislature. A week later fifty towns of Hampshire County held a convention to decry the government's "selfishness," foreclosures by the courts, the unfair taxes that fell primarily against the poor, and a host of other complaints. If the state would only print paper money, many of these grievances would be redressed. The intent of the convention was to seek redress legally, but within two weeks it had become an armed uprising.

The leader of the rebellion was Daniel Shays of Pelham, a veteran of Bunker Hill, Ticonderoga, and Saratoga, who had been commissioned a captain in 1777. Like many of his neighbors, he was now bankrupt. On August 29, 1786, Shays led five hundred men, armed with bludgeons and muskets, to prevent the Court of Common Pleas in Northampton from sitting. At Great Barrington another group closed the court and broke open jails to release debtors. Houses were searched, "enemies" driven out of town. In late September Shays marched to Springfield and put his men in front of the Supreme Court Building. By now the state had rallied a militia contingent under General William Shepard, but there was no disposition to fight. Shepard and Shays agreed to withdraw their forces on condition that the court adjourn.

The authorities, as well as upper-class circles, were quickly frightened and distraught. "What is to afford us security against the violence of lawless men?" asked General Henry Knox. "Our government must be braced, changed, or altered to secure our lives and property." Hat in hand, the State of Massachusetts had to solicit funds from the wealthy—since its own treasury was bare—to pay the troops to suppress the rebellion. On January 25, 1787, Shays and 1,200 men moved toward the Springfield arsenal where there were 7,000 muskets and 450 tons of military stores. He hoped to link up with his first lieutenant, Luke Day, but their communications broke down and Day was routed by the "regulars." Thus cut off, Shays's main body was defeated at Petersham in a blizzard on the night of February 2.

The rebellion was over, but it had put a scare in the leaders of the new nation. Surveying the situation that hectic year, Washington wrote "something must be done or the fabric will fall, for it is certainly tottering." The rebels were not without sympathy. When their leaders were sentenced to death, the matter became a heated issue in the gubernatorial campaign, with John Hancock—one of the candidates—promising he would pardon the condemned men if elected. This pledge helped return him to the governor's office and he kept his promise. Thomas Jefferson, writing to William S. Smith, son-in-law of John Adams, many months later asked, "Can history produce an instance of rebellion so honorably conducted?" He had some doubts about its motives but ascribed them to "ignorance, not wickedness." "God forbid," he said, "we should ever be twenty years without such a rebellion." The average man, both in Massachusetts and the rest of the nation, understood well what Shays' Rebellion was about.

II

It was against this background that Alexander Hamilton persuaded the states (all but Rhode Island) to revise the Articles of Confederation. The fifty-five delegates who assembled for the historic Constitutional Convention in Philadelphia, from May to September 1787, were for the most part men of property—owners of public securities, merchants, lawyers, moneylenders, slaveholders, land speculators. The leftists were conspicuously absent. Patrick Henry, though elected, refused to attend because he "smelt a rat." Sam Adams was not chosen. Jefferson was in Europe, as was Tom Paine.

The Constitution that was drafted during the secret sessions was, by the standards of 1787, highly democratic. It had to be, to stand any chance of ratification at the hustings. But the sentiments of a vast majority of the participants was unquestionably with the moneyed classes. Had they been free of popular pressure, they would have erected an aristocratic structure much different from what they did. Elbridge Gerry of Massachusetts ascribed all the nation's troubles to an "excess of democracy." Hamilton asserted that "all communities divide themselves into the few and the many. The first are rich and well-born and the other the mass of the people who seldom judge or determine right." The nation should be ruled, he suggested, by an executive chosen for life who would appoint all state governors. Both would possess veto rights over all legislation in their province, thus assuring virtual one-man rule.

Class consciousness was evident throughout. "The Senate," said Chancellor Kent of New York, "should be the representative of property, of landed interest, and its security against the caprice of the motley crowd of paupers, immigrants, journeymen, manufacturers, and those undefined classes of inhabitants a state and a city like ours is calculated to invite. Universal suffrage jeopardizes property and puts it into the power of the poor and the profligate to control the affluent." Governor Randolph of Virginia favored representation in Congress based on the taxes paid by each state—wealth, in other words—rather than the number of voters. That most of these proposals were not incorporated into the Constitution was a tribute to general sentiment rather than the wishes of the participants at Philadelphia.

Even the document that finally carried, and which was submitted to the states for ratification, aroused nationwide resentment on the part of the radicals. For one thing, it provided an edifice too centralized for the taste of men who had fought George III's centralism. For another, it had conspicuously omitted a Bill of Rights. Richard Henry Lee denounced "the strong tendency to aristocracy." George Mason of Virginia led a minority of delegates who refused to sign the document. Amos Singletary, a politician from Massachusetts, summed up the indignation of the rural folk thus: "These lawyers, and men of learning, and moneyed men, that talk so finely, to make us poor illiterates swallow down the pill, expect to get all the power and the money into their hands and then they will swallow up all of us little folks, like the great leviathan." Patrick Henry, who had once shouted, "Give me liberty or give me death," cast his ballot against ratification. Luther Martin, of Maryland, cried: "I'll be hanged if ever the people agree to it." Sam Adams voted for it, but grudgingly. Jefferson expressed reservations that the President, aided by the army, might form a dictatorship. He changed his mind later, but there were many old leftists who fought it to the end.

The votes reflected their disenchantment—particularly over the omission of the Bill of Rights. The dissidents of Rhode Island would have nothing to do with the project. In North Carolina the jovial backwoods leader, Willie Jones, convinced his state to stay apart. A young radical, James Monroe, took up the cudgels against the document in Virginia and won a respectable number of "No" votes. The proposition squeaked through by 89 to 79. In New York Hamilton's followers, favoring the Constitution, won a razor-thin victory, 30 to 27. In Massachusetts the vote was 187 to 168, in New Hampshire 57 to 47, for adoption. Describing sentiments in Massachusetts, General Knox noted those who favored the handiwork of Philadelphia included "the commercial part of the state, to which are added all the men of considerable property, the clergy, the lawyers," while in opposition were "insurgents or their favorers, the great majority of whom are for the annihilation of debts public and private." His description was apt for the other states as well.

In due course Washington appeased the radicals by having a Bill of Rights incorporated into the Constitution. The conflict, however did not end. The classes that had made the Revolution together were now quarreling with each other over the direction of that Revolution. Should it be in the interests of the "many" or the "few," the "common man" or the "rich and wellborn," the radical or the conservative? It was a dispute that was to continue in new forms each generation.

III

What did the words "life, liberty, and the pursuit of happiness" mean in specific terms? The government was charged with promoting the general welfare, and what the government did, then and now, could be decisive. But was it promoting general welfare if it gave a poor man a patch of land from the public domain free of charge? Or should the government sell the land in large plots and use the revenues to build roads? The determination depended not merely on pragmatic considerations but on the philosophy behind it.

On a summer day in 1792 three men sat around the table in a Philadelphia house discussing just such a problem and manifesting two clearly opposite approaches. One was President of the United States, George Washington. The other two were the strong men of his cabinet, bitter political enemies: Thomas Jefferson, Secretary of State, and Alexander Hamilton, Secretary of the Treasury. Hamilton was still a young man, only thirty-five; Jefferson was a year shy of the half-century mark. Both men were redheads, charming and brilliant, but there the similarity ended.

Hamilton had been born in the West Indies, poor, and had become the spokesman for the wealthy of America. Jefferson had been born to wealth but had become the spokesman for the impoverished. Hamilton had been an invaluable aide to Washington, had fought well, ridden recklessly into the battle at Monmouth. Jefferson's talents had been used primarily in diplomacy, and of course in drafting the Declaration of Independence. Washington was closer to Hamilton in sentiment, but as he looked at his Cabinet members he wondered if there were a compromise between their views.

At Hamilton's invitation, the three men rose and took a coach into New Jersey. There, as they rode, Hamilton explained how he would harness the power of waterfalls to operate textile mills. The industrial revolution was not yet under way in the United States. The first textile machinery had been built here by a Pawtucket blacksmith only in 1790. How far the trend would go was anyone's guess. Hamilton's famous Report on Manufactures had been sent to Congress in December 1791 and he was anxious to win Jefferson to the view that factories based on laborsaving devices represented a major part of the American destiny. Knowing Jefferson's attachment to agrarian democracy, Hamilton argued that agriculture itself would be enhanced if the government would stimulate manufacture. He was clearly attracted to the factory system of England. In his report he had noted that four sevenths of the workers in British cotton factories were women and children "of whom the greatest proportion are children, and many of them of a tender age." Far from being disturbed by this, Hamilton felt that "women and children are rendered more useful, and the latter more early useful, by manufacturing establishments, than they would otherwise be." As they talked, Hamilton's ardor for manufacture as the pivot of economic development became abundantly apparent. He foresaw the government aiding manufacture with protective tariffs, monetary help, restriction on rival imports, encouragement of inventions, and the building of roads and canals.

For Jefferson the Hamilton vision was a desecration of the democratic goal. He had seen the factory system on his travels to London and Paris, and far from being impressed, he was appalled by what it was doing to women and children. As he saw it, and as he stated it, democracy depended on a group of loosely connected states, each self-governed, with its own customs and traditions. The backbone of the nation, therefore, must remain the small independent producers, mostly on the land, with some in manageable workshops.

The notion that land ownership was the guarantor of equality and democracy was not confined to Jefferson. Charles Pinckney, member of a prominent political family in South Carolina, told the Constitutional Convention in June 1787 that the United States was blessed with "a greater equality than is to be found among other people . . . because in a new Country, possessing immense tracts of uncultivated land . . . there will be few poor, and few dependent." Access to land was expected to act as a bulwark against both poverty and "dependence." It was considered, indeed, the fulcrum for the good life.

Jefferson, of course, eventually yielded to the industrial onrush. But the conversation that summer day testified to the different angles from which the two men viewed the problem of their times. The manufactory would rob a formerly independent farmer of his independence, subjecting him to the will of another man, and could reduce little children to misery before their time. Jefferson opposed it on that account, disregarding what it would do to enhance the gross national product. For Hamilton manufacture was not only linked to the development of a strong nation, but, even more, to the concept of society in which the interests of the "rich and well born" were paramount. Jefferson could write: "I consider the class of artificers as the panders of vice, and the instruments by which the liberties of a country are generally overturned." Liberty was the key component for his decisions, and if he could be shown—as he evidently was later on—that the factory and democracy could coexist peacefully he would accept it. But with Hamilton, whose reservations about democracy were monumental to begin with, questions such as freedom or the common man were distinctly secondary.

The period from 1789 to 1801 has been called the "Hamiltonian period," even though Hamilton was not in the government all this time. But his philosophy was at work throughout. Carefully but fastidiously, the man from the West Indies began fashioning a nation along the businessman's—rather than the small farmer's—pattern. To assure a supply of labor for that businessman he placed obstacles in the path of would-be smallholders. No land of the public domain was to be sold in plots of less than nine square miles, at two dollars an acre. Such sums of course were far out of reach for the average citizen. Many who would have moved west had to stay behind to work in the manufactories and textile mills that were beginning to dot the nation. By funding the $56 million debt of the national government and the $18 million debt of the various states, Hamilton made it possible for the entrepreneurs to accumulate venture capital. (Interestingly enough, the $100 million in semiworthless Continentals, owing for the most part to farmers and laborers, was repudiated.) By doubling the duties on finished goods, Hamilton gave protection to nascent capitalists who were building factories. And by establishing a United States Bank, in a country that had only four functioning banks, he made large-scale credits available to the favored business community.

The radicals opposed such measures because they raised prices on consumer goods, increased taxes on the poor, and created a class of pauperized laborers in the burgeoning cities. But their opposition was negative and defensive. They had no blueprint to counterpose to that of Hamilton and his Federalist friends. They were not prepared for the towering role that business and manufacture was to play in future decades. In the womb of history was an industrial revolution which posed new problems and demanded new answers, but few leftist malcontents offered such answers. To be equal in an agrarian society meant to own a piece of land like that of your neighbor. But how did one achieve equality in an industrial society where one man owned the machines on which a hundred others labored? Future leftists found the solution in *collectivism* of one form or another, but in Jefferson's day radical sights were still set on individualism. Here and there, as in Rhode Island, there were suggestions for state ownership of trade facilities. A few religious groups had formed communitarian societies in which "all things were common." But these were notions that did not catch on—as yet.

Thus, while the radicals remained a powerful force in and out of government, and while they won many democratic concessions, they were hampered by a lack of clarity over the dimensions of the future.

IV

Beginning in 1792, laborers and militant farmers, the kind that had fought with the Sons of Liberty two decades before, formed

Pilgrims leave from Plymouth, England, September 1620. Their Mayflower Compact, signed by all forty-one adult males, spoke of majority rule and promised "just and equal laws" in the New World.

Freed from the tyranny of the Established Church in England, the Puritans set up a tyranny of their own in Massachusetts. Roger Williams, a rebel preacher, fled the colony to escape persecution, and was sheltered for the winter by the Narraganset Indians. From them he purchased the land on which he founded Providence, R.I.

*Imposing levies to pay for England's war debts, the Stamp Act united
the opposition of the colonists for the first time. Throughout the
colonies the Sons of Liberty organized a wave of demonstrations and
riots. Above, a crowd protests the Stamp Act in New York, November 1, 1765.*

Leading strategist of the American Revolution, Sam Adams knew how to combine traditional politics with mob action. He wrote petitions to the crown and made fiery speeches in government assemblies. But he relied most heavily on mass demonstrations—boycotts, parades, "tea parties."

Sons of Liberty met in four ports to protest the Tea Act of 1773. In Boston, a large group of Sam Adams' followers, disguised as Indians, boarded British ships and dumped $75,000 worth of tea into the harbor. As a result, the British tightened their control over the colony. The port was closed, town meetings were prohibited, and armed gunboats policed the docks.

On March 5, 1770, a crowd in the Boston streets threw snowballs at British soldiers. The Redcoats opened fire, killed five Americans and wounded six. Feeling ran so high over this "Boston Massacre" that the troops had to be removed to an island.

Orator Patrick Henry inspired the rebels with his memorable words. In the Virginia assembly he warned, "Caesar had his Brutus; Charles the First his Cromwell; and George the Third may profit by their example." To his listeners' shouts of "Treason!" he responded, "If this be treason, make the most of it."

In the spirit of the revolution, New Yorkers raised the liberty pole on July 4, 1776. Here the Sons of Liberty hold a rally at right, and King George's picture is removed from a tavern signpost, left.

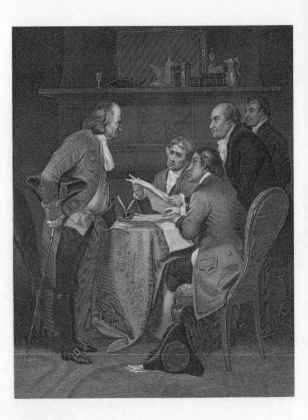

The ideas of the revolution were forcefully expressed in the Declaration of Independence, drafted by (left to right) Franklin, Jefferson, John Adams, Livingston, and Sherman. Below, the Declaration is announced at the State House in Philadelphia, July 8, 1776.

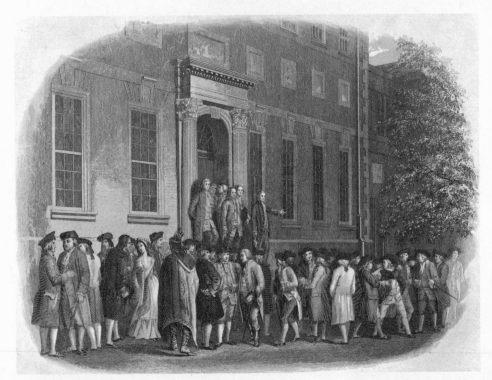

Democratic Societies and Republican Clubs as vehicles to express their resentment. The first such society was organized in Philadelphia and spread quickly to the large cities and towns until all fifteen states were blanketed. To Jefferson's banner flocked crusty mavericks such as Sam Adams and John Hancock of Massachusetts; liberal gentlemen like James Monroe and John Taylor of Virginia; idealistic followers of Rousseau like Albert Gallatin of Pennsylvania; George Clinton and the Livingston family in New York; and stormy petrels from the backwoods everywhere.

The Democratic Societies saw before them a twin danger—the aristocratic tendencies of the Hamiltonians in America and the offensive of the European monarchs against the French Revolution, which had started in 1789. In their minds the two were linked indissolubly. An address "To the People of the United States" by one of the leftist clubs stated: "Shall we Americans who have kindled the spark of Liberty, stand aloof and see it extinguished when burning a bright flame in France, which hath caught it from us? Do you not see if the despots prevail, you must have a despot like the rest of nations? If all tyrants united against the people, should not all free people unite against tyrants? Yes, let us unite with France and stand or fall together."

Poland had already been stifled by the monarchial federation, its cry for liberty squelched. If the bastion of European freedom, France, were to follow, there was little hope for the United States. The Democratic-Republican societies modeled themselves along the lines of the Jacobin Clubs of Paris, held meetings, and wrote pamphlets to popularize the revolutionary cause. When news came of Dumouriez' victory against the French royalists at Valmy, there were wild demonstrations in the United States. Boston mechanics held a barbecue. New Yorkers, rallying to the newly formed Society of the Sons of St. Tammany, staged parades. A Virginian, William Wirt, recounting the excitement years later, said: "My blood runs cold, my breast swells, my temples throb, and I find myself catching my breath, when I recall the ecstasy with which I used to join in that glorious apostrophe to Liberty in the Marseilles Hymn."

When the French king was killed there were more parades, more "ecstasy." The Jeffersonian crowds wore cockades and addressed each other as "citizen." Every symbol of privilege was deemed a regression to monarchism, and a threat to survival of the American

Revolution. Titles assigned to government leaders, such as "Sir," "Honorable," "Excellency," sounded to the Republicans like the language of Europe. When an innkeeper in Philadelphia hung a picture of the queen of France on his door, the Democrat-Republicans forced him to paint a streak of red around her neck and daub her clothes with splotches of blood. Radicals in New York forced the city to rename King Street as Liberty Street, and in Boston, Royal Exchange Alley was transformed by similar pressure into Equality Lane. Washington denounced the Democratic Societies; editors called their members "filthy Jacobins," "frog-eating, man-eating cannibals." But a large segment of America, following Jefferson, identified the French Revolution with their own.

Such sentiments reflected a pervasive fear that the democratic ideals of 1776 were being dissipated, that "inalienable rights" were being taken away. In the 1790's, as in the 1780's, the passionate dispute between Left and Right was something less than effete. On occasion it took violent form, such as in the Whisky Rebellion by western Pennsylvania farmers in 1794. Because roads were so bad, the farmers of the western sections of Pennsylvania, Virginia, and North Carolina converted their corn and rye into whisky, since it was easier to transport whisky than the bulkier grain. According to some estimates, there were five thousand distilleries in these areas. When Hamilton imposed an excise tax on whisky, he ran into the full fury of these backwoodsmen. The fury was so great that Congress had to modify its act to abolish the tax on *small* stills. This relieved the farmers of Virginia and North Carolina, but not of western Pennsylvania. They refused to pay the new impost, burning the offices of the collectors, much as the colonists had done in the days of the Stamp Act. Washington decried the "rebellion" as "the ripe fruits of the Democratic Societies." When a federal marshal tried to arrest some of the offenders in the summer of that year, the "rebellion" reached a higher peak. Hamilton himself accompanied a strong armed force to the scene of violence. A few men were arrested and put on trial, two convicted—later to be pardoned by Washington. The discontent of the Jeffersonians, however, was not allayed. Soon they were involved in a broader struggle, of a more meaningful nature.

Over in Europe, revolutionary France and Britain were at war. Its repercussions were felt in the United States, for Britain seized

American ships trading with France and its colonies, while France retaliated by capturing merchantmen doing business with Britain. When these maraudings became known in America, party tempers flared consonant with the divergent philosophies of the disputants. The Federalists (Hamiltonians) could see evil only on the French side; the anti-Federalists, on the British side. When France, under an old treaty of alliance made in 1778, asked the Americans for help against Britain, the argument reached a new climax. The Hamiltonians, fiercely hostile to French radicalism, insisted the obligations had ended with the death of the French king. The Jeffersonians continued to urge help for the republican cause in Paris.

Timothy Dwight, president of Yale, accused the Jeffersonians of becoming "the disciples of Voltaire and the dragoons of Marat." Another New Englander condemned the Virginian and his friends for spreading "the atheistical, anarchial, and in other respects immoral principles of the French revolution." For their part, the Democrat-Republicans distributed a pamphlet by Tom Paine, written from France, claiming that "the principles of America opened the Bastille."

During all this tumult the French Revolution had taken a turn to the right and President John Adams had decided that it was in the best interest of the United States simply to sit out the crisis, to avoid entering the war. Had matters ended here, there would have been little further conflict. But to the militant Federalists this seemed like a propitious moment to settle accounts finally with the Republicans. To quell radical agitation, it was decided in 1798 to introduce two acts which civil libertarians have ever since considered as a travesty on the democratic spirit, the Alien Act and the Sedition Act. The former empowered the President in the interests of "public safety" to expel or imprison aliens in times of war or emergency. It also increased the period required for an alien to become a naturalized citizen, from five to fourteen years. This was obviously directed at the growing body of Irishmen fleeing to America after the Irish rebellion, since they sympathized with France against the enemy, Britain. To the Federalists these anti-British refugees were the "most God-provoking Democrats this side of Hell." Fortunately the Alien Act was little enforced.

The Sedition Act, on the other hand, was applied with vigor. It imposed jail sentences and fines on anyone penning "malicious" statements against the government. One man was sentenced to eighteen months in prison and fined four hundred dollars for writing that "there has been an actual struggle between the labouring part of the Community and those lazy rascals that have invented every means that the Devil has put into their heads to destroy the labouring part of the Community." Editors were jailed. Men who attended meetings where derisive remarks were made about Federalist policies were heavily fined. Since the courts were packed with Federalist judges, it was not difficult to secure convictions.

In the streets of Philadelphia mobs marched past Jefferson's home shouting threats. So-called patriotic societies beat up artisans and small farmers who aligned themselves with him. Printing presses of editors favorable to the Jeffersonians were unceremoniously smashed. Cartoons pictured the future President as "mad Tom in a rage" and one paper predicted that "Jefferson's head will be rotting cheek by jowl with that of some toil-killed Negro slave." The tide became so strong that even Hamilton recoiled from it. "Let us not establish a tyranny," he pleaded. "Energy is a very different thing from violence."

The Republicans fought back by invoking the First Amendment of the Constitution, which guaranteed free speech and press. They prevailed on the legislatures of Virginia and Kentucky to pass resolutions declaring the two acts null and void. Virginia even appropriated money for arms. The Alien and Sedition Acts became issues in the Presidential campaign and helped turn the tide against the very Federalists who had introduced them. Jefferson's victory was due in no small measure to the hated acts, and with his accession to power the dispute died. The two laws, effective for only a limited period, were permitted to lapse. Those still in prison under its provisions were pardoned by the new President.

V

After a decade and a half of Hamiltonianism the radicals were again in the seat of power. But Hamilton's legacy was inviolate. The industrial revolution, though its effects were confined to New England and the Middle States, was irreversible. Whatever Jefferson's misgivings about centralism and the factory system, he bowed gracefully to exigency. When the opportunity offered itself to buy the territory of Louisiana from Napoleon, he accepted it, even though it conflicted with his abstract principles of decentralism. For fifteen million dollars he doubled the territory of the United States and added to its domain the picturesque port of New Orleans.

The merchants and businessmen had been edged aside by Jefferson's alliance of small farmers, planters, backwoodsmen, and mechanics, but neither the third President nor his successors, Madison and Monroe, did anything to hamper business affluence. They adjusted both to the protective tariff and the Bank. Twenty-five years after Madison had led the legislative assault against the first Bank, he himself formed the second one. It was enough to gladden an old Federalist heart. Jefferson himself, whatever his doubts in 1792 or 1809, could write in 1816 that "experience has taught me that manufactures are now as necessary to our independence as to our comfort."

But if the Jeffersonians could not realize their vision of an agricultural utopia, they did extend the democratic *élan*. Court etiquette was pruned, titles such as "excellency" forsworn. Property qualifications for voting were revoked in one community after another. When frontier states such as Ohio, Kentucky, and Tennessee applied for admission to the Union, universal manhood suffrage was taken for granted. Negro slavery was abolished in Massachusetts, and gradually in Pennsylvania. White indenture lingered a while but was gradually abandoned. New lands were opened up for the farmer and restless mechanic. Criminal and debtor laws were improved, some aid given to the unsteady labor unions.

The momentum of the Revolution carried over for a long time. Compared to France, whose revolution had been contained by Carnot and Napoleon, and compared to England, before Chartism, the United States was a radical nation indeed. If any danger lurked on the horizon, it was that this Revolution, like all revolutions, would institutionalize, and that the forces of privilege that had been given impetus by Hamilton and were entrenching themselves further, would stifle democracy's expansion.

It was an omen of the times that when Tom Paine, the great pamphleteer of the Revolution, died in 1809, in an obscure house at 59 Grove Street, New York, only six people followed his casket to its last resting place.

CHAPTER V

UTOPIAS AND WORKIES

WHEN Frances (Fanny) Wright and her sister Camilla came to the United States in 1818, they were elated "with the sound of political liberty, the absence of bayonets, and constrained taxation." Fanny, the more striking of the two, was a tall, slender girl with flashing eyes and close-cropped hair, a rich contralto voice, and a commanding personality that was to make her a leading figure of her time. Her Scottish father, an articulate liberal and a disciple of Tom Paine, left his three children a substantial inheritance, part of which Fanny later used in a dozen radical ventures. Twenty-three at the time she embarked for America, she was already an enthusiastic friend of the country "consecrated to freedom," and particularly of the principles in the Declaration of Independence. Coming here, she admitted, had been her "fixed but secret determination" for years, and on this first visit she was not disappointed.

For two years Fanny and her sister made a leisurely tour of the United States. The girls, as befits members of the affluent class, were wined and dined by the best people. Fanny's play *Altorf*, a tragedy dealing with Switzerland's struggle for freedom, was performed in New York and attracted the praise of Thomas Jefferson. The sisters visited western New York, got a taste of its wilderness, saw a bit of Canada, Philadelphia, Washington, and Virginia. On returning home, Fanny published her letters and observations in a little book that attracted the attention of George Washington's old friend, the Marquis de Lafayette. The book was so strongly pro-American, it pictured a nation of spotless cities and happy countryside with hardly any problems. The Revolution of 1775 was portrayed by her as if there had been no opposition to the patriots. Even her biographer, Paul R. Baker, is constrained to note that it was "distorted . . . by her prejudices and enthusiasms."

When Fanny returned to the United States in 1824 with her affectionate friend Lafayette (he once considered adopting her as his legal daughter), she had a chance to make "a more minute inspection." Since Lafayette was on a triumphal tour in honor of his contribution to the American Revolution, Fanny also had an opportunity to meet Jefferson, James Madison, John Quincy Adams, and Andrew Jackson. This time her reactions were far more critical. The slave system, which she examined for the first time in Virginia, repelled her terribly. She was equally discouraged when former President Madison commented that he saw no solution in the offing. She was still convinced that in the United States were "enshrined all the liberties and all the hopes of the human race," but now she was ready to admit that she had mistaken "the restlessness of commercial enterprise" for "the energy of enlightened liberty." On closer view, it seemed that America was a combination "both [of] the excellences that are, and those that are yet wanting."

Fanny became a foremost radical, trying to change "those that are yet wanting." She established a utopian community in Nashoba, Tennessee, to free the Negro. She published a newspaper with Robert Dale Owen in New Harmony. She was active in the workingmen's parties of the late 1820's. She was a feminist, an advocate of free love and abortion, and a promoter of the "free enquirer" plan, by which she hoped to make the United States an egalitarian society. For some years the term "Fanny Wrightism" was synonymous with the word "radicalism."

If Fanny Wright, therefore, could be confused about the character of the new nation, it could only have been because in the first half of the nineteenth century it was in a state of bewildering transition. It was in the kind of flux that defies simple description.

II

When the century began, the national direction was not clear. The industrial revolution was just catching on; the West was opening up; the Southern plantation system was turning toward a new crop, cotton. For a while there was an Era of Good Feeling, as leaders of the North, South, and West—Daniel Webster, John C. Calhoun, and Henry Clay—found adequate compromises to satisfy everyone. This was called the "American system," betokening stability and a feeling of national destiny. But before long it was obvious that what was presumably one nation was in fact three subnations, held together by the most tenuous threads. Except for the West, where nationalist feelings remained strong, one or another of these subnations periodically threatened to secede.

With the unfolding years, the divergencies became pronounced and irrepressible; each section—remarkably vibrant and dynamic in itself—was moving in its own special way. The West was filling out. So many migrants streamed into the valley of the Mississippi that by the time President Monroe retired in 1825 nine new states had been carved out, with one third the country's population. As the market grew for its crops, it turned from self-sufficiency farming to commercial agriculture, developing a small elite and a sturdy democratic mass. The North, though crippled by political alignments in Congress for much of the period, moved with steady purposiveness toward its industrial future. From 1820 to 1860 capital invested in factories rose from fifty million to a flat one billion dollars; and with it came the transport revolution—turnpikes, canals, and railroads—that was even more impressive. As for the South, it was transformed just as dramatically by cotton and the cotton gin. In Washington's day the planters produced a trickle of two million pounds of the white substance; by the Civil War it had increased a thousandfold, to two billion pounds. The number of Negro slaves, feeding this prosperity, enlarged from seven hundred thousand to four million.

Since each region was developing its own specific character, the three-way regional conflict was accompanied, inevitably, by three different class struggles—between capitalist and worker, slaveowner and slave, debtor and creditor. In the era of transition, the spirit of 1776 and the Jeffersonian vision of an agrarian utopia lurked in the national subconscious, but gave ground constantly to new spirits and new visions. What was left of the Hamilton-Jefferson dispute over centralism and manufacture was simply two clashing moods, one favoring the "rich and well born," the other the common man. The present linked itself to the past only in a continuing war against privilege, but the forms of radical response altered significantly. Backwoods revolt blended toward Jacksonian democracy and populism; the slave rebellions toward the abolitionist movement; the struggles of the Sons of Liberty and the Democratic Societies toward unions, labor parties, and utopian socialism.

Of the three simultaneous dramas, the one enacted in the big cities of the North was the most portentous. As industrialism was grafted on to the agrarian society, it changed the way of life as well as the structure of power. An old farmer was his own boss, working at his own tempo, at his own discretion. The colonial laborer, though his right to decision making was partly curtailed, was moderately close to his employer. The typical worker was a skilled craftsman—carpenter, printer, baker, cabinetmaker, shoemaker. He learned his trade by serving for some years as an apprentice, working his way up to journeyman. His master usually employed only two or three journeymen besides himself and worked side by side with them with the same elementary tools. There was little quarrel over wages, because wages were determined by the price charged the customer. If it were more, earnings rose; if it were less, earnings declined. This kind of wage system was patterned to the relationship with the purchaser. Most work was "custom" or "bespoke" work—custom-made. The buyer came to the shop, chose the leather (if she wanted shoes, for instance), picked the style, and had herself measured. The craftsman then made the product to order.

But as demand increased sharply after the Revolution, a new person entered the industrial picture—the merchant-capitalist, a sort of combined manufacturer and wholesaler. Instead of waiting for the customer to order in advance, the merchant-capitalist bought raw materials and sent it out for fabrication, either to a worker's home or a manufactory, to his own specifications. This ready-made commodity, or shopwork as it was called, was sold to retail stores and then to the final consumer. Because it was produced in large quantities, shopwork was cheaper. But it tended to drive the master craftsman out of business and it changed significantly the relationship between journeyman and master. Wages no longer were determined now by the price list in the master's shop but by what the merchant-capitalist would pay, and it was figured on the basis of time—by the day or by the week. The gulf between labor and capital grew apace.

With the advent of the factory system and the industrial capitalist, the problem became more acute. The early craftsman—let us say a shoemaker—had been a moderately independent person, proud of his workmanship. But with the machine he became a semi-skilled operative, working under entirely different conditions. As Jefferson had foreseen, women and children flooded the factories, and worked under the most unsanitary and depressing conditions. The typical workday was from sunup to 10 P.M. in the summer, a few hours less in the winter. For this, men earned from $2.50 to $5.80 a week; the women $2.25; and children under twelve, 50 cents plus board. The factory girls were required to live in boardinghouses and were severely controlled—much like female operatives in pre-World War II Japan. If they stayed out beyond a certain time at night, they were discharged. If they were a few minutes late, they were fined 12½ cents. They had to agree in advance that they would not "engage in any combination" (union) to improve their lot. And if they did, they agreed to forfeit their wages. Since wages were paid only twice a year in many places, this threat was a potent one.

Concomitantly, the social scene was also modified. Factory towns sprang up everywhere, in which a single company controlled the local politicians, churches, newspapers, police. The country prospered greatly with the influx of industry, but it also was desperately hurt by frequent and enervating depressions—every decade or less, beginning with 1819. The result was a widening gap between wealth and poverty.

According to the editor of the *Niles Register*, a business publication, there was one pauper for every 250 people in 1815. During the depression that began four years later, there were 12,000 on the streets of New York alone; by 1845 it was estimated that 20 percent of the population of that city was in need of public charity. The specter of unemployment plagued the laborer from cradle to grave. Twenty thousand men and women, perhaps half the breadwinners, found themselves jobless in Philadelphia in the first great depression. Their mood is typified by this statement of a skilled printer who brought his wife and children to New York in 1820: "I had barely two dollars in my pocket when I got here with my family. We lived eight days without tea, sugar or meat—on bread and butter only with cold water. It is pinching times." The industrial whirlwind brought power, profit, and affluence to the United States, but it also brought far too many "pinching times."

"That the factory system contains in itself the elements of slavery," said a workingman's paper during this period, "we think no sound reasoning can deny. . . ."

To escape from "wage slavery"—or at least make it tolerable— became the preoccupation of simple workers as well as social philosophers. The first instinct was for workers to group together—form unions—and pit their power against that of the employers. Strange as it may seem, this was a new idea when it was first tried by American workers. The first unions in the world originated here.

Their evolution is clouded in some controversy, since the initial combinations of workers were tenuous affairs in which the artisans and mechanics joined together for a specific objective and then dispersed. Sketchy records of "unions" and "strikes" go back to pre-Revolutionary days, not only in the North but in the South. A Charles Town Mechanics Society, for instance, was the core of the South Carolina Liberty Party, which urged independence back in 1766. The first modern-type strike, however, is said to have occurred in Philadelphia in 1786. Journeymen printers, aggrieved by rising prices, petitioned their employers for a dollar-a-day wage scale. When the employer refused, they *turned out,* and won their demand. House carpenters in Philadelphia went on strike in 1791 to reduce their workday from thirteen hours to ten. The turnout— strike—soon became a frequent weapon of sailors, shoemakers, masons, printers, and other craftsmen. After 1792 journeymen began to form *permanent* societies. The first, that of Philadelphia shoemakers, survived but a single year, but was reorganized and continued until 1806. Early unions had neither full-time officials nor offices. When a worker joined, he took an oath to accept no wage scale less than that prescribed by the society, to help other members find jobs, and to keep union affairs a secret. Initiation fees were forty or fifty cents, dues six cents to ten cents a month.

The first unions were small affairs. The Philadelphia Typographical Society in 1809 had 119 members; the following year it shrank to 55, after it lost a strike. The New York Typographical Society had only 84 members in 1817, of whom 45 were in arrears in their dues payments.

Added to their woes was the fact that they were condemned by employers as illegal "conspiracies," and harried by the courts. In 1806 Philadelphia shoemakers, on strike for a wage increase, were haled before the bar in the first of a continuing number of conspiracy cases. The prosecutor argued that while a man might ask for a raise for himself, he could not enter into a "conspiracy" with another artisan to jointly make the request. The court held with the prosecutor, fined the men one dollar and costs, and ordered their union disbanded. From 1806 to 1815 there were six such conspiracy trials, four of them decided against the unions. Only in 1842 did the courts finally recognize the right of laborers to form their own organizations.

Under these circumstances, though unions continued to operate, they were too small, too tenuous, and, in a sense, too pragmatic. Occasionally they moved beyond the narrow limits of unionism, to engage in what labor historian Helen L. Sumner calls "retaliatory cooperation." For instance, when the Philadelphia carpenters went on strike in 1791, they formed a cooperative offering their services to customers at 25 percent below what the employers charged. They shared the profits equally. After the Philadelphia shoemakers were convicted in the 1806 conspiracy case, they established a cooperative shoe warehouse. On occasion journeymen united to do a single job—publish a book, for instance—then dissolved their cooperative relationship to return to private employment. But these ventures were pragmatic reactions rather than the result of philosophic outlook. The unions, though they were to outlast all other working-class institutions, were not the stuff out of which dreams are made. They did not offer the workingman or his middle-class friends the vision of a beautiful tomorrow which would be free of strife and want.

What was needed to contain the industrial monster, as some visionaries saw it, was something more meaningful than a few hours less work per day or a few pennies more in wages. What was needed was an image of a different kind of society, based on cooperation rather than individualism, love rather than profit—in a word, a utopia. Utopian ideas and utopian communities gripped the imagination of innumerable people in the first half of nineteenth-century America, forming a special chapter both in the history of radicalism and the nation.

III

In 1824 there arrived in the United States an unusual man named Robert Owen. With long nose and rugged features he was far from handsome, but he carried himself with the grace of an athlete and there was an aura of self-confidence to him which was infectious. At the age of fifty-three, Owen was a phenomenal success in business, with a reputation that stretched the length of Europe. He had been born to poverty, the son of a saddler and ironmonger from Wales. His education had been fragmentary. At the age of nine he decided to leave the narrow confines of the village of Newton—population one thousand—to seek his fortune. At the behest of his parents he delayed until his tenth birthday and then, with forty shillings in his pocket, left for London to take a job as apprentice to a linen draper. His pay, typical of the times, was nothing for the first year besides room and board, eight pounds the second year, and ten pounds the third. If the wages were negligible, they were compensated for in part by the good-sized library of his employer, which permitted young Owen to proceed with self-education.

After four years in London, the draper's apprentice moved on to Manchester, where he changed over to factory employment for a few years, formed a partnership with a wire manufacturer, moved on to his own modest business, and then—not yet twenty—took on the task of managing a cotton-spinning factory with five hundred employees. The young man had extraordinary organizing talents, a sharp analytical mind, imperturbable temper, and was uniformly courteous to other people. Though he looked younger than his age, he so strongly impressed his new employer, Peter Drinkwater, that he was able to pry him loose of a higher wage than any of the other applicants had asked. Within six months he had improved the product so much that Drinkwater offered him a future partnership. Seven or eight years later Owen made a marital and business coup simultaneously. He convinced David Dale, who owned a textile mill in New Lanark, Scotland, to sell him part of his interest and hire him as manager; and he married Dale's daughter Caroline.

By the standards of 1800 these mills were among the best in Britain, offering what was then considered humane treatment for the sixteen hundred to two thousand operatives who worked there. But work was so taxing and pay so small that only the neediest were willing to accept employment at New Lanark. Of the employees, five hundred were foundlings, aged five to seven, who labored from 6 A.M. to 7 P.M. The town itself was filthy; its people saddled with debt to the tavern owner or storekeeper, given to drink, brutality, thievery, sexual promiscuity.

In a few years Owen had transformed New Lanark beyond recognition. The high-priced stores were replaced by Owen's own stores where merchandise was sold at cost. Saloons were moved out of the village, streets were cleaned, homes built, child labor abolished, free public schools provided for the youngsters, working hours reduced, wages raised, and punishment replaced by advice and counseling. On one occasion when there was a cotton shortage and the mill had to close down, Owen paid the workers full wages, an unheard-of generosity in industrial towns those days. Police, magistrates, lawsuits, poor laws went by the boards. New Lanark emerged an exhibition place for liberals and reformers from all over the world who flocked to see the miracle wrought by Owen. Included among the visitors was the future Czar Nicholas I of Russia.

But Owen soon realized how inadequate were the efforts of a single employer, no matter how good his will. What was wrong was not that employers were greedy per se, but that competition forced them to keep wages and conditions as low as possible, if they would survive. The answer to this dilemma of the industrial system lay in cooperation. No principle, he concluded, had "produced so much evil as the principle of individualism. . . . Until the individual system shall be entirely abandoned it will be useless to expect any substantial, permanent improvement in the conditions of the human race." Men should live together in cooperative communities, work together, and share all things in common.

Owen's rudimentary socialism was not new. Many religious sects lived in communitarian societies both before and after Owen. A group of German Anabaptists formed a community in Lancaster County, Pennsylvania, in 1732, which was to survive for 175 years. The "United Society of Believers in Christ's Second Coming" established fifty-eight communities between 1780 and 1874 as havens for their religious concepts of celibacy, confession, and common property. Religious socialist societies originated from the belief of certain Protestant sects that they were separate and consecrated bodies opposed to the sinful, mundane, world. They aimed, as Arthur Eugene Bestor, Jr., has noted in his book *Backwoods Utopias,* "to withdraw from all contact with the State, with force and secular power, and in a voluntary union to realize the evangelical law of God." They chose to build a "society within a society." Owen and his successors, however, were trying to build a new society out of the old one. He saw the secular socialist community as the ultimate form of society. He was convinced he could proselytize both capitalist and worker to give up the private profit system for the cooperative commonwealth. Why not? "The rich and the poor, the governors and the governed," he said, "have but one interest." That interest was to achieve a common happiness, which they could build together. There was no need to fight each other, no need of a class struggle, when salvation was so close at hand.

"These establishments," he wrote in an appeal to American entrepreneurs, "will enable the capitalists and men of extensive practical experience to solve without difficulty the Great Problem of the Age, that is, how to apply the enormous and ever-growing new scientific powers for producing wealth, beneficially for the entire population, instead of allowing them to continue, as heretofore, most injuriously to create enormous riches for the few and to impoverish the many, driving them toward a desperation that will ultimately, if not timely prevented by this measure, involve the over-wealthy in utter destruction."

It was as simple as that: the capitalists, if they were intelligent enough, must realize that unless they formed the cooperative society now, they would soon be swept aside by a social tornado— revolution.

Naïve as Owen's notions sound today, they were strongly welcomed in the United States in 1825. No proposal for the remaking of society had ever received so polite a hearing. On two occasions Owen addressed the House of Representatives, while President James Monroe and President-elect John Quincy Adams sat and listened. His lectures, from New York to New Orleans, were assiduously reported in the press. His proposal enrolled only a few tens of thousands into its practical experiments, but it gained sympathy the length and breadth of the land from many hundreds of thousands, and eventually drew to it most of the great intellectuals of the era— Emerson, Thoreau, Whitman, Greeley, Albert Brisbane, to list a few.

IV

If Robert Owen chose the United States for his experiment, it was because in England the same men who praised him as a forward-looking capitalist, when he was renovating New Lanark, looked askance at him when he proposed socialism. Across the ocean, Owen felt, there was hope that "fifty years of political liberty had prepared the American population . . . to govern themselves advantageously."

In Indiana there existed in 1825 a religious communistic settlement of six hundred Germans, called Harmony. Established in 1814 under the leadership of George Rapp, it had prospered to the point where thirty thousand acres of land had been cleared, and homes, factories, mills, and other appurtenances built. It was ready made for the new social order, and Owen cheerfully paid over $150,000 to begin his crusade. The Rappites, pocketing their windfall, moved to Economy, near Pittsburgh, while Owen began his labors for the beautiful tomorrow.

For a man who had been so competent in private business, it is incredible how loose and ineffective Owen became in this utopian venture. Turning from reformer to prophet, he was in a "lunatic hurry"—as one writer puts it—and thus too preoccupied to take elementary precautions. He did not try, for instance, to make a detailed estimate of how much more money would be needed once the project was under way. He made no attempt to screen the applicants, to determine if they were fit for such a life and if they believed in his principles. Six weeks after New Harmony was proclaimed, it had eight hundred members ready to transform a simple community into a brotherhood of man, but they were too assorted in interests and views to make a compatible lot. Some were dedicated idealists anxious to create a socialist society; others, restless men seeking to escape an unhappy plight elsewhere; a few, outright crooks. Robert Dale Owen, son of Robert Owen, who arrived at New Harmony the following spring, referred to the colonists as "a heterogeneous collection of radicals, enthusiastic devotees to principle, honest latitudinarians and lazy theorists, with a sprinkling of unprincipled sharpers thrown in." Among the experimenters were intellectual giants such as William Maclure, president of the Philadelphia Academy of Natural Sciences; Thomas Warren, inventor of a rotary press; Thomas Say, entomologist; Gerard Troost, renowned Dutch chemist and geologist; and Charles Alexander Lesueur, the French naturalist.

The array of talent was awesome and some of the innovations inspiring. Inhabitants received all necessities from the community store. At a time when free public education was a fervid cry of the lower classes, New Harmony educated, clothed, and boarded 130 children. For culture, the society had its own band, which gave concerts on Friday evenings and played for dances on Tuesdays. An apothecary dispensed medicine free of charge.

New Harmony operated in many respects like the *Kibbutzim* in Palestine a century later. But where the Zionist experiment was held together by the glue of nationalism, the Owen project showed strong centrifugal tendencies. It lacked the harmony it propounded. People lounged around and argued, rather than worked. Petty disputes led to disaffiliation, as in 1826, when a few members broke away to establish a second cooperative community two miles from town.

A man named Taylor put up a distillery, against Owen's wishes, and when asked to leave, defrauded the society of a considerable sum. New Harmony was a delightful place to live. But it foundered, as Josiah Warren—one of the colonists—pointed out, "on pecuniary affairs." The only manufacturing that produced more than was consumed was soap and glue. New Harmony was not carrying its weight financially, and as each crisis arose there were reorganizations and more reorganizations. Things went so badly that democratic councils were sometimes dissolved and either Owen or a committee installed as "dictators." Dissension over how the property should be disposed of was endless.

On June 4, 1826, Owen delivered his famous Declaration of Mental Independence: "I now declare to you and to the world, that Man, up to this hour, has been in all parts of the earth a slave to a Trinity of the most monstrous evils that could be combined to inflict mental and physical evil upon his whole race. I refer to Private or Individual Property, Absurd and Irrational systems of Religion, and Marriage founded on Individual Property, combined with some of these Irrational systems of Religion." But within a year these idealistic words vanished before the sweep of reality. Owen found it necessary to sell property to individuals, and the greater part of the town was soon composed of private plots. A private grocery store opened up opposite the tavern, both an affront to the cooperative principle. Before long, small capitalist ventures were operating in manufacture and trade. "Everything," as A. J. MacDonald, a New

Harmony member, wrote, "was getting back into the old style."

Within three years the first secular utopia in America disintegrated. Owen's son, Robert Dale Owen, attributed the debacle to the fact there was too much liberty and equality, introduced all at once. The father concluded "that families trained in the individual system, founded as it is upon superstition, have not acquired those moral qualities of forbearance and charity for each other which are necessary to promote full confidence and harmony among all the members, and without which Communities cannot exist." He left the country, momentarily disappointed, to become a reformer and trade-union leader in England, where he died at the age of eighty-seven. Robert Dale Owen remained in the United States as one of its foremost radicals, a collaborator of Fanny Wright. The eighteen other Owenite groups established in New York, Ohio, and Indiana in 1826 and 1827 all went the same way as New Harmony.

Fifteen years after the dissolution of the utopia in Indiana, one of its members visited the town, and recorded that "socialism was unpopular. . . . The people had been wearied and disappointed by it; had been filled full with theories, until they were nauseated, and had made such miserable attempts at practice, that they seemed ashamed of what they had been doing. . . . Mr. Owen said he wanted honesty of purpose, and he got dishonesty. He wanted temperance, and instead, he was continually troubled with intemperance. He wanted industry, and he found idleness. . . . He wanted desire for knowledge, but he found apathy."

V

A variation of the Owen principle was applied by Fanny Wright in an effort to free the American Negro. Undaunted by former President Madison's comment that there was no solution to slavery, Fanny applied herself with typical vigor to find it. She had met Owen in Washington and was immensely attracted by his views. Based on her discussions with him and a visit to New Harmony, the energetic feminist evolved a Plan for the Gradual Abolition of Slavery Without Danger of Loss to the Citizens of the South, which won plaudits not only from Madison, but Jefferson, Monroe, and, it is said, even Chief Justice Marshall, who was hardly a radical.

The plan was daringly simple. White benefactors would buy

slaves from their owners and pay off the purchase price from the profits they hoped to earn from a cooperative plantation. On this plantation, white emancipationists would work side by side with their Negro friends, meanwhile educating them in the three R's, and training them in various skills for future self-support. Fanny's first project was to cost $41,000 and bring a profit—she estimated—of $10,000 a year. In her exuberance she visualized full freedom for the slaves within five years.

Little did Fanny anticipate the difficulties ahead. The original prospectus called for fifty to a hundred slaves to work a two-thousand-acre plantation at Nashoba, Tennessee. Unfortunately there was barely enough money to buy five Negroes, and though a South Carolina planter generously contributed an entire family of bondmen, the number never exceeded thirty. Five white intellectuals, including the Wright sisters, who were terribly unaccustomed to physical labor, threw themselves into the operation with unbounded enthusiasm. With the Negroes, they cleared land, planted corn, built fences—undeterred by the intense heat and malarial conditions. To their surprise, however, they found that the would-be freemen lacked the same determination. Robert Dale Owen reported after a visit to Nashoba that scarcely a hundred acres had been cleared, and that the slaves—"released from fear of the lash"—worked indolently. Malingering was a constant source of friction and led to one community meeting after another, where votes were taken as to whether to accept the slaves' excuses. An entry in the community's record of June 13, 1827, noted: "Willis having reported to us that Henry declined coultering today on the plea of a pain in his knee joint to which he is subject—we met the slaves at breakfast time and told them that though we do not doubt that Henry's knee gave him more or less pain, we had not sufficient confidence in his veracity to trust to his statement regarding the degree of the ailment, that we would therefore take their vote respecting the capacity of Henry to follow the oxen today."

To add to the usual financial problems, Nashoba ran into two others. The project leader, Fanny Wright, fell dangerously sick from overwork and left for Lafayette's home in France to recuperate. With this loss, leadership fell into the hands of an erratic person, James Richardson, who felt he must fight many causes simultaneously. With a flare for exhibitionism, he published in an emancipationist journal, salacious details of Nashoba's sex life. Thus he recorded in printer's ink that he and a quadroon, Mamselle Josephine, "began to live together," that "Maria . . . now cohabits with Henry," and that Redrick went to the bedroom of Isabel "uninvited and endeavoring without her consent to take liberties with her person." Fanny, though her own views on sex were not puritanical, was shocked when she heard of this "publicity" and wrote Richardson a stinging letter. But the damage was done and could not be undone. Even an emancipationist called Nashoba "a great brothel." The term "Fanny Wrightism" became a stigma signifying loose morality.

By the time Fanny returned to her experiment she had had second thoughts about such means for freeing the slave. Though only thirty-two, she realized she was incapable of heavy pioneering labor, and so were her friends. Anyway, she concluded there would soon be an influx into the South of white free labor from the North that would make slavery obsolete. The Negro would be liberated through education and "racial amalgamation" rather than projects such as Nashoba. When Robert Dale Owen invited her to help him edit his paper the *Gazette,* she betook herself to New Harmony. A year and a half later she abandoned Nashoba entirely. She discharged her obligations to the thirty slaves by escorting them to Haiti, where they began life anew, as free citizens.

VI

The death of Owenism (it was to be revived in other forms later) coincided with the birth of a new type of radicalism. The first labor parties in the world sprang from American soil in the late 1820's, just as the first unions had three decades before. Unlike utopian socialist experiments, which were based on preconceived blueprints, the Workingmen's Parties—or "Workies," as they were called— evolved from the crucible of labor-management conflict. Where the former began with a vision that sought reality, the latter began with mundane grievances and worked its way toward the dream. Utopian socialism made no distinction of class; it was a no-class or a multi-class movement, inviting worker and capitalist alike to join it. The Workie was an instrument for a single class, the wage laborers.

One summer morning in 1827, six hundred carpenters in Philadelphia, tired of working from sunup to sundown, put down their tools to seek a ten-hour day. They wanted a shorter workday, they said, not only for more personal leisure, but to improve their citizenship. The long day prevented them from engaging in public affairs, leaving the field open to the wealthy and idle. They noted, in passing, the lack of free education, which kept the children of the poor in a condition of ignorance. The strike was unsuccessful, but it spurred unionists in Philadelphia to form the Mechanics' Union of Trade Associations, composed of delegates from all labor organizations in the city. This "union of unions" sought the ten-hour day, of course, but went far beyond it. "The real objective of this association," said its constitution, "is to avert, if possible, the desolating evils which must inevitably arise from a depreciation of the intrinsic value of human labor . . . and to assist . . . in establishing a just balance of power, both mental, moral, political and scientific, between all the various classes and individuals which constitute society at large."

What began in Philadelphia spread rapidly to Pittsburgh, Lancaster, Harrisburg, Cincinnati, New York, Wilmington, Newark, Trenton, Albany, Buffalo, Boston, Providence, and even Portland, Maine, and Burlington, Vermont. From 1828 to 1834 sixty-one Workingmen's Parties blossomed, and sixty-eight labor newspapers, many of them dailies, saw the light of day to sound off working-class views. Some of the parties were relatively subdued in their pronouncements; others were extremist. The words of the Working Men's Republican Political Association of Penn Township, Pennsylvania, were a foretaste of Karl Marx's *Communist Manifesto* two decades later: "There appear to exist two distinct classes, the rich and the poor; the oppressed and the oppressor; those that live by their own labor and they that live by the labor of others; the aristocratic and the democratic; the despotic and republican, who are in direct opposition to one another in their objects and pursuits. . . ."

The vague sympathy of the Workies for revolution was made evident when the second French Revolution took place in 1830. New York unionists marched in a parade three miles long. The mood was so tempestuous that in May 1830 the *Newark Village Chronicle* claimed—much too optimistically, as it turned out—that "from Maine to Georgia, within a few months past we discern symptoms of a revolution, which will be second to none save that of '76."

If there were to be no new revolution, however, there were many uncompleted tasks left over from the first one, and these became the platform for labor party agitation. Emblazoned on the Workie banners, first of all, was the demand for a free public-school system. This had been a recurring issue since the 1790's but was still unappeased. The few free schools that existed carried the "pauper" stigma and were grossly inadequate. As late as 1834 it was estimated that a million and a quarter school-age children were illiterate. Education, said the Workies, was not a matter of "charity" but of "right and duty" to prevent "the fabric of Democracy from being crushed beneath the weight of a monopolized and monied aristocracy."

Another irritant was the militia system. All male citizens were required to take part in military training three times a year. The man who failed to report was fined twelve dollars, and if he did not pay the fine, was put in jail. Since the wealthy could evade their obligations by paying this small sum, the burden was squarely on the laborers for whom twelve dollars represented two to four weeks' pay. Abolish the militia system, cried the Workies. Imprisonment for debt must also be ended. Under this ancient practice, there were seventy-five thousand in jail in the United States, one half of them for debts of twenty dollars or less. Persecution of this sort was "inconsistent with the spirit of our republican institutions," said the Workies.

The range of labor complaints was extensive. The legal structure lacked a mechanics' lien to protect a worker when his employer went bankrupt. Mechanics lost from $300,000 to $400,000 a year because wages were not considered, as today, the first obligation of a defunct company. Convict labor robbed workers of jobs and tended to reduce wage standards. A contractor in the 1820's could arrange for work in prison at wages ranging from ten cents a day for weavers, to twenty-five cents a day for more skilled shoemakers. Unequal taxes, property qualifications for holding office in some states, and similar grievances, were also brought up by the Workies for remedy.

One of the most persistent issues they dealt with was that of the chartered companies and chartered banks. It is now forgotten, but for almost a century American workers and farmers resisted the formation of limited liability companies—corporations. Early corporations were permitted to own limited amounts of property, were required to operate in a single line of business and for specific periods, say twenty or thirty years, after which they were required to dissolve. Monopolistic banks were conceived of as vehicles to "perpetuate an aristocracy which eventually may shake the foundations of our liberties and entail slavery upon our posterity." Such charges were not based purely on theory. Small farmers, when they could get credit at all, were being charged usurious interest rates, which the wealthier classes could absorb and pass on in higher prices. The worker was being paid in bank notes issued by private banks which had to be cashed at a discount. Wages varied in purchasing power from day to day and week to week, depending on the foibles of Wall Street. Employers often bought notes at reduced rates on the Wall Street market and then paid them out as the full coin to their workers. The unionists demanded now that wages be paid in specie—in coin or in bills of unvarying value.

By themselves, the concrete planks of the Workingmen's Parties were not revolutionary, but reformist. Most of them became law by the time "Old Hickory" Jackson and Martin Van Buren had departed from office. Imprisonment for debt and the militia system were done away with, free public schools functioned in most states, mechanics' lien laws were passed, even the Bank had fallen under Jackson's offensive. Their enactment was a monumental victory for the Workies' agitation in the few short years that they had functioned. But for many of the labor party leaders of that day reform was only a down payment for revolution. The ultimate liberation of the proletariat would come only with a basic change in society per se.

VII

The center of radical spirit was in New York, where those two stalwarts Robert Dale Owen and Fanny Wright, joined by Thomas Skidmore and George Henry Evans, were leading the crusade. Skidmore was a machinist; Evans was editor of the *Working Man's Advocate*. As in Philadelphia, the New York Working Men's Party grew out of mundane despair. The year 1829 was the second of a serious economic downturn. *The Morning Courier* of February 26, 1829, stated that "it is almost impossible to imagine and consequently beyond the reach of our pen to describe the suffering under which the poor of our city are at this time laboring by reason of

Cold and Hunger." New York was then the only city where employers recognized the ten-hour day. But with many unemployed, management decided this was a favorable moment to lengthen the hours to eleven. Union leaders responded by calling a mass meeting at which six thousand workers protested the change and elected a Committee of Fifty to organize a general strike. This determination persuaded the employers to yield on the issue. Simultaneously it encouraged the New Yorkers to form a new party. In due course they nominated a slate for the State Assembly and polled a surprising 6,000 votes out of 21,000 cast. One Workie member, a carpenter, was elected.

The success, however, could not dampen the fervid doctrinal dispute that embroiled the New York party. Skidmore, a self-educated, single-minded man, was most responsible for the formation of the labor party. In his thinking the election of good men to office was valuable but not a panacea. Nothing less than an uprooting of property relations would bring security to the workingman. A book Skidmore was writing gives some clue to his philosophy. It carried the long and imposing title: "The Rights of Man to Property! Being a Proposition to make it Equal among the Adults of the Present Generation: and to Provide for its Equal Transmission to Every Individual of Each Succeeding Generation, on Arriving at the Age of Maturity." Under Skidmore's plan, every man twenty-one or over, and every unmarried woman, would receive 160 acres of land, to be held as long as he or she tilled it. Such land could not be disposed of either by sale or rental. Those who currently owned more than the allotted 160 acres would not be disturbed, except after death. Then an inheritance law would expropriate everything over 160 acres. "Inasmuch as great wealth," said Skidmore, "is an instrument which is uniformly used to extort from others their property, it ought to be taken away from its possessors on the same principle that a sword or pistol may be wrested from a robber. . . ." Though he urged the poor to appropriate cotton factories, iron foundries, and industrial property in the same way as land, his philosophy was called agrarianism and his theories likened to those of Thomas Paine in his *Agrarian Justice*. In fact, however, it came closer to the revolutionary views of Karl Marx, in that it favored an expropriation of property. Where he differed from later socialists was that he did not conceive of state operation of industry or of cooperative farming.

[77]

The American economy was as yet too rudimentary to suggest these alternatives.

Skidmore was able to win the Committee of Fifty to his philosophy, but he was soon challenged by others with different panaceas. Robert Dale Owen and Fanny Wright, having recently given up their communitarian exploits, propounded a new thesis for proletarian liberation. The younger Owen was twenty-eight, short, blue-eyed, sandy-haired—a man of forceful character like his father. Despite his clumsiness in speech and an unpleasing voice, he made a deep and sincere impression on his audiences. Fanny Wright, whom Walt Whitman described as graceful, deerlike, and "whose very appearance seemed to enthrall us," was an indefatigable orator. With George Henry Evans, a printer by trade and editor of the most important labor paper of the time, they criticized Skidmore's scheme as "crude communism." Instead of expropriating property, the road to equality, said these Free Enquirers, lay in "State Guardianship Education."

According to this plan, the state would adopt all children after they reached the age of two. Both the children of the poor and the children of the rich would be placed in great boarding schools and be educated together. The cost would be borne by taxes on real property and the parents, as well as by work performed by the older students. This kind of education, said Fanny and her followers, would result in "the salvation and regeneration of human kind," for young people who grew up in an atmosphere of equality were bound to transform society in the same leveling direction. The Free Enquirers called for "equal food, clothing and instruction at public expense" and though they admitted that the public school without boardinghouses might do some good, it was "not practically democratic," since it did not do away with a society where "one class produces, while another consumes."

Though there was a utopian quality to this scheme, it represented a deepening of Fanny and Owen's radicalism. They were now committed to the notion of class conflict. "What distinguishes the present from every other struggle in which the human race has been engaged," argued Fanny, "is that the present is evidently openly and acknowledgedly, a war of class. . . ."

The differences between the two radical factions—both of which agreed with the reform planks of the Working Men's Party—turned out to be irrelevant. Though the conservative press raved about "The Fanny Wright Party," "The Infidel Party," "the barbarous dispossessed," the "scum," the "ring streaked and speckled rabble," and Fanny herself was called "a crazy atheistical woman," American capitalism was safe from either agrarianism or state guardianship. The *Working Men's Advocate* of November 7, 1829, could exult that the elections had "proved beyond our most sanguine expectation favorable to our cause," but the internal discord had already doomed the party for which it spoke. As indicated, a carpenter was elected to the Assembly, and three other candidates lost by small margins of 25, 26, and 31 votes. In Salina, upstate New York, the Farmers and Mechanics' Party elected its whole slate the following spring; in Troy and Albany all but one ward went to the Workies. But the party itself was under too much outside pressure to survive its internal factionalism. A sulking Skidmore, defeated on an organizational motion, withdrew from the Workie and formed his own sect with its own paper. The Owen-Wright-Evans faction, belabored from pillar to post for its extremism, lost support constantly. The moderate element charged Fanny was trying to foist on workers the "doctrine of infidelity" and urged them "to preserve the civil institutions of your country from the baneful, levelling system of a fanatical set of foreigners." When the smoke had lifted, the moderates controlled the most sizable of the three Workies. Each ran its own slate in the 1830 elections. But together they polled one third of what the combined group did the year before.

Workies everywhere flamed into existence and sputtered out almost as quickly. The Philadelphia party was able to elect twenty of its fifty-four candidates for city and state office—all of them simultaneously running either with Jackson's Democrats or the Federalists. Workie enthusiasts believed they were so strong they would be a permanent balance of power. But by 1830 charges in the press that the party was "anti-religious," "agrarian," and "Fanny Wrightist" —all untrue—had the desired effect of intimidating its adherents and decimating its ranks. In one of the suburbs, Northern Liberties, the labor party elected eight commissioners. But the movement had lost its momentum. Next year it elected no one.

As the depression of 1828–31 came to an end, radical ardor dampened. Workingmen, disquieted over the factory system, the Bank, and other features of the society in transition, nonetheless found

[79]

sufficient triumph through trade unions and in emotional identification with that man of the people in the White House, Andrew Jackson, to still their extremism—until the next time. In the prosperous days that followed there were many gains for the workingman on the industrial front. The strikes of 1833–34 resulted in sizable wage increases. A walkout by seventeen Philadelphia unions for a "six-to-six" workday the next year was a grand success and was followed by similar outpourings in a dozen centers from Baltimore to Hartford. Strikes for additional wage boosts brought skilled mechanics benefits as high as 50 percent. In the balm of victory two hundred labor societies were rebuilt, city central bodies emerged again in a dozen cities, and in 1834—another historical first—a national union of unions was formed, the National Trades' Union, with a claimed membership of three hundred thousand.

The tall, thin man, with wrinkled face and white hair, occupying the Presidential seat, was also a source of refreshment for the common man, both in the city and village. Andrew Jackson gave the grass-roots citizen a feeling of belonging again. He discarded what was by now the safe term, Republican, and referred to the party of Jefferson by the flaunting term "Democrat"—which still had a trace of anarchism associated with it. All the Presidents before him, whatever their political philosophy, had come from propertied families. All, except Washington, had a college education. None had ever worked with his hands for a livelihood. But Jackson was born of impoverished folk in South Carolina. He was rough in manner, his grammar was incredibly bad, he smoked an old unseemly pipe, chewed tobacco, told ribald stories, and knew painfully little about tariffs and similar details of politics. But he was a grand success story, a military hero, and a man of the people from head to toe. His taunting class consciousness was a delight to the average man. When he vetoed the bill to recharter the Bank of the United States in July 1832, he made no bones about his predisposition: "It is to be regretted that the rich and powerful too often bend the acts of government to their selfish purposes. . . . When the laws undertake . . . to make the rich richer and the potent more powerful, the humble members of society, the farmers, mechanics, and laborers, who have neither the time nor the means of securing like favors to themselves, have a right to complain of the injustice of their government." As might be deduced, Jackson did not believe in the consensus theory of governing.

With such a man at the head of the Democratic Party, fighting the Bank, extending the vote, solidarizing himself with the little man, the mechanic and laborer could endorse it, even where—as in New York—there was a taint of corruption. Many of the Workie leaders joined with the Jacksonian wing in the Democratic Party. In Indiana, Robert Dale Owen ran for the legislature as a Democrat and was elected under its banner. In this circumstance there was a pause for a few years, while agrarianism, utopianism, and "Fanny Wrightism" lay dormant—though not forgotten. As late as 1858 an Alabama congressman referred to "Socialism and agrarianism and Fanny Wrightism" as the scourge which brought about "mobocratic misrule."

CHAPTER VI

THE DREAMS OF
MIDPASSAGE

IN THE 1834 election for mayor of New York City workingmen went to the polls singing this song:

> *Mechanics, cartmen, laborers*
> *Must form a close connection,*
> *And show the rich Aristocrats,*
> *Their powers at this election*

Fear that rich aristocrats were in the process of re-forming an "aristocracy" persevered from the end of the Revolution well into the nineteenth century. That fear centered for a long time on two new phenomena—"the machine" and "the bank." Each in its own way seemed to be regrouping the forces of privilege, and threatening to reduce the status of the common man.

This was a period when neither the industrial capitalist nor the banking financier was as yet taken for granted. As a matter of fact, both were still considered an intrusion against the "normal" way of life, which included neither steam-driven machinery nor bankers. Back in 1811 British workers in Nottingham had formed secret bands of masked men—known as the Luddites—to invade textile mills and smash machinery. The movement became so strong in four or five areas, and had so much public support, that the government had to pass repressive laws, call out the troops, and hang some of the Luddites before machine breaking was stopped. American workers never resorted to machine breaking, but their suspicion of the new monster paralleled that of their British brethren. They were not hostile to the machine as such, only to what it was doing to their society. "The steam engine," wrote Thomas Skidmore in 1829, "is not injurious to the poor, when they can have the benefit of it. . . ." The trouble was that the "benefit of it" went to the wealthy—those who would become a new lawless aristocracy. Machinery, said John Commerford, a New York trade-union leader in 1835, must be under society's, rather than the capitalist's, jurisdiction. When that happens "machinery will not . . . be used, as it is now, for the benefit of the few, but for the mass. Governments will become the legitimate guardians of its improvements, and they will be compelled to keep machinery in operation for the comfort and convenience of the people." These were not isolated views in the era of transition prior to the Civil War. They were buttressed by the increasingly impersonal attitude taken toward employees by management. "So long as they can do my work for what I choose to pay them," said one millowner of his workers, "I keep them, getting out of them all I can. . . . When my machines get old and useless, I reject them and get new ones and these people are part of my machinery."

A second focal point of hostility, evoking even greater bitterness, was the chartered bank. Again, it was not a small group of "outsiders" that expressed such sentiments, but a popular spectrum running from the slum dweller to the inhabitant of the White House. The existence of the Bank of the United States, Thomas Jefferson had said in 1803, ran "against the principles and form of our Constitution." Martin Van Buren, when he was governor of New York, had denounced the chartered bank as a monopoly, injurious to "the laboring classes." He proposed, as early as 1817, that banks be forced to compete with each other. Jackson's veto of the bill to recharter the national Bank made him a universal hero, unbeatable in his campaign for a second term.

The worker knew, of course, that institutions for deposit and exchange were necessary. But when a government gave bankers a charter, they were giving them exclusive rights to issue all the currency notes that their president and cashier could sign. This currency tended to decline in value, reducing real wages as it fell. Further, when the government deposited its funds in the Bank, it was giving it a hidden subsidy, for the Bank used these monies to make loans at interest. Even more ominous was the fact that control over large sums of money made it possible for the bankers to wield political power far out of proportion to their number. As George Henry Evans, that perennial crusader, said in his paper the *Man:* "Is not this fact enough to alarm the American people? A *Bank* in the heart of the Republic with its branches scattered over the Union; wielding two hundred millions of capital; owning an immense amount of real property; holding at its command a *hundred thousand debtors;* buying up our newspapers, entering the field of politics; attempting to make Presidents and Vice-Presidents for the country. . . ." The Bank was not merely the fountainhead of economic privilege but an instrument of the "rich and well born" to win state power.

As far as the laboring man was concerned, banks and bankers were associated with just about every antisocial project known. "We want little more to convince us," said a resolution of thousands of New York workingmen at a meeting in 1834, "that the cause of the Bank is aristocratic and unjust than the simple fact that we find the same men arrayed in its favor who have always been opposed to our interest; who endeavored to deprive us of rights of suffrage; . . . and almost every other democratic measure that has ever been brought forward in our state or general government." The issue in the 1832 elections, as the *Working Men's Advocate* saw it, was "whether the Bank or the people shall rule the country."

The answer to the twin menace of bank and machine, threatening to restore aristocracy to America, was a doctrine that received considerable support in the 1830's—equal rights. As defined by William Leggett, a newspaper editor and a friend of Van Buren, equal rights implied that "the property of the rich be placed on the same footing with the labors of the poor." That meant that taxes must not be placed on the impoverished while "the rich go free," or that special rights be granted chartered corporations which entrenched monopoly while imposing burdens on the poor. Ely Moore, president of the New York General Trades' Union and the first leader of organized labor to serve in Congress, brought out the issue sharply in his maiden speech before the House of Representatives when he urged a "government founded on persons, and not on property; on equal rights, and not on exclusive privilege."

Among the equal rights legions were many of the leaders of the old Workie in New York—George Henry Evans, Commerford,

Moore, Alexander Ming. Though they were now working within Tammany and the Democratic Party, they were not doing so uncritically. They looked askance at those Tammany sachems who, while they opposed the national Bank, favored state banks in which they held shares of stock. To curb these elements in the Jacksonian party, the radicals grouped into a caucus, the Democratic Working Men's General Committee, to challenge the might of all banks, bankers, friends of bankers, and any Tammany sachems who curried favor with the bankers. This division within the Democratic Party led to the formation a year or so later of a short-lived and somewhat vague radical force that spread from New York to various other areas.

II

In October 1835 a mass meeting was scheduled at Tammany Hall to ratify a slate of candidates. Ordinarily this was a perfunctory affair, the machine's selection receiving unqualified approval. This time, however, trouble was brewing. Workingmen insurgents had been chafing over Tammany's increasing cordiality with the "lawless aristocracy" of New York. They had, in fact, formed another caucus within the Democratic Party—called Equal Rights Democracy—to control and decimate banker influence. But the slate that was being presented was made up from stem to stern of bankers and bankers' friends, and the radicals were as determined to upset it as the official claque to uphold it.

Tammany Hall was a unique institution, reflecting to some extent the conflicting forces within the nation. Before the Revolution the Sons of St. Tammany were a counterpart of the Sons of Liberty, with much the same objectives. Tammany—or Tamanend—was the name of a wise old Indian chief, and had been chosen to ridicule the followers of King George, who were forming societies in honor of numerous saints—such as St. George, St. David, St. Andrew. The Sons of St. Tammany were dissolved when the United States became independent, but an upholsterer, William Mooney, rescued the name from oblivion when he founded the Society of St. Tammany in 1789—again to fight off the encroachments of the aristocrats who would subvert democracy. The various leaders were, in Indian tradition, called sachems, and the chief leader, grand sachem. Tammany did not become an active political movement until 1800, when it campaigned ardently—in line with its principles —for Jefferson. Then in 1806 it was designated the official representative of the Republican (or, as it was later called, the Democratic) Party. Whatever its noble origins, however, by the 1830's Tammany was in the process of metamorphosis. It catered to the working masses from whom it received its votes, but it showed increasing trends toward the corruption that finally became its hallmark.

By six thirty on the evening of the date scheduled to approve the slate, a restive crowd gathered outside Tammany Hall, and when the doors were opened, swamped the seats nearest the rostrum. As each nominee's name was called off, the crowd greeted it with a chorus of hoots and catcalls. Nonetheless, the badly outnumbered conservatives ruled their slate approved and retired from the hall. Practically, it was the only maneuver left to them since there was no chance of winning a vote. Perhaps in the confusion the meeting would break up and the wrangle would come to an end. But if this was the strategy, the radicals were not to be dismayed. They raised their own banners with their own leftist slogans, and installed Joel Curtis, a former Working Men's Party leader, in the chair. Another maverick, Alexander Ming, Jr., jumped on a table ready to address the assemblage. Before he could open his mouth, however, the gas lights were turned off—a time-honored technique by which Tammany's sachems squelched opposition. Again, the wiley insurgents were prepared. From their pockets they drew out candles, and lit them with a friction match called locofoco. While fifty candles lined the platform, spreading an eerie glow over the hall, the spirited gathering nominated its own ticket, appropriately nicknamed by an amused public the Locofoco ticket. Thus began another political cleavage between radicals and moderates. The Locofocos did not win that year, though they garnered a respectable vote of 3,500, nor did they cause the defeat of Tammany. But they did make the race too close for comfort, and they continued in the ensuing months to try to capture Tammany.

Meanwhile two other events propelled the Locofocos to an independent course. The first was Mayor Cornelius Lawrence's use of the militia against a stevedore strike. The second, more important, was the conviction in 1835 of twenty-five union tailors on a charge of "conspiracy." There had been half a dozen similar rulings in various parts of the country, but Judge Edwards' reference to the tailors as "foreigners" raised tempers to the boiling point. The poet John Greenleaf Whittier denounced the decision as a doctrine "borrowed from the feudal aristocracy of Europe. If carried into practice generally, as it has been in New York, the condition of the free and happy laborers of our country will be little better than that of the Hungarian miner, or the Polish serf." An anonymous leaflet calling for a demonstration was headed "The Rich Against the Poor!" and advised workingmen: "A deadly blow has been struck at your liberty! The prize for which your fathers fought has been robbed from you! The freemen of the North are now on a level with the slave of the South! with no other privilege than laboring that drones may fatten on your life blood!"

One of the greatest protests in the young nation's history followed. Twenty-seven thousand gathered at City Hall Park to vent their fury. Judge Edwards' decision was condemned as a "concerted plan of the aristocracy to take from them [the workers] that Liberty which was bequeathed to them as a sacred inheritance by their revolutionary sires." Not surprisingly, they compared their protest with that of the men who threw "into Boston Harbor the tea that had branded upon it 'Taxation without Representation.'" A Committee of Correspondence, again reminiscent of Sam Adams' days, was elected to plan a convention that would cut "loose from both political parties" and run "a truly workingmen's ticket." In the ensuing weeks, despite the acquittal of shoemakers in Hudson, New York, on a similar charge, there were demonstrations in Poughkeepsie, Troy, Albany, and Hudson.

In September 1836, ninety-three delegates meeting at Utica drafted a "Declaration of Independence" and formed the Equal Rights Party "separate and distinct from all existing parties and factions." Isaac S. Smith, a former member of the Working Men's Party, was nominated for governor. If the specific planks of the Equal Rights program seemed tepid—election of judges for three-year terms, legislation to assure the rights of workers to organize, and opposition to paper money and bank notes—the general tone of the conclave was radical. The *Union,* organ of the New York General Trades' Union, described the pending elections as "a second Revolution" comparable to the one of 1776. "The Revolution of 1776," it claimed, "was against the monarch and aristocracy of England, this of 1836 is against charters and monopolies."

Locofocoism, though it did not produce the same kind of radical pronunciamentos as came from the pens of Fanny Wright or Thomas Skidmore, was nonetheless an important spur to Jacksonian reformism. It inspired Jackson and Van Buren to speed the pace of change, and it helped keep in line the two major parties. Often it was the balance of power in local elections. Tammany received a stinging rebuke in the mayoralty and aldermanic polls the following spring, primarily because the Equal Rights forces drained away working-class votes. The Locofocos shed few tears over this circumstance, even though it assured victory for the more business-minded Whig Party. They "could see no great difference in principles between the National Bank Whigs and State Bank Democrats."

The Equal Rights revolt was duplicated not only in twenty counties in New York but in Philadelphia, Massachusetts, and the West. Old insurgents who had fought with the Workies helped split the Democratic Party wherever it was becoming a spearhead for monopoly—and usually with Jackson's and Van Buren's blessing. Locofocoism was a major driving force for democracy, even in the West, where men such as Robert Dale Owen advanced the Jacksonian cause. The depression of 1837 reinforced its legions. As Arthur Schlesinger, Jr., records: "In the forties, as the dominion of the new finance crept westward, the radical Democrats grew stronger, and Locofoco ideas played a vital and sometimes dominating role in the state constitutional conventions of that and the next decade. . . . The East remained the source of the effective expression of Jacksonian radicalism, and Eastern ideas rose to supremacy in Washington as Jacksonianism changed from an agitation into a program."

An interesting side show to Locofocoism was the rebellion led by Thomas W. Dorr in Rhode Island. As late as 1840 this state, founded by Roger Williams, disfranchised half its citizens through a property qualification. Dorr and his lower-middle-class friends marched in great parades demanding this be changed and free suffrage instituted. Their banners blazed with such slogans as "No taxation without representation," "Liberty or Revolution." When they were unable to correct the situation through normal channels, they summoned a rump convention and drafted a "People's Constitution." In 1842 Dorr called his own elections in opposition to the official ones. Two separate governments emerged, each claiming to be the legal organ. The conservatives declared martial law; Dorr and his followers armed themselves and tried to seize the state arsenal. But the rebels, as in Shays' Rebellion of 1876, were dispersed, Dorr was arrested and sentenced to life imprisonment at hard labor.

The Dorr uprising had no links with the Locofoco movement, but it won Locofoco plaudits and support. New York workingmen passed a resolution that "we consider the cause of Dorr and Free Suffrage to be peculiarly the cause of the workingmen without re-gard to party. . . ." Had Rhode Island not granted a more liberal constitution the following year, it is likely that the Dorrites and Equal Rights advocates would have forged durable ties. Their pur-suit of equality was interlinked.

By the time of the Dorr Rebellion, however, it was already clear that the cry for equality by itself was too vague an idea to cope with industrialism. The Locofocos, in fact, were more of a mood than a movement. They lacked ideology, thus giving their efforts a defen-sive rather than forward-looking tone. And though their influence on Van Buren was substantial—in establishing a treasury system inde-pendent of the banks, for instance, or in the decree of a ten-hour day for certain federal employees—neither they nor the Jacksonians were able to formulate a program for the depression of 1837. The "Hideous Monster of Locofocoism," as the conservative Democrats and Whigs called it, was a challenge to some of the evils of nascent capitalism but not to capitalism itself.

III

With the panic of 1837—worldwide in scope—many men began to look to new nostrums. It was a dispiriting event for the working class, for with only a short interruption in 1842–43, it was to last for a decade and a half. By February 1837 the situation was dire. A "bread, meat, rent, and fuel" meeting, called by the Equal Rights Party in Chatham Square, New York, erupted into the famous flour riot. Part of the crowd drove the police and mayor to cover while it stormed and sacked a flour warehouse. In May the banks called a halt to specie payment, refusing to honor their paper notes. Six hun-dred banks closed down in a single year, and more thereafter. The twenty thousand unemployed who demonstrated in Philadelphia were, as one observer wrote President Van Buren, "more deeply agitated and roused" than he had ever seen before. By January 1838 there were tens of thousands unemployed in New York alone, and two hundred thousand living "in utter and hopeless distress with no means of surviving the winter but those provided by charity." One third of the laboring class was idle, most of the rest working part time. By 1839 wages had fallen 30 to 50 percent, and in the next two years there were actual incidents of families starving and freezing to death. At one time nine tenths of the New England factories were out of operation. This was the period when Horace Greeley urged the jobless to "fly, scatter through the country, go to the Great West, anything but stay here."

In these pitiful circumstances unions disappeared overnight as men fought for any available job, whatever the pay. Those who still had work were hesitant to form unions or go on strike when there were so many unemployed ready to take their places. Nor did political action offer much hope, for neither the Equal Rights movement nor President Van Buren seemed to have adequate answers. Inevitably then—here as in Europe—people began to listen to middle-class idealists who would fashion a new type of society, basically different from the existing one. Disoriented by the factory system, these men tried to recapture a vanishing epoch in which sturdy producers on the farm and in small workshops controlled their own destinies. They drew blueprints of a beautiful tomorrow, whose logic they thought was unassailable. Even the capitalists, they felt, could not resist.

The utopian doctrine which most captivated Americans in the late 1830's and 1840's was elaborated by the Frenchman Charles Fourier, and called Association. By Fourier's thesis, there was an ever-present power that drew men together for joint action. Unfortunately, this intrinsic attractiveness had been subverted, plunging mankind into antisocial behavior. Once the hurdles were removed, a universal harmony would ensue, men would develop a love of labor, and eliminate both economic waste and the chaotic system under which humanity was shackled. All that was needed was to find a form of social organization under which men could give vent to their inner passions. There were twelve such passions: the five senses, four "group passions"—friendship, love, family feeling, and ambition—and three "distributive passions"—passions for planning, change, and unity. These passions could be harnessed for the social good, so as to make work pleasant and greatly increase wealth. By way of example, Fourier conceived of "Little Hordes" of children whose passion for playing with dirt could be diverted to useful activity such as shining shoes, spreading manure, and cleaning streets. To make the tasks even more attractive, the youngsters would be designated a "Militia of God" and placed in the front lines of each parade.

The organizational form for achieving the ultimate harmony—and in Fourier's view, passing from human infancy to seventy thousand years of adulthood—was the *phalanx*. Essentially, the phalanx was a utopian community, in essence much like Robert Owen's New Harmony, but it was spelled out in far greater detail to take advantage of passional attractions. In each phalanx four hundred to two thousand men and women would live together in a large central building with common kitchen and common dining hall, called a *phalanstery*. The members of the community would unite into groups of seven to nine, who shared common tastes, known as a "series," and in larger units, called "groups." Each group would do a specific job, for instance, planting corn, while each series would undertake a part of the function, for instance, seeding or harvesting. To avoid monotony or boredom, an individual would be free to move from one series or group to another. Since everyone would be doing what he enjoyed, there would be no need for policemen, lawyers, or soldiers, and no possibility of crime. There would be only a small place for government because men would develop their natural harmony. The head of a phalanx would be called a "unarch," the leader of the world's phalanxes, with headquarters in Constantinople, an "omniarch," but beyond that few administrators would be necessary. Under these ideal conditions, according to Fourier, productivity would increase four or five times from present norms, so that a man would be able to produce enough in ten years, from age eighteen to twenty-eight, to live in comfort the rest of his days.

Fourier was no communist or socialist, in the strict sense of the word, for he did not propose to abolish classes. The capitalist and the worker would remain, but there would be a harmony between them. Under this plan a certain amount was to be allotted each person for his necessities. Beyond that, five twelfths would go to labor, four twelfths to capital, and three twelfths to talent. Labor was further divided into three classes—necessary, useful, and agreeable —with those doing the "necessary" work receiving the greatest rewards, and those the "agreeable" work the least.

Fourier personally was an eccentric bachelor whose ideas ranged from the bizarre to the brilliant. He actually visualized a day when lions would be tamed to draw carriages across the country, and whales to pull vessels across the seas. On the other hand, his analyses of monopoly, speculation, and adulteration of merchandise were highly competent, and he foresaw such "unbelievable" projects as the building of great canals not unlike Suez or Panama. He was certainly a single-minded person. The story is told that he once announced he would be at home at a certain hour every day to receive any philanthropist who would give him a million francs to set up a Fourieristic colony. For twelve years thereafter he waited each day punctually at noon for the generous donor, but no millionaire appeared.

Fourier, unlike Robert Owen, did not come to the United States to organize phalanxes or lecture to the House of Representatives. He died in fact in 1837, two or three years before his teachings began to take root here. The man responsible for introducing the theories of Association to Americans was Albert Brisbane, a figure as intriguing as Fourier himself. Only son of a rich landowner in Batavia, New York—what was then considered a frontier environment—and father of the future renowned Hearst journalist, Brisbane had a dreamer's mien. He loved the outdoors. He sported a thick beard, was tall, with high brows and piercing eyes, and so intensely dedicated to whatever he was doing that he was eventually called the Great Disciple. He was no leader of men, lacking the required charisma. He was mild in manner, modest, a student and dreamer rather than an activist, but his uncompromising dedication to finding a better way of life sometimes had a mesmeric impact on his listeners.

At the age of fifteen, Brisbane had what he called a "spontaneous intuition." It suddenly became apparent to him that "it is not right for the individual to work for himself." Each man belonged to a vast army in which he had a specific place and function; and if he left the ranks of this army to deal with his own personal concerns, he was flouting the common purpose. Men had to help each other, or else life had no meaning. Four years later, in 1828—he was nineteen—Brisbane decided to make the rounds of Europe to find out: "What is the destiny of man and what can I do to accelerate it?"

While eating ice cream during an intermission at the Paris Opera the following year, Brisbane had a second "intuition," namely, that "a certain class in society lived on the labor of the masses." Messianic as this sounds, it was not unique; many young people of this generation—William Lloyd Garrison, for instance—tied their philosophy to divine or mystic promptings. Not being too immersed in the real world of strife and torment, Brisbane came by his views in flashes of revelation. He believed God had not intended that men should suffer, and it was his task to alleviate it. For a few years he dabbled in Hegelian and other European philosophies, but none convinced him until one day someone gave him a copy of Fourier's latest book, *Treatise on Domestic and Agricultural Association.* "For the first time," he wrote subsequently, "I had come across an idea which I had never met before—the idea of dignifying and rendering attractive the manual labor of mankind, labor hitherto regarded as a divine punishment inflicted on man." Hurrying to Paris to make Fourier's acquaintance, he arranged for the aging utopian —he was then sixty—to give him private instruction. Then in 1834, after six years of travel, still only twenty-five years old, Brisbane returned to the United States ready for his mission.

Illness delayed his labors for a few years, but by 1839 the Great Disciple had organized Fourier study groups in New York and Philadelphia, and the following year he published a persuasive study on Association, the *Social Destiny of Man.* The central point Brisbane made—one which has been repeated by social scientists to this very day—was that "hired labor between man and man, as it exists in civilization, is degrading, besides being a source of petty tyranny, persecution, quarrels and litigation without end." What he proposed to do was to make labor desirable. "We assert, and will prove, that Labor, which is now monotonous, repugnant, and degrading, can be ennobled, elevated and made honorable—or in other words, Industry can be rendered Attractive!" When he showed this manuscript to Horace Greeley—whom he had never met before—Brisbane made an immediate and important convert. Greeley, editor of the *New Yorker* and later the *Tribune,* accepted a regular column by Brisbane. Since the *Tribune* in 1842 had a daily circulation of twenty thousand, quite large for the time, this was an important spur to the Association movement. In the next few years, as one writer put it, "Fourierism became one of the topics of the time." To its banner flocked such men as Parke Godwin, son-in-law of the poet William Cullen Bryant, the Reverend George Ripley, Ralph Waldo Emerson, William Ellery Channing, Nathaniel Hawthorne, Henry James, James Russell Lowell, Margaret Fuller, Bronson Alcott. The Fourierists were indeed a who's who of the literary world, as bright a list of luminaries as ever clustered around any idea.

The phalanxes themselves were less important than the aspirations they stirred. During the decade after Brisbane's campaign began, thirty-four were established, hardly enough to bring about the "radical change in our social economy," which Horace Greeley had envisioned. Only eight thousand Americans invested time or money in them. But Fourieristic educational societies fanned out far and wide. Pamphlets such as the one published by the Rochester Fourier Society in 1843—*Labor's Wrongs and Labor's Remedy*—struck a resonant chord with innumerable proletarians. The working class, it stated, "has too many idlers to support who think it dishonorable to work." The solution clearly was to flee to the phalanx, where a worker could be assured from the beginning "at least one-fourth more than in the best circumstances" otherwise. Brisbane, after a tour of New York, reported "the greatest enthusiasm and energy" for the dissemination of his doctrine. The convention of the New England Workingmen's Association in 1845 spent most of its deliberations discussing Fourierist philosophy.

Whatever the fate of Fourierism in practice, therefore, its circle of influence was much wider than the few thousands who ventured into the cooperative communities themselves. Its prestige vaulted, in particular when it converted to its cause the Brook Farm in New England. This was by far the most spectacular experiment of its time—not because of its economic success, but because of the great literary figures who supported it. Back in the 1830's an informal group of writers and thinkers met periodically in Boston to discuss social problems. Their detractors called them "transcendentalists" because—in the words of George Ripley—"we believe in an order of truth that transcends the sphere of the external sense." Before long the truth-seeking transcendentalists—Ripley, Emerson, Hawthorne,

Henry D. Thoreau—were talking of establishing socialist colonies as a means of liberating man from his drudgery. "We are a little wild here . . . ," Emerson wrote to Thomas Carlyle, "not a reading man but has a draft of a new community in his waistcoat pocket."

Inevitably these discussions were bound to take practical form. Under the initiative of George Ripley, who resigned his post as a Unitarian minister, Brook Farm began as a stock company—in which many bought shares—and raised fifteen thousand dollars to purchase a two-hundred-acre milk farm, nine miles from Boston. Among the twenty early participants was Nathaniel Hawthorne, who played "chambermaid to a group of cows" and declared lyrically that "such a delectable way of life as that in Brook Farm was never seen on earth since the days of the early Christians."

The Brook Farm Institute for Agriculture and Education proposed to substitute "a system of brotherly cooperation for one of selfish competition." The community limited work to ten hours a day, and undertook to support all children under ten, adults over seventy, and the sick. At its peak, it had seventy participants. But its way of life charmed the many thousands who became acquainted with it. Despite the hard toil there was time for music, intense literary and scientific discussions, excursions, and the frequent visits by its famous friends—the feminist Margaret Fuller, Brisbane, Greeley, Parke Godwin, Emerson, and innumerable others. The Brook Farm school was world famous, and many a prominent scholar received part of his education there.

Early in 1844, under the prodding of Brisbane and after a national convention of Associations, Brook Farm adopted *in toto* the Fourier principles, and changed its name to the Brook Farm Phalanx. Shortly thereafter the Associationist weekly newspaper, the *Harbinger,* transferred to Brook Farm. By this time thousands of visitors each year were making a pilgrimage to the community and not a few Brook Farmers were lecturing in the outside world on the glories of Association. The Farm itself was prospering modestly, and its members preoccupied with finishing the unitary Phalanx building, or "Palace," as prescribed in Fourier's teachings. But one fine spring evening in 1846 the Farmers were drawn by the shout, "The phalanstery is on fire!" The loss proved fatal. Brook Farm never recovered.

The other phalanxes established in this period, though better run than the Owenite experiments of two decades before, suffered from the same shortcomings—lack of adequate preparation, a dearth of cash, quarrels, inexperience in agriculture, poor management. Fourier's model phalanx required $400,000 in capital and at least 400 participants. None of the 34 American ventures reached such a figure, and so far as is known, only the Wisconsin Phalanx in Fond du Lac County was able to show a profit for its organizers when it ceased operations in 1850.

The first phalanx, Sylvania, was founded in western Pennsylvania by mechanics formerly of New York and Albany. Each subscribed a minimum of twenty-five dollars and appealed to the "opulent and generous" to help in what they considered a sound business effort. But, as with Fourier himself, no millionaires knocked at the door; money remained in short supply. There were other problems too. The climate was poor and it was difficult to find markets for the shoes and industrial goods that the mechanics produced. On August 10, 1844, Brisbane made the doleful announcement that "the Sylvania Association, having become satisfied of its inability to contend successfully against an ungrateful soil and an ungenial climate . . . has determined on dissolution."

The best-run experiment was the North American Phalanx, carefully planned by Brisbane, Greeley, Ripley, Godwin, and William Ellery Channing. On a sizable tract near Red Bank, New Jersey, the Fourierists built a three-floor phalanstery, planted a large orchard, and erected a gristmill. Here, as in the model plan, they divided into series and groups. If they deviated from the master's plan, it was in setting wage scales—the maximum being ten cents an hour. For the rest, they hewed close to orthodox principles of Fourierism and did moderately well. Earnings were not high, obviously, but the cost of living was low and living standards adequate. Natural forces, however, were unkind to the colonists, for in 1854 the twelve-thousand-dollar mill went up in flames, and with it the hopes of American Fourierism.

By late 1844, two years before the fire at Brook Farm, it was already obvious that the Fourier movement was in decline. Brisbane, however, refused to believe it. He insisted there had been no fair test, that not a single one of the phalanxes had sufficiently followed Associationist principles. For forty years thereafter, Brisbane, the Great Disciple, continued to rebuild his movement, but in vain. He died in April 1890, at the age of eighty-one, a lonely and forgotten man.

IV

Viewed in retrospect more than a century later, the utopian experiments of the 1840's appear naïve. But no drama can be understood outside its setting. This was a period of transition, from an agrarian to an industrial society, in which all the established values seemed to be falling apart. The concepts of brotherhood and community were being corrupted in unexpected ways. In this spiritual vacuum, what else was there to do but look for new forms of social organization? The "paradise-builders" were not necessarily impractical and certainly not dull. If they drifted far afield looking for answers, it was a time that demanded far-afield answers.

Fourierism was clearly the dominant radical philosophy of the 1840's, but there were other communitarian doctrines as well—each seeking its own road to the good life. Two former Brook Farmers, Bronson Alcott (father of Louisa May Alcott) and Charles Lane fashioned a community called Fruitlands, which combined communist property principles with food fadism. A distinction was made between food that grew in the air ("aspired"), such as wheat, corn, or fruit, and food that grew into the soil, such as beets or turnips. The latter, Alcott and his Fruitlanders would not touch. Nor would they eat animal substances, including butter, milk, or meats. The use of manure in farming was eschewed because it was felt that it would "force nature." Yet queer as all this sounds, it had its own logic. Alcott was a man who believed that happiness came from renunciation—"we plan to grow only enough of chaste supplies for bodily needs." He was, says V. F. Calverton, "far more like Christ than Thoreau, or any other New Englander; Christ's philosophy of poverty not only appealed to him, it fitted in with his whole psychology." In his view of the good life, man must blend with nature, not destroy it or "force" it. Despite the failure of Fruitlands, Alcott searched for a utopia of this kind to the end of his days.

The Oneida Perfectionists, whose guiding star was John Humphrey Noyes, combined communism in economics with communism in sex. Noyes, a graduate of Dartmouth College, turned from the study of law to theology. While taking courses at Yale and Andover, he evolved the principles which were later to be called Perfection-ism. This demanded immediate and total cessation of sin. It was a doctrine of ethical purity which demanded of its followers that they turn their back on a government which tolerated such iniquities as war, slavery, capital punishment, inequality. In 1834 Noyes re-turned to Putney, Vermont, where he formed his sect and by a process of recruitment he enlarged it to forty followers in 1847. The following year the Perfectionists established a communistic society at Oneida, New York. They not only farmed, but manufactured steel traps, traveling bags, satchels, silk, and silverware. By 1874, twenty-six years after its foundation, the community owned three hundred acres of good land and did a profitable business.

What distinguished Oneida, however, was not this business acumen—so rare among the utopians—but the views of the Perfec-tionists on sex. Just as all property was owned in common, so were all men and women married to each other. They cohabited promis-cuously, each man considered the husband of every woman, and each woman the wife of every man. For Noyes there was nothing evil or vulgar in this combined polygamy-polyandry. In one of his writings he explained that "when the will of God is done on earth, as it is in heaven, there will be no marriage. . . . In a holy community there is no more reason why sexual intercourse should be restrained by law, than why eating and drinking should be—and there is as lit-tle occasion for shame in the one case as in the other." Concomitant with this theory of free license Noyes, however, demanded "male continence." If all men were free to have sex relations with all women, they were not free to propagate children as they pleased. That was the task of the community at large, which paired people off on what was considered a "scientific basis" to produce the best progeny. On all other sexual occasions the male was required to pro-long the act for long periods to satisfy the woman, but to contain his own orgasm. Noyes's theories on sex failed to become popular—on the contrary—but they were the subject of discussion for many dec-ades; even Havelock Ellis a long time later saw great virtues in "male continence." Whether man is or ever will be ready for Noyes's notions of perfection is another matter.

A movement of an entirely different nature from the utopian com-munities was the Time Store. Where Fourier or Brisbane had be-lieved that workers and capitalists could cooperate harmoniously in the phalanxes, the anarchist Pierre Joseph Proudhon and his American apostle, Josiah Warren—once a member of New Harmony—considered the two classes totally hostile. Indeed, capitalists and bankers were the ultimate villains of society; their removal was a *sine qua non* for progress. The way to undercut them was to establish "mutual banks" so that commodities could be exchanged on the basis of their true labor costs, without middlemen or financiers to skim off the cream. In a complex society you obviously could not have a barter system, since there was too much to be exchanged. But why sell your product to a middleman, who is financed by a banker, and have him sell it to someone else at a profit? Why not make the exchange more direct? Warren devised an ingenious institution called the Time Store, in which customers received "labor notes" for their own products and used these labor notes to buy goods of equal value. Under this plan banks would be prohibited from issuing money. The only form of exchange would be a note listing the amount of time a worker had spent fabricating a product. This note could be exchanged for wares in which an equal amount of time had been spent. A typical labor note might read: "Due to bearer, Eight Hours Labor in Shoe-Making, or One Hundred Pounds of Corn." Only those who were producers should have, in Warren's thinking, the right to issue money, not nonproducers such as bankers. The anarchist leader, in due course, opened a Time Store in Cincinnati and later an anarchist colony, called Modern Times, on Long Island, both of which foundered.

An interesting feature of the anarchist tenet was "individual sovereignty." Each man would be guided in his behavior solely by his own conscience rather than by law. There were to be "no rules or regulations but such as each individual makes for himself and his own business; no officers, no prophets, no priests." If there were any meetings to be held, they were not for the purpose of formulating common plans but purely "for friendly conversation" or other pastime.

Two other means developed in the 1840's and 1850's to escape the capitalist vise were the producers' and consumers' cooperatives. The producers' cooperative had been tried by unionists ever since the opening of the century—especially after defeated strikes. It differed from cooperative communities in that members did not live together in isolated areas, but they did operate a workshop jointly. The movement was spurred by the French Revolution of 1848, when Louis Blanc proposed that the government set up workshops and factories, jointly run by the workers themselves, to compete against private capitalism. He was sure workers could be more efficient and would ultimately drive the capitalists out of business. Many labor papers in the United States, such as the Lowell, Massachusetts, *Voice of Industry*, seized on the idea as a cure-all. During the winter of 1847–48, even before Blanc had announced his plan, twenty iron molders near Cincinnati set up a stove foundry with a capital of $2,100 and loans from wealthy friends. Three years later the producers' cooperative was still thriving, its capital now $8,000 with forty-seven workers employed at union scales. Horace Greeley, who visited it, noted that while laborers in private industry worked "off and on," according to employer whim, no molder in the Cincinnati cooperative had been idle since it was established. Ironically not long after he made this visit the cooperative failed.

A similar venture was undertaken by Boston tailors in 1849 (also after a defeated strike); by iron foundrymen in Pittsburgh; nail cutters in Wheeling; seamstresses in Boston, Philadelphia, and Providence. Without exception, they met the same fate as the phalanxes, but they continued in the forefront of unionist programs for decades.

Cooperative stores were another feature of the times. They were initiated by Boston mechanics in 1845, under the title "Protective Union." Members paid an initiation fee of $3 and monthly dues, which allowed them to buy groceries and other items at low cost, and provided them with $3 a week when sick, as well as $7.50 a week pension after sixty-five. Soon there were forty such operations, and by the time the movement reached its zenith in 1854, eight hundred in New England, Michigan, Illinois, Wisconsin, New York, even Canada. But beginning with 1855, the stores began to fail for lack of capital and as a result of price wars. By the time of the Civil War they were gone.

Whatever the reason, cooperation as a substitute for competitive capitalism was a failure—both on the farm and in the city. Social scholars attribute this to insufficient aid by the state. They argue that the cooperative system can work, as in Scandinavia or Israel, only when it has the active support of the government. It needs low-cost loans and other forms of protection to carry it over its initial hurdles. At any rate, cooperation did not take root in the United States. The momentum of private enterprise was inexorable.

V

The one panacea of the pre-Civil War period that turned out to be more than a dream was "new agrarianism"—to distinguish it from the "old" agrarianism of Thomas Skidmore. Its mentor was George Henry Evans, an English-born radical of considerable durability. George Henry, born in 1805, and his brother Frederick, born three years later, had migrated to New York State in 1820. Both were avid readers of Thomas Paine, both "instant" radicals in their new land. Within two years George Henry was editing a leftist sheet in Ithaca, called the *Man*. Later in the decade he was associated with Fanny Wright and Robert Dale Owen, publishing the *Working Men's Advocate*. When the New York Workie disintegrated and George Henry's health broke down in 1836, he bought a farm in Granville, New Jersey, both to regain his vigor and revise his views. Periodically he published another leftist sheet, the *Radical,* in which the agrarian philosophy began to take form.

Early in the new decade George Henry renewed his activity, gathering together some of his old cronies in the Workingmen's Party to launch the National Reform Association and propounding a land reform program as the answer to the factory system. "If a man has a right on the earth," wrote Evans, "he has a right to land enough to raise a habitation." It was only because a few people controlled large tracts of land that landless workers were under the thumb of employers. "The poor," said Evans, "must work or starve in the manufactories as in England, unless they can cultivate the land." Because there was so much land available in the United States—unlike England—there was still a chance to save the proletarian from the indignity of the capitalist system. Evans did not rule out union activity, such as strikes, to ameliorate the laborer's plight, but the limitless land resources of the West seemed to him to offer the only final escape from low wages and cyclical depressions. As workers fled to the West, employers would be forced to improve wages for the ones who stayed behind. "Those who remain," he said, "as well as those who emigrate, will have the opportunity of realizing a comfortable living." To this end he proposed that the government give plots of 160 acres from the public domain to anyone who wanted them. When enough artisans had accepted land in the West, the cities of the East, with their slums, would just decay, leaving behind nothing but "warehouses, shipyards, and foundries to accommodate international commerce. . . ." Evans elaborated a timetable by which in 1900 the United States would be a "Nation of Freeholders" and the doctrine of the Declaration of Independence would be "fully recognized and practiced." "And all this," said Evans, "can be obtained by a simple vote, if the workingmen throughout the country will unite."

Evans' slogan "Vote yourself a farm" was plastered all over walls in New York and other cities. Workers in the North, West, and even the South flocked to his National Reform Association, organized clubs in their wards, and pledged not to vote for any man who did not vote them a farm. In addition to the homestead program, Evans also campaigned for such items as equal rights for women, abolition of slavery, abolition of the United States Bank and monopoly.

The Evans panacea was so appealing that, in diluted form, it was adopted by the new Republican Party and enacted by Lincoln in 1862 as the Homestead Act. It did not, as the radical philosopher had envisioned, liberate the working class, but it did ameliorate the plight of tens of thousands and kept wages higher here than in Europe. To this extent at least, Evans' vision achieved reality. His was one of the few successes, insofar as the radicals were concerned, of the decade or two preceding the Civil War.

CHAPTER VII

THE OUTSIDE AGITATORS

WHILE "wage slavery" occupied the attention of Owen and Brisbane, Skidmore and Evans, the Workies and Locofocos, chattel slavery was producing a parallel though different kind of radicalism.

The Revolution, despite the many changes it wrought in American society, had failed to obliterate this lingering blot on the American escutcheon. Jefferson, in drafting the Declaration of Independence, had included a passage denouncing slavery and berating the king for failing to halt the traffic in slaves. But when Georgia and South Carolina objected, the section was deleted. After the war was over, liberal laws for manumission were passed, under which Washington, Jefferson, and other Founding Fathers freed their slaves. Washington urged abolition not only "on the score of human dignity," but because he could "foresee that nothing but the rooting out of slavery can perpetuate . . . our union." Patrick Henry chided his fellow Americans that "in a country above all others fond of liberty" they tolerated "a principle as repugnant to humanity as it is inconsistent with the Bible." North of the Delaware River, actually, one state after another abolished human bondage. Many believed that the institution would die a natural death, because until the cotton gin there was no overriding need for it. Even in the South, except for the Carolinas and Georgia, enthusiasm for slavery was waning. Yet slavery had existed for a long time on this earth —ever since the inception of civilization, in fact, thousands of years before—and while it was repugnant to the enlightened, many tended to take it for granted. Former President Madison, it will be recalled, told Fanny Wright he saw no way as yet to abolish it.

[105]

What made the issue so complicated by the time Madison offered Fanny his opinion was Eli Whitney's cotton gin. Without this machine a slave extracted the seeds from only one pound of raw cotton a day; with it he raised his output to fifty pounds, and when the machine was improved and put to steam, a thousand pounds a day. In Washington's time only two million pounds of cotton were grown annually; by 1860, as already noted, the figure rose to two billion pounds. Cotton, which in 1810 accounted for only 22 percent of the nation's exports ($67 million), was responsible for 57 percent in 1860 ($334 million). How then could you disturb the slave system when slave labor was bringing in so much of your foreign *valuta?* The South was producing seven eighths of all the world's cotton— and slavery offered the cheap labor to make it profitable. The investment in a good field hand grew progressively higher from decade to decade, but upkeep was only fifteen to forty dollars a year, on the average seven cents a day. For that sum the master bought himself six days a week of labor, from dawn until dark. For this the slave received nothing but a little corn and bacon, a hut in the back of the plantation, some clothing, and medical attention if he were seriously ill.

Theoretically, one could prove that the cost of a slave—$1,400 to $2,000 in 1860—was so high that free labor, in the end, would probably have cost less. But the plantation owner had already made his investment and immediate abolition would have driven him into bankruptcy. Theoretically too, one could show that of the six or seven million white people in the South in 1850, only 350,000 owned slaves, and of these only 1,700 owned 100 or more. But the big slaveholders were precisely the ones that ruled the South and elaborated its political rationale.

Southern leaders taunted the North—in the words of Senator James H. Hammond of South Carolina, for instance—that "the difference between us is that our slaves are hired for life and well compensated; there is no starvation, no begging, no want of employment. . . . Yours are hired by the day, not cared for, and scantily compensated, which may be proved in the most deplorable manner, at any hour in any street of your large towns." Just as colonial Tories defended aristocracy as the will of God, so Southern Bourbons made the same claim for slavery. "We learn from the Holy Scriptures," said a Southern congressman in 1858, "that Abraham and many wise and good men of that day not only held slaves but exercised acts of ownership over them; and that God Himself, after he had rescued the children of Israel from the house of bondage, sanctioned and recognized slavery both in principle and in practice." Whether everyone agreed with such theses—repeated over and over again in the critical years—the fact is that as cotton became king, slavery became its alter ego. Few people, either in the North or South, could visualize its demise.

II

During the long saga from colonial times to the Civil War American slaves were not quiescent. Rather than accept their lot, some black men fled to the swamps to die of hunger or illness. Others killed their masters and then committed suicide. A document advising planters how to handle would-be suicides noted that Negroes sometimes "stifle themselves by drawing in the tongue so as to close the breathing passage, others take poison, or flee and perish of misery and hunger." Whole families of Negroes made compacts to deliver themselves beyond this world to the grace of God. One mother, it is recorded, strangled every one of her thirteen children rather than have them grow into the bitter bondage she herself had endured.

On at least two dozen occasions before and during the nineteenth century, Negroes moved from individual resistance to concerted revolt. In 1822 a free Negro, Denmark Vesey, organized nine thousand slaves for an insurrection in South Carolina. It was a remarkable bit of planning, with each conspirator assigned a specific task. One made two hundred and fifty pike heads, another fitted them to handles. Slaves who had access to horses laid plans to steal them. As Vesey read the Bible to his followers, telling them how the children of Israel escaped from Egyptian slavery, he prepared meticulously to liberate every Negro in an area fifty miles around Charleston. The grand plot, however, was betrayed by a house servant, just as the conspirators were making their final plans. One hundred and thirty-one warriors for freedom were arrested, thirty-five executed, and more banished to other states.

That there were similar conspiracies being hatched is attested to by the comment of J. R. Gilmore, a visitor to South Carolina in 1860.

"There exists among the blacks," he wrote, "a secret and widespread organization of a Masonic character, having its grip, password, and oath."

In 1831 a deeply religious Negro, Nat Turner, led a rebellion seventy miles from Richmond, Virginia, which he hoped, by the Lord's will, would spread throughout the South. Armed with scythes and broadaxes, the slaves marched to battle, picking up followers and fighting along the way. It was a bloody affair—fifty-seven whites and seventy-three black men died in battle. Turner himself eluded arrest for six weeks, but he was apprehended and executed along with seventeen others.

Turner's martyrdom had curious results. For one thing, it momentarily terrified the state's officialdom. "Before I leave this Government," vowed Governor John Floyd, "I will have contrived to have a law passed gradually abolishing slavery in the state." (Needless to say, he changed his mind when the initial anxiety passed.) For another, legislation was enacted in various states ameliorating conditions. A worried South Carolina passed legislation limiting the workday of slaves to fifteen hours in the warm weather and fourteen hours in the cold seasons. Louisiana provided two-hour dinner periods from May to November and an hour and a half at other times. Georgia imposed penalties for mistreatment of slaves. On the other hand, Georgia enacted legislation making it a crime to teach a slave to read and write. Many a Negro was killed on mere suspicion he was plotting revolt. Anyone cited for rousing the "spirit" of insurrection was subject to the death penalty, whether insurrection did or did not take place.

But despite men like Turner and Vesey, the Negro people as a whole were not yet prepared to liberate themselves. What few leaders they had were thinking less in terms of revolt than reform or amelioration. Frederick Douglass, son of a Negro mother and white father, though greatly beloved, confined himself to constitutional and political action, spending his time lecturing and publishing various journals. Harriet Tubman, called the "greatest heroine of her age" and the "Moses of her people," concentrated on individual liberation. Having escaped from bondage herself, she resolved to lead others to the promised land. When she discovered that her father was in trouble because he had helped a slave run away, she made her way to the South, and guided her parents north to

Canada—the refuge for thousands of Negroes. Subsequently she made a dozen and a half similar journeys, each time liberating still more black chattels. Slaveowners were so harried by this former slave that in 1856 they offered a reward of $25,000 for her capture. But beyond such efforts, Negroes themselves played a secondary role in emancipation.

The mandate of history fell on white men to rouse the American conscience. A motley force of pacifists, religious leaders, Quakers, unionists, and intellectuals mounted a campaign which for sheer moral force has seldom been equaled. At first the center of white agitation was in the South. As late as 1830, four fifths of the anti-slave societies were in the plantation states. North Carolina probably had ten times as many enrolled antislavers as New England and New York combined. But the Southerners, for a variety of reasons, could not give the movement its impulse. Most of them were gradualists. Some believed in colonization schemes to send the Negro back to Africa. Turner's rebellion terrified them, as did William Lloyd Garrison's cry for *immediate* abolition. In addition, they were subjected to severe repression. Louisiana enacted legislation imposing life imprisonment or death simply for printing antislavery tracts. Postmasters confiscated "subversive" material. Schoolbooks were rigorously censored. Southern hysteria can be gauged by the warning of one of its economists, George Fitzhugh, that abolition agitation was "a surrender to Socialism and Communism—to no private property, no church, no law, to free love, free lands, free women and free children."

The crusade against slavery, therefore, was conducted not where slavery flourished, but hundreds of miles away where it had already been abolished. It was the "outside agitator" who had to do what the Southerners would not, and the slaves could not.

III

The messiah of the abolition movement, William Lloyd Garrison, was a many-faceted and contradictory revolutionary. Bald headed, with even features that made him almost handsome, wearing round-rimmed glasses, he might have been mistaken for a self-effacing bookkeeper. But his pen dripped with vitriol, his phrases bristled with anger. His public image was of a harsh, unyielding, bitter, and unkind polemicist, but innumerable people who met him were surprised to find that he was tactful, modest, even witty in private conversation. The famous British author, Harriet Martineau, was astonished by "a countenance glowing with health and wholly expressive of purity, animation and gentleness." Many people hated Garrison and once or twice there were efforts to lynch him, but his sympathetic eloquence could bring unrestrained tears to the eyes of Negroes listening to him at a meeting in Providence. And Negroes in Boston, concerned for his safety, would follow behind him, armed with cudgels, to offer him unsolicited protection as he trod home.

Garrison was the born crusader. The abolition of slavery was his consuming concern, but he was also a pacifist, opposed to war. He was an advocate of temperance—abstinence from liquor and tobacco. He was enamored of John Humphrey Noyes's Perfectionism. He favored the Free-Soil movement. Yet—in his earlier days, at least—he viewed with suspicion the labor movement as an attempt "to inflame the minds of our working classes against the more opulent." As an individualist he felt that once a man was free, the rest was up to himself. Garrison was an excellent husband and father, but a poor provider. He was a hypochondriac who often thought he was on his last legs and who would try almost any patent medicine. Yet as his leading associate, Wendell Phillips, testified: "His was the happiest life I ever saw. . . . I never saw him unhappy." He was totally inflexible in his fundamental beliefs, yet in daily life he tended to procrastinate, to put off until the next day what he could do today.

Garrison was born in Newburyport, Massachusetts, in December 1805. His father was an easygoing, ruddy sea captain who deserted his wife and children when William Lloyd was only three. His mother was a pious Baptist nurse who sometimes went to church three times on Sunday. Lloyd, as his mother called him, was a poor student and was left-handed to boot, a circumstance which his schoolteacher "corrected" by rapping him on the knuckles. At the age of seven he could be seen roaming in a crowd selling his mother's molasses candy, or making a humiliating daily visit to the rear entrance of a wealthy home on High Street to accept leftover food. "He is a fine boy . . . ," his mother wrote, "and every Sunday he goes to the Baptist church, although he has so far to walk." But he was also extremely combative, ready to defend any youngster being harassed by a bully, even if the odds were weighted against him. It was this unyielding quality which characterized his whole life.

At the age of thirteen the future abolitionist was apprenticed to a cabinetmaker for the usual seven-year period, but he ran away after six weeks. His master, after catching the boy, was entitled to give him the customary flogging, but instead permitted him a legal release. On his return to Newburyport, Garrison became a printer's apprentice, a task he enjoyed more, and was soon immersed in his master's library with the avidity that was so typical. After finishing his apprenticeship in 1826, he convinced his employer to loan him money to buy out a friend and begin publication of a weekly paper, the *Free Press*. At twenty, Garrison was probably the youngest editor and publisher in the country. One of his discoveries on the *Free Press* was the Quaker poet, John Greenleaf Whittier, whose poetry he published regularly. After a number of other journalistic ventures, Garrison's path crossed that of a slender Quaker, Benjamin Lundy, who was then publishing in Baltimore the only antislavery sheet in the United States—a paper with the unwieldy name of the *Genius of Universal Emancipation*. Lundy was already a seasoned campaigner for the cause, having visited—by foot and horseback—nineteen of the twenty-four states. He was impressed by Garrison's editorials against slavery and came to see the young man to induce him to coedit his paper.

Garrison arrived in Baltimore in the summer of 1829, and with his first editorial laid down the gauntlet. Lundy had been advocating "gradual" abolition over a period of time—which was radical enough. He also felt that if he could assure the slaveholders that the freed slaves would be colonized outside the country, say in Haiti, Texas, or Canada, they might more willingly release them. But Garrison demanded "immediate and unconditional emancipation." A few weeks later he shocked his readers further by insisting that the slaveowners were not entitled to any compensation—"it would be paying a thief for giving up stolen property. . . . No, let us not talk of buying the slaves—justice *demands* their liberation."

One day, while reading the newspaper, Garrison learned that a man named Francis Todd, of his own home town, Newburyport, had carried seventy-five slaves from Baltimore to New Orleans on his ship *Francis*. Slave breeding was then a large business, with Virginia alone raising and "exporting" to other states some forty thousand slaves, valued at $24 million, a year. All told, ninety thousand Negroes annually were sold by slave-breeding to slave-consuming states. Garrison was of course outraged by this industry, but his anger spilled over when he learned that a New Englander was engaged in the practice. He wrote a blistering editorial calling slave traders, including Todd, "robbers and murderers" who should be "sentenced to solitary confinement for life." For this the zealous editor was haled before a tribunal, charged with "gross and malicious libel" and convicted by a jury after only fifteen minutes' deliberation. He was fined fifty dollars and assessed a similar amount in costs. Since he did not have the money, he had to sit in jail for seven weeks until a wealthy New York merchant and abolitionist, Arthur Tappan, put up the money for his release.

While incarcerated, Garrison's determination grew stronger, so that on release he made his way from the border state to the more propitious climate of Boston. There the twenty-five-year-old youth was to make a whole nation listen. Boston was more receptive than Baltimore, but when Garrison tried to hire a church hall to deliver three lectures he had drafted while in prison, he found them closed to him; only a society of atheists would make its facilities available to this devout Baptist. The meeting place was filled to capacity, and included some of Garrison's stanchest future supporters, Bronson Alcott, Samuel J. May, a Connecticut minister, and Samuel E. Sewall, a Boston attorney. After the session Alcott invited Garrison and some of the fascinated listeners to his home, where they discussed plans for a future newspaper.

IV

On January 1, 1831, without a single advance subscriber or penny of capital, Garrison began publication of the *Liberator*. It was never a towering success, either financially or in circulation. The first year it attracted five hundred paid subscribers, and at its peak only three thousand. But for thirty-four years its words stung the slothful and inspired the righteous. "Our Country is the World—Our Countrymen are Mankind," read the masthead. "I *will be* as harsh as truth," said the opening editorial, "and as uncompromising as justice. On this subject I do not wish to think, or speak, or write, with moderation. . . . I am in earnest—I will not equivocate—I will not excuse—I will not retract a single inch—AND I WILL BE HEARD."

For many months Garrison and an associate slept on the floor of the room where they published their paper. Small as the operation was, however, it had a wide impact. Virginia authorities charged that Nat Turner had read passages of the *Liberator* to the Negroes he was preparing for insurrection. A vigilance committee in Columbia, South Carolina, offered fifteen hundred dollars for the conviction of anyone "distributing or circulating the *Liberator*." Georgetown, in the District of Columbia, imposed a twenty-dollar fine and thirty days in prison for any Negro taking Garrison's paper. In November 1831 the legislature of Georgia offered a five-thousand-dollar reward for anyone who could "arrest, bring to trial and prosecute to conviction" the *Liberator's* editor.

Nor was the hostility to Garrison and his abolitionists confined to the South. Violence was used frequently to dampen the ardor of the antislavers. In 1835, an angry mob of "gentlemen of property and influence" tied a rope around Garrison's waist and dragged him through the narrow byways of Boston toward the City Hall. The mob had been looking to "snake out" George Thompson, a British abolitionist, and had offered one hundred dollars to anyone who would "lay violent hands on him" so that he could be tarred and feathered and his skin dyed dark. When Thompson was unavailable, the mob seized Garrison, tore off his trousers, ripped his shirt, and might have killed him if he had not been rescued by two brothers and placed in jail by the police for his safety.

Another time, after returning from England, Garrison was met at the New York pier by five thousand jeering citizens. In Boston leaflets were circulated calling on the people to tar and feather him, and a mock gallows was erected in front of his home with the inscription: "By Order of Judge Lynch." The Reverend Samuel May, one of his disciples, was attacked six times. A particularly odious incident which had repercussions nationally occurred in Illinois in 1837. Mobsters twice smashed the printing presses of a Presbyterian minister, Elijah P. Lovejoy, when he protested the lynching of a Negro in St. Louis. On the third occasion the crowd, armed with muskets and waving torches, shot Lovejoy dead and threw his press into the Mississippi. In New York it was a rare occasion when Garrison's followers could meet without being attacked by hoodlums such as the notorious Captain Rynders, who were in the pay of Southerners and spurred on by a hostile journalist, James Gordon Bennett. Indeed, almost until the Civil War, abolitionists had to contend with frequent physical abuse.

But Garrison's tenacity was as steadfast as his vehemence. The *Liberator* continued to carry some of the most biting attacks in the history of journalism. No one was spared. Great national figures who would compromise the issue, like Webster or Clay, were rebuked with the same sharpness as lesser men. The *Liberator* would have no truck with gradualism. "Has not the experience of two centuries," argued Garrison, "shown that gradualism in theory is perpetuity in practice? Is there an instance, in the history of the world, where slaves have been educated for freedom by their taskmasters?" There were no sacred cows for Garrison.

After he had been won over to the no-government doctrine of Noyes's Perfectionists, Garrison disavowed the Constitution. In 1842 he called for dissolution of the United States and characterized the Constitution as a slaveowners' document—a "covenant with death and an agreement with hell." The *Liberator*'s masthead that year blared: "A repeal of the Union between Northern liberty and Southern slavery is essential to the abolition of the one and the preservation of the other." At a rally in Concord, Garrison said: "I am for revolution, were I utterly alone. I am there because I *must* be there, I *must* cleave to the right. I cannot choose but obey the voice of God."

Just a year after the *Liberator* was born, Garrison called a meeting in Boston to form an antislavery society. It was a terrible night, bedeviled by snow and sleet, and only fifteen people had the courage to brave the weather—a fifty-year-old Quaker named Arnold Buffum, a few editors of small papers, a few lawyers. The chairman read a statement of principle which began: "We, the undersigned, hold that every person, of full age and sane mind, has a right to immediate freedom from personal bondage of whatsoever kind. . . ." The three lawyers expressed the view that immediate emancipation was "premature" and refused—momentarily, it turned out —to join. The other twelve elected Buffum as president and formed the New England Anti-Slavery Society. Garrison told the audience: "We have met tonight in this obscure schoolhouse; our numbers are few and our influence is limited; but mark my prediction, Faneuil Hall shall ere long echo with the principles we have set forth."

Within the next few years two thousand branches of the Anti-Slavery Society were formed, with almost a quarter of a million members. Among them were some of the most notable figures of the time—Wendell Phillips, a golden-voiced rebel who was born to luxury but devoted his life to every cause of the oppressed; the Quaker poet, John Greenleaf Whittier; another poet, James Russell Lowell; and familiar mavericks such as Horace Greeley and Albert Brisbane. All of them did what Garrison was doing—write, lecture, agitate, argue—in the hope that somehow the glare of publicity would demolish the demon slavery. Strange as it seems—it worked. By 1837, only six years after Garrison's campaign began, former President John Quincy Adams could record in his diary "the public mind in my own district and state is convulsed between the slavery and abolition questions, and I walk on the edge of a precipice in every step I take." Daniel Webster noted that antislavery sentiment could not be "trifled with or despised." Garrison's single-mindedness, his "impracticality," had caused a drastic change in mood. His agitation had to be joined by John Brown's acts of guerrilla warfare and by the economic needs of Northern industry before it achieved its goals. But Garrison did taunt the conscience of a morally weak nation, and in so doing eroded its misgivings until a John Brown or an Abraham Lincoln became possible. If history helped Garrison, he prodded it mercilessly.

V

As the nation drifted toward civil war, abolitionist agitation turned into action. Garrison himself refused to vote or form political parties. But some of his followers were not so purist. Encouraged by the collection of 300,000 signatures to an antislavery petition—which John Quincy Adams presented to the House of Representatives—zealous abolitionists in 1844 formed the Liberty Party to press their cause. It received a mere 65,000 votes out of two and a half million cast, and though it drained off just enough votes from Henry Clay to give the Presidential nod to Democrat James K. Polk of Tennessee, it was a humiliating defeat. It dissuaded the abolitionists from ever trying this technique again, for it was abundantly clear that while the populace might oppose slavery, it would not cast its vote on a single issue. People might read with avid sympathy—as they did years later—the great novel by Harriet Beecher Stowe, *Uncle Tom's Cabin*, which described in poignant simplicity the indignity of slavery, but they failed to translate their reactions at the polling booth. In 1852, while *Uncle Tom's Cabin* was being discussed everywhere, the Democratic Party, running on a proslavery platform, carried all but four states in the Presidential elections.

If the ballot box were foreclosed as a medium of protest, however, there were other ways to fight the abolitionist battle. Some men, mostly Quakers who from the early days of America had been associated with humanistic ventures, tried to organize a boycott against Southern cotton and other products produced with slave labor. They opened stores where "free goods" could be bought. Petitions by the thousands were circulated, signed, and presented to the lawmakers in Washington. Pamphlets and newspapers were published, and legislatures were pressured to grant fugitive slaves legal rights such as trial by jury.

Most dramatic, of course, was the laying out of circuitous routes —called underground railways—by which Negro slaves escaped from the South in droves. The "lines" by which they fled their bondage ran from Kentucky and Virginia across Ohio, and from Maryland through Pennsylvania to New York and New England. Characteristically, a small group of slaves, accompanied by a guide, would travel as far out of sight as possible, stopping for food and accommodations at the homes of sympathizers, until they made their way to freedom, preferably to Canada, where they felt secure from extradition or recapture. A fugitive song of the period went:

> *I'm on my way to Canada,*
> *That cold and dreary land;*
> *The sad effects of slavery,*
> *I can no longer stand.*

Just how many bondmen escaped via the underground railway is not known, for it was inevitably a secret operation without opportunity for statistics gathering. But it is estimated that the number was between forty thousand and one hundred thousand, a sizable figure when one remembers that there were four million slaves at the time. At the peak there were two thousand a year making the exodus.

Andrew Jackson stood for the rights of the common man when he vetoed the recharter of the Bank of the United States. The first President born to poverty, he used bad grammar, told ribald stories, and chewed tobacco. But he extended the vote and attracted the working class to the Democratic Party.

Architect's drawing for an American utopia. British mill owner Robert Owen dreamed of building a community along these lines when he founded a socialist colony at New Harmony, Indiana. But his plans never worked out, and within three years the experiment failed.

Members of the "Perfectionist" community at Oneida, New York, playing croquet. The Perfectionists practiced common ownership, not only in economics, but also in marriage. All colonists at Oneida were free to mate with all members of the opposite sex. But while promiscuity was encouraged, propagation was controlled. Couples were paired off on a "scientific" basis to produce the best children.

After he came to America, Robert Owen (above, left) addressed Congress, made lecture tours, and drew many intellectuals to his utopian socialist cause. One of his disciples, "Fanny" Wright (above, right), helped edit the newspaper in New Harmony and crusaded for public boarding schools, freelove, abortion, and the abolition of slavery. John Humphrey Noyes (left), founder of Perfectionism, lost his ministerial license for his radical ideas on religion and sex.

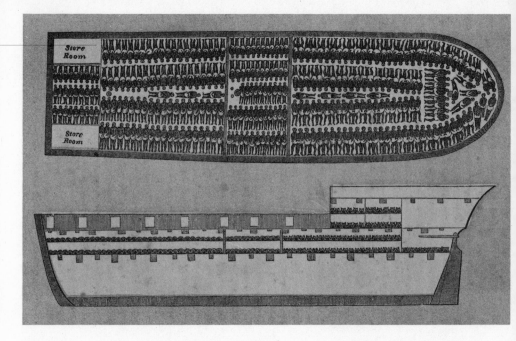

By 1860 the slave trade was booming. The cost of a slave rose to about $2,000, but up-keep remained inexpensive—about seven cents a day. On slave ships (see deck plan, above) Negroes were chained together and crammed into the narrow spaces between decks. Below, a trader drives a group of slaves past the Capitol in Washington.

With the invention of the cotton gin the South became increasingly dependent on slavery. A slave working by hand extracted the seeds from about one pound of cotton per day. With the machine he could separate a thousand times as much. As a result cotton grew to a 334-million-dollar business, responsible for more than 50 percent of the nation's exports.

The arrest of Nat Turner. In 1831, Turner led a rebellion of Negroes in Southampton County, Virginia, that he hoped would spread throughout the South. More than a hundred people of both races were killed, and Turner was executed along with seventeen others.

Leaders of the antislavery movement. Known as the "Moses of her people," Harriet Tubman led Negroes out of the South to freedom in Northern states and Canada. Frederick Douglass, son of a white father and Negro mother, incited feelings through his writings and lectures. Harriet Beecher Stowe, author of Uncle Tom's Cabin, *described in poignant fiction the injustices of slavery. Journalist Horace Greeley urged New York workingmen to help the Negro cause.*

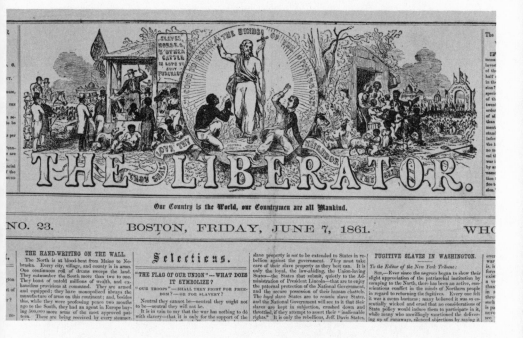

Our Country is the World, our Countrymen are all Mankind.

NO. 23.　　BOSTON, FRIDAY, JUNE 7, 1861.

"*Our Country is the World, our Countrymen are all Mankind*," read the masthead of The Liberator. *Though its top circulation was only 3,000, this paper carried on for 34 years a steady and dramatic campaign against slavery. Its effects were felt everywhere. Southern states passed laws restricting its distribution, and Georgia offered a reward for the arrest and conviction of its editor, William Lloyd Garrison (below).*

His truth went marching on, but John Brown went to the gallows on December 2, 1859. In the most dramatic incident before the war, he had attempted to capture arms from a federal arsenal at Harpers Ferry to free slaves in the South. His plans failed, and he was captured, tried, and sentenced by the State of Virginia.

Philadelphia alone gave aid to nine thousand runaways. Thomas Garrett, another Quaker, is personally credited with helping twenty-seven hundred Negroes to freedom. Levi Coffin, unofficial "president" of the movement, settled in Ohio, where his home became a meeting center for three "lines." It was highly exciting, this snatching of Negroes from the shackles of bondage, and it doubtless added fervor and hope to the antislavery societies. In the term popularized decades later by the anarchists, it was a "propaganda of the deed," as effective as "propaganda of the word" in drawing attention to slavery's iniquities.

Together, the words and the deeds ultimately changed American opinion. A businessman in Boston had once told Garrison: "It is not a matter of principle with us; it is a business necessity; we cannot afford to let you succeed; we do not mean to allow you to succeed; we mean to put you down by fair means if we can, by foul means if we must." But with time such views changed, for antislavery blended with capitalist interests. Industrialists and businessmen decided finally that lucrative trade with the Southern plantation owner was less important than long-term interests. To prosper, Northern capitalism needed the protective tariff, government subsidy to construct railroads and highways, opening of the public domain to settlement and exploitation. The South, a raw material area, opposed the tariff because it raised prices for consumer goods, opposed aid for public works because it raised taxes, opposed opening the public domain unless slavery were tolerated therein. The two subnations were going in diametrically different directions, each conscious that what added to the power of one detracted from the power of the other.

For threescore years the differences had been amenable to compromise. The Founding Fathers had tolerated slavery under the implicit doctrine of states rights, permitting three fifths of the bondmen to be counted for the purpose of allocating seats in Congress. Thirty years later, after slavery had been abolished in the original Northern states, Missouri was accepted into the union as a slave state on condition that Maine—then part of Massachusetts—be accepted as a free state. Secession was again avoided in 1833 when the two sides compromised the issue of tariffs. The next crisis was over a resolution introduced by David Wilmot in 1846 banning slavery from Texas as well as any other area to be seized from a prostrate Mexico. The resolution was voted down and might have been forgotten except that in the meantime the war with Mexico had resulted in the annexation of half its territory, posing again the question as to whether the seized area should be free or slave. The border genius, Henry Clay, had to use all his persuasive powers to effect another—his last—compromise: California entered as a free state and the issue was postponed elsewhere. After 1850, however, there were to be no further accommodations between the rival sections.

The workingman's position also grew firmer. Unskilled Irish-Americans at first feared that freed Negroes, emigrating northward, would compete with them for jobs. The *Freeman's Journal,* a Catholic publication in New York with wide influence among the Irish, had decried abolitionism as "an import from England." Ely Moore, president of the New York General Trades' Union, ordinarily a liberal man, opposed the emancipationists on the ground that they would divide the Democratic Party and thus play into the hands of "the pro-Bank, anti-Jackson aristocracy." But in due course more and more laborers began to understand the true significance of the chattel system. Wages for artisans and the few factory hands in the South were 25 to 50 percent lower than in the North. If this disparity should spread to new states entering the Union, such as Kansas or Nebraska, it would eventually lower wage rates in New York and Philadelphia as well. More and more workingmen saw the link between chattel slavery and "wage slavery."

In January 1845, Robert Dale Owen, Brisbane, and Greeley, held a massive meeting of twenty-five thousand laborers in New York in which they denounced, to thundering applause, "slavery in the abstract, slavery in the concrete . . . slavery absolute, slavery feudal, and the slavery of wages. . . ." The New England Workingmen's Association called on the slaves to rebel and promised that they would not join any army to subdue them. A mass meeting of union men to hail the European revolutions of 1848 rang with the slogan: "Down with both chattel slavery and wage slavery!" Delegates to a Workingmen's Association convention in 1846 resolved that "American slavery must be uprooted before the elevation sought by the laboring classes can be effected." German-American workers, strongly under Marxist influence, confidently predicted that liberation of the Negro not only would erase a sordid social disease, but would propel the proletariat itself to political power.

A mixture of idealism and self-interest, therefore, drew Northerners to Garrison's abolitionism. As the plantation system threatened to spread its tentacles, it provoked crisis and tension until the rift grew into a chasm. Texas was annexed as a slave state. But the Missouri Compromise was repealed, so that Kansas and Nebraska were opened to the potential of slavery. A stronger Fugitive Slave Law was passed, putting the government into the business of ferreting out Negro escapes. The Dred Scott decision by the Supreme Court ruled that a slave, Scott, who had been taken by his master to upper Louisiana where slavery was still forbidden, must return to bondage when he was taken back to Missouri. The Negro, said Chief Justice Taney, had no rights which a white man must respect. Even more, Congress had "no power to abolish or prevent slavery in any of the territories." With each such decision or event tempers grew taut. The Fugitive Slave Law caused riots in Boston, Philadelphia, Syracuse, and recruited many to work with the Underground Railroad. Five thousand crowded the Broadway Tabernacle in New York to condemn the legalization of slavery in Nebraska as "a base breach of compact and an attempt to degrade free labor." There were similar outpourings in Manchester, Pittsburgh, and Newark.

The moral campaign, initiated by Garrison in 1831, thus metamorphosed into a political one—both in the streets and at the ballot box. The Kansas-Nebraska Act of 1854, revoking the Missouri Compromise, was the signal for a great realignment in national politics. The farmer-labor unity, forged by Jackson but dominated in its latter days by the slavers, fell apart. So did the Whig Party, which temporized on the slave issue. In Ripon, Wisconsin, a former union leader, Alvin E. Bovay, called together radicals, reformers, and businessmen to organize a third party, the Republican Party. When the Republicans nominated John Charles Frémont for the Presidency in 1856, American toilers marched under banners calling for "Free Soil, Free Labor, Frémont." "The truth is," exclaimed the *Boston Courier*, "that Republicanism is neither more nor less than Radicalism." Virtually every radical in the country, from Garrison to the newly arrived followers of Karl Marx, voted for Abraham Lincoln in 1860.

VI

The most dramatic attack against slavery prior to the Civil War was engineered by a remorselessly dedicated man, religious to his bootstraps, tall, gaunt, humorless, a practitioner of violence and guerrilla warfare, who carried the prosaic name, John Brown. Descendant of pious frontiersmen who had worked for emancipation themselves, he grew up to a fierce hatred of an institution he considered "the sum of all villainies," a repudiation of God. Until he was twenty-six, he refused to be enrolled in the army and refused categorically to carry a gun. A perpetual failure in business, father of twenty lusty children by two wives, he was convinced at first that slavery would be extirpated through education. But the murder of Lovejoy in 1837 changed his mind. It was clear then that the slave-owners would not give up their human property willingly. Brooding inside himself, he determined to invade "dark Africa" and liberate the Negro at the point of a rifle. Beginning in Virginia, he would enlist a band of abolitionists to attack the plantations, carry the Negroes to safety in the surrounding mountains, and then move on until the last slave had been freed and the last bastion of slavery uprooted.

Never voluble, given to solitude, Brown felt little kinship for the prolix Garrisonians. He kept his plans secret, therefore, confiding only in a few men such as Frederick Douglass. When the Fugitive Slave Law was passed, Brown wrote his wife that it was "the means of making more abolitionists than all the lectures we have had for years," and he formed a League of Gileadites to "make clean work" of anyone who tried to seize a fleeing slave. Forty Negroes joined the single branch in Springfield, Massachusetts, and applauded Brown's dictum to "stand by one another, and by your friends, while a drop of blood remains." But none of them was ever to follow the heroic credo of his mentor or risk his life for Negro fugitives. The Gileadites passed into limbo, while a fanatical white man read the works of military leaders, pored over maps, and disengaged himself from mundane business affairs to be ready for "the day."

That day came when the Kansas-Nebraska Act was passed. Congress decreed in 1854 that these territories, when admitted to the Union, would determine for themselves whether to tolerate slavery in their borders. For the abolitionists this was a blatant repudiation of the Missouri Compromise, since both territories were north of the old line that separated slave from free states. They decided to colonize Kansas to keep it from being overrun by the slavers. On the other side, the plantation men in nearby Missouri, who owned fifty thousand slaves, were equally determined to make slavery the dominant way of life in the territory next door. The Missourians, being closer to the scene, were able to control the territorial government at first by stuffing the ballot boxes and by making it difficult for known abolitionists to pass through their state. But in a matter of months the free-soilers began settling in large numbers. They held conventions, drafted a free-state constitution, and refused to accept the existing government. It was a situation bound to explode in violence. The slavers had an armed force of Border Ruffians and a leader, Senator David R. Achison, who considered the abolitionists worse than a "horde of our Western savages," and they were ready to treat them accordingly.

Among the emigrants to Kansas were five of Brown's sons. Like their father, who had breathed antislavery into their nostrils from childhood, they were dedicated to keep the state free and implored their parent to send them Minié rifles. The request determined John Brown—age fifty-four but looking much older—finally to implement his long-conceived strategy. On arrival in Kansas he declared with the fierceness of a prophet, "I am here to promote the killing of American slavery." Only a few of the free-soilers, however, were ready to enforce abolitionism by violence. They had indeed arranged a truce with the Border Ruffians, which Brown could neither understand nor countenance.

But in May 1856 Brown went along with his eldest son and a volunteer force to defend Lawrence, Kansas, from the Ruffians. When they learned that the town had already been ravaged, they decided in despair to turn back—all but John Brown. With four of his sons—blindly faithful to their father to the end—and three others, he set out to do what he felt God had told him he must do. Hiding until Sunday, so he could do the Lord's work on a holy day, he led this crew to a proslavery village on the Pottawatomie. There, with a list of those slavers against whom he would wreak retribution, he wakened the victims in the middle of the night and killed five of them. He did not know the men, was not even sure they had engaged in any specific act against the free-soilers, but he had to make an example, and these were a warning to others. He had no pangs of remorse.

The story of Pottowatomie shocked many abolitionists and simultaneously drew the Ruffians into counteraction. Among those killed were two of Brown's children who had not taken part in his massacre, but the toll of dead was only beginning and would eventually grow far higher. Brown, by all accounts, became a master at hiding his small bands, striking when least expected, exacting a far greater toll on the slavocrats than he himself lost. His victories mounted. At Black Jack, he defeated and captured the captain of a much larger force than he himself commanded. His exploits now had the effect of galvanizing other free-soilers into action, and Kansas blazed with gunfire.

The high point of John Brown's warfare in Kansas was the battle at Osawatomie. His son Frederick had been murdered at daybreak while feeding his horses. The father, some miles away at the time, grouped 40 men to fight the 250 Ruffians. Against such odds John Brown could not prevail but his courage inspired people everywhere. His name, as his friends boasted, became "equal to an army with banners." Antislavery raids continued and mounted, throwing the Ruffians into disarray, even while a sick John Brown had to betake himself elsewhere.

It was around this time that the warrior of Osawatomie decided on his most audacious gesture. The few abolitionists to whom he confided considered it a folly or a crime, or both. But Brown could not be dissuaded by anyone short of God himself. He talked with Garrison in the spring of 1859, but would not confide in him because Garrison believed in nonviolence. Nor did he take into his confidence Wendell Phillips, who had been lukewarm during the Kansas campaign. "These men are all talk," said Brown, "what is needed is action—action." On June 30, 1859, with two of his sons he rented a farm in Maryland under a false name, and began collecting forces to invade Virginia. It was a simple plan. The motley group of sixteen white men and five Negroes, well trained and disciplined, was to capture the arsenal at Harpers Ferry, five miles away, arm Negroes nearby, and march deeper into the South, until all black men were liberated. Despite all the estimates of those with whom he discussed his project that the Negro was too weak and intimidated to rise up,

Brown believed to the end that he would be joined by thousands of black men, ready to die with him.

On October 16, 1859, during the night, the band began moving. When the sun had risen the town and the arsenal were in their hands, as were a number of prominent citizens, taken as hostages. But the Negroes failed to rise with John Brown and in his zeal he committed a number of military errors. He failed to cover a river that stood between him and the hills, permitting the Virginia Guard and federal troops, under Colonel Robert E. Lee, to seize these positions. He also permitted a train to pass through his territory, thereby prematurely notifying the authorities what was amiss. After two days of fighting, Brown's two sons and eight others were dead; many had fled; and Brown and four others were under arrest.

The proud antislaver, defiant to the end, told a hostile court: "I am ready for my fate. I do not ask for a trial. I beg for no mockery of a trial." He was ready to die, as he had lived, for the one cause that consumed him. Within a week the State of Virginia had condemned its prisoner to death. Brown's words, before sentence was pronounced, like the words of so many martyrs, had that ring of selflessness that makes history: "Had I so interfered in behalf of the rich, the powerful, the intelligent, the so-called great . . . it would have been all right. Every man in this Court would have deemed it an act worthy of reward rather than punishment. . . . I believe that to have interfered as I have done, in behalf of His despised poor, I did no wrong, but right. Now, if it is deemed necessary that I should forfeit my life for the furtherance of the ends of justice, and mingle blood further with the blood of my children and with the blood of millions in this slave country whose rights are disregarded by wicked, cruel and unjust enactments, I say, let it be done. . . ."

Wendell Phillips began a campaign to win Brown's release. In a speech at Beecher's Plymouth Church in Brooklyn, which gained national attention, he called Harpers Ferry "the Lexington of today." A few conspiratorial souls offered to help Brown escape from prison. But he disdained all help or all requests for clemency. "Jesus of Nazareth was doomed in like manner. Why should I not be?" he said. His words that "the crimes of this guilty land will never be purged away but with blood" was to turn out all too prophetic.

Of John Brown's martyrdom, Bronson Alcott undoubtedly echoed the views of millions when he said: "This deed of his, so surprising, so mixed, so confounding to most persons, will give an impulse to freedom and humanity, whatever becomes of its victim and of the States that howl over it." Both before and after he died on the gallows, many who could not condone his methods nonetheless hailed his sacrifice. Emerson called him "that new saint who will make the gallows glorious like the cross." A song was written about John Brown's body "a-mouldering in the grave, But his soul goes marching on." His act unquestionably galvanized public opinion as nothing else did toward that irrepressible conflict. "In firing his gun," said Garrison, who disapproved of violence but recognized Brown's service to the abolitionist cause, "he has merely told us what time of the day it is. It is high noon, thank God!"

VII

Two years after Harpers Ferry, Abraham Lincoln became President. Eleven Southern states seceded from the Union and the most enervating fratricide in American history ensued. Almost a million men out of a population of thirty-five million died in battle. On January 1, 1863, Lincoln signed the Emancipation Proclamation, granting freedom to over three million slaves in the states that had seceded. Their "value" in prewar prices was two billion dollars. Two years later the South laid down its arms, in utter defeat.

For Garrison the crusade was over. On the thirty-fifth anniversary of the appearance of the *Liberator* it ceased publication. Garrison, nominated again for the presidency of the American Anti-Slavery Society, demurred on the ground that slavery was finished, abolitionism had no further tasks to perform.

But the great apostle was wrong. Southern leaders introduced Black Codes, which required Negroes to go to bed early, rise at dawn, speak respectfully to their employers, do no skilled work without a license. Idle Negroes were imprisoned and forced to work out their prison charges with a private employer. The codes, said the Freedman's Bureau, "actually served to secure to the former slaveholding class the unpaid labor which they had been accustomed to enjoy before the war." To enforce economic degradation, such organizations as the Ku Klux Klan practiced unbridled violence against the Negro. Mass lynchings became commonplace. In Memphis, in May 1866, forty-six ex-slaves were slaughtered. In just one year in one state, Kentucky, one hundred were killed. It was enough to make the Left-wing Republicans bitter to the point of fury. For a while they proposed to give every freed Negro forty acres of land and a mule, so that economic independence would sustain political freedom. But their efforts were frustrated.

Led by Thaddeus Stevens, the radical Republicans finally imposed military rule on the South. Twenty thousand soldiers were sent to police five military districts and to protect Negro rights. With such support, by 1867 Negroes controlled the legislature of South Carolina. That year there were more Negro voters in the Southern states than whites—703,000 to 627,000. A few Negroes became United States senators, congressmen, judges. The Black Codes were abolished. The Fourteenth Amendment to the Constitution guaranteed to the Negro that he would not be deprived of "life, liberty, or property, without due process of law." The Fifteenth Amendment assured him that the right to vote would "not be denied or abridged by the United States or by any State on account of race, color, or previous condition of servitude."

But these were ephemeral victories. The scepter passed in time to the Right-wing Republicans and to a coalition which feared a Negro-poor white alliance more than it feared the defeated plantation owner. In 1877 Rutherford B. Hayes made an agreement with the South which nullified most of what the Negro had gained. Hayes, a Republican, ran for President against the Democrat Samuel Tilden. Tilden had 300,000 more popular votes than Hayes, but there were four states whose electoral vote was in dispute, enough to tip the scale. The issue had to be turned over to Congress for resolution. To win the necessary support Hayes offered the Southerners a deal: if they would cast their ballot for him, he would withdraw federal troops from the South and permit the old landowners to reassert their status.

The Solid South was thus re-formed. The Negro's right to vote was abrogated by poll taxes, literacy tests, and other devices. He went to work for the plantation owner as a free—but cowed—man, only slightly better off than he had been in the past. The schools he attended were segregated, greatly inferior to those for white children. The life he lived was segregated, his income far lower than that of his white brethren. His citizenship became more nominal than real.

A long time later, far into the twentieth century, a second crusade for freedom would begin, this time led by the Negroes themselves.

CHAPTER VIII

THE GILDED AGE

MARK TWAIN called the period following the Civil War the "Gilded Age." Industries mushroomed, railroads crisscrossed the nation, some men made fabulous fortunes. The merchant-capitalist of the first half of the century was considered rich when he owned a few hundred thousand dollars. The industrial capitalist of the last half measured his wealth in millions, sometimes tens of millions, of dollars.

Statistics of growth were breathtaking. Population tripled—from twenty-three million in 1850 to seventy-six million at the turn of the century. From 1859 to 1919 the value of manufactured goods increased by thirty-three times. Giant corporations and trusts dotted the country. Heavy industry, such as steel, replaced in importance light industry, such as shoes, cotton goods, flour. The industrial revolution was finally in full swing, remaking the country in its own image.

If there were any leftists who had visions that the Civil War would result in the "ascendancy" of the working classes, they were to be sadly disillusioned. The leading radical of the time, William H. Sylvis, entertained the hope that "if we can succeed in convincing these people [the Negroes] to make common cause with us . . . we will have a power . . . that will shake Wall Street out of its boots." The Left-wing Republicans, too, expected the Negro, liberated politically and sustained economically by "forty acres and a mule," to become a bastion against reaction. But the poor-white, poor-black alliance was never consummated. Even President Andrew Johnson, far from a radical, could note in 1866 that "an aristoc-

racy based on nearly $2,500,000,000 of national securities has arisen
in the Northern states. . . . The war of finance is the next war we
have to fight."

The Civil War certainly uprooted old institutions and changed
power relations within the country, but it entrenched industrial
capitalism, not the proletariat; it consolidated the power of business,
not the lower classes. Neither the white workers nor the black
showed the unity or the sense of purpose of their capitalist contemporaries. If the Negro's liberation was, in some respects, a
Pyrrhic victory, that of the financiers and manipulators was real—
and substantial. Economically they reaped a bonanza; politically
they crowded left-of-center allies out of Republican Party leadership until it became—like Alexander Hamilton's Federalist Party—
the exclusive domain of the "rich and well born."

When hostilities began, business was in a slump due to the loss of
Southern markets and Southern repudiation of three hundred million dollars in debts. But all this changed from bleak to sunny as war
orders filtered into the economy and created large numbers of
millionaires overnight. Never before had the United States been
caught up in such an orgy of corruption and thievery. Men like
Gould, Vanderbilt, Hill, Harriman, Cooke, and Morgan flouted all the
rules in a display of materialism unmatched before. Typical was the
transaction of J. P. Morgan, by which he bought defective rifles, already condemned, *from* the government for $17,500 one day, and
resold them *to* the government the next day for $110,000. Or—
Philip Armour, just twenty-six, who bought pork at $18 a barrel and
sold it in quick turnover for $40. Or—the burgeoning railroads
which charged Lincoln's government 50 percent more for traffic
than it did private customers. Shoes and knapsacks sold to a hard
pressed regime were so shoddy they had to be discarded. Guns,
vended by unscrupulous contractors, exploded in the hands of soldiers; uniforms disintegrated in the rain; sugar turned out to be part
sand; coffee, a mixture of bean and rye; and ships delivered to the
Navy were made of green lumber and outfitted with worthless
engines.

Nor was this all. Much of the land which anxious workers and
hopeful immigrants had expected to be their heritage was siphoned
off by speculators and railroads. The Homestead Act, passed in 1862
after decades of agitation by men such as George Henry Evans, was

certainly a boon to the poor. But much of the public domain—which in 1860 encompassed a billion acres, or more than half the country's area—found its way, through bribery and land-grabbing, into the hands of the wealthy. By 1890, for instance, 375,000 homesteaders had received forty-eight million acres of land from a generous government, but land-grant railroad companies were quietly awarded more than four times as much as the 375,000 combined. Three western railroads, chartered between 1862 and 1864, not only were given—with the aid of bribed congressmen—federal loans for each mile of track laid but outright gifts of seventy million acres.

The loopholes by which men made fortunes were depressingly obvious but patently weighted on the side of the speculator. Greenback currency, for instance, since it had no gold backing, fell in value to fifty or sixty cents on the dollar—at one time as low as thirty-nine cents—playing havoc with workingmen's wages. But the wary businessman could take those same depressed greenbacks and convert them into solid gold bonds that paid one hundred cents on the dollar. While prices doubled, according to the *New York Tribune,* and wages lagged far behind, the profits of venturesome entrepreneurs often pyramided to 300 or 400 percent a year. It was a wild era for which the robber barons were infinitely better prepared than the lower classes—and they scampered away with the fruits of victory.

A symbol of his time was Jay Gould, who began his career by cheating two partners in a leather factory. Later he made a fortune manipulating stocks on the New York Stock Exchange. In 1867, at the age of thirty-two, he printed and sold counterfeit shares of stock in the Erie Railroad. When the fraud was discovered in New York, he and his partner Jim Fisk slipped away to New Jersey with $6 million in cash and the Erie financial records. Later he bribed New York legislators to pass a law making his act legal. With the haul from the Erie Railroad defalcation Gould set about to corner the $15 million gold then circulating. It was a delicate operation which would founder if the government put any of its own $95 million gold hoard on the market. To assure the support of President Ulysses S. Grant for this scheme, Gould bribed the President's brother-in-law. Though Grant refused to go along, Gould was still able to pocket a handsome $11 million profit.

The age of the robber barons was an age of abysmally low political morals. During the Grant administration the Secretary of the Navy was able to bank $320,000 from profits on naval contracts. A railroad construction company, the Credit Mobilier Company of America, headed by a member of Congress, Oakes Ames, swindled the government—which was paying the bills—out of $44 million in building the Union Pacific Railroad. The congressman had bribed some of his congressional colleagues with free stock which realized 625 percent dividends in a single year. On the local front, there was the crooked politician looting the treasury of his city just as the politicians of a higher order were looting the federal till. Boss William M. Tweed, Grand Sachem of Tammany Hall, made off with an estimated $200 million in illicit income from the fair city of New York. And though his was the most artistic of the brigandage, it was far from the only one.

Attaining wealth became a religion for all too many people, so much so that it terrified even some capitalists. Andrew Carnegie, the steel man, assaying his own situation, wrote: "To continue much longer with most of my thoughts wholly upon the way to make more money in the shortest time, must degrade me beyond hope of permanent recovery."

Not all the entrepreneurs, or even a majority, were as bereft of conscience as Jay Gould, but the tide of war and postwar swept the most tawdry speculators to lofty heights. Their moral tone was indicated by Cornelius Vanderbilt when he shouted: "What do I care about the law? Hain't I got the power?" Or by Gould, when he boasted that "I can hire one-half of the working class to kill the other half."

It would be false to say the mass of Americans failed to benefit from the Gilded Age. Real wages did go up, and whatever the plight of the fifteen million immigrants, they were certainly better off than in Europe. But it was an uneven gain, interrupted and marred by perennial depressions, and by disparities between the unskilled and skilled, the foreign born and the native. The gap between wealth and poverty, the conspicuous consumption side by side with dreary existence, the flamboyant success stories of a few amidst the dashed hopes of the many—all this elicited an angry response. If anything, the industrial system looked more bleak to the lowly worker in the last half of the century than in the first. And he responded to it sometimes in cold blind fury—as in the violence of the Molly

Maguires or the 1877 railroad strikes—or in more traditional forms ranging from simple unionism (unionism that concentrated on simple goals such as wages or hours and eschewed radical politics) to money schemes and independent politics.

II

During the Civil War, with labor scarce, business booming, and profits plentiful, it was expedient for employers to grant union demands for wage increases. The raises never seemed to catch up with the rise in the cost of living—76 percent in five years—but they sufficiently appeased proletarian appetites to keep labor's loyalty focused on simple unionism. "The workmen of almost every branch of trade," commented a New England newspaper in March 1863, "have had their strikes within the last few months. . . . In almost every instance the demands of the employed have been acceded to." Molders, machinists, carpenters, printers re-formed labor unions that had been swept away by prewar depressions, content to fight for realizable immediate demands—wages and hours—rather than for broader objectives, such as political reforms or social revolution. By 1865 unionism had grown to two hundred thousand members in three hundred local unions, not a few of which were amalgamating into national unions and city central bodies.

But this was a peak of prosperity. Within eighteen months after Appomattox, as military production was curtailed and two million demobilized men swelled the labor market, the economy entered a valley of depression. The usual postwar letdown caused the usual unemployment, hardship—and union busting. Employers devised appropriate means to fend off the labor "conspirators." They formed associations—such as the Iron Founders' Association or the American National Steel Manufacturers—to coordinate antiunion efforts. They exchanged "black lists" of active union men, denying employment to those on the list whenever they applied for work. They hired spies and detective agencies—such as Pinkerton or Burns—to infiltrate labor's ranks and break strikes. When other means failed, they simply closed their doors, and laid off their men until they forced them to terms. Postwar strikes tended to run on for long periods, and with far less assurance of success than during the war.

Thus again in the inexorable rhythm of social protest, as palliatives proved inadequate or inaccessible, radical activists turned to the broader panorama. One of the leftist ideas put forth during and after the Civil War was for an eight-hour day. Ira Steward, who initiated the eight-hour movement, was a Boston machinist with a flair for the writings of John Stuart Mill. He became an eight-hour enthusiast when, as a machinist's apprentice at the age of nineteen, he was discharged for demanding a shorter workday. From then on he devoted his time to lectures, letters to the editor, and pamphlets dealing with a reduced work schedule. That he was convincing is evidenced by the fact that after a five-hour talk with Senator Charles Sumner, the senator announced he was dropping his opposition to an eight-hour law; and a minister who also had deep reservations declared that he had never met a college professor or writer on political economy "but could learn wisdom" from Steward.

With irrepressible conviction Steward argued that his single reform would alter the life not only of the worker but of the community in every respect. Wages, said Steward, depended on a worker's wants as a consumer. So long as he was tied to his workbench twelve to fourteen hours a day, he lacked the imagination, energy, or time to want more. Give him leisure and he will increase both his wants and his wages. He would do this, on the one hand, by demanding more: "Change and improve the daily habits of the laborers," said Steward, "and they will raise their own pay in spite of any power in the universe." Steward's wife Mary wrote a little jingle to emphasize this point:

> *Whether you work by the piece or work by the day,*
> *Decreasing the hours, increases the pay.*

On the other hand, as leisure brought about a "higher standard of popular intelligence," the worker would urge—rather than oppose —introduction of more and better laborsaving devices. With increased productivity, wages could be increased still further. The eight-hour plank, in Steward's pliable hand, became a panacea not merely to alleviate drudgery but to change society. With additional time for himself, the worker would become politically oriented and would guard democracy against the "corruption of capital." Ultimately he would bring about, through his pressure for change, a judicious social system and a total human emancipation. All that was needed to begin with was a national law for the eight-hour day.

Wendell Phillips, the abolitionist leader, was so impressed by Steward's reasoning that he made a generous contribution to his movement. Others flocked to the standard and soon the Eight-Hour Leagues were the most exciting attraction in the reformist camp. California alone had more than fifty such Leagues by 1868. In Illinois, Michigan, Iowa, and Indiana the separate groups federated into Grand Eight-Hour Leagues, and in New York City into a Central Eight-Hour League. Their platform was so uncomplicated it was bound to appeal to pragmatic Americans.

Another panacea was "Kelloggism," whose foremost proponent after the Civil War was A. C. Cameron, editor of the *Workingman's Advocate* of Chicago. Edward Kellogg, a well-to-do drygoods merchant in New York who lost his fortune during the 1837 crash, believed that labor's travail was caused exclusively by the fact that bankers controlled the supply of money and credit. By making available or withholding that supply, they held the farmer and wage earner in a viselike grip. To break this vise, Kellogg would have the federal government establish a National Safety Fund in every state to issue paper money. The money would be backed by real estate, and bear an interest rate of only 1 percent. By this means "all agriculturists, manufacturers, mechanics, planters, in short all who wish to secure a support by honest industry" would have all the capital they needed. The unions too would be able to secure funds to bolster producers' cooperatives, so that in due course the capitalist system would wither and die. It was an elaborate theory that was the forerunner of another type of money reform, Greenbackism, and it had its fervid devotees, arguing endlessly over nuances of its application.

There were other reformers plowing the fields, those who were disillusioned with the Republican Party and proposed a labor party; the suffragettes of Susan B. Anthony; the producer cooperative zealots; and many more. None were to succeed—at least not right then.

The man who brought the reformers together—perhaps because he subscribed to almost all of their nostrums—and welded them into a single movement, was a medium-sized iron molder, with blond sideburns and incisive blue eyes, the outstanding radical of this period, William H. Sylvis. Second son of a Pennsylvania wagonmaker who was never quite able to take care of his ten children, the younger Sylvis was taught the alphabet by his first employer at the age of eleven. Though he headed the most important union of his time, he never had enough money to gain a respite from bill collectors or poverty. His clothes usually were worn down to bare thread, and both he and his family (wife and five children) knew the pangs of hunger all too frequently. When he died prematurely at the age of forty-one, there was not enough money in the house to bury him.

Sylvis could have lived moderately well had he wanted to, for a molder was a privileged worker those days. His pay, twelve dollars a week for seventy-two hours, was four times that of an unskilled girl in the textile mills. But Sylvis was the true believer, the selfless idealist who would sacrifice anything for his beliefs. "I love this union cause," he said in an often-quoted speech. "I hold it more dear than I do my family or my life. I am willing to devote to it all that I am or have or hope for in this world."

"This union cause" was an isolated and harried cause in the mid-nineteenth century. Depressions had gnawed it to bits. No national labor federation had come to the fore since the National Trades' Union had foundered in 1837. For the most part the existing unions were local in scope, lacking even the ties of a national association in their own craft. But during the 1850's local unions began to federate nationally—first the printers, then the hat finishers, spinners, iron puddlers, blacksmiths, machinists. In the wake of this trend, Sylvis, having recently become a member and then secretary of the molders' union in Philadelphia, embarked on a similar campaign of amalgamation. Under his tutelage twelve of the seventeen scattered molders' groups in the country came together to set up a federation later known as the Iron Molders' International Union.

A labor leader, surveying the tempest of the war years, could hardly avoid a truculent suspicion. The anxieties leading to war reduced trade, closed factories, and caused unemployment; many unions disappeared as if caught in the eye of a tornado. This slump, on the heels of the one in 1857, convinced Sylvis that a compromise was needed between North and South to save the workingman from disaster. He took the initiative, therefore, in December 1860 to form a Committee of Thirty-Four to mobilize working-class sentiment to "preserve the union." He explained that "under the leadership of political demagogues and traitors scattered all over the land, North,

South, East and West, the country is going to the devil as fast as it can. . . ."

When hostilities began, Sylvis helped enlist molders in the Northern cause and served in the army himself for a while. But what he saw around him was the chicanery of a new group of freebooters, while his own union was in difficulties. "Worse than traitors in arms are the men," read a Congressional committee report, "who, pretending loyalty to the flag, feast and fatten on the misfortunes of the nation." While the Goulds and Morgans were growing rich, Sylvis in 1863 went to work full time for his union to prevent it from disintegrating. With $100 advanced by his Philadelphia organization, he traveled 10,000 miles—often hitching rides in engineers' cabs—to revitalize his half-defunct union. So lean were the financial pickings that he collected only $899 on his three trips that year, of which he sent home $279 for the support of his family. His union, however, grew to 53 local affiliates and a total of 7,000 members, and Sylvis was heartened by the results. But once the war ended, the old problem was there again—unemployment, bad times. "There was a prostration of our trade," Sylvis records, "unparalleled within the recollection of the oldest among us."

It is not surprising, therefore, that a man like Sylvis should have evolved a thoroughgoing class-conscious philosophy. In the face of this changing order of things, how could anyone say there was an identity of interests between labor and capital? "If workingmen and capitalists are equal co-partners, composing one vast firm by which the industry of the world is carried on and controlled," asked Sylvis, "why do they not share equally in the profits? Why does capital take to itself the whole loaf, while labor is left to gather the crumbs?" Northern labor and capital were jointly involved in a civil conflict, but far from narrowing the division between them, the war actually widened it precipitously. "Our recent war," Sylvis was to write, "has led to the foundation of the most infamous money aristocracy of the earth."

To checkmate this aristocracy, Sylvis, along with two confreres, William Harding of the coachmakers' union and Jonathan Fincher of the machinists, decided once again to form a national federation of labor. Unless labor centralized its efforts, it would be at the mercy of the employing class. As a labor paper in Rochester put it: "The longer action is delayed, the more difficult it will be for the workingmen to secure the end they seek. . . . The late war and what has grown out of the war, made Capital stronger. It has made millions all at the expense of the labor of this country, and the capital thus concentrated is to be used in a greater or less degree to defeat the objects sought by the workingmen." With such thoughts in mind, Sylvis early in 1866 issued the call for a labor convention, and in August that year seventy delegates assembled in Baltimore to form the National Labor Union. The delegates represented sixty thousand workers.

The National Labor Union, though it was made up entirely of union representatives, except for six members of the Eight-Hour Leagues, was not exactly a union, or perhaps, more properly, it was something more than a union. Its founders argued heatedly over a wide range of subjects—strikes, apprenticeship, Negroes, education, the eight-hour day, money reform, public lands, and a national labor party. It was obvious from the outset that what they were groping for, in addition to the organization of more workers, was a platform for social change. They seemed to have little faith in strikes, for they resolved to use this weapon sparingly and to rely increasingly on arbitration. They side-stepped the Negro question, catering to the fears of unskilled workers that the Negro would take their jobs. It is noteworthy that of the three thousand words in the Declaration of Principles, nineteen hundred were devoted to money reform. The eight-hour day received the loudest approval: "The first and great necessity of the present to free the labor of this country from capitalistic slavery is the passing of the law by which eight hours shall be the normal working day in all states of the American Union."

Inevitably, in this confusion over which strategy to concentrate on, Sylvis and his friends tried a number of approaches simultaneously. One of them was the producers' cooperative. Based on the experience of the Molders' Union, Sylvis came to the conclusion that strikes were a weak reed to lean on. Union members had to be assessed hundreds of thousands of dollars to pay strike benefits, yet even if the strikes were won, the gains were seldom permanent. Machinery continued to make skilled men redundant and employers constantly tried to reduce wages or increase work loads. It was a losing fight that promised only "continual trouble and taxation." After the war the Molders' Union had conducted strikes against the members of three employer associations, the first two ending in victory, but the last one in so abysmal a defeat that the union's treasury was drained dry and the union itself almost driven out of existence. Such disasters caused Sylvis to detour sharply toward cooperation, rather than strikes, as the main answer to "capitalist slavery." When the employers in the Albany-Troy district of New York posted notices they would no longer recognize union committees, Sylvis retaliated by raising $26,000 to form a cooperative foundry. For a while the cooperative functioned exceptionally well. It employed 35 workers regularly, and in addition to union wages paid them $2 a day as their share of the profits. The $25 or $30 a week that the men earned was higher than anything that prevailed in the industry just then. In the first six months profits were $6,000 and in the following year, when the work force was doubled, $17,000.

The success of Troy stimulated other cooperatives. By 1868 a zealous Sylvis had organized eleven and had twenty more in the process of formation. "Divide the profits," he urged his followers, "among those who produce them and drive the non-producers to honorable toil or starvation." It was an idea that caught on. Bakers, coachmakers, shipwrights, mechanics, boilermakers, shoemakers, hatters, printers, even Negro laborers and women seamstresses followed the molders' example. At the 1868 convention of his union, Sylvis was so enamored of this means of bringing "peace and prosperity" that he changed the name of the organization to the Iron Molders' International Cooperative and Protective Union of North America. Unionism, said Sylvis, attacks only the fringes of labor's problem. "The cause of all these evils is the WAGES SYSTEM. We must adopt a system which will divide the profits of labor among those who produce them."

Despite an auspicious beginning, however, the cooperatives could not withstand competition from capitalist establishments. They were never quite able to raise the capital for improved equipment. Not all the ventures were failures, to be sure. A shoe factory operated by the Knights of St. Crispin in Philadelphia enjoyed prosperity until 1871. The Coopers' Union was able, for a period, to sustain seven shops which produced barrels for flour mills. But eventually all foundered.

Sylvis died before the final disappearance of some of his brain children, but even while he was alive he was not demoralized by the failure of many cooperatives. He refused to concede that the idea was inoperative; all it needed, he concluded, was "state aid." The 1867 convention of the National Labor Union resolved: "WHEREAS, the Congress of the United States have from time to time made appropriations of large sums of money and grants of public land for the social benefit of Railroads and other monopolies . . . be it Resolved that we respectfully petition Congress at its next session to appropriate $25,000 to aid in establishing the eight-hour system, cooperation."

The political activity which most absorbed the energies of the National Labor Union was lobbying for eight-hour-day bills. By the time of its second convention, the NLU could report that six states had passed eight-hour laws and that the House of Representatives had approved such a bill for government employees. Unfortunately, the state laws were designated as "frauds on the laboring classes" because they were universally disregarded. The campaign continued, however, as did agitation for money reform, a better land policy, and many other items.

Sylvis died suddenly on July 26, 1869, of a stomach ailment that had made him bedridden for only four days. His death caused something of a panic among the leadership of the NLU, and in fact the organization was never able to renew its momentum. Just before his death, Sylvis had penned the call for the NLU's next convention. It read in part: "We are engaged in a huge struggle. Honesty versus corruption, freedom versus tyranny, the people against a monied aristocracy . . . that is fast reducing the whole industrial people of the country to mere vassals to contribute to Wall Street and its satellites. Who Shall Win? Let the People Answer."

Who shall win? The odds after Sylvis was gone did not seem too favorable.

One of Sylvis' pet projects had been the formation of a labor party. How else, he asked, could you implement monetary reform or the eight-hour day unless you had your own party? The 1867 convention of the NLU, under Sylvis' prodding, had called on the working classes to "cut themselves aloof from party ties and predilections and organize into a National Labor Party."

A local labor party was formed in Massachusetts, sponsored by the Knights of St. Crispin, among others. It won a big victory in 1869, receiving 13,000 votes and electing 23 men to the legislature. The following year it nominated the perennial crusader, Wendell

Phillips, for governor and he too did moderately well, polling 22,000 votes as against 80,000 for the winning Republican. Two years later, however, the tide receded; E. M. Chamberlin, running for the same post, garnered only 7,000 votes, and the party split between those who favored the eight-hour panacea and those who favored currency manipulation.

On the national level, a National Labor Reform Party was projected in 1870, but by the time nominations were due in 1872, it was rent with so many schisms it is virtually impossible to unravel what happened. One group decided to back the Liberal Republicans, who had split away from the main branch of Lincoln's party and had nominated Horace Greeley. Another chose David Davis of Illinois, who promptly deserted to support Greeley. Still another segment ran Charles O'Connor of New York, a man with questionable attitudes on the race question, and secured 29,489 votes under the original banner, National Labor Reform Party. Finally, a small minority, led by A. C. Cameron, decided just to sit it out.

With this political fiasco as its epitaph, the National Labor Union, then composed of two thirds of nonunion men, passed into oblivion. It had survived six confusing years.

III

The same year that Sylvis died, a different kind of drama was reaching its climax in the rich anthracite fields of Pennsylvania. There, tens of thousands of Irishmen, twenty-two thousand in Schuylkill County alone, worked in semidarkness, knee-deep in water, at the most dangerous job of the day. Their lot, as one mining clerk put it, was "little better than semislavery." One quarter of the workers were children, seven to sixteen, paid one to three dollars a week for separating coal from slate as it came down the chutes. Pay for adults was computed by the cubic yard of coal mined, or by the ton or car, with a base of only eleven or twelve dollars a week. Opportunities for cheating the wage earner were endless—for instance, by claiming more slate in the coal than there actually was, or by short-weighing. Hours were long, from dawn to dusk, sanitary conditions impossibly bad.

Worse than the wages was the rate of accidents. In one seven-year period, 566 miners were killed, 1,655 injured in Schuylkill County.

On September 6, 1869, at the Avondale Mine in Luzerne County, 175 men perished when fire broke out in its only shaft. The men were trapped only because the mineowners had failed to erect a safety exit. John Siney, leader of the Workingmen's Benevolent Association of Schuylkill County, echoed the universal bitterness when he addressed widows, orphans, and friends at the mine gate: "Men, if you must die with your boots on, die for your families, your homes, your country, but do not longer consent to die like rats in a trap for those who have no more interest in you than in the pick you dig with."

Periodically the miners tried to form unions, with almost invariable setbacks. Blood flowed freely in the abortive strikes of the 1840's and 1850's as state troopers and coal and iron police, paid by the operators, beat and killed miners with impunity.

In this inclement climate resort to violence became axiomatic. From 1860 or thereabouts to 1875, terror and counterterror was a frequent adjunct to coal mining. Many of the Irishmen belonged to an organization called the Ancient Order of Hibernians, which a hostile press nicknamed the Molly Maguires, after a picturesque figure in Ireland. Molly, it is said, carried two pistols under her red petticoat which she used liberally in the 1840's to dissuade tyrannical landlords and bailiffs from evicting tenants. Molly's assassinations were so effective a warning that parts of Ireland—again, according to hearsay—became uninhabitable except to her followers.

Cut off from more pacific means of protest, the Irish miners who belonged to the Ancient Order of Hibernians responded to the terror around them by terror of their own. By and large the men in the Order were solid, God-fearing men who otherwise led exemplary lives and abided by its purpose to "promote friendship, unity, and true Christian charity among the members." But the Mollies increasingly became embroiled in violence against the mine superintendents, strikebreakers, and even, on occasion, union leaders and socialists they felt had betrayed them. The killings were neither random nor indiscriminate, but carefully planned and executed. A Molly who had a grievance against a boss took the matter before a committee—meeting in the basement, perhaps, of a tavern owned by another Molly—and there a decision was arrived at. Assuming that the committee concurred, the "job"—beating or killing—was thereupon assigned to a Molly from another town, to best avoid detection. Lest this sound more frightening than it actually was, it should be noted that most Molly activity was confined to threats. An obnoxious superintendent would receive a crude picture of a coffin or a pistol—or both. The copy read, typically: "Mr. John Taylor—We will give you one week to go but if you are alive on next Saturday you will die." If Mr. Taylor took the hint and departed, he was safe; otherwise he had to fend for himself, usually against superior odds.

They were a peculiar lot, these Mollies. Moral, devout, religious, they finished an assignment for murder with prayer. On occasion they killed a socialist because he expressed atheistic sentiments, or a union leader who was too friendly to the boss. Never did they resort to organized violence to settle personal grudges. Never did they inform against each other—until their ranks were finally infiltrated by a Pinkerton spy. They were sufficiently influential to elect local officials here and there, and to secure the appointment of police chiefs and high constables. In its own way theirs was an inverted form of idealism. As the Socialist leader, Eugene V. Debs, wrote of them later: "It is true that their methods were drastic, but it must be remembered that their lot was hard and brutalizing; that they were the neglected children of poverty, the product of wretched environment."

The events which led to the entrapment of the Mollies and their dissolution began in 1869–70, when the coal operators signed the first written contract with the miners' union. It covered thirty thousand men—85 percent of the work force in the anthracite fields—and tied the wage rate to the price of coal. The minimum was to be three dollars a ton. But as the bottom fell out of the market with the depression of 1873, Franklin P. Gowen, leader of the operators and president of the Reading Railroad, which owned extensive holdings in the coal fields, decided to cut the rate below this figure. On January 1, 1875, the miners responded to Gowen's reductions with what was to become known as the "long strike." It lasted six bitter months. Thousands were reduced literally to bread and water. Children went into the woods every day to pick herbs and dig roots to nourish themselves and their parents.

Gowen was determined to smash the union—and the Mollies. Two years before the strike he called in Allan Pinkerton of the soon famous detective agency and gave him a hundred-thousand-dollar retainer to smash the Mollies. Pinkerton, an immigrant from Scotland who had once been a radical and was just beginning a career in union busting and industrial spying, assigned an agent to insinuate himself into the Ancient Order of Hibernians and collect evidence on the Mollies. The agent, James McParlan, who assumed the name McKenna for his task, was "a broth of a boy," twenty-nine years old, a native of Ireland. He sang well, danced a tolerable jig, told a good story, and drank with the best of them. After a while he gained the confidence of the Mollies and was initiated into the society in April 1874.

While McParlan was busy preparing a case, Gowen was also arming a band of his own terrorists, known as the "Modocs." Together with the coal and iron police, the Modocs ambushed, beat and killed quite a few strikers. A union leader, Edward Coyle, was murdered in March 1875. Another one met a similar fate at the hands of a Modoc named Bradley. At Tuscarora a union meeting was assaulted by vigilantes and one man left dead, others wounded. A particularly militant union man, Charles O'Donnell, was killed in his home, along with an innocent woman who happened to be visiting. The Mollies, as might have been anticipated, replied in kind. Strikebreakers, imported into the mines from outside the area, were frequently found dead in ditches. Any striker who entertained notions of going back to work was warned in stern language he would soon meet his maker. That the Mollies were more the victims than the victimizers is attested to by Marvin W. Schlegel, an assistant state historian of Pennsylvania, who wrote a favorable biography of Gowen. In it he argues that "the facts show that there was much more terror waged against the Mollies than those illiterate Irishmen ever aroused."

Whatever the toll between the Mollies and the Modocs, however, the strike itself was defeated by hunger. "Since I last saw you," a striker wrote in a letter, "I have buried my youngest child, and on the day before its death there was not one bit of victuals in the house with six children." The union was smashed. The miners went back to work at wages 20 percent below what they had before.

With the strike over, Gowen concentrated on settling accounts with the Mollies. His agent McParlan was an insider now and claimed to have knowledge of a number of murders as well as their perpetrators. He personally had been part of a group assigned to murder one man, but his associates botched the job and the man, though wounded, survived. Based on this information, various arrests were made, trials held, and nineteen men sentenced to death, others to prison terms. Gowen was so intensely involved in this campaign to exterminate the Mollies that he had himself appointed prosecutor in some of the cases. Eliminate the Mollies, he told one jury, and "we can stand up before the whole country and say: 'Now all are safe in this country. . . .'"

The Mollies no doubt had committed acts of vengeance, but whatever their misdeeds, there is serious question about the means used to convict them. McParlan was the main witness in all the cases, testifying that the accused had confessed to him. Corroboration was usually by men who were themselves charged with murder and won their freedom by testifying against their fellows. In what was perhaps the most important of the trials, five miners, all active in the "long strike," were accused of killing a patrolman named Benjamin Yost. The corroborating witness was a man who had also been arrested for this crime, Jimmy Kerrigan, but he gained immunity by implicating the others. His own wife testified that the real murderer was Kerrigan, who was now accusing "innocent men to suffer for his crime." But the five were convicted. (Thirty years later, oddly enough, the same Pinkerton agent McParlan was able to get another man accused of murder to testify against William D. "Big Bill" Haywood and two others much as Kerrigan did in 1876. This time, however, the jury brought in a verdict of not guilty.)

There were other suspicious circumstances to the conviction of the Mollies. An eyewitness to one murder specifically stated that the man being tried, Thomas Munley, was not the one he saw at the scene of the crime. Yet Munley was convicted. One miner, Jack Kehoe, was found guilty of a killing that occurred fourteen years before. The murdered man, a breaker boss, had been stoned to death by a crowd of miners, but Kehoe was singled out and eventually executed, though no evidence was ever brought forward that he threw a single stone.

The first ten Mollies were hanged in June 1877, the last two in January 1879, many of them protesting their innocence to the end. A *New York World* reporter who was present at some of the executions wrote that "the demeanor of the men on the scaffold, their resolute and yet quiet protestations of innocence . . . were things to stagger one's belief in their guilt. . . . They were arrested and arraigned at a time of great public excitement, and they were condemned and hanged on 'general principles.'" Nevertheless, with the executions the Molly Maguires passed out of existence, a strange movement that has no counterpart in American history.

IV

Less than a month after the first Mollies were laid to rest, the United States was shaken by the first nationwide strike in its history. Gowen's prediction that the country would be safe if the Mollies were subdued proved premature, as did an article in a business publication, the *Commercial and Financial Chronicle*, which boasted that "this year . . . labor is under control." The Great Riots of 1877 were actually a greater menace to the established order than anything since the Civil War. The *New York Tribune* referred to them as an "insurrection." Other papers called them a "communist conspiracy." One saw in them "the awful presence of Socialism, which has more than once made Europe tremble on account of its energy, its despotism, its fearful atrocities." It took twenty thousand armed men to suppress the strike.

Conditions had been improving steadily for a few years after the postwar depression when suddenly there was a new panic. The best-known banking firm in the country, Jay Cooke & Company, went bankrupt. In the three years after 1873, twenty-three thousand businesses closed their doors. Within seven years real wages were down to almost half what they were before. Three million out of a population of forty million were without work. "Never," wrote the Washington *Inter-Ocean*, "was a time . . . when a greater amount of misery, poverty and wretchedness existed than at the present time. . . . There are hundreds of well-born, well-bred, and well-informed men walking the streets without a cent, and without knowledge of where to get a dinner or a bed." So bad did conditions become that during the first three months of 1874, ninety thousand people in New York sought shelter in police stations. Huddled together on hard benches, they slept in damp clothes and left at daybreak, tired and unfed.

It was against this background that a minor incident, involving only forty brakemen and firemen of the Baltimore & Ohio, flared into bitter class war. The company, like other railroads, had just announced another wage cut of 10 percent. On the afternoon of July 16, 1877, the forty men, arriving at Camden junction near Baltimore, decided they would not work. It was a personal protest on their part; they had no idea of fomenting a general strike or anything approximating it. But they evidently expressed latent feelings of all railroad men, for the strike spread and spread until it stretched from Baltimore to San Francisco. Twelve hundred men of the same line halted operations in Martinsburg, West Virginia, almost immediately. When the mayor and police arrested the leaders, a large crowd gathered—including miners from nearby towns—and released them. This was to happen throughout the strike. Hostility to the railroads for discriminatory rates, watered stock, and other practices was so pronounced that innumerable nonstrikers joined the fray—miners near Pittsburgh, twenty thousand workers of different trades in Chicago, Negro sewermen in Louisville, farmers in West Virginia, and of course the jobless everywhere.

After Martinsburg, the walkout assumed serious proportions. Governor Matthews, responding to the railroad's request, immediately sent in the state militia. On the following morning, July 17, shots were exchanged and a fireman wounded. Townspeople and farmers thereupon staged another sympathy demonstration, but this time two companies of militia—and their officers—went over to the strikers' side, refusing to shoot. The governor, alarmed by the mutiny, appealed to President Rutherford B. Hayes in Washington for federal troops, and the President obliged at once. Soldiers were dispatched to the scene, arrested the leaders, and broke the strike at this single point. The trains began to move; the crisis seemed to be over.

But in fact it was only beginning. In a nonce it fanned out to Ohio, Kentucky, Maryland. When soldiers marched to the railroad station in Baltimore to entrain for strike duty in Cumberland, they were met by thousands of workers seeking to prevent their departure. In the melee that followed, twelve men were killed, eighteen wounded. Again, a governor appealed for federal forces, and again the request was answered at once. Strikers who sought to persuade workers to leave their trains were quickly arrested, many shot at. By July 22 the Baltimore & Ohio strike was smashed.

Still the crisis would not abate. The Pennsylvania, New York Central, and many other lines were now affected by the virus. In Pittsburgh the railroad workers took their locomotives to the roundhouse and went home. As word of the strike flashed to the general public, many thousands took to the streets—miners from nearby Wilkensburg, unemployed from the city itself. On July 21 the sheriff read the riot act to the assembled men but they refused to move. Worse still, the Pittsburgh militiamen refused to fire on them. The governor then sent in militia from far-off Philadalphia, young men anxious for a little action. They got their wish soon enough. On arriving in Pittsburgh and being met by a large crowd that hissed them, the soldiers shot into it with careless abandon. Twenty people died, twenty-nine were wounded. "The sight presented after the soldiers ceased firing," reported the *New York Herald*, "was sickening. Old men and boys . . . lay writhing in the agonies of death, while numbers of children were killed outright. Yellowside, the neighborhood of the scene of the conflict, was actually dotted with dead and dying; while weeping women, cursing loudly and deeply the instruments which had made them widows, were clinging to the bleeding corpses." One of the soldiers told a newspaper reporter the next morning: "I served in the War of the Rebellion and have seen wild fighting . . . but a night of terror such as last night I never experienced before and hope to God I never will again." A grand jury later termed the incident "an unauthorized, willful, and wanton killing . . . which the inquest can call by no other name but murder." In the wake of the shootings, the enraged strikers, buttressed by factory workers and miners (encouraged even by businessmen), set fire to hundreds of boxcars, the roundhouses, and shops. Five million dollars of equipment went up in smoke and the *New York World* reported that the city was "in the hands of men dominated by the devilish spirit of Communism." The murders continued. At Reading thirteen were killed, twenty wounded in a single exchange.

President Hayes ordered soldiers out to guard the Capitol. At a Cabinet meeting someone suggested that Pennsylvania should be declared in a state of insurrection and seventy-five thousand volunteers enrolled to police it. Still the surge of desperate railroad men continued—heedless of all the defeated strikes in the mines and textile mills of this period. It consumed the Erie of New York, New York Central, Lake Shore. At Buffalo another company of militia joined the strikers. William Vanderbilt of the New York Central was so disturbed he promised the Buffalo men a 26 percent raise (which he later repudiated) and doled out $100,000 to aid the unemployed.

When the strike reached Chicago and St. Louis, it found organized leadership for the first time. A Marxian socialist movement had been taking root in the United States since the 1850's. As part of its evolution, three groups came together in July 1876 to form the Working Men's Party of the United States. The new party, of course, gave its blessings to the railroad strikes from the outset and called on the government to nationalize the railway and telegraph lines. In Philadelphia, Newark, New York, and Brooklyn it had held meetings to express sympathy "for the families and friends of those who have been shot down while fighting the battle of oppressed labor." In Cincinnati it appointed a committee to give aid to the strikers. But it was in Chicago and St. Louis where the party was sufficiently entrenched so that it gained control of affairs. A mass meeting of twenty thousand called by the socialists stirred the Chicago workers as few incidents of that period. They carried banners inscribed "Why Does Overproduction Cause Starvation?" "We Want Work Not Charity." Albert Parsons, a handsome young Texan, a member of the Working Men's Party who was later to become a prominent anarchist, spoke ceaselessly at strikers' meetings.

On July 23, 1877, switchmen of the Michigan Central in Chicago, whose wage rates had already been reduced from sixty-five to fifty-five dollars a month, rebelled at the prospect of another cut. Within a day the midwestern transport system was in paralysis, and workers in innumerable factories and shops, caught by the mood, joined the parade. "The City in Possession of Communists," was the headline of the New York Times. Next day police, cavalry, and strikers met in bitter battle at the Halsted Street viaduct. At one point twenty thousand men on both sides were under arms. Fifty separate mobs were fighting the authorities, closing saloons, attacking residences, destroying locomotives, marching toward City Hall. At least thirty were killed and almost one hundred wounded.

Simultaneously the tornado moved on to St. Louis, where again the Working Men's Party was the spearhead of events. On July 22 the party issued a circular for a mass meeting in which it said: "We are asking the public to condemn the government for its action in sending troops to protect capitalists and their property against the just demands of railway men." Inspired by the Marxists, the railroad workers voted to down tools. This was the first effort at advance organization. In the face of it, the employers offered a compromise —to restore part, but not all, of the wage cuts. The men rejected it with disdain.

In this taut situation, with the railroad strike as a spur, other workers too became involved. The socialists called a general strike in St. Louis, which included among its demands not only wage increases but the eight-hour day and a law prohibiting the employment of children under fourteen years of age. By July 29 the city was closed tight, business at a standstill, and the Executive Committee of the socialists practically the only instrument of law and order. When Governor Phelps threatened to invoke martial law, the Executive Committee informed him that "nothing short of compliance" to its demands would "arrest the tidal wave of revolution." The party seemed convinced its moment of glory had arrived, that the liberation of the proletariat was at hand. But the combined power of the militia, police, private vigilantes, and federal troops was able to regain control of the city. Seventy-three men were arrested at the party's headquarters. Many were held without charges and four were subsequently sentenced to five years' imprisonment and a two-thousand-dollar fine. By August 2 the strike was over; the last bastion had fallen.

In two-and-a-half weeks proletarian rancor had reached proportions that in other countries, less endowed in wealth and potential, would have spilled over to revolution.

The Gilded Age, it seems, was not so gilded after all.

CHAPTER IX

ENTER KARL MARX

PRIOR to the Gilded Age, American leftists, despite unending frustration, enjoyed a certain status as "insiders." Jefferson, Jackson, Van Buren, Lincoln were, by and large, *their* Presidents.

The end of the Civil War, however, marked a great divide, a definitive end to one period, an introduction to another. The dispossessed, to be sure, would batter against the doors of the establishment time and again. The nationwide strikes of 1877 or 1894 might be called—if one exaggerated a little—near-revolutions. The United States, however, was on the road to stability. It was never again to witness an actual rebellion like 1775 or a civil conflict with social overtones like 1861. The radicals became distinct "outsiders." Through links with reform movements, such as the Greenbackers or Populists, they won many concessions for the lower classes, but they never came close to their ultimate aspiration, a revolutionary reconstitution of society itself.

In Europe, on the other hand, the nineteenth century was one of marked instability. Revolutions came in cycles. There was the cycle of 1830, in which Frenchmen ousted the last of the Bourbons, Charles X; Belgians rebelled against the Dutch; Poles rose against the czar; seven German states (out of thirty) dethroned their rulers; and three Italian states challenged the temporal power of the Pope. There was the more tempestuous cycle of 1848, in which Frenchmen removed still another king, Louis Phillipe; Austrians forced out of power that leader of European reaction, Prince Metternich; Hungarians fought Austrians; Croats fought Hungarians; and Germans and Italians made still another abortive attempt to achieve national

[*149*]

unity. In 1863 the Poles once again tried to assert independence; and after France's defeat at the hands of Germany in 1870, the Parisian proletariat formed what Karl Marx considered the model of revolution, the ill-fated Commune.

This continuing upheaval inevitably produced a bevy of colorful figures and a wide variety of social remedies. There were revolutionary conspirators like the Frenchman Louis Blanqui; the Russian Michael Bakunin; the Italians Garibaldi and Mazzini. There were the giants of intellect like Fourier, Louis Blanc, Pierre Joseph Proudhon, Ferdinand Lassalle, Karl Marx, and Friedrich Engels. These were the legions of change, each in his own way seeking to fashion the ideal society, most of them producing sects not only in Europe, but conterparts in the United States of America.

Of these figures, the man who was to leave the deepest imprint with the Left wing of both hemispheres was Karl Marx. No revolutionary before or since has had so enduring an effect. His theories of "historical materialism" and "surplus value" were to form the ideological bedrock for anarchists, syndicalists, Socialists and Communists, whatever their disagreements on other matters. His theories and personality are therefore a pertinent feature of the unfolding saga of radicalism both in the United States and elsewhere.

Marx was not an organizer or popular leader of masses in the street. He did not direct great strikes or organize unions, and he never successfully guided an actual revolution. His contribution to the radical cause was primarily intellectual—and overpoweringly so. He was the scholar par excellence, the man with an orderly, logical, sternly analytical mind, who possessed an extraordinary grasp of historical detail. Before him leftist thought was, in the words of Harold J. Laski, "little more than an inchoate protest against injustice." Marx lent an aura of science and sophistication to radical doctrine. He rooted it in history and economics, rather than in religion or abstract humanism, and by doing so gave his followers hope instead of desire.

The father of "scientific socialism" was born in the Rhineland in 1818 of a solid middle-class family which converted from Judaism to Christianity when he was six. His early life followed a predictable pattern—elementary schools, the right universities. But Marx had an avidity for study which made him the perennial scholar. "My clever and gifted son Karl," wrote his father, "passes wretched, sleepless nights, wearying body and mind with cheerless study, for-bearing all pleasures with the sole object of applying himself to abstruse studies. . . ." At the age of nineteen he was translating Greek and Latin, voraciously studying the philosophy of Hegel, and, strangely enough, writing three volumes of poetry. Like many another radical—Trotsky, for instance—the desire to write fiction and poems was a strong first instinct.

Marx's fate, however, was neither with fiction nor the academic world. After being awarded his doctorate, he was forced to turn to journalism when the University of Bonn refused him a position as lecturer. He became editor in 1842 of a little paper begun by a friend of his, the *Rheinische Zeitung*. A year or more later, after he married the cultured daughter of a government privy councilor, he went to Paris to assume a similar post with the *Franco-German Year Books*. Journalism, it turned out, was not to be his career either, but this short stint gave Marx an opportunity to become acquainted with the economic theories of French socialism, and—equally important—with Friedrich Engels, a German businessman, two years his junior, who lived in Manchester, England. Engels was to be Marx's closest friend, associate, and benefactor rolled into one. Without his financial support, says biographer Max Beer, "Marx, with his unpractical, helpless, and, at the same time, proud and un-compromising disposition, would most probably have perished in exile." It was in this brief period of 1843–44 that Marx plunged him-self into the study of socialist writings and emerged a self-made convert.

But if Marx was a socialist, he did not yet belong to a socialist movement. The opportunity came in 1845. The Prussian govern-ment complained to the French authorities that a number of Ger-mans, including Marx and Heinrich Heine, were writing inflamma-tory articles against it for a Parisian publication called *Vorwaerts*. Thereupon Marx was expelled from the country and forced to betake himself and family to Brussels. There he came in touch with a small group of German workers who had been functioning under the enigmatic title, League of the Just, since 1836. In due course the group, rechristened the League of Communists, commissioned Marx and Engels to formulate a new program for it. The forty-page docu-ment produced by the two men, the *Communist Manifesto,* is still the "bible" of radicalism for millions on all continents.

"A spectre is haunting Europe," it began, "the spectre of communism." Applying the Hegelian dialectic—thesis, antithesis, and synthesis—to the process of history, the authors proclaimed that all of history had been the outgrowth of a struggle between classes. "Freeman and slave, patrician and plebian, lord and serf, guild-master and journeyman, in a word, oppressor and oppressed, stood in constant opposition to one another, carried on an uninterrupted, now hidden, now open fight, a fight which each time ended either in a revolutionary reconstitution of society at large, or in the common ruin of the contending classes." Here was a new view of history which, like Darwin's concept of evolution, showed it as something in flux, following specific laws of development.

As Marx conceived it, there was a flow from one social system to another, always accompanied by class struggle and climaxed by rev-olution. The tribal society—primitive communism—makes way in the historical ladder to a system of chattel slavery. Chattel slavery yields to feudalism, feudalism to capitalism, and capitalism is des-tined to be replaced by an era of socialism. (Communism is the "highest stage" of this era, a stage in which the state has withered away and classes have disappeared.) In each cycle the new society is progressive at first, superseding one which has become reaction-ary and intolerable, only in its turn to lapse into the same institu-tionalized rigidities itself. Marx and Engels did not argue that capitalism had been an unmitigated evil since its inception. On the contrary, capitalism, too, in its formative period, "has played a more revolutionary" role. "It has accomplished wonders far exceeding Egyptian pyramids, Roman aqueducts, and Gothic cathedrals. . . . During its rule of scarce one hundred years, [it] has created more massive and more colossal productive forces than have all preceding generations together." But as it has evolved, it has been consumed by periodic crises of overproduction causing ever greater misery for its proletariat. Thus it has been creating "its own gravediggers" who will replace it with a system in which society as a whole, rather than individuals, will own the means of production.

Communism was certainly no new doctrine. It had been preached by thinkers since the dawn of time, including the early Christians and, later, religious savants of the Middle Ages. But what Marx added was historical scope, something which gave it the taste of destiny. Marx denied that it was automatic—the workers would have to organize to seize power from the bourgeoisie. In some places, where democracy flourished, as in the United States or England, they could accomplish it through the ballot box; in others they would have to counter the violence of the class enemy with violence of their own. But the tide of history clearly was running with the oppressed, a tide which they had only to join to assure victory. Where other philosophies of the beautiful tomorrow were based on human desire, Marxism was based on a recitation of history which made success seem virtually certain. Capitalism would fall not so much through the personal will of men—though that would enter the equation—as through the impersonal momentum of history. Towering as this capitalism might seem, it carried within it the seeds of its own destruction.

In a small library of books and pamphlets, Marx subsequently enlarged on the theories in the *Communist Manifesto*. The heart of his doctrine was that man's evolution was triggered primarily—though not exclusively—by economic factors. "The mode of production in material life," Marx argued, "determines the general characteristic of the social, political, and spiritual process of life." As that mode of production changes, social relations similarly change. "The hand mill creates a society with the feudal lord; the steam mill a society with the industrial capitalist." The steam mill obviously takes man a few steps farther along the road to economic security. But capitalism has an inherent defect which at a certain stage thwarts this process. That defect, according to Marx, springs from something called "surplus value." Other theorists before Marx had explained the value of commodities in terms of the labor-time involved in their production. A pair of shoes, for instance, which takes three hours to make (including the time that must be expended for raw materials, plant, machinery) is exchanged for money which, in gold equivalent, also takes three hours to mine and mill. It is all fair and square, even though the price—as distinct from the true value—may fluctuate a little, depending on supply and demand.

But if it is all fair and square—if a man exchanges something for its equivalent in value—how does he earn a profit? This was the point which other theorists failed to explain. The answer is to be found, said Marx, in the peculiar nature of labor-power. "Labor-power is . . . a commodity which its owner, the wage-worker, sells to the capitalist." As a commodity, labor-power too is exchanged for its equivalent in money. It is exchanged "for the value of the nec-

[*153*]

essaries required to produce, develop, maintain and perpetuate the laboring power." The difference between the commodity "labor-power" and the commodity "shoes," however, is that shoes do not produce anything, while labor-power produces not only enough to cover its own cost (wages) but a surplus which goes to the capitalist as profit, rent, or interest. It is the only commodity with this characteristic. Let us assume, by way of example, that a worker received fifteen dollars a day as the price for his labor. But the worker takes raw materials and by applying his labor-power adds value to the raw materials. That additional value is likely to be twenty-five dollars, thus leaving a *surplus value*—over and above his own wages—of ten dollars, which is the capitalist's profit.

This is the fly in the ointment. The worker has produced values for which he has been partly paid and partly unpaid. Not only is there a moral question involved in this, but more important, an economic dilemma. The worker who received fifteen dollars a day but adds twenty-five dollars in value can buy back only part of what he produces. For the rest, the market is limited, since businessmen, bankers, landlords obviously do not spend all the *surplus value* they extract; they put some of it in the bank or under the mattress. Thus in due time the market becomes glutted. The warehouses are full but there are not enough customers to buy. The system becomes victim to overproduction, and in its wake there is a chain reaction that is shattering. With a shortage of customers, the capitalist must curtail production and lay off part of his staff. In the midst of plenty, millions become jobless and go hungry. The proletariat lives in indescribable misery and anxiety.

Eventually, of course, the wheels begin to turn again, but not without social catastrophe. For one thing, "the modern laborer . . . instead of rising with the progress of industry, . . . becomes a pauper, and pauperism develops more rapidly than population and wealth." For another, the "big fish eat the little fish"—larger capitalists absorb the businesses of smaller ones driven to the wall, thus creating larger monopolies. Finally, the capitalist nations, finding the markets at home inadequate, seek outlets abroad. They subdue weak, underdeveloped nations, to assure the export of goods and capital, as well as a source of raw materials. This works well for a while, but when the great powers have finished carving up the world between them, a moment arrives when the "have-not" industrial nations go to war with the "haves" to change the balance of power. Depression and misery at home are therefore compounded by imperialism and war abroad, driving the masses ultimately to revolt.

With "historical materialism" and the theory of "surplus value" as his anchor, Marx could assure the proletariat that socialism was not only morally right, but was almost inevitable. He offered hope that was grounded not in human wish or religion but in the sciences of history and economics, as predictable, according to Marx, as Newton's apple falling to the ground or Darwin's anthropoid evolving to man. Life has proved some of Marx's concepts wrong—notably the "immiserization" theory, which held that the worker would become progressively pauperized—and some theories inadequate. But beginning with the *Manifesto,* Marx—in the words of Laski—"freed socialism from its earlier situation of a doctrine cherished by conspirators in defiance of government and gave to it at once a purpose and an historic background." He gave the workers "at once a high sense of their historic mission and a realization of the dignity implicit in their task."

In the more than a hundred years since Marx and Engels issued their *Manifesto* a vast majority of radicals, in Europe as in America, have accepted it as the cornerstone of their faith. It has had for them the ring of a clarion: "Let the ruling classes tremble at a communistic revolution. The proletarians have nothing to lose but their chains. They have a world to gain. Working men of all countries, unite!"

II

On the practical side, Marx's efforts were less fruitful than in the intellectual arena. When the 1848 cycle of revolutions began, he was banished by the Belgian government for fear he might help spread the February revolution in France northward. The situation was now reversed; French leftists, flush with a new (though temporary) freedom, invited Marx to their soil once more. Here he reassembled members of the League of Communists and sent them back into Germany to further the revolution there. In June 1848 he and Engels also returned to the Rhineland to begin publication of the *Neue Rheinische Zeitung.* In their optimism they called on the working class to rise up against the bourgeoisie, disregarding the fact that Germany was still a divided nation, pockmarked with feudal characteristics. For such a nation to jump a historical stage directly to socialism was premature. Marx and Engels themselves later conceded "cheerful deceptions and almost childlike enthusiasms." After a year and a half in Germany, as the continentwide revolution was overpowered by counterrevolution, Marx emigrated, by stages, to his permanent home, London.

For the next decade and a half the perennial scholar pored over tomes in the British Museum, exchanged correspondence with his friend Engels, and for a couple of years around the time of the Civil War in the United States, did some writing for Horace Greeley's *New York Daily Tribune*. At the end of this period Marx participated in the launching of the first international body of radicals. On the organizational plane, though not the intellectual, the foundation of the International Workingmen's Association—popularly referred to as the First International—represents the high point of Marx's career. He was not the initiator of the movement, but he quickly became its dominant figure. The First International is also part of the "American story" for it helped both to unite and divide radicals here.

In July 1863 London unionists arranged a giant rally to protest Russia's terror against Polish nationalists. Attendance by several French labor leaders inspired the British to propose formation of an international confederation of workingmen. It was not at first conceived as a revolutionary movement but as an instrument for collaboration between unionists of different countries. "Whenever working men of one country are sufficiently well organized to demand higher wages or shorter hours," read the address of the Englishmen to their French brethren, "they are met by the threat of the employer to hire cheaper foreign labor, and this evil can only be removed by the international organization of the working class."

But when the organization reached reality in September 1864, it was found that though the unionists were in predominant number, it was the radical intellectuals, many of them exiles, who held sway over the deliberations. They comprised a mosaic of forces, ranging from revolutionary nationalists to utopians and a half-dozen varieties of socialism. Marx, with his scholarly precision, however, towered there as he had with the League of Communists. It was he who was assigned to draft the inaugural address and declaration of principles; it was he who remained the guiding spirit until the First International was quietly interred in far-off New York twelve years later. Treading lightly because of the conglomerate character of the assemblage, Marx proclaimed a set of principles in less flamboyant terms than the *Communist Manifesto*. To have done otherwise would have immediately alienated the revolution's hostile children. But the direction was clear: "The emancipation of the working class must be accomplished by the working class itself."

The European press, which dismissed the International cavalierly to begin with, was soon alarmed. The first multinational body of laborers gained affiliates in France, England, Germany, Austria, Belgium, Denmark, Portugal, Italy, Spain, Holland, Poland, even Australia. Sylvis' National Labor Union in the United States decided to adhere. When the International raised funds for striking bronze-workers in Paris and tailors in London, its stock rose sky-high. The French affiliate alone reached an estimated peak of two hundred thousand members.

Expansion, however, was followed by decline, as one ideological segment after another seceded or was expelled. Mazzini, who believed in conspiratorial societies and could not stomach Marx's notions of an open mass movement, withdrew. The Blanquists, also dedicated to secret organizations, were expelled. The Proudhonists, who believed in a labor bank and anarchism, were defeated in open debate. Marx won every ideological battle—but lost the war. The crisis of the International coincided with a revolution in France and the formation of the Paris Commune. Though this body was not Marx's handiwork, he greeted it lyrically as a foretaste of the future. For staid British unionists this was anathema. All but one promptly withdrew from the International's highest councils. Simultaneously, as the Commune was suppressed and various other labor bodies in Europe suffered the lash, a lingering argument between Marx and Michael Bakunin shattered whatever unity still remained in the movement.

Bakunin, the subject of many future novels, was as romantic a figure in radical history as one can find. Scion of an aristocratic Russian family, energetic, eloquent, he was the impulsive activist, the foot-loose conspirator. He was a leading participant in leftist conspiracies in France, Germany, Austria, and Russia before 1848. Condemned to death after the Saxon revolt of 1849, he was extradited to his native land and shipped to Siberia, from which he escaped to London in 1860. Eight years later he formed the Alliance of Socialist Democracy, which contained within it a secret section of national "brothers"—and above it one hundred international "brothers"— whose purpose was to uproot by violent revolution all existing forms of government. Where Marx opposed only the present state, because it was capitalist, Bakunin declared war on all states because they were "born historically . . . of the marriage of violence, rapine, pillage, in a word, war and conquest. . . ." Ready to make revolutionary coups at the drop of a hat, Bakunin inevitably came into conflict with the methodically logical Marx, who placed his revolutionary faith in *mass* rather than conspiratorial revolt. The road to power, for Marx, was through strikes, political action, demonstrations, open revolt in which large numbers of people were engaged; not in a quick thrust by fifty or a hundred men assassinating a tyrant or capturing the government offices.

At the 1872 convention of the International, though Marx's followers still predominated and passed a resolution favoring political action, they decided to ship the headquarters to America, to keep it out of Bakunin's reach. It was a useless precaution, for by that time the German and French affiliates were disappearing under governmental repressions and the general mood was one of decline. After four solitary years in the States, far removed from the base of operations and still consumed by petty squabbles, the First International folded its tent.

III

It was as part of this larger drama, with its enervating disputes between Left, Right, and Center, that Marxism came to the United States. The first adherents, understandably, were German-Americans. Among the three million Germans who deserted their fatherland in the first half of the nineteenth century were many who flocked to New York, Milwaukee, Chicago, St. Louis. At one time the flow here was two hundred thousand a year. Many were simple journeymen, disillusioned with conditions at home, seeking their fortunes elsewhere. Quite a few, however, were experienced revolutionaries fleeing certain imprisonment at home. Many had been associated with Marx and Engels personally, either in Brussels or London. Wherever they went, they transplanted their radical seed with unabated fervor. They formed unions and study circles as a matter of course. Even their gymnastic clubs, such as the *Socialistischer Turnerbund* in the United States, were politically oriented and extreme leftist. The big cities were filling up with a tidal wave of immigrants (about two million each decade, five million in the 1880's), who constituted half to three quarters of the population. But of these the Germans were far and away the most consistent rebels. In St. Louis the "forty-eighters"—German immigrants who arrived after the 1848 revolutionary fiasco at home—became the leading trade-union force, as they were to be in so many other cities.

Prior to the Civil War many of the German radicals had a tendency to be diverted into byways. Herman Kriege, an associate of Marx's in Europe, got lost in the land reform movement of George Henry Evans, much to the discomfiture of his mentor. Wilhelm Weitling, a magnetic personality who also knew Marx, decided to proselytize for "labor exchange banks." It was only with the arrival of Joseph Weydemeyer in 1851 that Marxism gained an orthodox spokesman and organizer. Weydemeyer enjoyed some success in uniting both German-speaking and English-speaking laborers into politically minded union federations, and in popularizing standard Marxist works in his journals. But by 1860 his organizations, as well as similar ones, such as the Communist Club of New York, were in disarray.

When the Civil War broke out, individual Marxists in considerable number joined the colors and served with distinction. They believed, as Marx put it in a letter congratulating Lincoln on his re-election, that "as the American War of Independence initiated a new era of ascendancy for the middle class, so the American Anti-slavery War will do for the working class." Weydemeyer, though in his mid-forties, joined the army to fight for the freedom both of chattel and wage slaves. August Willich, who had been a member of the London Communist League in 1848, enlisted as a private and rose rapidly to the rank of brigadier general. Another Marxist, Robert Rose of the New York Communist Club, worked his way up to major. The *Turnverein*—gymnastic clubs—enrolled 40 to 50 percent of their able-bodied men in Lincoln's legions. This support for the Union's cause was noteworthy because not a few American workers of other ethnic strains, infected by Copperhead propaganda, were either hesitant or defiant. In 1863, for instance, New York workingmen, angered by a Conscription Act which exempted rich men from duty if they paid a commutation fee of three hundred dollars, rioted for three days, causing the death and maiming of four hundred people and property damage of five million dollars. But the German socialists were steadfast. One of their groups distributed a leaflet urging laborers to "Stand by the Union, the Constitution and the Laws! . . . Keep honestly at your work!"

The Marxist movement, like many unions, failed to thrive during the war. But once it was over, and encouraged by the birth of the International in London, American Marxists were soon re-forming their ranks. The first to join the International—Sylvis' National Labor Union voted to affiliate, but never actually did so—was a group launched on New York's Bowery in January 1868. Under the imposing sobriquet, the Social Party of New York and Vicinity, it ran an independent slate in the elections that year, and on receiving discouraging results went out of business. In its place there emerged the General German Workingmen's Association, which simultaneously adhered to Sylvis' National Labor Union and to the International. It was called Section 1 of New York, and was followed in short order by thirty other sections—French, Bohemian, Scandinavian, Irish, as well as German.

Though small in numbers—about five thousand all told—these men and women were what Eric Hofer has called true believers. They exerted significant influence on many workers, such as the thirty thousand Pennsylvania anthracite miners during the "long strike." It was they too who called the unemployed demonstration at Tompkins Square, New York; conducted the hunger march in Chicago; and, as already related, played a prominent role in the 1877 railway strike.

The most interesting section of the nascent Marxist movement, if only because of its amusing origin, was an English-speaking one, Section 12. It played no role in the history of American socialism, but typified one of its problems—its lure to off-beats. The key figures in Section 12 were two seductive sisters, Victoria Woodhull and Tennessee Claflin. Victoria and Tennessee were born in Homer, Ohio, of parents who, to say the least, were eccentric. The mother was a spiritualist and a believer in mesmerism. The father had been suspected of arson and left town only two steps ahead of the sheriff, deserting his family in the process. The eleven Claflins thereupon became a traveling wagon show in which Tennessee and Victoria told fortunes and gave exhibitions of spiritualism. The two girls later posed as clairvoyants in Cincinnati, before moving to the greener pastures of New York in 1868. Somewhere along the line, the Claflin sister developed an enlightened view on sex. They were both married for the first time in their teens, and were to be married again. But they were devotees of free love, both in theory and even more so in practice—a fact which was to figure prominently in their success.

Not long after arriving in New York, Tennessee, the least ladylike of the two ladies, arranged to meet the railroad tycoon Commodore Vanderbilt, and after applying some of her magic treatment became his mistress. With the aging commodore to back them, the two sisters set themselves up as "lady brokers" and were an immediate sensation. Vanderbilt's tips on the market were like money in the bank and the male stock speculators were attracted like flies to honey. One of the men Victoria met at the height of her financial adventures was a mild scholar, just about to turn sixty, Stephen Pearl Andrews. Andrews was a linguist, reputed to be adept at thirty-two languages, including Chinese, Sanskrit, and Hebrew, and he was working on a universal language to be called Alwato. He had been associated with Josiah Warren in his Time Store but had broken with his mentor on the question of free love, which he favored and Warren spurned. Andrews also dabbled in spiritualism, and to round out his philosophical leanings, was a sympathizer of the First International. With Andrews and Victoria's lover, a certain Colonel Blood, to help them, the sisters launched a newspaper called the *Woodhull and Claflin Weekly*. In it they regaled their readers with articles on abortion, prostitution, free love, and, on occasion, the amorous exploits of prominent citizens. An issue in which they exposed the love affair between the prominent minister Henry Ward Beecher and the attractive wife of journalist Theodore Tilton was gobbled up so fast that single copies sold at black-market rates as high as forty dollars. But their interests did not end there, particularly for Victoria. The weekly was also the first journal to publish in English the *Communist Manifesto*. With Andrews as their intellectual guide, Victoria and Tennessee joined the International and became the focal point of Section 12. Thus by a circuitous route, a frost-bitten American capitalist, Commodore Vanderbilt, had spawned a small revolutionary cadre bent on overthrowing his cherished system. Needless to say, Victoria and Tennessee were not as successful here as in the brokerage business. They soon alienated the staid German workers, especially the German *Hausfrauen,* and were expelled, bag and baggage. Victoria thereupon called together a convention of all "male and female beings of America" to found an "Equal Rights Party," for which she was the candidate for President of the United States, and the famed Negro reformer Frederick Douglass candidate for Vice-President.

The socialist movement repeatedly had to cope with such off-beat elements. But this was only a minor irritant compared to doctrinal warfare. The movement, here as in Europe, was beset with three approaches to achieving political power. One school was composed of the followers of Ferdinand Lassalle, son of a rich wholesale merchant in Germany, who had majored in philology at the universities of Breslau and Berlin. Lassalle's views on history coincided with Marx's but he disagreed with the father of modern socialism when he designated the state as the "executive committee of the ruling class." For Lassalle, the state was of a classless character—"to help the development of the human race towards freedom." From this he drew the conclusion that if the proletariat could gain the unhampered right to the ballot box, it could elect itself to office without the need for strikes or revolutions as its major weapon. Electoral activity was the only road to liberation, said Lassalle, because by the "iron law of wages" there was always, under capitalism, a surplus of labor driving wages downward, and making economic action futile. Though Lassalle was killed in a duel over a lady two months before the First International was formed, his beliefs exercised appeal both in Germany and the United States long after his death.

At the opposite pole were the firebrands who followed the Russian anarchist Bakunin. They accepted neither Lassalle's nor Marx's definition of the state. Any kind of a state was the enemy per se, even—if such a thing were possible, which they denied—a working-class state. And since the state held a monopoly of the instruments of force, it was obvious that it could be disloged only through violence. Unlike such philosophical anarchists as Henry D. Thoreau, who preached nonviolence, the anarcho-Communists believed there was no other alternative. The world they sought for tomorrow was to be one of peace and harmony, but the road there led through fierce and unavoidable struggles in which the people would have to counter the violence of the state with defensive violence of their own.

The triangular Lassalle-Marx-Bakunin hassle was re-enacted in America with typical energy. During the panic of the 1870's, Lassalleans formed the Labor Party of Illinois and a Social Democratic Workingmen's Party of North America in New York. In 1876 the two groups, plus one or two others, held a unity convention to found the Working Men's Party of the United States—the one involved in the 1877 railroad strike—which the following year changed its name to the Socialist Labor Party of North America (SLP).

If this bewildering saga gives the impression that Socialists were doing nothing but dividing and uniting, it is only partly true, for within the ranks of the SLP were many who played decisive roles in the American labor movement. There were Adolph Strasser, leader of the cigar makers' union (whose protégé Samuel Gompers was to be the long-time president of the American Federation of Labor); Peter J. McGuire, head of the influential carpenters' union; Albert Parsons and most of those who guided the labor movement in Chicago, New York, St. Louis, and other major cities. The influence of these Socialist unionists is reflected in the first preamble to the constitution of the American Federation of Labor, which reads like the text of Karl Marx's *Manifesto:* "A struggle is going on in the nations of the civilized world between the oppressors and the oppressed of all countries, a struggle between capital and labor, which must grow in intensity from year to year. . . ."

The dispute over strategy was actually an outgrowth of the frustration of such men in their day-to-day activity. Some SLP members felt the most fertile area for their endeavors was at the polling booths. SLP candidates, in fact, did tolerably well in the elections of 1878, garnering 8,000 votes in Chicago and electing two aldermen. In St. Louis the party won three seats in the legislature, and in New York, though it secured only 4,000 votes, this was twice as much as in the election before. With the return of good times the following year, however, the party slumped and the more extreme faction demanded something more virile than election campaigns. For this

[163]

group it was the union, rather than the franchise, which was the fulcrum for revolution.

The center of controversy then and for a long time to come was the most radical city in the country, Chicago. Here the SLP was blessed with top-notch union tacticians of the caliber of Albert Parsons and G. A. Schilling, who had wide support among the working masses. To them the exhortations of the SLP's national leader, Phillip Van Patten, to effectuate "a revolution in the minds of the people," seemed tepid. Police, vigilantes, and soldiers were bashing in the heads of strikers with intolerable regularity. To wait until the populace could be convinced to vote the Socialists into office was, in the face of this, not a convincing nostrum. As early as 1875, SLP militants had grouped for self-defense into armed bands called Educational and Defense Societies (*Lehr und Wehr Vereine*). Van Patten disavowed these paramilitary squads on the ground that they were trying "to accomplish by force what they could not obtain by the ballot." But the extremists grew both in size and influence. Before long they were forming Revolutionary Clubs outside the party, and in October 1881 they held a convention in Chicago at which they unveiled the Revolutionary Socialist Labor Party—to distinguish it from the reformist Socialist Labor Party. Its platform called for creation of unions along "communistic" principles and decried the ballot as "an invention of the bourgeoisie to fool the workers."

Into this cauldron was now thrown a bombastic orator and alumnus of European prisons, Johann Most. Here was a man fierce and brilliant, whose hatred for authority was unbridled. Son of an impoverished subaltern officer, Most was born in Augsburg, Germany, in 1846. His childhood and youth were miserable ones. He was a puny youngster enervated by five years of sickness. An operation permanently deformed his face. His stepmother showed little understanding for his problems and his first employer was a man of marked cruelty. Growing up in this way it is not surprising that Most compensated with a strong sense of social concern. He overcame his scant education by voracious reading, and he managed in due course to travel to various parts of Europe. It was while in Switzerland that he became acquainted with the socialist doctrine of the First International, and he preached it wherever he went.

In the summer of 1869 Most was sentenced by the authorities in Vienna to a month in jail for making a bombastic speech, and, a little later, to five years on the charge of high treason, for organizing a free speech demonstration. Pardoned, but expelled from Austria, he returned to Germany, where for the next seven years he was a prominent figure in the socialist movement. Twice he was elected to the Diet, in 1874 and again in 1877. Other men in such circumstances tended to mellow, but not Most. He continued making inflammatory speeches and continued going to jail. After the passage of the anti-Socialist laws in 1878 he was sent packing from Berlin, and like many another radical pilgrim, he settled in London, where he published a weekly magazine *Freiheit* (Freedom). Then his views shifted steadily from socialism to anarchism. He was enthralled by sensational revolutionary deeds; "propaganda of the deed," the anarchist byword, intrigued him more than "propaganda of the word." When Alexander II, czar of Russia, was assassinated in 1881, Most published an article not only extolling the act but urging others to emulate it. For this he was sentenced to sixteen months hard labor by the British, and on being released in October 1882, departed for new adventures in America.

When Most landed in New York, his reputation as a martyr and hero had already preceded him. His tour of the major cities late in 1882 and early in 1883 was a notable success which received considerable notice in the press and helped enlarge the anarchist contingent. Many a wavering Socialist was drawn to anarchism by Most. Out of this burst of activity, a potpourri of anarchists and Left-wing socialists from twenty-six cities came together in October 1883 to proclaim the International Working People's Association —or, as it was better known, the Black International. Its manifesto illustrated its disillusion with moderation. "We could show by scores of illustrations," it stated, "that all attempts in the past to reform this monstrous system by peaceable means, such as the ballot, have been futile, and all such efforts in the future must necessarily be so. . . . Since we must then rely upon the kindness of our masters for whatever redress we have, and knowing from them no good may be expected, there remains but one recourse—FORCE!"

The anarchist bark, history was to prove, was worse than its bite —the number of violent deeds committed was surprisingly small— but the emphasis on terror in its verbal stockpile was unmistakable. Not long after he arrived, Most published a pamphlet called *Science of Revolutionary Warfare—A Manual of Instruction in the Use and*

Production of Nitroglycerine, Dynamite, Gun-Cotton, Fulminating Mercury, Bombs, Fuses, Poison, Etc., Etc. On April 8, 1885, *Die Arbeiter Zeitung* informed it readers: "Here is something worth hearing. A number of strikers in Quincy, yesterday, fired upon their bosses, and not upon the scabs. This is recommended most emphatically, for imitation." On May 5, 1885, it implored: "Workmen, arm yourselves!" Albert Parsons, who had also been caught in the sweep of anarchism, carried an article in this paper, "Alarm," on the virtues of explosives: "Dynamite! Of all the good stuff, that is the stuff! Stuff several pounds of this sublime stuff into an inch pipe (gas or water pipe), plug up both ends, insert a cap with a fuse attached, place this in the immediate vicinity of a lot of rich loafers who live by the sweat of other people's brows, and light the fuse. A most cheerful and gratifying result will follow. . . ."

The stage was thus set for anarchism's climactic moment—Haymarket.

I V

Between the Great Riots of 1877 and the Haymarket affair of 1886, much had happened not only within the working-class movement but among farmers and the abused middle classes. The Knights of Labor, founded in 1869, and now headed by the former mayor of Scranton, Terence V. Powderly, was gaining momentum. This vain but able man considered strikes a "relic of barbarism," counseling workers instead to concentrate on the familiar remedies, electoral action and cooperatives. The Knights was an admixture of labor unions and "general assemblies," which welcomed not only members of the working class but of the middle class as well—all but bankers, lawyers, gamblers, stockbrokers, and saloonkeepers. Since Powderly believed there was no essential conflict between labor and capital, this was consistent with his philosophy. He could not prevent episodic strikes by the unionists in his ranks, but he discouraged them, and lent his energies to building two hundred producer and consumer cooperatives. This, not strikes, was the road to eventual emancipation. Ironically, however, it was a successful strike and boycott against Jay Gould's railroads which propelled the organization from 53,000 members in 1883 to 700,000 three years later.

Powderly reaped the harvest of these events but his basic hostility to the labor walkout remained unappeased. When 340,000 unionists struck on May 1, 1886, to secure the eight-hour day he ordered them back to work. The good will gained in the electrifying strike against Gould was dissipated overnight, and the Knights slipped rapidly within two years to less than a third its size. By 1893 it was on the road to extinction.

But if the "uplift unionism" of the Knights of Labor failed to capture proletarian hearts, traditional unionism recorded impressive gains. With the end of the depression of the 1870's, trade unions resumed their march foward. The bricklayers' unions grew from 200 to 9,000 in three years; the printers' doubled their membership, from 6,500 to 13,000; and the cigarmakers' zoomed from 4,400 to 13,000. Encouraged by these developments and alienated by Powderly's pomposity, a number of Socialists like Peter McGuire and Adolph Strasser, and sympathizers like Samuel Gompers, took the timid step in 1881 of forming the Federation of Organized Trades and Labor Unions. In 1886 they enlarged and converted the Federation into the first stable union movement in the nation's history, the American Federation of Labor.

It was a favorable time for the AFL to begin operations. The 1880's was a decade of rising expectations all round, with business booming as never before, and radicals and reformers waiting in the wings to right accumulated wrongs. Sensing opportunity—even before the AFL was officially proclaimed—Samuel Gompers and his associates had initiated a campaign to win the eight-hour day through either negotiations or strikes by May 1, 1886. The call had an electric effect; workers bought "Eight-Hour Shoes," and smoked "Eight-Hour Tobacco." An "Eight-Hour Song" went like this:

*We mean to make things over;
    we're tired of toil for naught
But bare enough to live on: never
    an hour for thought.
We want to feel the sunshine; we
    want to smell the flowers;
We're sure that God has willed it,
    and we mean to have eight hours. . . .*

Conservative newspapers damned the agitation as "communism, lurid and rampant," which could only encourage loafing, gambling, drunkenness, or worse. In Chicago the anarchists were at first hesitant about joining the movement, on the ground that "to accede the point that capitalists have the right to eight hours of our labor is more than a compromise, it is a virtual concession that the wage system is right." But, stirred by the mood, the radicals formed the Eight-Hour Association and became the primary advocates of the shorter workday.

On May 1, 1886, in 11,500 establishments throughout the nation, 350,000 workers laid down their tools. Slightly more than half won their demand—an eight-hour day with no reduction in pay. In Chicago, the anarchists prepared the way by sustained propaganda in advance. The first and second of May passed tensely but without incident. On May 3, however, there was trouble. The McCormick Harvester plant had locked out its employees three months before. That day 300 strikebreakers, guarded by 350 police, entered the plant. The strikers held a mass meeting near the factory, where an anarchist, August Spies, addressed them on their own problems as well as the eight-hour day. It might have ended peacefully, but during his talk a whistle blew and the strikebreakers, finished with the day's work, were let out of the plant. In the ensuing battle of stones, bricks, and fists the police opened fire and at least four men were killed, many more wounded.

The anarchists responded with white fury. *Die Arbeiter Zeitung's* headline read: "BLOOD! Lead and Powder as a Cure for Dissatisfied Workers—This Is Law and Order!" A circular in English and German read: "Revenge! Workingmen, to Arms!!!" Despite these implorations, however, no workers were observed arming themselves or forming battalions against the police. The protest meeting called at Haymarket Square on May 4 proved unexpectedly tame; three thousand men, women, and children listened solemnly to an array of speeches. Albert Parsons devoted himself to an innocuous exposition of how labor receives only 15 percent of the product of its toil, while capital grabs the remaining 85 percent. Mayor Carter H. Harrison, a fat cigar in his mouth, mingled with the crowd and satisfied himself that "nothing is likely to occur to require interference."

By this time drops of rain had begun to fall, and all but five hundred of the crowd had gone home. Samuel Fielden was on the verge of closing the meeting when a police inspector ordered 176 policemen to stop the proceedings. Captain Ward, sword drawn, moved toward the speaker, shouting, "I command you in the name of the people to immediately and peaceably disperse." Fielden was pleading with the officer that "we *are* peaceable" when suddenly there was a blinding flash. From the alley near the speaker's stand someone had thrown a bomb close to the police detachment. Soon the scene was utter chaos, policemen shooting at the demonstrators, and at each other. Within two or three minutes, sixty-seven police were wounded, seven dead. The demonstrators suffered casualties two or three times as great.

No one has ever determined who threw the bomb. The anarchists ascribed it to an *agent provocateur* hired by the police. Others said it had been thrown by a brother-in-law of one of the anarchists. A third theory held that it was an act of vengeance by a relative of a citizen abused by the police in another matter, unrelated to anarchism. Haymarket opened a reign of persecution which hurt both labor unions and the Socialists for some time to come. The anarchist movement, of course, was a shambles. The dead had hardly been carried off when hundreds of Chicago workers were arrested, homes were searched without warrant, meeting halls and printing establishments were invaded indiscriminately.

The role of the police in planting dynamite in anarchist offices has never been officially admitted. But three years after Haymarket, Chicago Police Chief Frederick Ebersold conceded it in a newspaper interview: "It was my policy to quiet matters down as soon as possible after the 4th of May. . . . On the other hand, Capt. Schaack wanted to keep things stirring. He wanted bombs to be found here, there, all around, everywhere. . . . After we got the anarchist societies broken up, Schaack wanted to send out men to again organize new societies right away." The subscription lists of *Die Arbeiter Zeitung* were seized, and gave the police excellent leads for new raids. Every time a home was entered, the inevitable ammunition, rifles, pistols, bayonets, billies, and anarchist literature were found, undoubtedly under Captain Schaack's careful planning. Each discovery merited a heavy newspaper headline. Once the rumor was spread that Johann Most was coming from New York to supervise further assassinations. Detectives were dispatched to the railroad station—making more headlines—but no Herr Most appeared.

It was in this kind of atmosphere that less than two weeks after the event a grand jury indicted ten men on the charge of murdering one of the policemen at Haymarket. Of these, one escaped and one turned state's evidence. The eight who stood trial—Parsons, August

Spies, Fielden, Michael Schwab, Adolph Fischer, George Engel, Louis Lingg, Oscar Neebe—were the bone and marrow of the anarchist movement in Chicago. Except for Fielden, none had been at the scene of the shooting when the bomb was thrown. They were not actually accused of throwing it. They were accused, instead, of provoking it by their inflammatory statements and articles. The trial, held only seven weeks after the event in a climate of raging hostility, was, in the opinion of people far removed from socialism or anarchism, a travesty of justice. The accused were tried not for their deeds but for their ideas, a fact which was attested to by the summation of State's attorney Julius S. Grinnell after a forty-nine-day trial. "Law," said Grinnell, "is on trial. Anarchy is on trial. These men have been selected, picked out by the grand jury and indicted because they were leaders. They are no more guilty than the thousands who follow them. Gentlemen of the jury: convict these men, make examples of them, hang them and you save our institutions, our society."

Never was the state able to show who made or threw the bomb or what association the accused had with it, except the nebulous one of having "inspired" the act. Parsons proved that he could not have anticipated violence and killing because he had taken his wife and children to the demonstration. Schwab, Lingg—a youth of twenty-two—and Neebe had not been present. Fischer and Engel were at home playing cards. But the jury convicted all eight men, seven to hanging, Neebe to serve fifteen years.

Protest movements all over Europe and America, involving some of the most prominent writers, jurists, and legislators in the world, resulted in the commutation of the sentences of two men, who along with Neebe were pardoned by Governor John Peter Altgeld six years later. One anarchist, Lingg, cheated the gallows by exploding a cartridge in his mouth. Four—Spies, Parsons, Fischer, and Engel—were hanged on November 11, 1887.

As the noose was being fastened around August Spies's neck, he cried out that "the time will come when our silence in the grave will be more eloquent than our speeches." He was not wrong. In commemoration of the events surrounding Haymarket, May 1 was declared a working-class holiday throughout the world, celebrated to this day by radicals of a dozen different hues.

CHAPTER X

THE UNCONSUMMATED
MARRIAGE

THE SOCIAL PANORAMA of the two decades leading into the twentieth century revealed an untamed American plutocracy arrayed against a baffling assortment of new personalities groping to challenge it.

The nation—and future historians—could view with pride the naked statistics of economic development. At the time of the Civil War the United States had ranked only fourth in the firmament of industrial nations. But by 1894 it had eclipsed all rivals, accounting for fully one third of the world's output of manufactured goods. American factory owners, so awed by Britain at the turn of the nineteenth century, were now fabricating twice as many wares as the previous world leader. The boom drew five and a half million immigrants to the country in just ten years, and increased the number of workers in manufacturing from less than three million to almost six million. Railway mileage almost doubled, so that the United States had more track than all of Europe put together. Statistics in coal, iron, steel, capital investment, were sensational enough to make a business publicist light up like a glowworm.

But on the grim side, what was emerging was what cynics called "the new feudalism." Growth and wealth, far from guaranteeing social justice, produced a widening and bitter inequality. President Grover Cleveland informed Congress in 1888: "As we view the achievements of aggregated capital, we discover the existence of trusts, combinations and monopolies, while the citizen is struggling far in the rear or is trampled to death beneath an iron heel. Corporations, which should be carefully restrained creatures of the law and servants of the people, are fast becoming the people's masters." Wherever one turned, the small entrepreneur who lived and died by his competitive acumen was being engulfed and destroyed by the rampaging trusts.

After the panic of 1873 many industries, notably the railroads, had devised a clever method for circumventing competition and raising prices. By means of a "pool" they apportioned the market—one firm allotted the business in one area, another elsewhere—so that each had a monopoly in its own sector and could charge what the market would bear. The Interstate Commerce Act of 1887 illegalized the pool, but by this time a more effective control was being established through the "trust." John D. Rockefeller, by arranging to have the New York Central, Pennsylvania, and other railroads transport Standard Oil's products cheaper than that of competitors, was able to drive most of them to the wall, and in 1882 to establish the oil trust. The majority of the holdings of forty companies was placed in the hands of nine trustees, who were given irrevocable power of attorney over them, while the stockholders were given powerless trust certificates. Thus 95 percent of the industry was thereby lodged in a single management, charging the public what it pleased. The oil trust was followed by trusts in cotton oil, linseed oil, sugar, whisky, lead, tobacco, cordage, and other industries. When the patience of the American people over the defalcations of the railroads and now the trusts reached a breaking point, Congress passed the Sherman Antitrust Act in an effort to halt this trend to monopoly. But again the "holding company"—a corporation which owned enough stock to control a number of corporations—was replacing the trust and the pool as the means of effectuating monopoly. In these circumstances free competition became a fiction in certain industries and the small entrepreneur—whom Jefferson had once considered the backbone of the country—a feather in the wind. The concentration of capital went far beyond anything that had ever been anticipated before the Civil War.

The obverse side of the surging wealth of this era was the depressing poverty. "There are too many millionaires and too many paupers," said the *Hartford Courant*. According to Samuel Gompers, the wages in 1883 were less than in 1870, and the United States Census figures indicated a decline in per capita income of 20 or 25 percent. With all the industrial progress, more than a million children, one sixth of the total in the country, were forced to go to work at a tender age. The mild depression in the first part of the 1880's saw almost a million workers lose their jobs, and the panic in 1893, far, far more. A study by *Bradstreets'* in 1885 showed that wages had been cut by 15 percent—in mining by 40 percent—as a result of the downturn. Eleanor Marx Aveling, daughter of Karl Marx, and her husband, making a tour of the United States in the 1880's, made this doleful report: "We have lived in English factory towns and know something of English factory hands; but we may fairly say that we have never in the English Manchester seen women so worn out and degraded, such famine in their cheeks, such need and oppression staring in their eyes . . ." as in the United States. Employers in many industries still levied fines against their employees for lateness, absenteeism, or excessive stay in the wash-rooms. Company stores in many places charged exorbitant prices for their products. Wages for Negroes in the South were as low as fifty to seventy-five cents a day, with payment frequently made in scrip redeemable only at the employer's store. The Negro found himself in debt from year to year with little possibility of rising beyond this peonage. Conditions in the rural West also reflected the pervasive malaise. The farmer, as usual, was at the mercy of the railroads and banks. "Never in our history," said the Greenback Party in 1884, "have the banks, the land-grant railroads, and other monopolies been more insolent in their demands for further privilege—still more class legislation." A Nebraska farmers' paper in 1890 claimed there were three crops produced in the state: "One is a crop of corn, one a crop of freight rates, and one a crop of interest. One is pro-duced by the farmers who by sweat and toil farm the land. The other two are produced by men who sit in their offices and behind their bank counters and farm the farmers."

As in all ages, conservative social theorists found a means of justi-fying the existing inequities. In accord with the writings of Herbert Spencer, they saw the root cause of poverty in the inability of the poor to adapt themselves. Just as Darwin had explained evolution in terms of "survival of the fittest," so apologists for inequality argued that the rich prevailed because they were more "fit." Poverty itself was a proof of indolence, vice, the squandering of money on liquor, and—as one economist put it—"excessive reproduction, sexually."

Wealth, on the other hand, signified that a man (or his father) had been provident, industrious, and had shown foresight. Those who did not justify poverty in Spencerian terms argued—under a "wages-fund" theory—there was just so much money for wages in any country, and this cannot be increased either by the action of government or unions. It was not the employer's fault that conditions did not improve; it was just a fact of economic life.

Fact or not, however, the "injured and oppressed" refused to be guided by such apologia. A discontented populace defended itself as best it could with a variety of techniques ranging from the mild to the extreme, the reformist to the revolutionary. The farmers organized the National Independent (Greenback) Party in 1876 to reduce their debt burden by the inflationary means of printing more money; and the People's (Populist) Party in 1891 to achieve the same aim through unlimited coinage of gold and silver at the rate of sixteen to one. The Greenbackers at their peak polled 300,000 votes and the Populists, in 1892, more than a million. But their influence was far broader, forcing the two major parties to make many concessions in their direction.

Moving beyond the farm leaders, Samuel Gompers, who had been nursed on socialism but had decided to keep it at arm's length, was, in this period, laying the first bricks of a strong elementary working-class organization, the American Federation of Labor. Henry George, the single-taxer whose book *Progress and Poverty*, published in 1879, had made him a minor messiah both in America and Europe, was able for a brief moment to unite such hostile forces as the Socialists and non-Socialist reformers, the AFL and the Knights of Labor. When the single-tax star began to dim, another writer, Edward Bellamy, lit the horizon with his novel *Looking Backward*, which formed the basis of still another utopian socialist movement, the nationalists.

"Thoughts and theories," observed novelist Elizabeth Higgins, "sprouted like weeds after a May shower." Simultaneously, the "thoughts and theories" translated themselves into independent third parties. Thirteen such parties, usually including the Knights of Labor, the Greenbackers, and trade unionists, operated in thirteen states during the 1886 elections. Labor tickets were put forth in no less than fifty-nine cities that year.

Moving farther in the radical direction were the spontaneous and semispontaneous eruptions, such as the Homestead and Pullman strikes, and the march on Washington by Jacob Coxey's army, which were radical in intent if not in leadership. Finally there was the radical movement itself, dominated in the 1880's by the Lassalleans and anarchists, and in the 1890's by Daniel De Leon and the Socialist Labor Party.

The United States economy might be running at higher gear than that of Europe and the standard of living might be many times better than that of Latin America, but the disparity between the few and the many, the rich and the poor, was so glaring it evoked irrepressible conflict.

I I

The Haymarket affair was an incident in this continuing "war." In its wake employers and employer associations took the initiative to drive the radicals and reformers to cover. Employers who had granted the eight-hour day in 1885 and early in 1886 now restored the ten- and twelve-hour day. Three hundred prominent citizens contributed $115,000 to wage a campaign against "anarchy" and pledged $100,000 more each year until the devil was laid low. Thomas Scott, president of the Pennsylvania Railroad, urged his fellow businessmen to "give the workingmen and strikers gun-bullet food for a few days and you will observe how they will take this sort of bread."

It was advice that did not go entirely unheeded. The *New York Sun* in September 1886 described a police attack against ten thousand men, women, and children during the streetcar strike, in which "men with broken scalps were crawling off in all directions and squabbling children were knocked every way by their daddies who were flying from the clubs." Hundreds of strikers were arrested and many charged with that ancient crime "conspiracy." Even peaceful picketing incurred the wrath of Judge Power of New York, who ruled that "any man who walks up and down in front of a man's place of business commits a species of assault."

The antilabor offensive weighed heavily on the unions and dealt a crushing blow to the anarchists. But despite the setback, the radicals and reformers found other means of registering their discontent. One of them was on the electoral front.

A minor strike in New York triggered the formation of a highly promising labor party in 1886 and for a fleeting moment flashed the star of Henry George across the horizon. A few months before Haymarket, musicians belonging to the Knights of Labor in New York had called a strike against the "concert saloon" belonging to George Theiss. The strike was a failure but it was followed by an effective boycott which brought Theiss to terms. He not only accepted union demands, but paid the organization one thousand dollars for the expenses it incurred in the campaign. Having made his peace, however, the salonkeeper turned on the committee and had it prosecuted for extortion and intimidation. In the mood of the country two months after the bomb at Haymarket, it was not surprising that the five men were convicted and sentenced to prison terms of from eighteen to forty-four months. The harshness of the decision for what was, after all, a legitimate labor activity brought cries of outrage from all labor and radical quarters. "The sentence passed on the boycotters," wrote *Der Sozialist*, organ of the Socialist Labor Party, "has poured flaming fire into the hearts of workingmen in New York, and has driven into the background all differences in labor's camp." These words were confirmed by the mass meeting held in Cooper Union a few days later and the subsequent launching of the Independent Labor Party of New York and Vicinity.

The man chosen to run for mayor on the new party's ticket was Henry George, still basking in the great popularity that came with the publication of his book *Progress and Proverty*. In this lucid work, George presented little that was new—Thomas Spence, William Ogilvie, and Thomas Paine had proposed the single-tax panacea a long time before. But George's book was clear and passionate. The ills of society, he claimed, are due to "the inequality in the ownership of land." There is inequality of course in other property as well, but "there is a fundamental and irreconcilable difference between property in things which are the product of labor and property in land." Society would be justified in confiscating or nationalizing the land. But let the owners keep it so long as there is placed a heavy tax on the rent they receive. This would be the only tax levied by the nation and would be sufficient for all public requirements. The single tax on land, chipping away at the source of evil, would, George felt, "raise wages, increase the earnings of capital, extirpate pauperism, abolish poverty . . . lessen crime, elevate morals. . . ."

This passionate exposition became a runaway best seller, appearing in one hundred editions and circulating to three million readers. It also elevated Henry George to the status of a minor saint, so that when New Yorkers sought an independent candidate, they rallied behind him in grand coalition. Hundreds of street meetings were held and a daily penny paper, the *Leader,* was printed in editions of one hundred thousand on the presses of the socialist *Volkszeitung.*

George did not win—though some of his zealots argued he had been given a fast count—but he received 67,000 votes to the winning Democratic candidate's 90,000. The Republican standard-bearer, Theodore Roosevelt, future President of the United States, polled only 60,000. It was enough to send spirits pyramiding, particularly since independent candidates were making dents, small or large, from Maine to Kansas. In Milwaukee the People's Party won the mayoralty and carried the county by 13,000 votes. The United Labor Party in Chicago, an amalgam of unions, Knights of Labor assemblies, and the People's Party Club, polled a respectable 25,000 out of 92,000 ballots cast for local offices. The Knights of Labor, still at its peak, was able to carry dozens of adherents to office, even in such far-off places as Leadville, Colorado, and Fort Worth, Texas. The AFL at its convention was so impressed by "the remarkable and extraordinary demonstration made by the working-men of New York, Milwaukee, Chicago, and other places," it promised "most generous support to the independent political movement of the workingmen." The blending of radicalism and unionism seemed inescapable. Friedrich Engels, in distant London, wrote with unmistakable satisfaction that "the first step of importance for every country . . . is always the constitution of the workers as an independent political party. . . . This step has been taken, much more rapidly than we had a right to expect. . . ."

But Engels was using a European measuring rod for things American. It did not work that way here. Time and again the American Left came close to cementing an alliance with the trade-union movement, or gaining control of it, only to fail in the end. It was not because the Left was inept—though it made its share of mistakes—but because American society had a much greater resiliency to it than its European counterparts. The natural wealth of the United States was unsurpassed. The Atlantic Ocean separated it from the warring powers of Europe, so that it was not enervated by European wars. Its neighbors to the north and south on this hemisphere were impotent. In this splendid isolation the United States could grow and flourish at a more rapid tempo than other powers and could grant concessions which they could not. Blessed by geography and resources, it could yield improvements and reforms just at the propitious moment when the temper of the workingman seemed to be shifting from moderation to extremism. This was approximately what happened in the 1880's, as it was to happen many times in the future.

By 1888 the independent political tide had spent itself, one labor party after another disappeared in the void. The United Labor Party, Henry George's vehicle, polled only 2,808 votes for President of the United States, and a Union Labor Party, which refused to accept the single tax as its platform, did even worse. In the dreary backwash that year the Socialist Labor Party ran its own ticket in New York State, its main base of operations, and attracted less than 3,000 voters. The same fate, or worse, befell Edward Bellamy's Commonwealth Party in 1890, which drew only 700 of the electorate—despite the enormous sale of Bellamy's masterpiece *Looking Backward*.

Here again was confirmation of the unique behavior pattern of American mavericks. *Looking Backward* sold a million copies in ten years and caused quite a stir in liberal and radical circles. It was a fantasy about a Bostonian named West who fell asleep in 1887 to wake up 113 years later in a bright new city unsullied by corruption or graft, extreme wealth or extreme poverty. By the year 2000 the United States was a Cooperative Commonwealth, a society in which monopolistic capitalism had given way to nationalized industry, the profit motive, violence, and the class struggle had all disappeared in favor of a universal equality. Soon after the book's appearance, Nationalist clubs appeared to popularize its principles—the term "nationalist" taken from Bellamy's program for nationalizing industry. By 1891 there were 162 such organizations. The Nationalists drew to their fold many who were timid about Marxian socialism with its thesis of the class struggle. Yet, while so many people read the utopian novel and were sympathetic to its offered solutions, few voted the Nationalist ticket. People have to be strongly motivated to make the leap from established parties and organizations to the unorthodox. It needs more than a feeling of malaise; it needs a sense of desperation, which evidently they did not have.

This was the problem facing socialism, both utopian and Marxist, as the 1890's opened.

III

The man who gave socialism an infusion of new vigor was a foreigner by birth, but unlike the German, Jewish, or Lithuanian leaders, a master linguist whose precise English not only made him seem like a native, but one of superior breed. Daniel De Leon, a distant descendant of the Spanish explorer Ponce de León, was born in the small Dutch protectorate off Venezuela, Curaçao. His father was a Spanish-American doctor of more than moderate means who could afford to send his son abroad to complete his education. When Daniel landed in New York in 1872, not yet twenty years of age, he had finished six years' schooling in Germany and Holland. He was not yet a Marxist—that path would take him the better part of two decades to traverse—but he was easily attracted to causes. Knowing Spanish, he volunteered to help edit a periodical published by Cuban revolutionists seeking to liberate their island from the Spaniards. When the newspaper went out of existence, De Leon successively took on a teaching job, studied law at Columbia University, from which he graduated with honors, and accepted a prize lectureship in international law for six years. In background, then, De Leon, like Marx, was a man of erudition who belonged more to the ivory tower than the slums of the proletariat. But he was also an intense person—a fact which caused his enemies to class him as impatient, and his friends as idealistic—who identified with the lowly and oppressed.

The Henry George campaign of 1886, which electrified so many people, carried De Leon with it. But his penetrating mind soon concluded that the single tax was, as he expressed it later, "half-antiquated, half-idiotic reasoning." Yet a brief time later De Leon joined the Nationalists for a short spell. *Looking Backward* stirred his imagination and made of him an immediate convert—though it too could not hold him. It was only in 1889, on reading some of Karl Marx's works, that he joined the Socialist Labor Party, and almost immediately became its dominating figure. To the foreign born in the SLP ranks, De Leon was a most welcome recruit, a man who not only was linguistic and worldly, but so impeccably upper class in background. It was a matter of pride to refer to a leader whose family had emigrated from Spain to America as far back as 1562. In 1891 De Leon became editor of the English organ of the SLP, *The People,* and together with Lucien Sanial and Hugo Vogt, the party's ruling triumvirate.

The SLP which fell under De Leon's spell was in an exceptionally poor state of health. It was trying to recover ground lost in its fight with the left-wingers and anarchists, which had withered it to a mere fifteen hundred members in 1883. By 1885 it still had less than four thousand. The decimation of the anarchists after Haymarket gave the SLP a new lease on life, but it could not shake loose of factionalism. It was wracked by the perennial dispute over whether to emphasize independent politics or trade-union activity. A New York group, centered around the newspaper *Volkszeitung,* held that the movement was too weak to dabble in elections, whereas the unions offered happier prospects. The official party papers, *The Workmen's Advocate* and *Der Sozialist,* on the other hand, tended to de-emphasize union activity in favor of concentration on the ballot box. The antagonism between the two factions reached an acrimonious stage where they sundered relations and began separate existences. It was at this point that De Leon joined the *Volkszeitung* faction (the other disappeared in a few years) and steered the party on a more clearly defined course.

The road to political power, as De Leon saw it, was neither exclusively through the unions nor the ballot box, but in a judicious combination of the two. Perhaps because of his legalistic training, he added a purist flavor to this concept. The SLP, he counseled, must not submerge its banner in the reformist parties, such as the labor party. It must instead fly only its own. In the past it had tied itself to the Greenbackers and similar parties but had never run its own candidate for President. It must now turn its back on such groups and go it alone.

When the People's Party (Populists) was formed in 1891, its program had a mild leftist tone. "Wealth," it said, "belongs to him who creates it, and every dollar taken from industry without an equivalent is robbery. . . . The interests of rural and civil labor are the

The "Gilded Age" following the Civil War was a period of growth and prosperity. But the rapidly growing economy was sometimes set back by financial panics. Two of the worst were Black Friday on September 24, 1869, (right) and the Great Panic of September 20, 1873 (below). Both drawings on this page show crowds on Broad Street, outside the New York Stock Exchange.

"*A world to gain.*" *Probably the most influential radical of all time, Karl Marx gave his followers a sense of hope and destiny. In the Communist Manifesto, he presented history as a series of class struggles that eventually would lead to a classless society: He urged workers to unite and throw off their chains.*

Henry George, a printer from Philadelphia, believed that the ills of society resulted from the inequality in the ownership of land. To benefit the farmer, worker, and small businessman, he advocated a single tax on the value of land. His book Progress and Poverty *became a best seller, and in 1886 the Labor Party ran him for mayor of New York. Although he was defeated, George polled more votes than the Republican candidate—future President Theodore Roosevelt.*

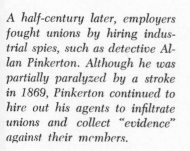

THE TRIAL

OF THE

BOOT & SHOEMAKERS

OF PHILADELPHIA,

ON AN INDICTMENT

FOR A COMBINATION AND CONSPIRACY

TO RAISE THEIR WAGES.

TAKEN IN SHORT-HAND,
BY THOMAS LLOYD.

PHILADELPHIA:
PRINTED BY B. GRAVES, NO. 40, NORTH FOURTH-STREET,
FOR T. LLOYD, AND B. GRAVES.
1806.

Title page for conspiracy trial, 1806. As unions grew, employers looked for ways to fight back and in many cases even challenged their right to organize. A group of Boot and Shoemakers in Philadelphia was prosecuted for "endangering the public interest."

A half-century later, employers fought unions by hiring industrial spies, such as detective Allan Pinkerton. Although he was partially paralyzed by a stroke in 1869, Pinkerton continued to hire out his agents to infiltrate unions and collect "evidence" against their members.

Suffragette Susan B. Anthony created a stir among delegates by attending the National Labor Union convention in 1868. She was seated only after labor leaders made it clear that they would not endorse her "peculiar ideas."

In the 1880's many a militant socialist was drawn to anarchism by a fiery German immigrant named Johann Most. He advocated violence, wrote pamphlets on the use of explosives, and organized an anarchist movement known as the Black International.

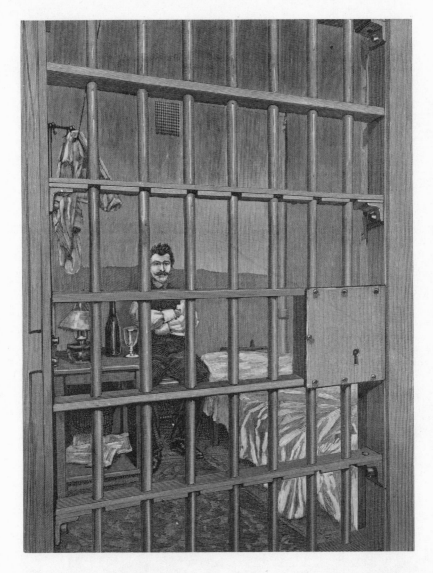

August Spies in jail after Haymarket riot. On May 4, 1886, a bomb exploded during an anarchist meeting in Haymarket Square, Chicago. The origin of the bomb was never determined, but the anarchist leaders were blamed for inciting violence and hunted down by the police. Four, including Spies, were hanged, one committed suicide. Three others were pardoned by Governor Altgeld six years later.

A secret meeting of the Mollies. Long oppressed and underpaid, Irish coal miners known as Molly Maguires carried out a wave of threats, beatings, and murders in eastern Pennsylvania. They attracted wide attention for their violent acts. Their power was broken by a Pinkerton spy who infiltrated their ranks and prepared a case against them.

In 1877 railroad workers across the country walked off their jobs in the first nationwide strike. Violence broke out in city after city and the government called out federal troops to suppress the strikers. In Pittsburgh railway workers halted trains, seized railroad property, and burned the Union Depot.

Terence V. Powderly, head of the Knights of Labor, was the advocate of "uplift unionism." He opposed strikes and urged his followers to form consumer and producer cooperatives. For a while the Knights were highly successful. At their peak in 1886 they claimed 700,000 members.

The American Federation of Labor, led in 1886 by former cigar maker Samuel Gompers, favored strikes where necessary. Less rigid than the Knights, the AFL eschewed long-range goals, but focused on such immediate objectives as the eight-hour day.

same; their enemies are identical." The Populists made strong ges-
tures in labor's direction, calling for shorter hours, abolition of
mercenary armies such as the strikebreaking Pinkertons, enforcement of laws against contract labor, and the like. But for De Leon, a
party that did not clearly speak up for the overthrow of capitalism
was on the other side of the fence. Populism, with its cries for a
graduated income tax, free coinage of silver and gold, a postal sav-
ings bank, government ownership of the railroads, and reclamation
of surplus land owned by speculators, railroads, and other corporations, was to make an indelible impression on millions of Americans
in the following years. It was the outstanding reform movement of
the nineteenth century, but in De Leon's view it was only "middle
class corruption."

Driven by a single-minded zeal, De Leon took the schematic
stand that reforms must not be sought within the context of the
hated capitalist system but only as part of the social revolution. If
the American worker did not yet understand this, the SLP and De
Leon would make it clear. But while the SLP picked up momentum
after the lean days of the 1880's, the Populists showed results that
were qualitatively of a higher order. In 1891 De Leon running for
governor of New York received 14,651 ballots. In 1892 the SLP,
running its first Presidential ticket, polled 21,500 in six states. By
contrast, the Populists garnered a million votes. Such success was
often more alluring to socialists than De Leon's preachments of purity. An SLP member in Independence, Kansas, wrote his leader that
he had "converted most of the Populists who were not already socialists," simply by working with them in the campaign. He recommended this tactic for others, but De Leon waived such frailty
aside. He believed that a farmers' movement oriented to immediate
benefits alone did not enhance but endangered the impending social
revolution. "Nothing short of socialism" must be the socialist's
credo, he said.

A similar tendency to purism was manifest in De Leon's adventures on the industrial front. He understood, naturally, that a socialist movement without a strong following in the unions can only
abort. If it is to undermine capitalism, it must rely on a large enthusiastic contingent at the "point of production." To win one, De Leon
had a choice either of building a new federation of labor, or trying
to wean to the SLP, ready-made, the Knights of Labor, the AFL, or

both. He decided on the latter course, for in both the Knights and the AFL, the SLP held strong bastions from which to advance. The Knights of Labor by 1893 were on the wane, with only a small number of its former membership left, but the largest, District Assembly 49 in New York, had a sizable socialist faction in it, under the spirited guidance of a pleasant Irishman, Patrick J. Murphy. By drawing in the Jewish tailors, also leftists, Murphy and De Leon were able to gain a commanding hold over "49" and designate De Leon himself as delegate to the 1893 convention of the Knights. There the former Columbia professor forged an alliance with a Populist, J. R. Sovereign, and together they succeeded in ousting from office that ancient apostle of "uplift unionism," Terrence V. Powderly. In gratitude, Sovereign promised to appoint Lucien Sanial, a socialist, as editor of the Knight's journal; a labor base seemed clearly within grasp for the Socialists.

The new allies, however, were unable to cement their alliance. Sovereign reneged on his pledge and before long the two groups were quarreling over programmatic planks. At the 1895 convention, by the slim margin of 23 to 21, the Populists refused to seat De Leon as a delegate, writing finis to his hopes in that quarter. The SLP denounced the Knights as "rotten to the core," and the socialist-led unions withdrew their thirteen thousand members, leaving—as they put it—"the remaining seventeen thousand to find their own way to oblivion."

The Knights of Labor, of course, was headed along this path even before De Leon entered its ranks, and whether he could have used it as a launching pad for socialism is open to question.

The AFL, on the other hand, was another matter. Its star was definitely on the rise. Samuel Gompers, its prime architect, a London-born cigar maker with prominent jaws and a stern chin, was not unfriendly to socialism—at least not to begin with. As a young worker in the dusty lofts of New York, he had read Marxist tracts to his fellow cigar makers. In his formative years he had been a socialist sympathizer, strongly influenced by the socialist head of his union, Adolph Strasser. In fact, he once considered joining the socialists. But on the advice of Karl M. F. Laurrell, an adherent of the First International, that he "go to their meetings, by all means, listen to what they have to say and understand them, but do not join the party," he held back. Eventually Gompers, watching American capitalism rise from fourth to first place in the roster of industrial nations, found socialism too visionary. And though the preamble to the AFL constitution had an unmistakable class-struggle tang, Gompers was quick to point out that "the ills of our social system can not be cured by patent medicine"—a dig at socialism as well as money reform and cooperative panaceas. Gompers insisted: "We have no ultimate ends. We are going on from day to day. We fight only for immediate objects—objects that can be realized in a few years." This was "simple unionism," as opposed to revolutionary unionism such as advocated by the anarchists or the "uplift unionism" of the Knights. Gompers' AFL, then and today, was the only important one in the Western world not integrally linked to radicalism.

Yet the AFL at first was not so much anti-socialist as *non*-socialist. Gompers inveighed against the profit system with the vehemence of De Leon himself. He described workers "as the lubricating oil for the machines that grind their very bones into cash to gratify the wishes of the insatiable monsters whose only deity was the almighty dollar." He kept up a cordial correspondence with such overseas socialists as Wilhelm Liebknecht, Marx's daughter Eleanor Marx Aveling, Victor Delahaye, and Friedrich Engels. In a letter to Engels giving his side of a dispute with De Leon, Gompers reassured the coauthor of the *Communist Manifesto* of his "respect for your judgement, having been a student of your writings and those of Marx." The hope for a *modus vivendi* between the AFL and the SLP, therefore, was not entirely misplaced.

What kept the mortar from hardening was the burgeoning industrial system, on the one hand, which made it possible for employers to grant concessions to the skilled laborers almost painlessly, and De Leon's low boiling point, on the other. The mortar might not have held anyway, but the socialist leader's intemperance did not help matters. The first dispute between socialism and simple unionism took place at the 1890 convention of the AFL. New York City at the time had two central labor bodies, one controlled by the socialists, the other by more moderate elements. Under Gompers' pressure the two were united, but the marriage did not take and the socialists withdrew, seeking to regain the charter for their own Central Labor Federation. Gompers was favorably disposed, but there was a complication. One of the affiliates of the Central Labor Federation was an English-speaking section of the SLP. In Gompers' view, political parties had no place in a labor union. They might be compatible but they had to play their own games in different arenas. Lucien Sanial of the socialists, however, was not appeased by this argument—the SLP, he said, was not just any old party, but *the* party of the working class. It merited a direct role in the AFL. When the matter was put for review before a convention committee, the AFL officials urged "cordial acceptance of the proffered fraternity of the Socialist Labor Party," and pointed out that "the hope and aspiration of the trade unionist is closely akin to that of the socialist." But it upheld Gompers' concept of separation.

Even at this point the rift could have been healed. The issue was not earth shaking and Gompers went out of his way to be conciliatory. He pleaded his case with native socialists and wrote to leftists abroad. In his note to Engels he denied that the AFL "placed its seal of disapproval upon socialism as a science, or a theory, or even as a system of society for the future. Such I beg to assure you is not at all the case." He was willing, he told one of Engels' friends, "to abide by his [Engels'] judgement." But Marx's collaborator refused to inject himself in the dispute. Many a rank-and-file socialist, including Thomas J. Morgan, leading spokesman for the party at the AFL convention, pleaded for acceptance of the decision in the interests of harmony. But De Leon remained adamant. Instead of narrowing the breach, he used his acid pen to excoriate the AFL hierarchy as "labor fakers," "agents of the capitalists inside the trade union," and "traitors to the cause of labor." By its attitude to the socialists, the AFL "has become a whited sepulcher, a living lie, a petrified mummy. . . ." At best, it was "a cross between a windbag and a rope of sand." The *People* counseled socialists in August 1893 to withdraw from the AFL on the ground that some of its officials "are ignorant, others are corrupt, all are unfit for leadership in the labor movement. To civilize and unite them is out of the question. The social revolution must march over the bodies of each and every one of them. . . ."

Individual SLP members, it must be noted, did not desert the fort so readily. They clung to it and that very year, 1893, won what was considered a great victory. It was a year, it should be recalled, of panic. Three million workers were jobless, lending credence to the socialist propaganda that labor had no future under capitalism. To talk of simple goals such as the eight-hour day in the face of such holocaust seemed like spitting against the wind. When Thomas J. Morgan, therefore, introduced a resolution at the AFL convention in Chicago, which included among its planks independent political action and "the collective ownership by the people of all means of production and distribution," he met little objection. There was some question as to whether the delegates were endorsing every jot and tittle of the eleven-point program, but the resolution tallied 2,244 votes against a mere 67. The socialists were elated. Their central thesis had been endorsed by the main body of labor. When the program was sent around to the individual AFL affiliates it was again overwhelmingly acclaimed—by the miners, steelworkers, cigar makers, glassworkers, tailors, a dozen state federations, and many others. Only one union, the bakers, rejected it. But in the face of this mandate, the following convention overrode the decision of the lower echelons by 1,345 to 861. Gompers had either had a change of heart or had a different interpretation of the original resolution. Whatever the reason, De Leon's argument that the "labor fakers" could not be won to socialism seemed vindicated.

In his best vitriol he denounced both the AFL and the Knights as "corrupt and decadent," urging decent unionists to leave their foul portals. On December 8, 1895, the Central Labor Federation of New York, the United Hebrew Trades, District Assembly 49 of the Knights, and the Central Labor Federation of Newark—all under SLP aegis—joined ranks to found the Socialist Trade and Labor Alliance. "If in the past," cried the *People*, "we have been unsparing with these outposts of capitalism—the labor bunco-steerers—we shall in the future smite them more relentlessly." A hundred local unions were enrolled, growing within three years to 228. But the total membership of the Alliance was a mere 20,000. Not only did it fail to carry along the unwashed nonsocialists, but many a Marxist as well, who preferred to remain in the AFL. In the West radical newspapers decried the venture in dual organization, as did die-hard socialist unions such as the brewery workers and printers. But none of this had any influence on Daniel De Leon.

For him the union movement was the embryo of tomorrow's society and it had to be patterned accordingly. It had to be revolutionary in outlook and centralized organizationally. "Industrialism," he wrote, "is that system of economic organization of the working class that denies that Labor and the Capitalist Class are brothers;

. . . that perceives that that struggle will not, because it can not, end until the Capitalist Class is thrown off Labor's back; that recognizes that an injury to one workingman is an injury to all; and that, consequently and with this end in view, organizes the whole working class into one union, the same subdivided only into such bodies as their respective craft-tools demand in order to wrestle as one body for the immediate amelioration of its membership and for their eventual emancipation by the total overthrow of the Capitalist Class, its economic and political rule."

For Gompers and for the working class generally this was heady medicine. Capitalism might be rotten but it was not senile. De Leon's campaign of verbal venom, therefore, was in direct proportion to the impotence of his Socialist Trade and Labor Alliance. He might call a machinist leader "a blatant and slick political faker," the head of the carpenters' union "a disreputable renegade and inebriate," and a socialist who disagreed with his strategy, J. Mahlon Barnes, "a cold-blooded, crafty villain." But the AFL grew from 265,000 in 1897 to 550,000 in 1900, while the De Leonists dwindled to insignificance. By 1898 it had only 114 affiliates, of which 54 paid their assessments.

The Socialist Labor Party under De Leon could record some gains in the 1890's. Its ranks grew from 70 sections in 1889 to 200 in 1896, and to 350 in 1899. But its fiasco with the Socialist Trade and Labor Alliance was to extinguish it as a viable force—even though it continues to exist, run candidates, and publish a small journal to this very day.

Four years after De Leon's death in 1914, the revolutionary journalist John Reed, who was closely associated with Lenin and Trotsky, noted that Lenin was "a great admirer of Daniel De Leon, considering him the greatest of modern socialists—the only one who had added anything to socialist thought since Marx." There is some dispute as to whether Lenin's words were misinterpreted, but there is little doubt of the stature of De Leon. He was erudite, a brilliant thinker even when he was wrong, and he wrote not only with fire, but penetrating historical insight. His speeches, such as the one he made in 1898 to striking textile workers, "What Means This Strike?" are classics of simplicity, down-to-earth expositions which few leftists before or since could emulate. His pen bristled and his voice thundered, but De Leon lacked that rare trait (which Lenin had, for instance), flexibility. It served to isolate him and his party from the main stream of labor as well as from the major class battles of the period.

IV

The conflict between labor and capital in the last decade of the nineteenth century was waged under auspices other than the Socialist Labor Party. There was the well-to-do businessman, Jacob S. Coxey, who led a tattered unemployed army to Washington; the colorful western miners, "Big Bill" Haywood and Vincent St. John, who engaged in a near civil war in the Rockies; the railroad worker from Terre Haute, Indiana, Eugene V. Debs, who directed the Pullman workers in what became known as the "Debs' Rebellion"; and finally the unheralded men who fought at Homestead, New Orleans, Tennessee, Buffalo, and elsewhere. While De Leon declaimed against the labor fakers who betrayed the class struggle, strikes—the overt expression of that struggle—came into their own as labor's primary weapon. Between 1865 and 1881 there had been less than five hundred walkouts; but from 1881 to 1905 there were no less than thirty-eight thousand, involving seven and a half million laborers.

The most frustrating of these strikes were in the giant industries, such as the railroads or steel. Unions made steady headway in decentralized industries, with many relatively small companies, such as construction or printing. But for more than a half century, during and after the Gilded Age, the untamed plutocracy resisted, with unrivaled fierceness, efforts to organize its major bastions. Time and again workers in the mass production industries and on the nation's railroads were driven to violence on a scale far outstripping anything in Europe. No country in the world has witnessed so many picket line battles and so many deaths on picket lines as the United States. Figures are fragmentary to document this point, but a survey made by *Outlook* magazine in 1904 gives some idea of how extensive was this phenomenon. In the thirty-three months prior to the survey—not a particularly exceptional period—198 men were killed on picket lines in thirty states, 1,966 injured, 6,114 arrested.

Symbolic of the bitter confrontation between the plutocracy and its wage earners was the strike at Homestead, Pennsylvania, in 1892, against Andrew Carnegie and his subaltern, Henry Clay Frick.

As has happened so often in the annals of labor, the conflict was defensive in nature, with workers fighting not to gain new benefits but to hold on to those already won. In 1889 skilled workers had won a strike by turning back one hundred deputies sent to guard "blacksheep"—nonunion men. A three-year pact had been signed for the eight hundred skilled employees (of a total of thirty-eight hundred), tying wage scales to the price of steel. If steel went up, wages went up; if it went down, wages fell. As the expiration date of the agreement drew near, Carnegie decided to settle accounts. He called in Frick, a notorious unionbuster, to manage his works, and wrote him a private memo instructing him that since the three thousand unskilled men were not represented by a labor organization "these works, therefore, will be necessarily non-union." In compliance with this directive, Frick handed union representatives an ultimatum one day to accept a wage cut ranging from 18 to 26 percent. There was no explanation for the reduction. Times were good—the depression was still a year away—and Carnegie was earning profits. When the men rejected Frick's proposal, he simply shut down operations and forced them on the streets in the hopes that because their ranks were divided—skilled versus unskilled, native versus foreign born—they would be unable to hold out.

The accepted technique for breaking strikes those days—and indeed until the 1940's—was to hire a detective agency to recruit "scabs" and run them into the plant under police or army protection. Frick hired the largest such firm, the Pinkerton Agency, and in time-tested fashion it assembled a force of three hundred men from New York, Philadelphia, and Chicago, put them on barges below Pittsburgh, and sent them silently up the river to Homestead. Frick had already taken the precaution, in advance of the strike, to erect a wire fence three miles long and fifteen feet high to protect the landing place. The fence, however, could not contain the strikers' anger. United in a common purpose, union man and nonunion man, skilled and unskilled, they stormed past the fence into the mill yard toward the landing. As the Pinkertons sought to embark, a shot was heard, then others; the battle raged from early morning to five in the afternoon. The climax came when strikers mounted a small brass cannon and set fire to barrels of oil which they poured on the water near the barges. Under this attack the Pinkertons ran up the white flag of surrender as if in actual war. At this point nine workers and three Pinkertons lay dead, about three times that number wounded. Shortly after five o'clock the strikebreakers marched sullenly to the skating rink of this town of twelve thousand, taunted and attacked by strikers' wives all along the way.

It was a grand victory for the strikers. Unions everywhere passed resolutions of solidarity, and in Pittsburgh glassworkers demanded from the city council that it return a million dollars Carnegie had contributed for a free library. In Congress, Democratic Party senators and representatives denounced the steel baron for pocketing vast profits as a result of 55 and 70 percent protective tariffs, while demanding a wage cut from his men. With a favorable public opinion the strike spread to two other Carnegie plants, raising hope of a compromise. But it was all an uneasy interlude. On July 10 the governor of Pennsylvania mobilized eight thousand National Guardsmen to establish "law and order." The general in charge referred to the strike as "revolution, treason, and anarchy," an index of his plans.

In the face of this overpowering force, the workers were virtually impotent. Management sent seventy recruiting agents to hire men in other parts of the country. Afterward they were escorted into the plant under the protection of the soldiers, put up in bunkhouses, fed in company dining rooms on the premises, so as to escape the wrath of the pickets. Though it could not operate well without its own experienced hands, the company set about to demoralize them through legal proceedings and starve them out. On July 18 seven strike leaders were indicted for the murder of a Pinkerton. On September 22 a grand jury handed down 167 true bills charging various leaders with murder, conspiracy, and aggravated riot. During this time the labor organizations of the nation were raising about ten thousand dollars a week to feed sixteen hundred Carnegie strikers. By October, however, the load proved too heavy, funds began to dwindle. Soon the sympathy strikes collapsed, and on November 20, after five long months, the men voted by 101 to 91 (most of the others having forsaken Homestead for greener pastures) to reapply for their jobs.

For Frick and Carnegie this was unconditional surrender, the sweet taste of victory. Yet Frick did not escape whole; in fact, he almost lost his life as a result of the strike. A young anarchist, Alexander Berkman, who was an admirer of the Haymarket martyr, Louis Lingg, and the lover of another colorful anarchist, Emma Goldman, decided to settle accounts with Frick. Hearing of the gun fight between the strikers and the Pinkertons, Berkman betook himself to Homestead on July 23 and burst into Frick's office. A Negro porter tried to stop him: "Mister Frick is engaged. He can't see you now, sir." But the anarchist slipped past him to confront three men sitting at a long table.

"Frick?" Berkman asked, drew his revolver, and aimed it at the black-bearded man's head. The shot misfired, cutting a serious wound in Frick's neck instead. It was a close call, but the mill manager survived. Berkman was subdued quickly and sentenced to twenty-two years in jail, of which he served fifteen. The strikers disassociated themselves from the vengeful deed, but not a few labor leaders considered the act an incident of the class war that merited defense. Even Gompers participated in the campaign that eventually effected Berkman's release.

Homestead was still in the headlines when an equally violent strike broke out in the Coeur d'Alene district of Idaho. The silver and lead mines of this area had been operated by the mineworkers themselves for a long time, either individually or in small partnerships. But in due course, as this rich bonanza attracted enterprising financiers, the mines were purchased and merged into larger ventures. Simultaneously the independent miners were reduced to wageworkers, and what is more, were forced to accept steadily declining rates of pay. A two-week strike in 1891 against the Bunker Hill mine, believed to be owned by Standard Oil, resulted in a full victory with the company agreeing to the union scale. That same year, however, the corporate owners decided to form a Mine Owners' Protective Association and announced wage scales 25 percent below previous ones.

The union, of course, rejected the cut, whereupon the Association locked out its employees and promised "never to hire another member of the miners' union." Strikebreakers were brought in by the hundreds, under armed protection. For a while pickets were able to dissuade many from accepting the work merely by meeting them at the trains or talking with them at company boardinghouses. Peaceful persuasion proved remarkably effective, causing about half of the potential scabs to turn back. But violence was well-nigh inevitable as twelve hundred strikers became more desperate and the Pinkertons more daring. On July 11, after a fight with the Pinkertons, the miners loaded a rail car with dynamite, and sent it hurtling into the Frisco mine. The strikebreakers were forced to surrender and leave town. Two days later Governor Willey declared a state of insurrection and used fifteen hundred National Guardsmen to defeat the strike. Six hundred miners were placed in bull pens at Kellogg and Wallace, while others, deciding to escape, fled to Montana. With so many men incarcerated, further resistance was impossible. Thirteen strikers were eventually sentenced to jail on various charges.

There were other strikes—in Buffalo, New Orleans, Tennessee— equally radical in tactics and import. If there had been a strong socialist movement to draw them together and give them political focus, they might have been more successful and given radicalism itself a stronger undergirding. But the radical *action* of the strikers and the radical *thought* of the De Leonists failed to intermesh. During Homestead, De Leon issued a statement that "it is the old struggle between capital and labor, which has been carried on and will be carried on in all parts of the world for a long time." But "the old struggle between capital and labor" is precisely the raw material that socialism usually tries to weave into finished fabric. In this instance at least, its machinery was out of commission. In actual fact the Homestead strike helped the Democrats and President Cleveland more than the socialists, for they used it as ammunition against the Republican protectionists. What was the sense of having a tariff to protect big industry, they asked, when men like Carnegie pocketed the profits therefrom but refused to share them with labor?

Nor did the socialists play a major role in the dramatic march by Coxey's army on Washington. In 1893, once again black clouds of depression hung ominously over the nation. Prior to the panic, Senator John J. Ingalls told the Senate: "We cannot disguise the truth that we are on the verge of a revolution. . . . Labor, starving and sullen in the cities, aims to overthrow a system under which the rich are growing richer and the poor are growing poorer. . . ." The bottom fell out on May 4, 1893, when the National Cordage Company, which only five months before had declared a 100 percent dividend, went bankrupt. It was followed by 16,000 other bankruptcies and

642 bank failures the same year. Thousands of factories closed down, more than a tenth of the railroad mileage went into receivership, and three million proletarians found themselves jobless and hungry.

Though the depression lasted half a decade, from 1893 to 1897, not a single state provided relief—only a few cities here and there. Workers in the prime of their lives—60 percent were under thirty-five—found themselves on the scrap heap with no place to look for help except an occasional dollar from their unions or from public charity. A conference of union delegates presided over by Samuel Gompers called on the cities and states to inaugurate public works projects and to initiate public relief. In his best oratorical style, Gompers denounced "the wealthy possessors of our country." Demonstrations flared in the streets of the big cities. One held in Chicago in the fall of 1893 attracted ten thousand men and was addressed both by Gompers and Henry George. At another one in New York's Madison Square Garden a few months later, early in 1894, Gompers was so distraught he uttered poetical words which few socialists would disparage:

> Let conflagration illumine the outraged skies!
> Let red Nemesis burn the hellish clan
> And chaos end the slavery of man.

It was against this background of "starving in a land of plenty" that Jacob S. Coxey, a horse breeder and manufacturer, a Populist in politics and a Theosophist in religion, decided to do something drastic. To pressure the government to issue enough greenbacks to finance a public works program, Coxey decided to lead the jobless to Washington. "On to Washington" became a magic call which captured headlines and stirred not only the rank and file of labor but the AFL leadership and, to some extent, the Knights of Labor. An AFL member in Richmond, Indiana, wrote a song called "Marching with Coxey":

> Hurrah! hurrah! for the unemployed's appeal!
> Hurrah! hurrah! for the marching commonweal!
> Drive the lobbies from the senate,
> Stop the trust and combine steal,
> For we are marching with Coxey.

We are not tramps nor vagabonds that's shirking honest toil,
But miners, clerks, skilled artizans, and tillers of the soil
Now forced to beg our brother worms to give us leave to toil,
While we are marching with Coxey.

Coxey's appeal, as one historian put it, "came as rain upon thirsty ground." In the spring of 1894 there were twenty thousand Coxeyites moving from all four corners of the country "On to Washington." Everywhere they went they camped on the outskirts of town, and solicited food from friendly farmers. In San Francisco a Coxeyite named Charles Kelly recruited an army of fifteen hundred in a single day. "We are witnessing now a spectacle," said former President Benjamin Harrison, "that our country has never witnessed before."

But the army tended to dribble away. Many small townsmen were fearful of the hordes of hoboes and unemployed who might take scarce jobs in their own communities. They gave Coxey's Army something less than a joyous welcome. So that by the time the army reached Washington—appropriately enough on May 1—it was decimated to less than one thousand. Coxey was given permission to hold a parade providing he did not enter the Capitol grounds. In defiance, he did just that and was sentenced to twenty days in jail. On release, the businessman from Ohio lingered on to lobby with Congress, but could find few friendly ears. The movement dissolved, despite its publicity and support, an abject failure. "What does it all amount to?" asked the Cleveland *Plain Dealer* when it was over. "The enterprise was meaningless when it started and is meaningless in its conclusion, except as an evidence of the unrest that is prevalent."

CHAPTER XI

THE MAN FROM
TERRE HAUTE

On June 20, 1893—between the time that Coxey's decimated army was encamping in Washington and the Coeur d'Alene strikers were blowing up the Frisco mine—fifty railroad unionists met in Ulrich's Hall in Chicago to map strategy. On their minds was the recent Buffalo switchmen's strike, which had gone down to defeat only because other railroad brotherhoods had refused to come to the aid of their beleaguered brethren. In the receding past was the memory of those terrible days of 1877, when the railroad men had paid a frightful toll, and more immediately there was the new depression which had begun the previous month. All fifty were unhappy with the craft unions, which sometimes fought each other as hard as they did the employers. Only one hundred thousand of the million men in the industry carried a union card, and with bad times on the agenda, there was dire need for something more dynamic. That is what the group was discussing.

That night a press release announced the launching of the American Railway Union (ARU)—an important, if ephemeral, milestone for both labor and radicalism. Unlike the old craft unions, it was to be industrial in structure, a single organization which combined under one roof all "white" workers regardless of occupation. (The exclusion of Negroes, traditional in the industry, was a blot against the ARU escutcheon, but it must be said that it carried only against the wishes of a near-equal minority.) Up to now each railroad union represented a single group—conductors, firemen, engineers, and so on. In critical moments they often were unable or refused to co-ordinate their actions. Now there was to be one union, one big union. It was to be open to all comers, even coal miners and long-shoremen who were peripheral employees of the railroads. Its dues were to be nominal—a dollar initiation and a dollar a year for the national office, with supplementary dues for the local lodges. Its purpose was direct and attractive—to protect wages and hours, pub-lish a daily paper and a monthly magazine, lobby for beneficial leg-islation, and provide low-cost insurance, a particularly sore point in this hazardous industry.

The officers of ARU, chosen that day, were a forceful group. There was George W. Howard, who had quit a supervisory job with the San Diego Street Car Company to head the Brotherhood of Conductors. There were L. W. Rogers, former editor of the *Railroad Trainman;* Sylvester Keliher, secretary-treasurer of the Railway Carmen; and, as president, a tall, impressive product of Terre Haute, Indiana, who was to be the cornerstone of the radical move-ment for the next quarter of a century, Eugene Victor Debs.

Looking at this array, the *Machinist's Journal* made the enthusias-tic assessment that "the new organization starts out with brilliant prospects ahead and under one of the brainest [*sic*] men of the present age." The "brainest" man, Debs, came from the Brotherhood of Locomotive Firemen (BLF), which he had served as secretary-treasurer and magazine editor, but from which he was resigning, de-spite a good salary, to take on the questionable task of founding an industrial union. For fourteen years he had been associated with the BLF, and had built up its magazine circulation from fifteen hundred to thirty-seven thousand. Now he was moving to uncertain pastures.

Unlike De Leon, who carried men along with his polemical ag-gressiveness and theoretical purity, Debs galvanized them by his deep-rooted humanism. As a theorist he was ambiguous, often vague, inferior both to De Leon, his political adversary, and to Vic-tor Berger and Morris Hillquit, his contemporaries in the socialist movement. But his humanity was overpowering, more so than that of any radical leader before or since. He could give away his watch to a jobless railroad worker or his last penny to an old woman who had lost her ticket, without fanfare or being patronizing. James Whitcomb Riley, the Hoosier poet, recognized in him:

As warm a heart as ever beat
Betwixt here and the Mercy Seat!

In appearance, Debs was over six feet in height, thin, with blue eyes, light hair—the little that was left of it—and a strong chin. He loved children, though he and his wife Katherine never had any themselves. "Childhood," he wrote, "What a holy theme! Flowers they are, with souls in them, and if on this earth man has a sacred charge, a holy obligation, it is to these tender buds and blossoms of humanity."

Debs was to lead the most revolutionary strike in American history and was five times to be the candidate of the Socialist Party for President, a man whose name was on the lips of millions, toasted and damned in the newspapers ceaselessly, but he possessed an empathy with the common man that no other American radical ever matched. He could defy the governor of Minnesota, who called him an "agitator, foreigner and anarchist" with the taunt: "I have never in my life worn the collar of a plutocrat, nor jumped like a jack when he pulled the string as you have done for Mr. Hill [of the Great Northern Railroad]. Now, Governor, I know something about railroads, and you may, with my consent, take the B Line and go to hell." On the other hand, he could tell a judge who was convicting him under the Espionage Act: "Your honor, years ago I recognized my kinship with all living beings, and I made up my mind that I was not one bit better than the meanest on earth. I said then, and I say now, that while there is a lower class, I am in it; while there is a criminal element, I am of it; while there is a soul in prison, I am not free." Though his Pullman strike went down to total defeat and he never headed another union, Debs was the most idolized labor leader America had produced. His impact on people was electric— perhaps because he appealed to their sense of individual importance. He once told a group of workers: "I am not a labor leader; I do not want you to follow me or anyone else. If you are looking for a Moses to lead you out of the capitalist wilderness, you will stay right where you are. I would not lead you into this promised land if I could, because if I could lead you in, some one else would lead you out."

One of ten children born of French-Alsatian parents, Debs went to work at the age of fourteen mixing paints for the Vandalia Railroad in Terre Haute. A year later he was promoted to locomotive fireman at a dollar a night. But the job was dangerous—a locomotive might hit another one or a freight train, boilers sometimes exploded, men were burned by escaping steam. When two of his friends were killed in a wreck, his mother prevailed on him to work in a grocery store. Debs, however, could not forget the railroad men. He attended the firemen's meetings and, though no longer employed in the craft, was elected secretary of one of its lodges. The young man made friends easily, inspired confidence, and moved quickly up the ladder. By 1877 he was assistant editor of the union's national magazine, and after 1880, when an officer of the organization disappeared with what remained of the treasury, he became secretary-treasurer. With the aid of his brother Theodore, a lifelong associate, and two sisters, Debs rebuilt the BLF, so that by 1883 it was out of debt and claimed eight thousand members.

The close ties of the Debs family to brother Eugene is evidenced by the fact that Theodore dissolved a partnership in a local haberdashery to become the union's bookkeeper at ten dollars a week, and Emma quit a schoolteaching job to become, along with sister Eugenie, the organization's unpaid office staff. Eugene Victor, typically, worked that year without pay, spending eight hundred dollars of his own money for the union.

Simultaneous with his union career, Debs was becoming somewhat of a political figure—though far from a Socialist. As a matter of fact, in 1877 he was even talking against strikes. "Our organization," he said, "believes in arbitration. All differences should be settled in this way for no good has ever or can ever come from resorting to violence and bloodshed." Debs's first political office was as city clerk of Terre Haute, elected on the Democratic Party ticket. In 1885, as a good Democrat, he took his elected seat in the legislature of Indiana, but the in-fighting and particularly the refusal to pass his bill to provide increased security for railroaders, repelled the future Socialist. "I am through with [this] business forever," he told his brother Theodore. His next six years were devoted exclusively to the cause of his firemen, but though the union prospered and his own wages were raised to the goodly sum (at that time) of four thousand dollars a year, there was a restless doubt stirring within Debs. Employers were amalgamating into trusts and were operating against labor through employers' associations, yet the AFL and the railroad brotherhoods refused to fuse their craft unions into a single industrial union. By a simple technique of *divide et impera,* management pitted one craft against another to the detriment of both. The refusal of the other railway crafts to join the strike of the Buffalo switchmen in 1892, when they were being harassed by eight thousand militia, convinced Debs he must find a new way.

Less than a month after the Buffalo setback Debs decided to resign his lucrative post with the BLF, and not long thereafter formed the American Railway Union. The ARU was an instant success. As a fledgling just a few months old, it conducted an eighteen-day strike against the Great Northern Railroad and forced management to restore almost the entire amount of three wage cuts—sixteen dollars a month. "That a corporation of so gigantic proportions," said the Salt Lake *Tribune,* "had to yield so quickly to their men indicates that the day has already come when the voice of united labor has to be heard in the matter of wages." Victory against a firm with 2,500 miles of track and 9,000 employees was so remarkable, especially in a depression period, that the ARU gained recruits at the rate of 2,000 a day. Within a year it had grown to 150,000 members, not much smaller than the AFL at the time.

The stage was set for the Pullman strike—and Debs's metamorphosis to socialism.

II

Pullman, Illinois, near Chicago, was considered in the 1890's a model town. Here six thousand workers produced the famous sleeping cars—Pullmans—which were attached to trains on almost all lines. Unlike other industrial sites, Pullman's streets were wide and clean; its neat brick houses were arranged around a square which was landscaped with lawns and flowers. But the façade hid from view an industrial feudalism. Workers at Pullman were required by the Pullman Palace Car Company to rent their homes from management at rates 25 percent higher than in neighboring Chicago. They bought groceries and clothing at the company stores; sent their children to company schools; attended a church owned by the company; and took relaxation in the company's park or theater. Even the gas and waterworks belonged to the company, and the sewage from workers' homes was pumped into Pullman's farm to be used as fertilizer. Since Mr. Pullman considered liquor an evil, the town of Pullman was dry. And since he was unalterably opposed to unions and the eight-hour day, these ideas, too, were *verboten* in his domain.

George M. Pullman, the monarch of this princedom, was of the school that believed he knew what was best for "his" workers, and woe betide any who questioned his judgment. His company was in excellent condition—it had paid $2.5 million in dividends for the year ending July 31, 1893, as against a total wage bill of about $7.2 million. Its assets were $62 million, of which $26 million were undivided profits. There was no reason to cut wages, except, of course, that such things were fashionable in bad times. On the heels of the depression, Pullman not only reduced his staff by 2,200 (out of 5,500), but lowered pay scales by 25 to 40 percent. He forgot, somehow, to lower his rents or the prices in his stores accordingly.

In March and April 1894, the Pullman workers began to form branches of the ARU, and in a nonce had enrolled four thousand members. When a committee of forty-six met with Pullman to urge restoration of the wage cuts, he refused to budge. Three of the committeemen were fired, causing the men—as might have been expected—to walk out of the shops. For a month the strike remained localized, with hungry workers offering to arbitrate and Pullman insisting "there is nothing to arbitrate." It was as yet a typical affair, not much different from what other proletarians were going through during the depression. The only possibility the strike had for succeeding was if it could "spread" to other Pullman shops and to railroads that carried the sleeping cars.

This was what the strikers proposed when the first national convention of the ARU met in Chicago on June 12, 1894. Debs had visited the model town and spent a few days in the homes of its workers, but he was hesitant to commit his untested organization to what promised to be an all-or-nothing battle not merely with Pullman but the whole industry. At his suggestion, committees again made the pilgrimage to the great man in Pullman, suggesting arbitration; but to no avail. Debs was swept with the tide and, on June 26, instituted a boycott against all Pullman sleeping cars. Wherever they were attached to a train they were sidetracked. A sympathetic strike was also called at the shops belonging to the company in St. Louis and Ludlow, Kentucky. The response exceeded Debs's expectations. Within a few days, 125,000 railroad workers were involved in the boycott, and when the employers refused to detach the sleeping cars, it was converted into a strike, since railroad men would operate no train that had a Pullman coupled to it.

Debs's adversary, it turned out, was not merely Pullman, but the General Managers' Association, a recently formed grouping of twenty-four railroads which controlled 40,000 miles of road, 220,000 employees (one fourth the national total) and $1 billion of capital. It was, so to speak, an industrial union of employers, just as the ARU aspired to be for the employees. The association opened headquarters in many cities to recruit strikebreakers, and set up a publicity bureau to create an image of anarchy. Every man who refused to switch Pullman cars was summarily discharged, and as each line took action, the union called its men out on strike, until the boycott had been converted into the first *organized* nationwide strike in American history.

At first it was a simple dispute between labor and management, testing whether the employers could mobilize enough strikebreakers or the union could stave off hunger. The craft unions—the rail brotherhoods—ordered their men to continue working and in some cases supplied strikebreakers. On the other hand, scores of local AFL unions and central city bodies, plus the strong miners' organization, pledged aid to Debs's legions. Gompers played a game of wait and see. Had matters remained thus, there is little question that the ARU would have prevailed, or at least that it would have effected a favorable compromise. Time after time Debs counseled restraint and nonviolence, pointing out that all the men needed to win was to stay off the job. But the employers had a trump card which Debs, a former Democrat (he was now a Populist) who had campaigned three times for President Grover Cleveland, had not anticipated—the United States government.

It happened that Attorney General Richard B. Olney had not only been a prominent railroad lawyer before taking office, but a director of a number of lines and a member of the General Managers' Association. To him a railroad strike was illegal per se and he set about to break it with cool determination. Using the argument that the government had to protect its mail trains—which the strikers had scrupulously permitted to pass—he took three measures to break the ARU offensive. The first was to appoint a railroad attorney, Edwin Walker, to deputize special deputies. "I feel," he wired Walker, "that the true way of dealing with the matter is by a force which is overwhelming and prevents any attempt at resistance."

The second was to secure on July 2 the most sweeping injunction against strikers ever known. Judge Peter Grosscup, one of the two judges in the case, had said only a few weeks before that "the growth of labor oganizations must be checked by law," so that his impartiality was open to question. The basis for the injunction— the Sherman Antitrust Act—was also of doubtful applicability in this instance since it had been passed at the behest of farmers and small businessmen to curb monopolies in "restraint of trade," not unions. It was never the intent of its author or of Congress that the bill be used to designate a labor union in "restraint of trade." But the injunction was issued nonetheless, forbidding strike leaders from taking any action on behalf of the strike, even to send telegrams or answer questions about it. Under its provisions, and similar ones in various states, a man in Albuquerque was sentenced to fifteen days in jail for refusing to get on an engine and fire it. Others were arrested for refusing to turn on switches.

The third Olney measure against the strike was a massive use of federal and state troops—on the theory that the mail was in jeopardy and the injunction had to be enforced. At one point there were militia on patrol in twenty states. Debs and J. R. Sovereign, of the Knights of Labor, jointly protested to President Cleveland that it was precisely this show of force that could lead to a revolt. The government, they said, "is soon to be declared a military despotism." Governor Altgeld of Illinois sent two stern telegrams to the President protesting the use of military forces. "Our railroads," he argued, "are paralyzed not by reason of obstruction, but because they cannot get men to operate their trains." Others pointed out it was the railroads themselves that were refusing to carry mail on trains to which Pullmans were not coupled. The President, however, swept aside such objections and dispatched the troops. Though violence had been sporadic and limited until then, it suddenly expanded. Chicago became an armed camp with thousands of men, both soldiers and civilians, carrying guns.

On July 5, after a signal house was destroyed and railroad tracks blocked in Chicago, regular soldiers made a bayonet charge, wounding several people. The next day $340,000 of railroad property was burned to the ground. A deputy deliberately shot a bystander a hundred yards from the scene of the riot, and when the man tried to rise, killed him. The bias of the soldiers was so flagrant that a group of officers met to draft a statement denouncing the strikebreaking role of the Army. Before they could publicize their views, they were arrested and held for court-martial. The court-martial was squelched, but the arrests had served their purpose of withholding the information from the press.

On July 7 a crowd, gathered to protest the moving of a train by the National Guard, was met with gunfire and twenty persons were killed. A headline in the Washington *Post* that day reported: "Chicago at the Mercy of the Incendiary's Torch." Similar difficulties occurred at Denver and San Francisco, where federal troops were on patrol. In three states, California, Iowa, and Michigan, state troops were called out. A proclamation against the right of assembly was issued by the President for eight states, from Illinois to California. The tension was reflected in such lurid newspaper headlines as "From a Strike to a Revolution," "Anarchists and Socialists Said to be Planning the Destruction and Looting of the Treasury," "Anarchists on the Way to America from Europe." Yet by and large the strikers had resorted to little or no violence if for no other reason than the fact they had the situation well in hand. Of the twenty-four railroads fanning out from Chicago, thirteen were entirely stalled and the other eleven were running only mail and passenger trains.

The callous behavior of the government inevitably stirred sympathy in the rest of the labor movement. Sovereign of the Knights of Labor made common cause with Debs. Within the AFL a ground swell began to build up for calling a nationwide general strike in all organized trades. Debs, on July 7, wired several local labor bodies: "We ask your cooperation . . . we are making a great fight for labor. . . . Capital has combined to enslave labor. We must all stand together or go down in hopeless defeat." The news coming in from various places added fuel to the flames. A carpenter was killed by the Army in Hammond, Indiana, near Chicago. The total of troops, deputy marshals, and police in Chicago and vicinity was reported at fourteen thousand. In this circumstance, workers everywhere felt the only hope for the Pullman strike—and peripherally for themselves, since the defeat of this strike would mean catastrophe—was to spread the walkout. At a large mass meeting in Chicago one hundred unions decided by a nearly unanimous vote to call a general sympathy strike in their city.

The same meeting urged Gompers to come to Chicago immediately to consider calling a national strike. The AFL leaders, however, could not bring themselves to take the decisive step that might have meant a near revolution in America. They showed their concern by voting a thousand dollars for the strikers and by sending a wire to President Cleveland asking him to come to the storm's center "so that the present industrial crisis may be brought to an end." But they postponed action on the call for a general walkout—perhaps because Debs himself was already willing to settle on the single condition that the employers rehire all strikers. Soon the city-wide strike in Chicago petered out, and the national railroad walkout began to sputter as well.

By July 10 the situation was bleak. Two more men were killed in Spring Valley, Illinois. The House of Representatives passed a resolution "endorsing prompt and vigorous action of the military forces in suppressing interference with the mails and interstate commerce." And a federal grand jury indicted the strike leaders, Debs, Howard, Keliher, and Rogers. They were immediately arrested. All told, 705 strikers were jailed either by federal or local authorities, charged with assault, intimidation, riot, burglary, inciting to riot. Against such sustained pressures, plus the recruiting of replacements by the craft brotherhoods, the insurgents began to give way. More and more men went back to work, more trains began to move. When Pullman's posted a notice on July 18 opening its shops to employees willing to return, only 325 showed up—less than half the minimum 800 crew that the company needed to resume operations. By August 1, however, the required 800 had been lured back. Out West, particularly in Sacramento, California, the ranks held firmer. But on July 20 the government withdrew its troops from Chicago and sent them westward to break the strike there. Finally, in the face of what amounted to organizational suicide, Debs called a special convention of the ARU for August 2 and officially pronounced the strike at an end. It had been utterly routed. As a symptom of the rout, only fifty-three delegates, nearly all from the West, were present for the proceedings.

The defeat of the strike was a traumatic moment for Eugene Debs. He was confronted, first of all, with a number of legal difficulties. He had been arrested on July 17 for "contempt of court"—violating the injunctions. In December Judge William A. Woods sentenced him to six months in jail. Two weeks later Debs was put on trial on the July conspiracy indictments, which the government dropped when a juror became ill.

Ruminating on the prison sentence, the smashing of his union, and the events of the strike, Debs could only wonder about his political views. He had been a Democrat for a long time. In 1894, at the last strike meeting, he had proclaimed: "I am a Populist, and I favor wiping out both old parties so they will never come into power again. I have been a Democrat all my life and I am ashamed to admit it." Sitting in jail in Woodstock, Illinois, where he was permitted enough freedom to edit his union paper and see many prominent visitors, Debs went further. He began to question the underlying assumptions of his philosophy. Was there any *modus vivendi* to be reached within the capitalist system? Was social revolution the only answer? Victor Berger, Socialist editor of the Milwaukee *Vorwaerts*, came by and left him a copy of Marx's *Capital*. Keir Hardie, the English union leader and Socialist, visited him together with Thomas J. Morgan, another radical. For a whole day in the prison yard they talked of socialism. Deep within him a conversion was taking place. On being released from jail—typically he had won the acclaim of his fellow prisoners who passed a resolution of "heartful thanks and gratitude for the many acts of kindness and sympathy"—Debs was met by a crowd of ten thousand and a special trainload of unionists who "fell upon their hero and kissed him in the sight of thousands." He was now ready to enter the third phase of his career—as leader of American socialism.

Unlike De Leon, who came by his socialist predilections as a scholar and intellectual, Debs's conversion was a by-product of his experience as a worker and a trade unionist. De Leon was the inflexible doctrinaire, searching for consistency; Debs was the humanist, more concerned with people than abstractions, and self-confident enough to overlook his own foibles if he were inconsistent. Both men could explain the most difficult concepts in simple terms that an unlettered man could grasp, but one got the feeling listening to De Leon that his clarity was the result of unexcelled erudition, while with Debs it seemed to bespeak his ability to place himself in the little man's shoes. The worker must feel De Leon as a man apart, while Debs always left the impression he was integrally linked to the crowd, one of the family. De Leon was essentially a brain, Debs essentially a heart. Perhaps the two movements they fathered reflected this difference.

III

The mood of America as the 1896 election campaign opened was an unhappy one. Farm products were lower in price than at any time since the Civil War. Factory workers were earning $406 a year and working 54 to 63 hours a week. Three decades of class war and frustration on the part of workers and farmers to secure a just share of the beneficence of industrialism had yielded inadequate results. Theodore Roosevelt, soon to become President of the United States, had a simple solution, which expressed the bitterness of the contending forces: "The sentiment now animating a large portion of our people can only be suppressed . . . by taking ten or a dozen of their leaders out, standing . . . them against a wall and shooting them dead. I believe it will come to that." President Cleveland had so alienated his fellow Democrats by his injunction policy that Governor Altgeld of Illinois was able to seize the machinery of the Democratic convention from him for a program of free silver, reduced tariffs, and control of monopolies. The Altgeld platform denounced "government by injunction as a new and highly dangerous form of oppression." Had Altgeld been native born, he would have been the party's candidate, but since he was not, the nomination fell to William Jennings Bryan, whose mellifluous voice and famous cross-of-gold speech had mesmerized the convention.

In the backwash of depression and the Pullman strike, the Populist movement too veered leftward. Henry Demarest Lloyd, a wealthy reformer and friend of labor, proposed a slate of Debs for President, Coxey for Vice President. The Ohio delegates chanted:

> One, two, three
> Who are we?
> We're for Debs, Eugene V.!

Victor Berger, a moderate Socialist from Milwaukee, busied himself mobilizing votes for the former jailbird from Woodstock. But Debs was not clear in his own mind that he wanted to tread the path of Populism rather than socialism. At the last moment he sent a wire to crestfallen friends: "Please do not permit use of my name for nomination." Instead of Debs, the People's Party accepted the Democratic choice, Bryan, and his free coinage slogan. Though Debs campaigned on Bryan's behalf with dozens of speeches, the golden-voiced candidate went down to an unexpected defeat as a bumper crop and rising economic hopes allayed farmer resentment. Altgeld, too, tasted the bitter brew as he lost the race for governor in Illinois.

Within two months after the elections, on January 1, 1897, Debs published his personal credo in the ARU's *Railway Times*. "The issue," he said, "is Socialism versus Capitalism. I am for Socialism because I am for humanity." Five months later he convened for the last time his ill-fated ARU. Where four hundred enthusiastic delegates had attended its first convention scarcely three years before, there were now barely two dozen, most of them officials. In line with Debs's own acceptance of socialism, the ARU, too, took the long leap. Dissolving itself as a union, it became, together with members of a motley group of other organizations, the Social Democracy of America. The new party favored public ownership of all monopolies and utilities, public works to make jobs for the jobless, a shorter workday, and as its major plank, an odd scheme for "colonization." Under this colonization plan, the Socialists were to choose one western state in which to concentrate their forces. By colonizing their members there, they hoped to win political power, form a "cooperative commonwealth"—in one state—and fan out "until the national cooperative commonwealth shall be established." It was a weird idea, reminiscent of Robert Owen and the utopian communities, but destined to even greater sterility. By June 1898, the colonizers had raised only $2,430.67 to colonize whatever zealots were available. Though the colonizers gained an ephemeral majority in Social Democracy at its second convention, their star dimmed as Debs (and Victor Berger) set up shop on their own, as the Social Democratic Party of America.

Meanwhile from three other directions the legions were converging to give meat and marrow to a socialist movement distinctly different from that of De Leon. Fifty-eight Jewish Socialists, representing twelve hundred De Leonists, disillusioned with his union policies, joined hands with Social Democracy. In August 1897

Berger and his Milwaukee "Independents," a solidly based group essentially of German extraction, similarly amalgamated forces with Debs.

Berger was a purposive man who was to build the most effective local machine the Socialists have ever forged in this country. An immigrant from Austria who blended well in Milwaukee with its large German population, a former secondary-school teacher, Berger was somewhat pompous and lacking in a sense of humor. But no one could ever dispute his effectiveness. His newspaper the *Social Democratic Herald* listed itself as the official paper of the "Federated Trades Council of Milwaukee and of the Wisconsin State Federation of Labor," a tribute to his concentration—and that of his comrades—on the trade-union movement. Berger was the machine man who eventually built an organization with roots in every precinct, capable of electing men to office. As a concomitant of this emphasis on electoral activity, Berger was a "gradualist" and in general a Right-winger. Socialism, as he put it, "is coming all the time. It may be another century or two before it is fully established." Left-wingers might be appalled at the idea of waiting one hundred years for their revolution, but Berger was an evolutionist, not a revolutionist. He prided himself on being the "American Bernstein." Eduard Bernstein was a German Marxist—Engels' literary executor—whose book *Evolutionary Socialim* proposed that the Socialists be a party of reform, rather than revolution. "The goal of socialism," he said, "is nothing. The movement everything." Berger was this kind of a Socialist. Like Debs, he favored industrial unionism, and he opposed De Leon's isolation from the main stream of labor, the AFL; but where Debs was to grow increasingly leftist, Berger became the spokesman of a Right-wing sector. Yet Berger had influenced Debs to become a Socialist, and in 1900 they could collaborate smoothly.

Plodding away steadily, Debs and Berger could report in March 1900 they had 226 branches and 4,536 members in 32 states. These figures underestimated their true strength, for behind them was a formidable influence in the union movement and the support of leftist newspapers, like the *Appeal to Reason,* which had scores of thousands of readers. The *Appeal to Reason,* founded by J. A. Wayland in the 1890's and edited by Fred D. Warren, had its own "army" which solicited subscriptions, as well as nickels and dimes in an emergency, to make it the most widely read radical publication the

United States has ever known. It carried Debs's weekly column and spread the Socialist message to a much larger milieu than the membership statistics of the party might indicate.

The third group to coalesce with Debs's movement was a dissident force in De Leon's party, comprising about half the membership and led by Morris Hillquit. Born in Riga, Latvia, in 1870, Hillquit came to the United States when he was fifteen, and like so many other Jewish immigrants, went to work in the needle trades, at shirtmaking. For a while he was secretary of the United Hebrew Trades, but he was soon enrolled in law school, and in 1893 embarked on a legal career for which he was almost as famous as for his socialism. As a member of the Socialist Labor Party, he was alienated by De Leon's all-or-nothing purism. At a meeting of AFL textile strikers in New Bedford, for instance, the SLP leader had denounced the struggle for higher wages and shorter hours. At the 1900 convention of the party, De Leon went further by removing "the tapeworm of immediate demands" from the party's platform. What remained was a simplistic single plank—revolution. To Hillquit and the "kangaroos"—as his faction was called—De Leon's policy would permanently isolate the movement from its working-class base. In February 1900, therefore, fifty-nine kangaroos met in Rochester, New York, and voted to unite with Debs's Social Democratic Party.

The fusion, however, was not consummated as easily as anticipated, for Debs and Berger entertained deep-seated suspicions of anything tainted with De Leonism, even if it were only residual. Representatives of both groups met in March and agreed, after a bit of maneuvering, to a joint national ticket for the Presidential campaign—Debs for President, Job Harriman for Vice President. All that remained to complete the marriage was to settle on a name, but this turned out to be a travesty of recriminations as each side held out for one that would give the appearance it was not being swallowed by the other. Finally, however, in the summer of 1901 at the Masonic Hall in Indianapolis, more than a hundred men and women rose to sing the "Marseillaise" and proclaim the Socialist Party of America.

After three decades of finding its way, American Marxism was close to its high-water mark. The new party began with some ten thousand members—a majority from Hillquit's group. Unlike previous Socialist conventions, it had a home-grown aura, with three quarters of the delegates being native born. "The number of young American-born delegates," noted A. M. Simons, "was a source of frequent comment." In its ranks was a broad spectrum, including western metal miners, a wing of the Populists, Christian Socialists, and for the first time at any Socialist convention, three Negroes. Under the Debs-Berger-Hillquit leadership, radicalism became a force with which to reckon.

IV

The vote for Debs in the 1900 elections was 95,000, four years later it had risen to 400,000, and by 1912 to 900,000—or 6 percent of the national poll. In slightly more than a decade the membership of the party was to increase twelvefold, to 118,000—more than any leftist party before or since. There were many who believed that it would emulate its British counterpart and become the main opposition force in America. It certainly was not out of the question, for the Socialist Party's influence in the unions was growing and it attracted to itself a large coterie of prominent intellectuals. Among the contributors to Socialist publications in the ensuing years were Sherwood Anderson, Walter Lippmann, Upton Sinclair, Jack London, Lincoln Steffens, Floyd Dell, Louis Untermeyer, John Reed, Mary Heaton Vorse, Max Eastman, and innumerable others. By 1912 it was propagating its views through thirteen daily newspapers, five of them in the English language. Of the forty-two socialist weeklies in 1916, one—*Appeal to Reason*—had a circulation of a half million. The *Forward,* a Jewish daily, had two hundred thousand readers, and the *National Rip-Saw,* a monthly, a similar number. Few magazine in history produced so outstanding a group of writers and artists as the *Masses,* which began publication in 1911. The socialist movement had its own educational institute, the Rand School of Social Science, and its own book publisher, Charles H. Kerr.

At one time there were 1,039 Socialist Party members holding public office, including 56 mayors, one congressman, and 300 local aldermen. In 1910 Emil Seidel won the mayoralty in the first big city captured by socialism, Milwaukee. Describing his feelings at the inauguration, Abraham Cahan, editior of the *Forward,* wrote:

"A thrill passed through the socialists present. It was one of those moments which are a landmark in one's life. There were tears in some eyes, tears of the highest joy known to man. . . . It almost seemed too good to be true. As Comrade Simons subsequently put it, 'Is this the United States?'" That same year Berger was the first Socialist elected to Congress. Meyer London, whose career ran parallel to that of Hillquit, having been born abroad, in Russia, and admitted to the bar in the United States in 1898, was elected to Congress in 1914 from the immigrant-packed East Side of Manhattan. The party, by and large, did poorly in rural areas (except in Oklahoma), but in the big cities it was no small factor. By 1917 it garnered a quarter of the votes in Buffalo; a third in Chicago; a fifth in Cleveland; almost half in Dayton, Ohio; more than a third in Toledo; almost a third in the Bronx. Paul H. Douglas, many years later to become senator from the State of Illinois, made a poll of fifteen cities that year, and found the Socialists had won 21.6 percent of the ballots. The Socialist Party of New York City sent ten assemblymen to Albany and elected Jacob Panken for a ten-year term as municipal judge. The party carried five wards in Chicago and many posts in such cities as Elkhart, Indiana, and Sandusky, Ohio.

This progress was reflected in a host of other ways as well. A Christian Socialist Fellowship, fathered by Dr. Harry F. Ward and Dr. Walter Rauschenbusch, carried the message to the religious community. The Intercollegiate Socialist Society, renamed the League for Industrial Democracy, exerted considerable influence among professors and students. Upton Sinclair's sensational book about conditions in the Chicago stockyards, *The Jungle,* after being serialized in the *Appeal to Reason,* gripped a whole nation and directed the gaze of many toward socialism. Jack London, who with Sinclair, had formed the League for Industrial Democracy, pubished *The Iron Heel* and the *War of the Classes,* and told students at Yale that in the United States there were "nearly one million who begin their letters 'Dear Comrade' and sign them 'Yours for the Revolution.'" Upper-class converts, like William English Walling and Robert Rives La Monte, joined the ranks of the proletarian revolution by the dozen. Walling, in fact, formed the Friends of Russia in 1905 to aid the abortive revolution of that country, and raised funds to send a shipload of arms to the comrades living under czarist terror.

Whatever its weaknesses, the Socialist Party showed thrust and momentum.

V

If there was a single cause for this success, it was the Socialist Party's decision to work for "immediate demands," for realizable reforms. The average worker could not be expected to accept the cooperative commonwealth at one fell swoop. He had to live through the experience of unionism and strikes before being convinced there was an inherent link between his struggle for higher wages and the ultimate demand for the abolition of the "wage system." He had to be shown the panorama piecemeal rather than all at once. To do so involved the risk that the socialist message would be diluted. Someone once coined the term "sewer socialist" to designate those Socialists who were so busy winning sewers for their constituents they forgot about the main objective, socialism. Many a party member, buoyant with the taste of political victory, bolted the ranks for the safer recluse of the Democratic Party. George R. Lunn, Socialist mayor of Schenectady, New York, for instance, deserted the Socialists to find a greener pasture with the traditional Democrats. But withal, the party leaders, ranging from the Left-wingers like Debs and Big Bill Haywood, to the Right-wingers like Berger, recognized the need to win for the downtrodden more wages, more leisure, more security, as a precondition for instilling revolutionary consciousness.

The opening to an immediate demand policy was obviously through the American Federation of Labor. Hillquit and Berger nourished the hope, like De Leon at one time, that they could win the AFL to socialism's cause, bag and baggage. It would not be easy, but it could be done. Back in 1898 Berger reported Sam Gompers had privately assured him: "I have read Karl Marx; I am as much a Socialist as you and I will vote the Social Democratic ticket and advise trade unionists to do so." In the wake of such assurances, Berger had convinced his party comrades not to oppose Gompers, as originally planned. The pure and simple unionist was on the road to conversion, just as the British Trades Union Congress leaders had recently been when they accepted a plank for the nationalization of basic industry. One had only to wait.

The following year things looked even better. Max S. Hayes, a prominent Socialist and a typographer from Cleveland, won adoption of a proposal that the AFL make a study of trusts and monopolies "with a view to nationalizing the same." A resolution to commit the union movement to collective ownership of the means of production gained support from sixteen national unions, including the important carpenters and brewery workers, plus one state federation of labor and nine city central bodies. At the next convention the teeth were taken out of this plank, but Hayes was certain that it was "only a question of a year or two before the Federation went on record for socialism." When in 1902 a socialist motion lost by the close vote of 4,897 to 4,171, there was further jubilation, even though the proposal had been much emasculated. But Berger and Hillquit had obviously miscalculated. Gompers was either not as close to them as they thought, or events had driven him farther apart. At the 1903 AFL convention, Gompers let loose a bitter barrage at the Socialists: "Economically you are unsound; socially you are wrong; and industrially you are an impossibility." There was no longer any question about the former cigar maker's intent.

The policy of "boring from within," as Job Harriman had called it, was not exactly a failure, for the Socialists made large numbers of converts inside the house of labor. They remained men of power in individual unions such as the miners, machinists, and cigar makers, as well as in numerous state and local bodies of labor. Victor Berger in Milwaukee; Adolph Germer, Duncan McDonald, and John Walker in the miners; J. Mahlon Barnes in the cigar makers held entrenched positions for considerable periods.

But the AFL, waxing fat on the good times brought in the wake of the Spanish-American War, was already institutionalized, moving from "simple" unionism to "business" unionism—unionism with a probusiness philosophy and unidealistic, sometimes corrupt methods. Increasingly it was unamenable to socialist arguments. Between 1897 and 1904 union ranks swelled almost four times, the AFL growing to 1.7 million. The miners' union expanded from 40,000 in 1899 to 260,000 five years later, and the carpenters' union from 20,000 to 155,000. It was, as AFL theoreticians put it, an "era of good feeling." And why not? Capitalists in many industries, assessing the costs of class warfare against those of class collaboration, found the latter preferable. Why fight when business was booming

—and additional costs could be passed on to the consumer? Often there was a *quid pro quo* between union leadership and management that was highly profitable. In 1897, for instance, an employers' association in Chicago granted the carpenters' union a closed shop —compulsory union membership—in return for a pledge by the union officials to call strikes against employers who refused to join the association or maintain its price scales.

Success mellowed the AFL and pushed it toward accommodation with respectable businessmen. One of the signs of the times was the participation by Gompers and other AFL factotums in the National Civic Federation. Formed in 1893 as a local Chicago group and expanded in 1900 to national proportions, the National Civic Federation was the brain child of such industrial titans as Mark Hanna and August Belmont, with the Rockefellers and Morgans active in the wings. Its stated purpose was to adjust "the differences of capital and labor," and on occasion the National Civic Federation did help resolve a dispute. When the coal miners threatened to strike in the summer of 1900, Hanna persuaded the operators to grant a one-year pact and a 10 percent raise, lest industrial warfare have a negative effect on the Presidential campaign of William McKinley. More often than not, however, the same forces that were behind the National Civic Federation fought labor tooth and nail when it tried to invade virgin territory. J. P. Morgan's United States Steel, created in 1901, smashed a strike of sixty-two thousand steel workers early in its career and the Rockefellers resisted with hammer and tongs attempts to organize their mines in the West.

Thus the cozy relations between some unions and some employers were counterbalanced by bitter ones between others. Twenty teamsters were killed in Chicago in a 1905 strike, four hundred injured and five hundred arrested. In Colorado the strikes of miners in Telluride and Cripple Creek were on the scale of a minor civil war. Governor James Peabody's declaration of "a state of insurrection and rebellion" belied the facts, but was testament to the inability of western miners to gain industrial justice without stern measures of self-defense. During the packinghouse strike of 1904, management recruited 1,400 strikebreakers from southern cities, most of them Negroes. Yet because the AFL was de-emphasizing the organization of unskilled and mass production workers, it was able to draw closer to big business, and correspondingly farther away from the Socialist militants.

Once again, therefore, socialism found itself in a dilemma. Should it build a dual union movement to challenge the AFL? Or should it be content to control a minority of the Federation and continue trying, against ever greater odds, to win the rest? One way or another it had to take a decisive step, for socialism without the support of unionism was like a tail wagging a recalcitrant dog. To the militants of the party, the AFL's policy of collaboration with the goliaths of business was treason. Even Victor Berger, a moderate who had tried to placate Gompers, showed signs of disillusion. "Sam Gompers," he wrote, "has more and more developed into an empty self-complacent fool who does not see that the AFL, from inertia and lack of movement, is hastening before his very eyes to a fatal apoplexy." Berger (and Hillquit) could not bring himself to a second round of dual unionism. The scars of De Leonism had not healed. Dual unionism, they felt, would further weaken labor in the industrial field, and alienate many sympathetic trade unionists from the Socialist Party.

Yet there were others in the party, including Debs, with whom the idea was taking hold. Though the socialist movement was to continue to make progress until the eve of World War I, it spun off a dual satellite in 1905—against the intent of most of its leaders. Once launched, that satellite—the Industrial Workers of the World—broke away from socialism to mold a movement more reminiscent of the 1886 anarchists than of either De Leon or Hillquit.

CHAPTER XII

ONE BIG UNION

THE FIRST DECADE and a half of the twentieth century has been called the "Progressive Era." After a long period of mounting class conflict there was, to an extent, an awakening of conscience. Muckrakers like Ida Tarbell and Lincoln Steffens mercilessly exposed great pockets of graft and corruption in government and industry. The momentum of the Populists, though defeated at the ballot box, carried on to Theodore Roosevelt's "Square Deal" and Woodrow Wilson's "New Freedom." Reforms that had been urged for a long time suddenly saw the light of day. Persistent suffragettes won the right to vote for women—a century and a half after the Revolution. Twenty-five states enacted legislation limiting the workday, and tens of thousands of workingmen won an eight-hour day through their unions. Thirty-eight states passed laws setting age limits for child labor and restricting hours. Thirty-five introduced workmen's compensation bills to provide payments for employees injured in industrial accidents. The Adamson Act proclaimed an eight-hour day for railroad workers and time and a half for overtime. The La Follette Seamen's Act limited the prerogatives of a ship captain over his crewmen. The Pure Food and Drug Act gave the public a measure of protection against unscrupulous hucksters. The Clayton Act closed loopholes in the regulation of monopolies and specifically exempted unions from prosecution as conspiracies.

The agitation of radicals and reformers finally seemed to be bearing fruit, both on the legislative and industrial fronts. The AFL grew to two million members, a small number compared to the millions who remained unorganized, but a large number compared to unions of the nineteenth century. Though there was some question as to whether wage increases outpaced the rise in prices, there was nonetheless a distinct improvement in rates and a concomitant reduction of the work week to forty-nine hours for the skilled and fifty-six for the unskilled.

Yet, on balance, the seamy side of the Progressive Era ranked with its sunnier one. There was a bedlam of strikes, picket line murders, strikebreaking, "open shop" campaigns, abuse of immigrants, and a hard vein of inhumanity that would not chip away. Two million children were still working as late as 1910 for pittances of two and three dollars a week—despite the improved legal situation. In 1914 alone, thirty-five thousand workers were killed in accidents on the job, at least half of whom, according to a U.S. Commission on Industrial Relations, could have lived if management had taken requisite safety measures. Seven hundred thousand were injured. The country was flooded with immigrants as never before, thirteen million arriving in the fourteen years prior to the outbreak of World War I. These foreign born, together with those who had come previously but were not yet "Americanized," comprised three fifths to two thirds the work force in such industries as steel, meat packing, coal, the needle trades, furniture, and oil refining. Though opportunity knocked here more than in Europe, they did not find quite the "golden land" they had expected. They lived in crowded, unseemly slums and worked in crowded, unseemly sweatshops.

Periodically a tragedy such as the famous fire at the Triangle Shirtwaist Company in New York laid bare the brutalizing conditions under which they labored. Just a few minutes before closing on this fateful day, March 25, 1911, the fire alarm rang. In this poorly ventilated shop which occupied the top three floors of a ten-story building, five hundred Jewish and Italian immigrant girls sat crowded back to back, the floor littered with inflammable material; garbage heaped everywhere. The sanitary facilities were so bad that workers had to leave the factory to reach the toilets. To prevent what management called "interruption of work," a steel door leading to the stairway had been locked that day. There were no outdoor fire escapes—the one in the light shaft proved a trap—and no sprinklers. The only means of exit turned out to be through the freight elevators, and before the girls could jam into them, 147 had perished, some jumping to their death, others burned to a crisp. The

fire resulted in the appointment of the New York State Factory Investigating Commission and some improvement in the fire laws, but
sweatshops like this continued to exist and made many immigrants
old long before their time.

Despite a growing awareness of social problems, there was no
doubt who ran the country. "The masters of the government of the
United States," declared President Woodrow Wilson in 1913, "are
the combined capitalists and manufacturers." There were forty-four
families who earned more than a million a year and had "fortunes of
a size never before dreamed of." But for each of the well-endowed
there were a hundred thousand at the edge of destitution. A government commission noted that the "largest private fortune in the U.S.,
estimated at one billion dollars, is equivalent to the aggregate
wealth of 2,500,000 of those who are classed as 'poor,' who are
shown . . . to own on the average about $400 each." The contrast
of wealth and poverty was as glaring as ever, probably more so,
while attempts of the common worker to remedy his plight were
met by employer campaigns for an open—nonunion—shop, as well
as naked terror. In 1903–4, during the fifteen-month strike at Cripple Creek, Colorado, 42 men were killed, 112 wounded, 1,345 held
in bull pens for many months without the right of habeas corpus,
and 773 forcibly deported. "The prime insurrectionist . . . against
the regularly established laws," wrote Henry George, Jr., "are the
governor and his soldiers . . . representative of . . . the mining
and smelting interests of Colorado." General Sherman Bell, whose
troops were being paid by the employers, refused to heed a judge's
order to release prisoners illegally held. "To hell with the Constitution!" he cried. "We're not following the Constitution!"

On Easter night in 1914, coal miners striking against John D.
Rockefeller's Colorado Fuel & Iron Company in Ludlow, Colorado,
were awakened to find company gunmen and National Guardsmen
drenching their tents with oil. They had moved into these improvised homes when the oil tycoon had evicted them from company-
owned dwellings. Regularly harried by soldiers' bullets, they had
taken the precaution of digging a cave inside the largest tent where
they placed thirteen children and one pregnant woman. All were
burned to death that night as the tent community went up in flames.
A father, stooping to pick up his dead son, was told by a company
man, "You red-neck son of a bitch, I have a notion to kill you." Six

adults also died that eerie night, and others were wounded in a
spray of soldier gunfire. But if the Rockefellers had any pangs of
conscience, it was not immediately evident. Two years later in another industrial dispute, this time at the Standard Oil plants in
Bayonne, New Jersey, Rockefeller guards killed two and wounded
twenty-nine.

There was, clearly, a duality about the Progressive Era—a bonanza of reforms and benefits for some sectors, such as the skilled
men in the AFL, compensated for by the anxious insecurity of much
larger sectors, such as the immigrants, western miners, and the unskilled generally.

II

No group could have captured the mood of this early century
bedlam like the Industrial Workers of the World (IWW)—or the
Wobblies, as its members were called. It was a revolutionary union,
formed in 1905, that answered fire with fire, gunshot with gunshot,
and wore overalls as a badge of honor. No radical force in American
history has been so earthy, so wedded to its beloved proletariat. The
Wobblies rode the rods, tramped the roads, marched off to jail defi-
antly. They fought and they sang, and their songs were eloquent
testimonials to a direct-action credo which anyone with a fourth-
grade education could understand. Their lyrics had both the bite
and the tang of America, eschewing all circumlocutions and va-
garies. They sang of "long-haired preachers" who promised "pie in
the sky." The moderate American Federation of Labor became, in
their revolutionary jargon, the American *Separation* of Labor. They
talked scornfully of "Scissor Bill," who "wouldn't join the union,"
and of "Casey Jones, the Union Scab," all with the flavor of Ameri-
cana. "Scissor Bill" referred—so it is said—to a term once used in
Arkansas to denote a man whose mouth went up and down, like a
scissors, but said nothing. "Casey Jones" was a cynical parody of a
well-known lyric about an actual, living railroad man named Jones
and nicknamed "Casey." Wobbly songs were usually based on old
tunes, many of religious origin, but given a radical twist. "Dump the
Bosses off Your Back," was a lyric written by John Brill to the music
of "Take It to the Lord in Prayer." The plaint of the proletarian

seeking a fair share was captured in this chorus of Ralph Chaplin's "Solidarity Forever":

> *It is we who plowed the prairies; built the cities where*
> *they trade;*
> *Dug the mines and built the workshops; endless miles of*
> *railroad laid;*
> *Now we stand, outcast and starving, 'mid the wonders we*
> *have made;*
> *But the Union makes us strong.*

Nothing, not even the tomes of history that have been written about them, so aptly describes the Wobbly philosophy as this refrain:

> *Tie 'em up! tie 'em up; that's the way to win.*
> *Don't notify the bosses till hostilities begin.*
> *Don't furnish chance for gunmen, scabs and all their like;*
> *What you need is One Big Union and One Big Strike.*

One big union, one big strike, it was as simple as that for the many thousands who flocked to the IWW because they felt there was no place else to go.

The roster of leaders who formed the IWW in 1905 was made up essentially of picket line fighters, usually with heavy shoulders and strong fists. There was Vincent St. John, successively a delivery boy, farmhand, tinner, printer, upholsterer, miner, who led the Telluride strike in 1901 and was to be beaten within an inch of his life during a dispute in Goldfield, Nevada, some years later. A direct actionist who shied from ballot box activity, he was to become the secretary-treasurer of the IWW and one of its pillars. There was Joe Ettor, a product of the Brooklyn slums, whose radical father had been badly wounded by the Haymarket bomb. There was Elizabeth Gurley Flynn, a young Irishwoman from New Hampshire, who was delivering socialist sermons from soapboxes while still in her teens. There was William Trautmann, whose father died in a mine disaster in New Zealand and who, on coming to the United States in 1892 at the age of thirty, became a leader of the socialist brewery workers. There was Arturo Giovannitti, born in Abruzzi, Italy, a well-educated poet, clerk, theological student, preacher, tramp, and editor of a small radical Italian sheet. There was the revolutionary priest, Thomas J. Haggerty, whom the church never got around to defrocking.

And there was the incredible Mother Jones, who bobbed up at every important strike for thirty years and was still marching on picket lines at the age of ninety. Mother Jones's autobiography notes that she "doesn't need a vote to raise hell," which is as accurate an estimate as any. Her labor career began after her husband and four children died tragically of yellow fever. For a while she was in the dressmaking business in Chicago, but beginning with the 1870's the gray-haired little lady who could—and did—swear like a trooper, began to "raise hell" for the Knights of Labor. Militant and sentimental, tough and vain, she could be seen thereafter organizing the coal miners and walking at the head of every picket line she could get to.

Most of all, however, the spirit of the IWW was that of William D. (Big Bill) Haywood, leader of the bloody Cripple Creek strike. Stoop-shouldered, blind in one eye, Big Bill nonetheless was six-foot-two and 225 pounds of muscle who could—and often did—knock a man unconscious with a single blow. During one strike a police captain's nephew hit an associate of Haywood's with a six-shooter— "lifting his scalp about three inches." "I knocked the young fellow back," records Big Bill, "and then had the whole bunch to deal with. . . . It was a fight for life. One of them struck me on the head with a gun. I dropped on my knees off the curb of the sidewalk, and drew my revolver. The captain's nephew was rushing up to give me another blow; I shot him three times in quick succession." Such melodramas, while not exactly commonplace, punctuated Haywood's life. He was no bruiser who hurt others for hurt's sake, but in the milieu in which he lived, toughness was a means of survival. It was a milieu of death, killings, and rootlessness.

Born in Salt Lake City in 1869, one of Haywood's earliest memories was at the age of three when he tried to push his arm into the fresh grave of his father so that he could touch the coffin. When he was seven, living in a mining town in Utah, he saw one man kill another in a gun duel. Later, at fifteen, he witnessed the lynching of a Negro, an incident which left him limp with tears. In the mines, where he began working that same year, miners all too often died of lead poisoning or in accidents. One day, fourteen hundred feet below the surface, Big Bill saw one of his own friends hit by a slab of rock. "We got the body out of the *stope* [a steplike excavation] on a timber truck," Haywood writes in his autobiography, "ran it to the station, and put all that was left of Louis in the skip. We rang three bells for the surface."

Growing up in such surroundings, Big Bill became tough in body and restless in spirit. How did a man find his place in this world? At the bunkhouse on his first job, just turned fifteen, he listened avidly to old radicals like Pat Reynolds, explaining the class struggle. He borrowed from other miners books by Darwin, Marx, Burns, Voltaire, Byron, and, above all, Shakespeare. By the time his character was formed, he could not only knock a man down with a single blow but recite poetry with grace and sensitivity. The mines those days were unorganized, but there were radicals and unionists who had been black-listed in the East, spreading the gospel. To an impressionable youngster the slogan, "An injury to one is an injury to all," had the sound of religion. When the Haymarket anarchists were executed, Haywood's friends discussed in reverent terms August Spies's last words, "The time will come when our silence in the grave will be more eloquent than our speeches." This was, Haywood recalled, "the turning point in my life."

Big Bill married Nevada Jane Minor when he was nineteen, and after fathering a girl, tried to settle down on a farm. Here at last was work he loved, work that catered to his sense of independence. The government, however, took the land to return to the Indians. In the midst of the 1893 depression, a disconsolate Haywood was forced to migrate. Circulating far and wide through the West, riding the freights, walking, hitching rides with ranchers, sleeping under the stars, Big Bill could ruminate there were thousands just like him, desperate, hopeless, willing to take any work they could get. The pragmatic facts of life were shaping him into a unionist and a radical. When he learned of the Pullman strike in 1894, he saw in it "a great rift of light" that echoed the "voice of the Haymarket martyrs."

The opportunity to follow this "great rift of light" came two years later when he was working in a mine at Silver City, Idaho. Big Bill had smashed his right hand and was living on contributions from his fellow miners when Ed Boyce, president of the Western Federation of Miners (WFM)—formed three years earlier—came through on

[223]

an organizing tour. Crippled hand and all, Big Bill became the spark plug of a union drive. When two of the one thousand workers refused to join, he personally drove them out of the camp. A forceful debater and writer, Haywood was immensely popular. He could fight and he could talk. He could get drunk with the boys and write a stinging article. Within four years he was secretary-treasurer of the WFM and had moved to Denver to handle its affairs.

Inevitably Haywood's path crossed that of Eugene V. Debs. They were kindred spirits who had come by their radicalism in the cauldron of experience rather than through academic exercise. Both were suspicious of Sam Gompers—the WFM had joined the AFL at birth only to secede four years later because of the latter's lack of militancy. Debs, for his part, could never allay the feeling that Gompers was an obstacle to teaching workers the connection between short-run objectives and socialism. The Socialist Party, which he had helped form in 1901, was committed to working within the AFL, but Debs felt a stronger bond to such groups as the independent WFM. When Haywood and Boyce, both of whom had just joined the Socialist Party, asked him to address the 1901 WFM convention, Debs jumped at the opportunity. Amidst lyrical enthusiasm, he gave the miners an exposition of socialism and urged them to endorse its tenets. The federation responded by putting itself on record for "a complete revolution of present social and economic conditions." That night Haywood and the unusual priest who worked with him, Thomas J. Haggerty, knocked on Debs's door with two bottles of whisky under their arms. After hours of swapping stories and wide-ranging political discussion, they cemented a relationship that endured until after they launched the Industrial Workers of the World.

Debs was not opposed to the AFL per se, but he felt that good Socialists ought to work outside, as well as inside, its ranks. He was disgusted with the AFL role in the National Civic Federation and its failure to organize Negroes or unskilled mass production workers. In 1902, therefore, he urged the Western Labor Union—a satellite of the miners dedicated to the unionization of nonminers in the West—to change its name to the American Labor Union, embrace socialism, and initiate a national campaign to form industrial unions. Haywood, of course, was elated with the suggestion. But within the Socialist Party the Debs-Haywood *démarche* caused deep consternation. That was the year when Socialists at the AFL convention had gained a surprisingly good vote for a resolution calling for "the overthrow of the wage system." Victor Berger was in control of the Central Labor Union of Milwaukee; Hillquit was attorney for a number of craft unions; and J. Mahlon Barnes was a key figure in Gompers' own cigar makers. To the right and center wings of the Socialist Party, dual unionism was anathema. They argued vehemently against Debs' position, but the man from Terre Haute was not to be deterred. In his mind a growing American Labor Union would eventually merge with the Socialists inside the AFL to form a new radical labor center. He did not consider it dual unionism but parallel unionism.

Two years later Debs was willing to go further. Together with five others, he issued a call to thirty radical leaders to "discuss ways and means of uniting the working people of America on correct revolutionary principles." After a preliminary conference in January 1905, the Industrial Workers of the World was ready for unveiling. Haywood, with the bitter experience of the fifteen-month strike at Cripple Creek behind him, was eager to explore this new road. It was to take him farther than he expected.

III

Precisely at 10 A.M. on June 27, 1905, Haywood mounted the platform at Brand's Hall in Chicago, picked up a loose piece of lumber, and gaveled the meeting to order. "Fellow workers," he said, "this is the Continental Congress of the working class. The aims and objects of this organization shall be to put the working class in possession of the economic power . . . without regard to the capitalist masters." On the platform were Debs and Lucy Parsons, widow of the Haymarket martyr. Sprinkled through the audience of some two hundred delegates and dozens of spectators were such well-known figures as Daniel De Leon; Charles Moyer, new president of the WFM; Trautmann; Father Haggerty; Mother Jones; and Left-wing Socialists like Ernest Untermann and A. M. Simons, editor of the *International Socialist Review*. Victor Berger and Max Hayes had been invited, but Berger had ignored the letter, and Hayes had replied that he still had faith in the possibility of winning the AFL to the Socialist banner.

After making a pilgrimage en masse to the grave of the Hay-market victims and passing a resolution endorsing the Russian Revolution then in progress (the first one, of 1905), the delegates wrote a constitution defining their aims. In succinct terms the preamble declared: "The working class and the employing class have nothing in common. There can be no peace so long as hunger and want are found among millions of working people and the few who make up the capitalist class have all the good things of life." The "one big union," it said, will serve "not only for the everyday struggle with capitalists, but also to carry on production when capitalism shall have been overthrown. By organizing industrially we are forming the structure of the new society within the shell of the old." Amidst enthusiasm and self-congratulations, the assemblage proclaimed the Industrial Workers of the World, with a claimed membership of fifty-two thousand. Hopes ran high, as the delegates departed, that the "one great industrial union embracing all industries" would "smash all labor fakers and traitors" in the AFL and emerge as the rallying force for the downtrodden, organized and unorganized. "We are going down in the gutter," shouted Haywood, "to get at the mass of workers and bring them up to a decent plane of living."

The IWW was only a few months old when Haywood and two others became involved in a sensational murder trial. On December 30, 1905, former Governor Frank Steunenberg of Idaho, a man who had been elected with miners' votes but had called out the militia against their strike at Coeur d'Alene, was killed as he entered his home. A fishing line with a bomb attached had been carefully tied to the gate so that when Steunenberg opened it, he was blown to bits. Within days there were offers of fifteen thousand dollars in reward for apprehending the murderers, a lure which attracted the Pinkerton Detective Agency. James McParlan, the spy who had foiled the Molly Maguires three decades before and was now one of the Pinkerton managers, came west and there extracted a confession from a man named Harry Orchard, an occasional bodyguard for President Moyer of the WFM. Orchard said he had been hired for the murder by Haywood, Moyer, and a Denver businessman friendly to the miners, George Pettibone. Furthermore, this was not his first crime on their behalf; over the years he had killed twenty-six mining bosses. Two months after Steunenberg's death, McParlan arrested another man, Steve Adams, who, according to the Pinkertons, corroborated Orchard.

On February 12, 1906, a county attorney in Idaho filed complaints against Moyer, Haywood, and Pettibone. Warrants were issued, but the problem was how to get the accused from Colorado to Idaho without long court proceedings over extradition. The governor of Colorado solved the matter nicely by signing extradition papers secretly on a Saturday evening, when the defendants could not get to a court, and having them hustled to the railroad station, bound for Idaho, without anyone knowing about it. They "will never leave Idaho alive," boasted McParlan to a Chicago *Tribune* reporter.

To the Wobblies, Socialists, and AFL these proceedings had all the stench of a frame-up. In the pages of *Appeal to Reason*, Eugene Debs wrote with passionate fury: "Nearly twenty years ago the capitalist tyrants put some innocent men to death for standing up for labor. They are now going to try it again. Let them dare! There have been twenty years of revolutionary education, agitation, and organization since the Haymarket tragedy, and if an attempt is made to repeat it, there will be a revolution. . . . If they attempt to murder Moyer, Haywood, and their brothers, a million revolutionists at least will meet them with guns." But Debs's threat had little effect in Idaho. A petition for a writ of habeas corpus on the grounds that the men were "kidnapped" was denied. Ten days later the United States District Court issued a similar decision. When the Supreme Court finally upheld the lower courts by an 8-to-1 vote, Debs wrote: "Kidnapping, then, being a legitimate practice, we all have a perfect right to engage in it. Let us take advantage of the opening. For every workingman kidnapped a capitalist must be seized and held for ransom." Seldom have Americans been so stirred in a civil liberties case as in this one. While the men languished in jail, Debs made hundreds of speeches from coast to coast arousing public sentiment. Demonstrations were held in all corners of the land. In Boston fifty thousand union men paraded, chanting:

If Moyer and Haywood die; if Moyer and Haywood die:
Twenty million workers will know the reason why.

As the trial neared, twenty thousand citizens of New York marched to Grand Central Palace to hear Morris Hillquit. The *Appeal to Reason* published special editions of a million copies each. Left-wingers and liberals, revolutionary unionists and simple unionists, recognized in the impending trial a threat to all that they were fighting for. The Illinois District of the United Mine Workers sent a five-thousand-dollar unsolicited contribution to the defense. Even Sam Gompers rose at the 1906 convention of the AFL to excoriate the authorities of Colorado and Idaho for kidnapping. De Leon's paper, the *People*, charged that it was the capitalists themselves who had conspired with Orchard in order to destroy the WFM. According to the Socialists, Steunenberg had been involved in land frauds and was killed by a business associate he had helped bilk. They showed their faith in Haywood by nominating him for the governorship of Colorado while he was in jail. When, on the eve of the trial, President Theodore Roosevelt called Haywood, Moyer, and Debs "undesirable citizens," college boys put buttons on their lapels: "I am an undesirable citizen."

On May 9, 1907, fifteen months after he had been spirited out of Denver, Big Bill Haywood went on trial. Clarence Darrow represented the defense; Senator William E. Borah, just elected to office, the prosecution. Fifty reporters from the United States as well as England covered the proceedings. The case itself, though it lasted many months, turned out to be anticlimactic. By this time Adams had repudiated his confession, blowing a gaping hole in the prosecution's case. Orchard, the state's main witness, was thus without corroboration, and he made a poor showing anyway. It turned out his real name was Alfred Horsely, that he had a long career—even before being associated with the WFM—as a bigamist, thief, arsonist. Several defense witnesses testified he had threatened revenge against Steunenberg for forcing him to sell his share of a mine which later yielded a rich strike. The defense showed that Orchard had committed perjury in courts before and had confessed to crimes he had not, in fact, committed.

In the climate of Boise, however, none of this might have availed if not for the masterly eleven-hour summation by Clarence Darrow. He berated those trying to kill the accused, "not because it is Haywood, but because he represents a class." "Don't be so foolish," he told the jury, "as to believe you can strangle the Western Federation of Miners when you tie a rope around his neck. If at the behest of this mob you should kill Bill Haywood, he is mortal, he will die, but I want to say that a million men will grab up the banner of labor where at the open grave Haywood lays it down. . . . I speak for the poor, for the weak, for the weary, for that long line of men who, in darkness and despair, have borne the labors of the human race. Their eyes are upon you twelve men of Idaho tonight. If you kill Haywood your act will be applauded by many. . . . But if your verdict should be 'not guilty' in this case, there are still those who will reverently bow their heads and thank these twelve men for the life and reputation you have saved."

Darrow finished his remarks at 10 P.M. The jury, made up for the most part of poor farmers, deliberated through the night and at 7:45 A.M., July 29, 1907, rendered a verdict for Haywood—"not guilty." Shortly thereafter Moyer and Pettibone were also freed. Orchard, by a special irony, was given a life sentence.

IV

When Big Bill Haywood emerged from the jail in Boise he was a proletarian hero of grand stature. He had survived what everyone left of center had considered a capitalist frame-up, and in so doing had added luster to the cause with which he was associated. It was a luster the IWW badly needed just then because it was rent with dissension. It turned out that common antipathy to the AFL was no mortar to bind a movement together. At the 1906 convention—while Haywood was in jail—the heterogeneous forces that had fashioned the IWW divided into "conservatives" and "radicals." The former were led, oddly enough, by delegates from the WFM; the latter by De Leon, Trautmann, and Vincent St. John. The "conservatives," while Left wing by AFL standards, were more interested in building an effective organization than in revolution. "The West," as one of their delegates put it, "does not want a *revolutionary* IWW." The radicals, of course, clung to the spirit of the preamble. Before the sessions had concluded, some of the "conservatives" had bolted, while the "radicals" removed "conservative" President Charles O. Sherman from office. As in so many leftist schisms, the aftermath was filled with recriminations, each faction claiming a majority and running to the courts to gain control of the organization's machinery. The "radicals," however, had the greater persistency, for even though repudiated by the judiciary, they emerged at the helm— largely because Sherman and his allies lost interest. By 1907, a badly divided WFM, the main bastion of the IWW, voted by a 2-to-1 margin to disaffiliate.

The feuding did not end there, however. Within the radical faction, too, there were deep fissures, between traditional Left-wing Socialists and syndicalists. In part this was a matter of temperament, in part philosophy. The western migratory workers who poured into Chicago in blue denim overalls, black shirts, and red ties, singing "Hallelujah, I'm a Bum," were not particularly enamored of the ballot box. It seemed like an effete trap to them—and to leaders like Vincent St. John, who verbalized their misgivings. How were you going to overthrow capitalism by casting your vote? The powers-that-be could be toppled only by force—direct action, sabotage, general strike. There was nothing wrong perhaps for an individual to vote in elections. But insofar as a revolutionary movement was concerned, the ballot box only drained off valuable energies that could better be used in fighting scabs or waging free speech fights. The syndicalists, like the Chicago anarchists two decades earlier, believed in Marx's doctrine of the class struggle and most of his other theories. Many of them, like Haywood, were simultaneously members of the Socialist Party. But they would limit IWW activity to the economic front—the point of production. In this they were following the philosophic path laid out by European intellectuals such as Georges Sorel, Gustave Hervé, Edouard Berth, and others. The rank-and-file Wobbly probably understood little of Sorel's "Social Myth," but his experiences with politics were so negative he veered instinctively to direct action, as against electoral maneuvering. For him it was more a matter of mood than ideology.

For De Leon, however, and other radical Socialists, the philosophy of anarcho-syndicalism was barren naïveté. For all his revolutionary stance, De Leon wanted to fight the enemy on a "civilized plane." On his insistence, the original IWW preamble had included a clause about the need of the toilers to "come together on the political as well as on the industrial field." But the "bummery" and "slum proletarians," as he called his syndicalist opponents, rescinded this doctrine. At the 1908 convention a split between the syndicalists and De Leon was finalized, with the latter again forming a rival group that survived in one form or another for seventeen years, but with the same sterility as the old Socialist Trade and Labor Alliance.

As the IWW took an irrevocable stand for syndicalism—Haywood, too, having been converted while on a trip to France—

old Eugene V. Debs was caught in a vise. As much as he was attracted to militant action, he was alienated by the apolitical trend of his brain child. His was a more wide-ranging radicalism. Yet, though he disagreed with the syndicalists, he could not bring himself to engage in the in-fighting of the IWW any more than he enjoyed in-fighting in the Socialist Party. Without fanfare he simply stopped paying dues, permitted his membership to lapse, and thus ended another chapter in his long career.

With such losses, it might have been expected that the IWW would rapidly disintegrate. But, on the contrary, it flourished. Unlike De Leon's Socialist Trade and Labor Alliance of a decade before, it did fight for immediate demands. Wherever there was trouble, there one could find the Wobblies battling it out with cops and scabs, and going to jail to win free speech. They were colorful, typically American, and though they might alienate De Leon because they wore overalls and rode the rods, they were thoroughly dedicated. Everything about them bespoke drama and a certain type of integrity. When William Z. Foster—later to become leader of the Communist Party—suggested that the fellow workers "bore from within" the AFL as well as ply their revolutionary unionism independently, he was hooted down. This kind of mundane maneuvering had an element of deception which did not sit well with the Wobblies. Critics considered them hopelessly romantic and blissfully feeble in laying permanent roots. In early 1912, for instance, during the Mexican Revolution, the global-minded IWW sent an "army" to seize Mexicali and Tijuana. A year after the sensational victory of twenty-five thousand Lawrence textile strikers —which Vincent St. John termed "the start that will only end with the downfall of the wage system"—the IWW local in town had fallen to a slender membership of seven hundred. By 1931 the IWW had issued one and a quarter million red cards, yet its peak membership never exceeded one hundred thousand. Withal, however, the Wobblies were fighting zealots whose willingness to go to jail or die for the cause had a mesmeric effect on hundreds of thousands of downtrodden. No one was too lowly for them to unionize—one of their first efforts was to enroll Western Union messengers in Goldfield, Nevada, something the AFL would not dream of doing. And their tactics always had an unusual flair—three decades before the CIO sit-down strikes of 1936–37, for instance, the Wobblies were conducting "stay-ins" at the General Electric plant in Schenectady, New York.

V

The list of IWW battles prior to World War I is far too long to record. It ranged the gamut from struggles of simple agricultural laborers to skilled mass production men, from one end of the country to the other. Typical, however, were the strike of steelworkers at McKees Rocks, Pennsylvania; the free speech fights out West; the Lawrence textile strike; and the upheavals among harvest and lumber workers which went on constantly.

The Pressed Steel Car plant at McKees Rocks in 1909 was a microcosm of American industry. Among its eight thousand workers were fourteen different groups of foreign born, each speaking its own language, each husbanding antagonisms gained in the Old World. Some had been prominent figures at home, Italians who had led resistance strikes, Russians who had been in the Duma in 1905, some who had played a role in the German metalworkers' union. But because of the language barrier they were easily divided, easily abused.

Early in 1909 management introduced a new method of pay. Under the "pool system," men with specific occupations, such as riveters or heaters, were lumped into gangs and compensated on the basis of total output rather than individual effort. It was a system that lent itself both to confusion and corruption. The foreman was allotted the pay for the entire gang. In turn, he doled it out as he saw fit, rewarding favorites willing to speed up the work, penalizing others. To pad his pocket, he extorted large sums from job applicants and often fired workers solely to hire others. After a few months of this intolerable state of affairs, forty riveters advised the company they would not work unless told specifically what their rates were. Half were discharged, the other half slunk back to work. The resentment, however, would not abate. Other departments joined the protest when the company refused to meet with them, and soon the plant was at a standstill. Two committees sprang up, the "Big Six" to run the strike, and another, composed of radicals who had been active in Europe, called the "Unknown Committee," to handle other matters. Sixty of the "Unknowns" invaded the plant at one point to drive out 350 men who were still working.

True to the tradition of the times, as soon as the strike began on July 14, one hundred deputy sheriffs and two hundred of the state constabulary—dubbed "cossacks" by the strikers—surrounded the plant and attacked the pickets. The authorities used rifles, the workers rocks and missiles. In the month of July, as one battle followed another, seventy-six strikers were wounded. One was killed. The Unknown Committee wrote the "cossack" commander a letter saying that "for every striker's life you take, a trooper's life will be taken." Meanwhile Secretary Trautmann of the IWW was called in to address the men and the Wobblies assumed charge. The determined radicals armed themselves for a final showdown.

On August 23 a group of strikers boarded a streetcar entering the strike zone in search of "scabs." A deputy sheriff on the car refused to get off, and when he fired his gun at the men, was killed. Then the troops were called out to settle accounts. In the ensuing melee, eleven lives were lost, some on each side. The "cossacks" avenged themselves by tying some of the strikers to their horses and dragging them through the streets. But the ranks had held too solid for the company to resist further. Public opinion was definitely against it as the facts of its operations became known. Transportation workers were refusing to haul strikebreakers, and not a few of the latter, terrified by events, were deserting. Management agreed to drop the pool system. Shop rules were improved and a 15 percent wage increase put into effect. Significantly, no attempt was made to prosecute anyone for murder. Six Wobblies were sentenced to sixty days in the workhouse, but that was all. It was a victory of towering proportions that had repercussions at Inland Steel, Republic Steel, and Standard Steel Car, where the IWW won similar gains under similar—but not so bloody—circumstances.

In the West, where episodic work in construction, lumber, and the harvest fields was a way of life, the Wobblies found themselves embroiled in another type of battle—the free speech fight—which was to become their special trademark. It began in a campaign at Spokane, Washington, against thirty-one employment sharks. These had an unsavory habit of mulcting jobless workers out of their last dollar. They sold jobs that did not exist or others that, by prearrangement, were to last only for a short time. The more discharges, the more new men could be placed—and the more fees for the employment agencies. Reaction against the fleecing companies was so intense that in January 1909 a mob of between two and three thousand men hurled rocks and chunks of ice through the windows of the Red Cross Employment Agency. To focus on this evil, James H. Walsh, IWW organizer, began to hold street meetings, urging the unemployed not to patronize the sharks, who then responded by having the city pass a municipal ordinance against outdoor gatherings.

So matters stood for a number of months, through the summer. Despite the fact the Wobblies believed in direct action and did not flinch from violence in self-defense, Walsh warned his followers that "you can gain nothing by resorting to mob rule." But when September rolled around and the city exempted the Salvation Army from the antimeeting ordinance, the Wobblies decided to test the law. In September and October a few meetings were held, speakers were arrested, but in each case were released. Finally in late October and November the real fight began. The *Industrial Worker* carried a headline: "Wanted—Men to Fill the Jails of Spokane." What followed was a mixture of comedy and tragedy.

As one IWW speaker was hauled off his soapbox and arrested, another took his place. On the first day alone, 103 were jailed—and beaten by police. Within a month there were 500 locked up, living on bread and water, refusing to accept bail, singing their lusty songs. Elizabeth Gurley Flynn, then only nineteen years old, chained herself to a lamppost, continuing her speechmaking until she was cut loose. Eight editors of the *Industrial Worker* successively put their paper to bed and then betook themselves to the soapbox—and jail. The prisons became inadequate to accommodate the prisoners; the overflow had to be put up in a school and at Fort Wright, generously contributed by the War Department. It was all made to order for national headlines, particularly such lurid charges as those of Miss Flynn that the women's cells were being used as a brothel, with police soliciting customers. When, on top of this, Vincent St. John announced another free speech day for March 1, 1910, the authorities beat a retreat. On March 3, civil liberties returned to Spokane, the prisoners were released, and nineteen of the more unscrupulous employment sharks had their licenses revoked.

The battle in Spokane was followed almost immediately by another in Fresno, California, where Frank Little was trying to organize fruit pickers. At the behest of the fruitgrowers in the immensely rich San Joaquin Valley, police arrested one hundred Wobblies while they were holding meetings. Thereupon a couple of thousand "blanket stiffs"—laborers who traveled from job to job carrying their own blanket rolls—embarked from Portland, Seattle, and as far away as Denver to the scene of the dispute. Faced with the choice either of finding new prison space, since their own jail was full, or giving in, the authorities decided to retreat.

The free speech fight at Everett, a medium-sized lumber city thirty miles from Seattle, introduced new tactics on both sides. Three AFL unions were on strike in this nonunion town in 1916 when the IWW Lumber Workers' Union No. 500 decided to open a headquarters to unionize the area. To head them off, the sheriff evolved the tidy tactic of arresting the Wobblies—as they came into town or as they rose to speak at a meeting—and deporting them out of the city. All told, three to four hundred IWW members were treated in this fashion before the denouement. Ever ready to accept a challenge, the revolutionary unionists decided that if they could not come into Everett by land, they would try it by water. Forty-one of them took a boat in Seattle but were met by the sheriff and his vigilantes, beaten and driven to the outskirts of town. On November 5, three hundred determined free-speechers tried anew. They boarded two ships and sailed for Everett, their voices raised lustily to the words "Hold the fort for we are coming. Union men be strong." At the docks one of the boats, the *Verona,* was met by a reception committee of two hundred vigilantes, who fired at them from the cover of a nearby warehouse for fully ten minutes. Some of the Wobblies obviously fired back because when the battle was over and the ship had been backed out, two vigilantes and five IWW's lay dead, and fifty, on both sides, lay wounded.

V I

The most notable event in the pre-World War I history of the IWW was the Lawrence strike. Lawrence, Massachusetts, a city of eighty-six thousand, was the citadel of the textile industry in 1912, with the American Woolen Company its major employer. Almost everyone over fourteen years of age worked in the mills, a large number of them Italians. Average wages were sixteen cents an hour; twelve to fifteen thousand of the less skilled earned as little as nine and a half to twelve cents an hour, or less than seven dollars for a fifty-six hour week. Since the AFL local in town concentrated exclusively on the aristocrats of labor, the skilled, it was clearly up to the IWW to offer shelter to the unskilled plebians. Actually it had been agitating in the industry since its inception, so that by 1912 roughly half the IWW membership was scattered through the mill towns of New England. The local in Lawrence had about a thousand members and was preparing a major strike for the summer.

But on January 1, 1912, a state law went into effect reducing the work week to fifty-four hours. Ordinarily a two-hour reduction in labor should have brought jubilation, but in this case it simply meant that employers paid only for fifty-four hours, thinning the pay envelope by thirty-two cents a week. Thirty-two cents bought eight to ten loaves of bread in those days. As the mill hands counted their money under the new work schedule, the cry went up like a cannonade: "Short pay! Short pay!" Next morning a sullen operative at the Everett cotton mill shouted, "Goddamn it to hell, let's strike! Strike!" Before anyone knew what was happening, workers were streaming past the machines in every department, pulling others out of the plants with them. In a few hours the cry had been taken up at other mills and within three days twenty-five thousand workers, of fourteen different nationality groups, were on the picket line.

Interestingly enough, the first act of the strikers, meeting at the Franco-Belgian Hall, was to telegraph Joseph Ettor, a member of the IWW General Executive Board, asking him to take charge. Joe, a handsome young man in his mid-twenties, eloquent and affable, was one of the brilliant tacticians of the movement. "Make this strike as peaceful as possible," he told the workers. "In the last analysis, all the blood spilled will be your blood." He was joined a week later by another colorful man, Arturo Giovannitti, a poet, editor of an Italian socialist sheet, *Il Proletario*, who constantly declaimed that "capitalism is the same here as in the Old Country. No one cares for you."

During the nine-week conflict all the usual techniques were employed against the strikers—police, soldiers, arrests, strikebreakers. After a mass picket line at two mills on January 15, the commissioner of public safety announced, somewhat indelicately, "There will be no more toying with these lawless strikers. . . . The soldiers . . . will shoot to kill." All told, twenty-two companies of soldiers, fourteen hundred men, were called in to patrol the city. On January 16, in an effort to reopen one of the mills, the militia charged a demonstration of pickets with drawn bayonets. Four days later police discovered dynamite in three different spots: a cemetery lot, a shoeshop, and a tailorshop near where Ettor got his mail. Immediately they accused the strikers and arrested seven of them, while Ettor called the episode a "plant." He was proved right. Subsequently a local businessman, John C. Breen, confessed he had planted the explosives at the urgings of the American Woolen Company, and he was fined five hundred dollars for the crime. But similar amateurish efforts to discredit the strike continued. A "citizens committee" of management officials, lawyers, and local politicians decried the walkout as anarchy. John Golden, the AFL textile union leader, denounced it as "a revolution," despite the fact that a thousand skilled workers had joined it. Four respectable citizens, including a minister, tried to tie up sorely needed relief funds by initiating court action. Three hundred and thirty-five strikers were arrested, most of them eventually released by higher courts.

But through it all young Joe Ettor kept his poise. The strike could not be won, he knew, by matching military strength with the authorities but only through economic power. To stave off hunger, he and Giovannitti formed a relief committee and collected seventy-five thousand dollars from Socialists and sympathetic AFL unions. It was not a large sum, judged by the needs, but it managed to keep the ranks intact. Soup kitchens and food stations were set up, one for each nationality group, to feed the strikers and their dependents.

On January 29, with the strike in the third week, Ettor held a large demonstration on the public commons, repeating again his exhortation to be orderly and peaceful. After a parade through the business district, the jubilant strikers dispersed for home. But as the sun was setting of a winter evening, shots rang out and an Italian weaver, Anna Lo Pizzo, fell dead, killed presumably by a policeman. Her death, instead of causing the police to tread warily, became a signal for reprisals. Two days later, with the city under martial law, Ettor and Giovannitti were arrested on the charge of being accessories to murder. They were held without bail.

If this was meant to decapitate the strike, it failed. As Ettor observed, "Bayonets cannot weave cloth." Within a few days Big Bill Haywood arrived in Lawrence, greeted by ten thousand at the railroad station, to take personal charge. With him were William Trautmann and the twenty-one-year-old Elizabeth Gurley Flynn. As the days dragged on, it became a question of endurance. Contributions were tapering off; the specter of hunger was becoming formidable. If it were just adults that were suffering they might, somehow, muddle through. But the children, already undernourished, presented a more disheartening problem. To meet it, Haywood and his associates devised a scheme that would not only deal with this challenge but would dramatize publicly the whole strike. Why not send the youngsters to be "adopted" by friends in other cities? Thereby not only would the pressure on parents be relieved but the children would be ambassadors to acquaint the whole country with what was going on in Lawrence.

One hundred and nineteen youngsters were sent to New York on February 10, where they were met by a crowd of five thousand, examined by doctors, and taken to the homes of sympathizers. A week later ninety-two arrived and paraded along Fifth Avenue. These pilgrimages by innocent victims of industrial conflict had a great effect on public opinion, something which caused growing concern with the authorities of Lawrence. When, on February 24, therefore, another group of children was taken to the railroad station, bound for Philadelphia, the police refused to let them pass. What followed was sheer tragedy. As the Women's Committee of Philadelphia reported:

"When the time approached to depart, the children, arranged in a long line, two by two, in orderly procession, with their parents near at hand, were about to make their way to the train when the police, who had by that time stationed themselves along both sides of the door, closed in on us with their clubs, beating right and left, with no thought of the children, who were in the most desperate danger of being trampled to death. The mothers and children were thus hurled in a mass and bodily dragged to a military truck, and even then clubbed, irrespective of the cries of the panic-stricken women and children."

If Lawrence officials had hoped to take the spotlight from the strike, their acts boomeranged. In Congress, Socialist Victor Berger, elected in 1910, had been demanding an investigation. It was now approved. On March 12, the American Woolen Company, faced with universal hostility, agreed to a two-cents-an-hour raise for the lowest paid and a penny an hour for those earning twelve to twenty cents an hour, plus time and a quarter for overtime. The proposal was agreed to and the strike ended on March 13, just about two months after it began. Within a few weeks IWW membership in Lawrence pyramided to fourteen thousand and not long thereafter the Wobblies were leading eighteen thousand operatives in Lowell, fifteen thousand in Bedford, and others, to similar victories. "The IWW," wrote a prominent clergyman, "leaves behind as hopelessly passé, the methods of the American Federation of Labor."

There still remained the Ettor-Giovannitti trial, which opened on September 30 in Salem. Both men urged the textile workers to take no action on their behalf, but in the spring and summer before the case was heard, large demonstrations were held and fifteen thousand responded to the call for a one-day protest strike. "Either open the jail doors," the textile workers cried, "or we'll close the mill doors." A defense committee raised sixty thousand dollars from radicals and liberals who were convinced no fair trial could take place in Massachusetts. They were wrong, however. After fifty-eight days of testimony, a jury pronounced the two IWW leaders "not guilty." Nothing expresses the Wobbly spirit more fervidly than Giovannitti's words to the jury before it began deliberations: "Let me tell you that the first strike that breaks again in this Commonwealth or any other place in America where the work and help and the intelligence of Joseph J. Ettor and Arturo Giovannitti will be needed and necessary, there we shall go again, regardless of any fear or of any threat. We shall return again to our humble efforts, obscure, unknown, misunderstood soldiers of this mighty army of the working class of the world, which, out of the shadows and darkness of the past, is striving toward the destined goal, which is the emancipation of human kind, which is the establishment of love and brotherhood and justice for every man and every woman on this earth."

VII

What distinguished the IWW was, as at Lawrence, an impressive ingenuity in tailoring tactics to circumstance. During a 1912 strike of construction workers against two railroads, the Wobblies put up a "thousand-mile picket line" from San Francisco to Minneapolis, preventing replacements from shipping out to their jobs. IWW missionaries hopped trains going to the strike sites, and induced potential strikebreakers to quit, leaving behind them ragged suitcases filled with bricks and newspapers, to deceive the employers that they were still at hand.

Another imaginative technique was employed when the IWW launched an extensive campaign to unionize harvest workers. As was well known, migrants do not stay long enough at any job to be enrolled in a union. But the effervescent Wobblies found a way around this dilemma. Since the field hands usually rode the freight trains from one job to another, or congregated in "jungles" (camps) awaiting new assignments, the IWW concentrated its efforts on the trains. Armed committees greeted harvest workers and persuaded them to accept the red card of the IWW. That card was the equivalent of a railroad ticket, for without it the migrant would not be permitted aboard by Wobblies on the freights. Using this device, the Wobblies were able to build the newly founded Agricultural Workers' Organization to eighteen thousand members by October 1916, and with this union as a base, to send organizers into the lumber areas of Montana, Washington, and Idaho, the construction camps throughout the West, and the oil fields of Kansas and Oklahoma. Had World War I not intervened, it is possible that for once the IWW might have carved a firm niche in the farming industry. A. C. Townley, president of the Farmers' Non-Partisan League, offered them a written contract, but before the parties could work out the details, the wartime repressions had begun and the IWW was in no position to continue negotiations.

Another ingenious tactic was adopted in the lumber districts. In these remote areas working conditions were abysmal, hours long, housing and living facilities inadequate, wages poor. Among the demands of the lumberjacks in one of their early strikes were such items as better food, single spring beds with mattresses, shower baths, elimination of overcrowding in the lunchrooms, as well as the usual ones for an eight-hour day and higher wages. When it appeared that walkouts, called in 1917, were foundering, the Wobblies decided to return to work and "strike on the job." Instead of laboring a full ten hours, they would stop work at the end of eight. Or they would slow down operations so that they performed only eight hours' work in ten hours' time. It was enough to drive management berserk, but it worked. When older crews were fired, new men, indoctrinated by the IWW, used the same tested methods. Faced with inefficiency and the high cost of labor turnover, the employers, prodded by the government, finally gave in.

Yet despite unexampled militancy and clever devices to check-mate the authorities, the IWW was unable to follow through with permanent organization. Unlike the AFL, it eschewed written con-tracts or the closed shop. To enter into a one- or two-year agreement with the hated boss only tied the union's hands, in their opinion. And the closed shop was a weapon of compulsion rather than free will. In all its widespread activity the IWW was unable to build an adequate treasury of its own to pay strike benefits or feed its mem-bers during a walkout. Whenever it faced such problems, it had to appeal to AFL unions, Socialists, and liberals. The result was that while the Wobblies were long on dedication and fighting spirit, they were short on durability. As at Lawrence, thousands would follow them in a moment of desperation, attracted by their concepts of di-rect action, only to become inactive in normal periods. A defeated strike, such as the one of twenty-five thousand textile workers at Paterson, New Jersey, in 1913, often wiped out a whole salient. Paterson, in fact, almost did for the IWW what the Pullman strike had done for the American Railway Union in 1894, namely, destroy it. Five workers were killed in this fracas, fifteen hundred were ar-rested. After five grueling months, with the 1913 depression exact-ing its toll in morale, the Wobblies had to concede one of their rare defeats. With this defeat the textile campaign lapsed into oblivion, and the revolutionary unionists had to turn their attention to a dozen fronts elsewhere—the Kelsey Hayes plant in Detroit, the Mesabi iron range in Minnesota, the Baltimore garment industry, the copper mines of Arizona and Butte, Montana, the lumber and harvest fields out West. It was the kind of hedgehopping that drew sensational headlines and brought many incidental victories, but only a tenuous base of operations. At its peak, therefore, the IWW never numbered more than one hundred thousand members.

By contrast, both its union rival, the AFL, and its radical rival, the Socialist Party, fared much better. In Chicago a young immi-grant, Sidney Hillman, led a dramatic strike against Hart Schaffner

& Marx in 1910, which laid the groundwork for an independent Left-wing union, the Amalgamated Clothing Workers. The International Ladies' Garment Workers Union, Socialist-dominated, called a halt to operations in the dress industry in New York at the height of the season in 1910, and forced management to yield a "protocol of peace." The AFL membership reached two million by the outbreak of World War I in 1914. Even the surprise confession in 1911 by the McNamara brothers, leaders of an AFL union, accused of dynamiting the Los Angeles *Times* building, did not appreciably slow down the AFL momentum.

As for the Socialists, Victor Berger had been elected to Congress in 1910. The removal of Big Bill Haywood from the executive committee of the Socialist Party in 1912 caused the defection of many thousands of other Left-wingers. At a private debate with Hillquit, Haywood had made the provocative statement that "a little sabotage in the right place at the proper time" was not out of order. Even Debs, normally friendly to Haywood, repudiated this position, and the 1912 convention of the party amended its constitution to provide for the expulsion of a member who "advocates crime, sabotage, or other methods of violence as a weapon of the working class. . . ." The amendment carried by about 2 to 1 vote, and as an aftermath, Right-wing members called for a referendum to sever Haywood from the leading committee. It carried again by 2 to 1 vote—23,495 to 10,944—and in its rancorous wake some sympathizers of Haywood deserted the fold. Yet Debs, running against Woodrow Wilson, William Howard Taft, and "Bull Moose" Theodore Roosevelt in 1912, garnered a record 900,000 votes, 6 percent of the total. That same year Max Hayes, leader of the Socialists in the labor movement, received a respectable 5,073 votes for the presidency of the AFL, against Gompers' 11,974. Aligned with the radical wing were such organizations as the machinists, fur workers, brewery workers, tailors, mine-mill, and sizable contingents of coal miners, carpenters, printers, and cigar makers from Gompers' own union.

The Wobblies, however, despite sensational campaigns among lumberjacks, harvest hands, and mass production workers could not break the numbers barrier. They were far more successful than De Leon's Socialist Trade and Labor Alliance or the Chicago anarchists of 1886. They offered a home for the homeless unskilled, and they lent an aura of nobility to the struggles of the underprivileged. But combined with this nobility there was also a note of tragedy surrounding them, symbolized best by the fate of such men as Frank Little and Joe Hill.

Joe Hill, poet laureate and song writer of the organization, was arrested in 1914 after leading a strike of Utah construction workers. He was accused of murdering a local grocer—an ex-policeman—and convicted. Executed in November 1915, despite the plea of President Wilson, the Swedish government, the AFL, and innumerable others, Hill's last words, "Don't mourn for me—organize!" were matched by the moving cadence of the Alfred Hayes–Earl Robinson song:

> *I dreamed I saw Joe Hill last night*
> *Alive as you and me.*
> *Says I, "But Joe, you're ten years dead."*
> *"I never died," says he.*
>
> *"Joe Hill ain't dead," he says to me.*
> *"Joe Hill ain't never died,*
> *Where workingmen are out on strike*
> *Joe Hill is at their side!"*

During the prolonged conflict between the Butte miners and the copper companies in 1917, Frank H. Little, a member of the IWW General Executive Board, was dragged out of his room by five gunmen—broken leg and all—and hanged from the trestle of a railroad. As a warning to others, the lynchers pinned the old vigilante numbers, 3-7-77, to his clothes.

Thus Big Bill Haywood's legions fought and died. When the United States entered World War I, they fought again—their last major battle.

CHAPTER XIII

IDES OF WAR AND REVOLUTION

LATE IN JUNE 1914 the Austrian Archduke Francis Ferdinand was shot to death by a Serbian student in Sarajevo, setting in motion a chain reaction of war and revolution that drastically altered both traditional and radical politics everywhere.

For the Socialist parties of Europe, World War I was a traumatic experience. In theory, they had clearly anticipated the great powers would someday go to war to redivide the world. Engels had predicted it as early as 1892. They had even sketched plans to meet the challenge. The Second International—formed in 1889 to succeed the First International—had determined at its 1907 congress at Stuttgart that should hostilities break out, they would "arouse the masses politically and hasten the overthrow of class rule." At the 1910 congress in Copenhagen, Keir Hardie of Britain and Edouard Vaillant of France introduced a resolution listing the "general strike, especially in the industries that supply war with its implements," as "among the means to be used in order to prevent and hinder war." Though a final decision on this issue was postponed, in large measure because of the misgivings of German Socialists who felt it might prevent them from gaining political power, most Socialists on both sides of the barrier fully expected that this was what their parties would do. As a matter of fact, a day after Austria declared war on Serbia, the International Socialist Bureau met in Belgium to plan *"guerre a la guerre."* It urged its members to widen and enlarge their antiwar demonstrations and work for a settlement of the as yet limited dispute by arbitration.

Socialism was by then a formidable movement in Europe. The German Social Democratic Party, for instance, commanded four and a half million votes and had 110 members in the Reichstag. Except for a few Christian and anarchist unions, the whole labor movement was safely enrolled in the Socialist cause. With such levers of power at their disposal the Socialists were expected to shut the factories, suspend railroad operations, and stop the war.

The actual course of history, however, did not proceed in this idyllic fashion. Instead of workers of the world uniting in a grand display of internationalism, the Socialist movement—except for such parties as the Italian and Russian, and certain individual leaders such as Rosa Luxemburg, Karl Liebknecht, Friedrich Adler, Ramsay MacDonald, Lenin, and Trotsky—turned chauvinist. The German Socialists who on June 25 had proclaimed that "not a drop of blood of a German soldier shall be sacrificed to the power itch of the Austrian rulers," voted war credits for the kaiser's armies on August 4. French, Belgian, and British leftists also rallied behind their respective flags. The British Labour Party argued that "the victory of Germany would mean the death of democracy"; while German Social-Democracy maintained that in Germany "much, if not everything, would be endangered by the triumph of Russian despotism." At the moment of decision the parties affiliated with the Second International could not bring themselves to place their unions, treasuries, and mass organizations in jeopardy. Extreme antimilitarists such as Gustave Hervé, Jules Guesde, or Henry Hyndman, all found a rationale to support their own government against the others. Nationalist emotions and sectarian concerns easily overpowered internationalism.

The American Socialists and Wobblies, unlike their European brothers, were not called upon to make an immediate decision, for it was almost three years before the United States became embroiled in battle. The government permitted considerable leeway, at first, for antimilitarist preachments. Other people, including the President, seemed to be speaking the same language as the radicals. A month after the European war began, Samuel Gompers proclaimed that "peace is the fundamental necessity for all governments and progress. . . ." As late as May 1916, in the fervid language that characterized his oratory, he reminded the League to Enforce Peace that "no class has more to lose and less to gain in war than the workers." President Wilson boasted "we are too proud to fight."

Yet as Senator Robert M. La Follette said in September 1915: "With the first clash in the great European War came President Wilson's solemn appeal, 'The United States must be neutral in fact as well as in name.' But when you can boom stocks 600 percent in manufacturing munitions, to the Bottomless Pit with Neutrality! What do Morgan and Schwab [head of Bethlehem Steel] care for world peace when there are big profits in world war? . . . Now we are about to engage in furnishing the Allies funds. We are underwriting the success of the cause of the Allies. We have ceased to be 'neutral in fact as well as in name.'" His fear that the United States was veering toward joining the fray was shared by many, including the five other senators and fifty congressmen who later voted against American entry.

President Wilson ran in 1916 on a platform that he had kept the country out of war, but almost before the campaign was over, it was clear that America was headed in the opposite direction. War was declared against the Central Powers in April 1917. In June, Gompers helped form the American Alliance for Labor and Democracy as a counterweight to the pacifist People's Council, and was pledging full AFL support to the war effort.

In this panorama of confusion the Socialist Party and the IWW increasingly felt the pangs of isolation. Unlike their chauvinist brothers in Europe, they steered an antiwar course both before and after the United States entered. "I am opposed to every war but one," said Eugene V. Debs early in 1915. "I am for that war with heart and soul, and that is the worldwide war for socialist revolution." In editorial after editorial he played the theme: "Never Be a Soldier." Morris Hillquit, leader of the center wing of the party, remained obdurate in his opposition, even when Socialist intellectuals like Charles Steinmetz, the electrical genius, John Spargo, novelist Jack London, William English Walling, and others became partisans of one side or the other. At the meeting of the party's executive committee in August 1914, the Socialists reaffirmed opposition "to this and all other wars." Party candidates for Congress that year ran on the slogan "Every Socialist ballot is a protest against war." By a 15 to 1 referendum vote, an amendment was tacked onto the constitution providing that any party member who held public office would be expelled if he supported military credits or war.

At an emergency convention of the Socialist Party in St. Louis one day after the United States became a belligerent, Morris Hillquit presented a resolution branding "the declaration of war by our government as a crime against the people of the United States and against the nations of the world." Of approximately 200 delegates present, 140 voted for Hillquit's statement, 31 for a similar but slightly altered one by Louis B. Boudin, and only 5 for a veiled prowar stand.

The IWW, which suffered few defections to the militarist camp, was equally if not more set in its antiwar stance. Soon after the guns began to roar in 1914, it repeated its commitment in time of war to "the general strike, in all industries." Whatever differences appeared in its ranks were over matters of strategy. A minority, including Frank Little, soon to be lynched, argued that the IWW should openly defy the draft and concentrate on antiwar propaganda. The majority held that since workers in other countries had permitted themselves to be put into uniform, the only fruitful way to undermine the war effort was to continue the class struggle for better wages and improved conditions. A Wobbly sticker, much in evidence, read: "Don't be a soldier, be a man. Join the I.W.W. and fight on the job for yourself and your class."

But adherence to principle, while it did honor to leftist determination, left the Socialist Party and the IWW highly vulnerable to government reprisal. After the *Lusitania* was torpedoed by a German submarine in May 1915, sending 124 Americans, among others, to a watery grave, prowar sentiments in the country mounted steadily. Olympian fear, generated first by the war and then by the Russian Revolution, blanketed the nation in hysteria from the summer of 1916 through the summer of 1920. Hysteria converted to hate, hate to repression, and woe betide any leftist caught in the whirlwind.

II

On July 22, 1916, twenty thousand people gathered in downtown San Francisco for a "preparedness parade." This was one of a number of parades in the larger cities called by business leaders, chambers of commerce, and patriotic societies to arouse interest in "national defense." A concomitant purpose, as one of the leading figures of the Law and Order Committee of San Francisco put it, was "to show the sons of bitches where to get off." The so and so's referred to were pacifists, radicals, and some labor leaders who were still talking about keeping the United States out of war. In particular, the questionable title applied to Thomas J. Mooney, a molder by trade, leader of the Left wing of the California Federation of Labor, and a friend of the anarchist Alexander Berkman. Only a few days before the parade, Mooney had led a strike of streetcar workers employed by the United Railways, and though the strike was unsuccessful, the utilities were sufficiently incensed to assign a private detective—as future Supreme Court Justice Felix Frankfurter concluded in an investigation for President Wilson—"to get" Mooney.

The crowd that day was thin. One hundred thousand had been expected, but the number was held down because the unions had refused to join with the antilabor employers who organized the demonstration. In midafternoon, with the governor and the mayor in the forefront, flags waving, bands playing, a detachment of the Spanish War veterans fell into line from a side street near the Embarcadero. At this moment, precisely six minutes after two, a bomb exploded near a saloon wall at Steuart near Market, leaving a shambles of bodies and limbs—six dead, forty wounded, with four more to die later.

Such a shocking deed would have evoked fury under any circumstances, but in the jingo mood of the period, it had an especially strong impact. Large rewards were offered for apprehending the criminals—already assumed by the press to be "radicals." The Law and Order Committee of the Chamber of Commerce, which had been formed by businessmen to fight a longshoremen's strike, called a mass protest meeting. Police raided offices of the anarchist sheet the *Blast*, subjecting its editor, Berkman, and some of his coworkers to long questioning. And behind the scenes, the detective—Martin Swanson—hired by the utilities "to get" Mooney, was gathering "evidence."

Within a few days the Bay City police made their haul. Included were Mooney; his wife Rena, a music teacher and a coworker of her husband in his labor activity; Warren K. Billings, a leftist member of the Boot and Shoe Workers' Union; Israel Weinberg, a leader of the Jitney Bus Drivers' Union; and Edward D. Nolan, a key figure of the machinists' union. Billings was a particularly good target because in 1913, when he was nineteen, he had been convicted of carrying dynamite during a lineman's strike. His trial came first, therefore, to be followed by that of Mooney in January 1917.

The prosecution's case rested essentially on two witnesses, both of whom were later found to have perjured themselves. An unemployed waiter, John McDonald, stated that at 1:50 P.M. on July 22 he had seen Billings deposit a suitcase near the saloon wall, after which he conferred for a few minutes with Mooney in the saloon doorway. Frank C. Oxman, a cattleman from Oregon, described how Mooney and Billings had arrived at the scene in a Ford that looked like Weinberg's jitney, along with three others, including a woman. As a good citizen, suspicious that something was amiss, he had carefully taken down the license number. It all sounded convincing until Mooney's lawyers produced a photo, taken during the parade, which showed the defendant and his wife a mile from the bombing, on the roof of the building where Mrs. Mooney had her music studio. A clock in the enlarged picture clearly read 1:58, which would have made it impossible, in that traffic, for the Mooneys to have been at Steuart and Market eight minutes earlier. But in the climate surrounding the trial, with the prosecutor denouncing Mooney as a dynamiter and a German agent, conviction was all but assured. The San Francisco labor official was sentenced to death by hanging; Billings, to life imprisonment.

Shortly after the trial Oxman's "frank" testimony was thoroughly impeached and he was tried for perjury. Instead of being at Market and Steuart, as he had claimed, it was shown incontrovertibly that he had been with friends in Woodland, California, nearly two hundred miles away. McDonald, years later, admitted he had testified falsely at the behest of the prosecutor and the detective Swanson. Investigation proved further that the foreman of the Mooney jury, William MacNevin, had been collaborating closely with an assistant district attorney, and that other witnesses too had committed perjury. The verdicts stood, however, while radicals, liberals, and the AFL—in a rare display of unity—held protest demonstrations throughout the country. Everywhere, here and abroad, millions were convinced that the two men were framed for their radical views.

Subsequent events reinforced this thesis. Rena Mooney and Weinberg were both acquitted in their trials, and Nolan released. When the prosecutor tried to indict the anarchist Alexander Berkman, as an accomplice to the murder, his effort to build an image of a grand "anarchist plot" was stymied by the governor of New York. The whole case was so clearly questionable that the governor refused to extradite Berkman, who happened to be living in New York just then. President Wilson showed his doubts by addressing an open letter to the California governor calling on him to grant a new trial, or, at worst, commute Mooney's sentence to life imprisonment. The President's commission which looked into the case stated that the evidence presented to them "would shake confidence in the justice of the conviction. . . ." The judge who presided in Mooney's trial pleaded with three successive governors to pardon the convicted men. The effect of all this was that Mooney was spared from hanging, his penalty changed to life imprisonment. But it was not until 1939 that Governor Culbert L. Olson, a New Dealer, finally released Mooney and Billings from prison.

The Mooney-Billings case was only one symptom of the national mood. The misnamed Espionage Act, passed in June 1917, was directed not so much against spies, for whose apprehension adequate legislation already existed, as against the radicals. Under its provisions the government gained the right to censor newspapers, ban from the mails those it deemed suspect, and prosecute anyone who "interfered" with the draft or enlistment of soldiers. The punishment in such cases was a maximum of twenty years in prison and a ten-thousand-dollar fine. Radicals were duly alarmed because the word "interfered" was loose enough—as events were to prove—to include anyone who made an antiwar speech. A month after the act's passage the Attorney General withdrew second-class mailing privileges from the *American Socialist* because it advertised a pamphlet which claimed that house of Morgan loans to the Allies ($1.9 billion before America's entry) were responsible for American involvement in the war. Before the war was over, almost all Socialist newspapers, similarly denied low-cost mailing rights, were forced either to mail at the much higher first-class rates or deliver their sheets by hand, house to house. It came to a point where the postmaster even refused to deliver mail addressed *to* the Milwaukee *Leader*.

Postal harassment, however, was mild compared to other repressions. Many states, bursting with patriotic fervor, enacted their own criminal-syndicalism laws, abridging the vaunted rights of free speech and assembly. Not by accident the first such bills were introduced in Idaho and Minnesota, where the IWW was engaged in extensive unionizing drives. Nor was this all. The nation was in so ugly a temper that authorities not only winked at extralegal action but often encouraged it. In June 1917, for instance, several hundred sailors from the Bremerton Yards were permitted time off by their officers to wreck the IWW headquarters in Seattle. In November, seventeen IWW members, deported out of town by the Tulsa police, were seized by a masked mob, beaten, tarred and feathered, and left half dead. Local store windows carried posters: "I.W.W. Don't let the sun set on you in Tulsa." Soldiers and sailors raided the Socialist office in Boston. Armed businessmen and mine executives corralled twelve hundred striking Wobblies in a ball park at Bisbee, Arizona, loaded them into cattle cars and sent them headlong into the desert.

Except for one minor incident—the "green corn rebellion"—the radicals engaged in no violent acts to overthrow the government. The one assault against authority occurred in Oklahoma where 450 poorly educated men belonging to two esoteric organizations called the Working Class Union and the Jones Family, decided to capture Washington. Oklahoma, with its crop of poor farmers, had been an exception for many years to the general rule that the Socialists were impotent in the rural areas. The party there was relatively strong, polling more than one third the vote in three of the most impoverished counties. Though it had nothing to do with the green corn rebellion, probably most of the poor rebels were Socialists at heart and had voted the Socialist ticket in past elections. The Working Class Union was a moderate group originating in Van Buren, Arkansas, in 1914. But since it was a loose organization, some of its branches were more extremist. The Jones Family was a native force, uniquely Oklahoman.

When the United States entered the war the angry farmers, who naïvely believed Wilson's pledge to keep out of the fray, felt betrayed. They planned to get together at a central point, win recruits, march on Washington, take over the government machinery, and thereupon declare the war terminated. Most of them had not the foggiest notion how far away Washington was or how formidable was their problem. Some had heard that other revolts were brewing and that there were 190,000 Wobblies in the city of Chicago ready to join with them. The name green corn rebellion comes from the plan of the rebels to subsist on green corn and barbecued steer. Needless to say, the revolt petered out quickly, just two days after it began on August 3, 1917—smashed by a few sheriff posses. Detachments that were assigned to blow up bridges and pipe lines were singularly inept. Most of the captured rebels were given suspended sentences; eight of the leaders, however, served long prison terms.

Apart from this one display of antiwar violence, there was no harm done. Yet the radicals of 1917–18 were in a vise, subject to terror by unlawful gangs and confronted by the obvious determination of Attorney General Thomas W. Gregory to behead the IWW, Socialists, and anarchist movements. On September 5, Department of Justice agents descended on IWW halls in fifteen cities, from Boston to Los Angeles, seizing literature and records. One hundred and sixty-two Wobblies, including Big Bill Haywood, Arturo Giovannitti, and Elizabeth Gurley Flynn, secretaries of the various industrial unions, editors, writers, and organizers, were indicted for violation of the Espionage Act. A few days later a raid was conducted against the national headquarters of the Socialist Party. "In America," wrote John Reed, "the month just passed has been the blackest month for freedom our generation has known. With a sort of hideous apathy the country has acquiesced in a regime of judicial tyranny, bureaucratic suppression and industrial barbarism which followed inevitably the first fine careless rapture of militarism."

The raids, arrests, and convictions did not stop, however, after this first attack. According to Haywood, two thousand Wobblies were rounded up in the first two months of 1918 alone, though not all were held. The four-month trial of 113 IWW defendants—before a biased Judge Kenesaw Mountain Landis, who was later to become czar of baseball—ended in the conviction of ninety-three, sentenced to terms from ninety days to twenty years and fined a total of $2.3 million. Among the convicted was Haywood, playing out his last major drama on the American scene. Two and a half years later, after his appeals were rejected and with his health failing, he jumped bail and fled to Soviet Russia. There he died in 1928, a tragic and disillusioned figure.

There were many other trials of Wobblies and many more convictions. But though the brunt of the repressions was against the IWW, the Socialists and anarchists did not escape unscathed. The two out-standing anarchists, Emma Goldman and Alexander Berkman, had formed a No-Conscription League to "resist conscription by every means in our power." They were arrested in June 1917, charged with obstructing the draft and sentenced to two years in jail, plus ten-thousand-dollar fines. In her speech to the jury Emma, using the court as a forum to explain her "propaganda of the deed" philoso-phy, said: "It is organized violence on top which creates individual violence at the bottom. It is the accumulated indignation against organized wrong, organized crime, organized injustice, which drives the political offender to his act."

Of the Socialists, Kate Richards O' Hare was given five years in jail for an antiwar speech in North Dakota during the summer of 1917. Rose Pastor Stokes received a ten-year sentence for a letter to the Kansas City *Star* in which she said: "No government which is *for* the profiteers can also be for the people, and I am for the people while the government is for the profiteers." Five members of the na-tional executive committee of the party, including Victor Berger, were sentenced to twenty years by Judge Landis. Some years later Landis said his only regret had been that he could not mete out a harsher sentence. He would have preferred, he said, "to have Berger lined up against a wall and shot." Fortunately for Berger the law was not as inhumane as Judge Landis, and the Supreme Court was judicious enough eventually to set the verdict aside. Notwithstand-ing, however, Berger, who had again been elected to Congress, was expelled by that petulant body in April 1919 by an almost unani-mous vote. A special election was called in his district for December that year, and again Berger won, only to be refused his seat still an-other time.

The repressive mood stretched out beyond the radicals even to pacifists and simple liberals. It included such organizations as the Nonpartisan League, a Populist group in the Midwest, individual antiwar professors and teachers, German farmers, and others. Mobs broke up meetings of the Friends of Irish Freedom. German-born folk were horsewhipped by enraged patriots. A twenty-year-old girl was sentenced to fifteen years for distributing leaflets against Allied intervention in Russia. Religious pacifists, according to Norman Thomas, were "forcibly clad in uniform, beaten, pricked or stabbed with bayonets, jerked about with ropes around their necks, threatened with summary execution, tortured by various forms of the 'water cure.'"

One of the high points of the government witch hunt was reached with the arrest of Eugene V. Debs on June 30, 1918. The Socialist leader had been inactive for fifteen months, watching developments from the side lines. He was immensely pleased by Morris Hillquit's impressive poll of 150,000 votes for the mayoralty of New York and by the election of ten state legislators and seven New York City aldermen. But he was equally sick at heart when the same seven aldermen came out in favor of the Liberty Loan drive, and when Socialist Congressman Meyer London said that President Wilson's objectives were the same as those of the Socialists. With the war in full swing, party stalwarts who had voted for the unequivocal St. Louis resolution in April 1917 were bending with the wind. A new faction fight between Left and Right seemed to be building up in the movement, particularly since the victory of the Russian Revolution.

In this situation Debs decided that something was needed to prop the hesitant and show his solidarity with antiwar critics being jailed. Although he was a tired man, gaunt, often ill, his eyes weak, he set out on a speaking tour deliberately designed to challenge the Espionage Act. At Canton, Ohio, while Department of Justice agents checked the draft cards of those in the audience, and a stenographer furiously recorded every word, a calm, smiling Debs, enjoying his reactivation and certain of his destiny, rose to make one of his most eloquent speeches. After paying homage to Mooney, Haywood, and other wartime prisoners, he came to the core of his remarks: "The master class has always declared the war; the subject class has always fought the battles. The master class has had all to gain and nothing to lose, while the subject class has had nothing to gain and all to lose—especially their lives." He finished with a note of evangelism: "Yes, in good time we are going to sweep into power in this nation and throughout the world. The sun of capitalism is setting; the sun of socialism is rising. . . . In due time the hour will strike and this great cause triumphant—the greatest in history—will proclaim the emancipation of the working class and the brotherhood of all mankind."

On June 30, Debs was again in jail—for the first time in twenty-three years. When released on bail, he went home to Terre Haute to deliver another two-hour speech against militarism. His activity gave the antiwar movement a much-needed hypodermic, and Debs a ten-year jail sentence.

As the court pronounced sentence on September 14, Debs delivered an oration—some of it pieced together from other speeches—which American radicals were to quote for many years: "Your Honor, years ago I recognized my kinship with all living beings, and I made up my mind that I was not one bit better than the meanest on earth. I said then, I say now, that while there is a lower class I am in it; while there is a criminal element, I am of it; while there is a soul in prison, I am not free. . . . Your Honor, I have stated in this court that I am opposed to the form of our present government; that I am opposed to the social system in which we live; that I believe in the change of both—but by perfectly peaceable and orderly means. . . . Let the people take heart and hope everywhere, for the cross is bending, the midnight is passing, and joy cometh with the morning."

Early in April 1919, although the drums of battle were already stilled, Debs entered his prison cell at Moundsville, West Virginia. While in jail, in 1920, he was nominated by the Socialist Party for the Presidency of the United States. His campaign, while prisoner Number 9653, was confined to issuing a single bulletin a week through the United Press, but he received 917,799 votes. On January 31, 1921, Attorney General A. Mitchell Palmer, though a rabid Red-baiter, recommended that the sentence of the sixty-five-year-old prisoner be commuted to expire on Lincoln's birthday. President Woodrow Wilson, on receiving the written suggestion, marked across it the single word: "Denied." It remained for his successor, the conservative Republican Warren G. Harding, to free Debs a few months later.

III

The repressions naturally had a negative effect on the radical movement, chipping away at its adherents, making it difficult to function. But there were other factors at work, both for good and ill, whose results were longer lasting. The war unleashed social forces of such extreme intensity, particularly in Europe, that it reshaped the lives of many nations and the radical movement everywhere. Too many men had died, too many people were hungry, too many economies were in ruin. The belligerent nations had suffered over thirty-seven million casualties—including more than eight million dead—at the front, and many more behind the lines. What had begun as an internecine war between capitalist states, threatened to undermine capitalism itself. The Russian Revolution in March and November 1917 was a stunning and surprising blow. It was followed by rebellions and general strikes in more than a dozen countries—Germany, Finland, Austria, Hungary, Bulgaria, and others. Even in far-off America people talked of "soviets" and "soviet republics," and strikers in at least three cities actually established what they considered to be revolutionary councils. For a long, critical moment the old order staggered—both in Europe and America. Winston Churchill expressed the anxiety of the existing establishments when he wrote Prime Minister David Lloyd George: "We may well be within measurable distance of universal collapse and anarchy throughout Europe and Asia." Though the Soviet revolution was the only one to survive, it drastically changed the world relationship of forces and gave millions of radicals elsewhere a new pole around which to rally.

Thus, despite the repressions, the end of hostilities offered the American Left an opportunity to recoup lost ground. Its ranks were enheartened by the Russian Revolution just at a time when a new militancy was beginning to grip native laborers. The immediate postwar period was typical, pronounced in its contrasts. Prices had doubled since 1913, while wages had increased by only 55 percent. On the other hand, the war had created twenty-thousand millionaires, and corporate profits were immense. The affluence just had not filtered down to the lower echelons. Average wages of blue-collar workers were twenty-one dollars a week, yet in the prevailing price-wage spiral they were hardly adequate for subsistence. After decades of struggle for an eight-hour day, 60 percent of the Carnegie Steel employees and 36 percent of those at United States Steel, worked twelve hours a day, six days a week. It was not only the leftist winds blowing in from Russia, therefore, but a homegrown malaise resulting from inequality of sacrifice, which produced a tornado of strikes and other forms of protest. For the next four years the industrial turf of the United States was torn up by pickets as never before—almost eight and a half million of them. In 1919 alone, one seventh of the working class was on strike.

Four days after the armistice, Sidney Hillman led a strike of sixty thousand clothing workers for a forty-four-hour week and a 15 percent raise. It lasted for three months, ending in a total union victory. A leftist clergyman, A. J. Muste, who had lost his church because he opposed the war, formed an independent union of textile workers and conducted still another strike at Lawrence. In Seattle, early in 1919, Socialists and Wobblies (carrying two cards, one in the AFL and another in the IWW) were involved in a general strike that resulted in the formation of a "soviet." Sixty thousand workers walked out in support of twenty-five thousand shipyard workers threatened with a wage cut. Lyrical with the notion they were emulating the Russian Revolution, the radicals among them formed a Workers, Soldiers, and Sailors Council, part of whose function was to patrol the streets and enforce order. The general strike did not last long, only four days, and the "soviet" was soon dissolved, but it indicates the line of thinking of militant unionists in 1919. "The trade union," said the *Union Record* of Seattle, "is to the American workers what the Council of Workmen and Soldiers is to Russia, Austria, and Germany. The labor council is the central soviet. . . ." Two days after the Seattle strike another "soviet" was formed in Butte, Montana, and in May still a third one in Toledo, Ohio. Proletarians of dozens of occupations, with varying degrees of radical leadership, "downed tools" in those four eventful years—harbor workers in the Port of New York; mill hands in Paterson, New Bedford, Fall River, Pawtucket; telephone operators in New England; actors, printers, even Boston policemen.

The national strike of 350,000 steelworkers in September 1919 was the largest one America had ever witnessed up to then. Led by thirty-eight-year-old William Z. Foster, who was later to become the head of the Communist Party, it was a pivotal incident both for the unions and radicalism. Like the Pullman and Homestead strikes, too, it was filled with drama and heartache. Every device that ingenuity could muster was used to smash the strike—armed deputies, beatings, arrests, killings, red-baiting, denial of free speech. At McKeesport alone, the authorities swore in three thousand men as special deputies. Along the Monongahela River, from Pittsburgh to

Clairton, barely twenty miles, twenty-five thousand deputies stood with guns at the ready to protect law and order from unarmed steel-workers. At Farrell, Pennsylvania, the constabulary killed three and wounded eleven, one of them a woman on her way to the butcher shop, in a single engagement. Gary, Indiana, near Chicago, was under martial law, patrolled by federal troops. All told, twenty men were killed, hundreds wounded.

Nor was this all. Local authorities in western Pennsylvania totally suppressed meetings and free speech, as if the country were under immediate siege. The Sherman Service, a strikebreaking detective agency, ordered its operatives in South Chicago "to stir up as much bad feeling as you possibly can between the Serbians and Italians." Ethnic differences were fanned to white heat and forty thousand Negroes were imported from the South to act as strikebreakers. Businessmen placed dozens of advertisements in local newspapers pointing out that the strike is "not between workers and employers, but between revolutionists and America." It was a "diabolical at-tempt of a few radicals to seize industry and plant Bolshevism in this country." Under such a concentrated assault the strike petered out, and was finally called off in January 1920. Most of the AFL unions which had formed the joint committee to conduct the cam-paign had contributed $100 each and then forgotten about it. The Amalgamated Clothing Workers donated $100,000 and the Ladies' Garment Workers $60,000, but all told, only $418,000 was forthcom-ing to feed hundreds of thousands of families.

Forty days after the steelworkers "hit the bricks," 400,000 miners walked out of the pits. Their chance of success was much brighter, for they had a solid union behind them with a twenty-year history as a functioning organization. But President Wilson declared the strike "unlawful" and secured an injunction to stop it. John L. Lewis, who had only recently assumed the presidency of the United Mine Workers, sent his men back to work. "We cannot fight the government," he declared.

In the ensuing years, still more strikes monotonously dotted the industrial horizon. Four hundred thousand railroad workers struck against a wage cut in July 1922. Attorney General H. M. Daugherty secured an injunction which was so far-reaching it left even the rail-road magnates breathless. The injunction outlawed meetings; pro-hibited the union from using its funds for strike purposes or picketing; and strikers from writing, speaking, telephoning, or in any way communicating with fellow workers to induce them to remain out. That same year six hundred thousand miners walked out in both the anthracite and bituminous fields, and near civil war raged in such places as Herrin, Illinois, and Mingo County, West Virginia.

The rumble of discontent in factory and mine was accompanied by a parallel disaffection in the rural communities, drawing farmers and laborers together in a new upsurge of independent politics. Back in 1915, A. C. Townley, a former Socialist, had founded the Nonpartisan League in North Dakota. It was a precursor of many such movements in the Midwest and Northwest, which culminated in 1924 with the nomination of Wisconsin Senator Robert M. La Follette for President. Working in the Republican primaries, ordinarily, the Nonpartisan League was able to elect a host of reformers and former Socialists to office. For two years the League controlled the state machinery of North Dakota, including the governorship, and its allies succeeded in placing a sizable number of men in the legislatures of Idaho, Minnesota, Montana, South Dakota, Colorado, and Nebraska. By 1918 the movement boasted 190,000 dues-paying members. Its left-of-center and prolabor tone was unmistakable. When the campaign against the Wobblies was at its height, Governor Lynn Frazier of North Dakota issued a proclamation guaranteeing the IWW right to free speech without interference. During the national coal strike of 1919 he proposed terms of settlement to the mineowners in his state, and when they turned it down, seized the mines under an emergency decree and operated them on terms favorable to the miners.

In 1918 the Nonpartisan League took a major step toward cementing relations with labor. A joint campaign in the Republican primaries with the Minnesota Federation of Labor resulted in victory for three quarters of the legislative candidates and a respectable 151,000 votes (out of 344,000) for its gubernatorial standardbearer Charles A. Lindbergh (father of the famous aviator). After the primary, the farmer-labor forces ran an independent candidate in the elections and came within 41,000 votes of success. Fifteen of its adherents were elected to the state senate and thirty-six to the lower house. Considering the wartime hysteria, the charge against the League that it was pro-German because of its antiwar stand, the suppression of meetings, and the tarring and feathering of some of its organizers, this was no mean achievement. Minnesota unionists, together with their allies, went on to organize their own political machine, pledged to work outside the two-party system.

The notion of a labor or farmer-labor party permeated a wide spectrum of rural and urban America from 1918 to 1924. In April 1919, John Fitzpatrick of the Chicago Federation of Labor, ran for mayor of Chicago on a labor party ticket and received more than 50,000 votes. Similar parties emerged in the states of Illinois, Indiana, Michigan, New York, Utah, and Pennsylvania. In November 1919, during the tragic steel strike, a thousand delegates from forty states came together in Chicago—over the stern opposition, it should be noted, of Sam Gompers—to form a national labor party. A year later the Farmer-Labor Party nominated Farley Christensen of Utah for President and Max Hayes, the well-known unionist and former Socialist, for Vice President, polling 300,000 votes.

To a greater extent than the Populist movement of a few decades back, the Farmer-Laborites were willing to dabble in socialist nostrums. "We demand," said the national program, "nationalization of railroads, mines, forests, water power, telegraphs, telephones, stock yards, grain elevators, packing plants, flour mills and of all basic industries which require large-scale production and are in reality on a non-competitive basis; these to be democratically managed." The banks, public utilities, and unused lands were similarly to pass into public hands, when and if the Farmer-Labor Party came to power. Not even Karl Marx could have asked for more. To attest to its internationalism, one of the party planks called for "a league of workers of all nations pledged and organized to enforce the destruction of autocracy, militarism, and economic imperialism throughout the world." To Left-wing Socialists, Communists, and Wobblies, the emphasis on electoral action rather than the "class struggle" was a strategical transgression, but the stated objectives of the Farmer-Laborites were not too different from those of Right-wing Socialist parties in Europe. Many of its leaders had been Socialists themselves at one time or another, and those who had not, were not unfriendly to the radical cause. Max Hayes, its president, had left the Socialist Party only because the Left wing of the party had seized his Cleveland local. Duncan McDonald, chief officer of the Illinois Federation of Labor, though he had also severed relations with the party, was still a Socialist in ideology. So was William Kohn of New

York. The key figure in the movement, the disarming and tough Irishman, John Fitzpatrick, was considered an unaffiliated radical.

IV

The postwar panorama, therefore, showed many bright spots for the radical movement. Though the strike wave ended in a setback and the AFL lost one fourth of its members, there were millions of workers in motion. It was a situation made to order for leftist proselytizing—for breaking out of wartime isolation. In John Fitzpatrick, who might have replaced Gompers as the leader of the AFL had the steel strike succeeded, the leftists had a strong ally in the labor movement. He had opposed the war, had refused to associate himself with the American Alliance for Labor and Democracy, had agitated for industrial unionism as against craft unionism, and was a radical in spirit if not in affiliation. The pyramiding farmer-labor sentiment, though it was considered reformist, nonetheless attested to widening leftist possibilities.

Most important of all, the radicals received an injection of new vigor from the Russian Revolution. From Right-wing Socialists to the irrepressible Wobblies, the Revolution was hailed with enthusiasm. Early in 1918 the Socialist Party executive issued a statement of unqualified approval: "They come with a message of proletarian revolution. We glory in their achievement and inevitable triumph." A conference of party leaders later that year stated buoyantly: "Since the French Revolution established a new high mark of political liberty in the world, there has been no other advance in democratic progress and social justice comparable to the Russian Revolution." On the first anniversary of the Revolution, Eugene Debs, waiting to go to jail, wired Lenin to salute "your great revolutionary triumph, the greatest in point of historical significance and far-reaching influence in the annals of the race." On another occasion he exclaimed: "From the crown of my head to the soles of my feet I am Bolshevik, and proud of it." Harold Lord Varney, acting secretary of the IWW, noted that "Bolshevism was but the Russian name for I.W.W." and Harrison George, another Wobbly leader, wrote the first pro-Soviet pamphlet published in the United States while sitting in Cook County jail awaiting sentence. Morris Hillquit referred to the Soviet Republic as "the vanguard of democracy and social progress. It is from top to bottom in the hands of the people, the working class, the peasants." He became legal adviser for a while for a Soviet government trade bureau in the United States. Even Right-wing Socialists heartily applauded the new experiment. Abraham Cahan, editor of the *Jewish Daily Forward,* wrote: "We have criticized them; some of their utterances often irritate us; but who can help rejoicing in their triumph? Who can help going into ecstasy over the Socialist spirit which they have enthroned in the country, which they now rule?"

For a harassed Left in America, Bolshevism was a cool rain after a long dry spell. And when it was followed by the revolt of German sailors at Kiel, and the Soviet republics in Hungary and Bavaria, it gave the impression of an inexorable tide. Mutinies took place in the French army; Italian workers, for a brief time, seized the factories in larger cities; English laborers formed a radical shop steward movement. The end of capitalism, foreseen by Marx seventy years before, was clearly at hand. Tens of thousands who had never heard the name Lenin until 1917 converted to Leninism overnight. There was hardly a radical meeting, whether Socialist, anarchist, or IWW, where the mere mention of Soviet Russia did not bring forth deafening applause. Little boys lined up to buy photos of new American heroes—Lenin, Trotsky, Liebknecht, Luxemburg.

Bolshevism, it seemed to many, would become a unifying force for a new Left, surging to state power. Eager young men in the Socialist Party were certain that their day had come. In 1917 an American Left-wing Socialist, J. C. Rovitch, ebulliently predicted that "the days are not far off when we shall have a Council of Workmen and Soldiers on the same pattern as the one in operation in Russia." The war had converted to revolution in one country; it was destined to do the same throughout the capitalist world.

CHAPTER XIV

THE LOST DECADE

THE GENERATION OF RADICALS of the post-World War I era was, like its predecessors, a blend of idealists and malcontents seeking the beautiful tomorrow. If it were dissimilar in any way, it was only because of its conviction that the revolution—at last—was close at hand. It was no longer a haze in the distance, as it had been for previous well-meaning leftists, but a delineated vision coming into immediate focus. It was already a reality in Russia; it had almost succeeded in Germany and Hungary; it could no longer be held back. The young radicals who became the core of the Communist Party were determined, therefore, to put an end to looseness and temporization. If you were going to storm the barricades, you had to have military discipline, clarity on minute details, a total unity of purpose. You could no longer leave the task of revolution to a generation of middle-aged men who tended to weaken under fire, to look for compromises and accommodations. Thus it was that temperament, as much as ideas, became a determinant of radical inner life.

Differences between Left and Right—between Debs and Berger, for instance—had caused dissension in the Socialist Party for almost two decades but had never led to actual splintering. Debs had arraigned himself against Hillquit and Berger back in 1905 over the issue of the IWW—the age-old question, that is, of dual independent unionism versus working in the AFL. In 1912 the party convention, again with Hillquit and Berger in the lead, rebuked Big Bill Haywood. He had the support of a quarter of the party, including such intellectuals as Walter Lippmann, Max Eastman, Louis B. Boudin, Rose Pastor Stokes, and state organizations in Texas, West

Virginia, Oregon, Nevada, Montana, Utah, Washington, and Tennessee, but even his removal from the national executive committee soon thereafter did not lead to a formalized break. Thousands let their membership lapse without trying to launch a new organization.

After World War I, however, disputes not only led to splits, but splits within splits. The issues were often the same as those of the past; should radicals bore from within the AFL or build dual unions; should they join with reformers and labor partyites or go it alone? But the tensions around each debate were far more demanding. The new and unknown young men who led the various Left wings insisted that followers accept a conformity in strategy and tactics. In self-defense, therefore, dissenters formed themselves into equally rigid factions, publishing their own bulletins, holding their own caucuses, and bringing themselves to the brink of permanent schism even on points of secondary consequence. What might have remained small differences magnified into mammoth ones, each one appearing less wholesome as the movement itself shrank to a shadow of what it had been at its 1912 peak.

II

The evolution of American communism from the Socialist chrysalis was the product of many forces and the handiwork of many people, but no one played a more significant role than a man whom the Communists themselves have long since forgotten, Louis C. Fraina. Communist histories, if they mention him at all, do so only in derogation, and it is doubtful if more than a handful can identify him. But he was a spark plug of the new Left by the time he was twenty-one. Fraina was born in a small town sixty miles from Naples in 1894—the year Debs was leading the Pullman strikers. His father, an impoverished Italian with republican views, emigrated to the United States two years after Luigi Carlo was born and brought his family to the slums of New York's East Side the following year. By the time Louis was six he was selling newspapers, shining shoes, helping his mother in a tobacco factory. He was a small boy, physically puny, but he was an incessant reader, with a brilliant mind. Five weeks after Fraina graduated from elementary school his father died, and though Fraina was to become a college professor at Antioch and write many books, this was the end of his formal learning. The library and then the radical movement became his university.

Fraina was a self-made convert to the revolution, lured to it after reading the works of such social critics as Jack London and Upton Sinclair. At the age of fifteen this volatile but highly talented young man joined the Socialist Party. He found it too tepid for his temperament, so he deserted it in six months for De Leon's Socialist Labor Party. Still a long way from the age of majority, he was already contributing articles to an agnostic publication and speaking to working-class audiences two or three times a week from the traditional soapbox. The De Leonists and De Leon himself were impressed. They made Fraina secretary of the New York committee, chose him to draft resolutions, appointed him organizer, and added him to the staff of the *Daily People*. For a half year in 1912, stirred by the Lawrence strike, Fraina joined the Wobblies. But neither the SLP nor the IWW could hold him. The IWW was not sufficiently political; De Leon was too much of a "Jesuit." In May 1914 the budding author and theoretician, twenty years old, joined the leftist magazine *New Review* as a member of its board of editors, business manager, and chief writer. In the articles he wrote for this magazine he berated militarism, American imperialism, liberals, and moderate Socialists with almost equal ferocity. He was the First American contributor to a Left-wing journal to denounce the Second International as a corpse and issue a call for a New International. The first International, it will be recalled, was formed on the initiative of British and French unionists in 1864 but dissolved in 1876 after the enervating dispute between Marx and Bakunin. Thirteen years later, in 1889, a Second International was constituted on an exclusively Marxian groundwork, but World War I had virtually immobilized it. Fraina was one of the first to call for its liquidation.

Oddly enough, though the Socialist Party in the United States was one of the few to take an unequivocal antiwar stand, it was steadily pelted with Left-wing criticism by Fraina, Louis Boudin, and many others. What irked the critics was not so much the party's pronunciamentos, with most of which they agreed, as the tendency to be conciliatory. Victor Berger and his Milwaukee Socialists, for instance, spoke in favor of a larger army to deter what they called the Asian threat. Former Congressman Meyer London, though he opposed the war before American entry, urged "national unity" should war be declared—which amounted to backhanded support to the war effort. Algernon Lee and six other Socialist aldermen in New York voted for the third Liberty Loan to finance military operations. By 1918 the Socialist needle trades' unions had openly endorsed American participation. The People's Council, a Socialist-dominated movement to mobilize pacifist sentiments, diluted its program simply to urge "clarification" of American war aims, rather than withdrawal from the war itself. "By the middle of 1918," writes historian Nathan Fine, "important sections of the Party were no longer seriously, if at all, opposed to the war." And even those who still were, such as the section around Hillquit, were not sufficiently forthright to suit the Left-wing tastes. A book published by Fraina in 1918, *Revolutionary Socialism*, demarcated those who favored "mass action" against the war from those who confined their activity to verbal darts and parliamentarism. The answer to war, as the critics saw it, lay in resistance to conscription, antiwar demonstrations, political strikes—militant deeds, in other words, leading to revolution, rather than passive renunciation. Neither Fraina nor his followers ever mobilized enough forces to make "mass action" meaningful, but the significance of this difference—if only theoretical— became more apparent as the conflict developed.

As has happened so often in the annals of the American Left— and America itself for that matter—overseas influences played a determining role in the emergence of the Left wing. As early as October 1914 the celebrated Dutch astronomer Anton Pannekoek, who was also a Socialist, published an article in an American journal raising the banner for a Third International. One of his associates, S. J. Rutgers, a civil engineer by profession who had lived in the Dutch East Indies, appeared in the United States in 1915 to preach the Pannekoek doctrine on the spot. Simultaneously the antiwar Socialists of Europe were reassembling what was left of the internationalists at conferences held in Zimmerwald and Kienthal during 1915 and 1916. Some of them or their emissaries made a pilgrimage to the United States and remained to play a part in the unfolding melodrama. Mme. Alexandra Kollontay made a lecture tour late in 1915 to popularize the views of her mentor, Lenin. She came again in 1916 and was on hand in 1917 when Leon Trotsky arrived for a short stay in New York. Trotsky, then thirty-eight, was already renowned as the head of the fifty-day Soviet that came to life during the ill-fated 1905 revolution in Russia. Though he was in the United States only two months, he made a deep impression on American leftists, in particular Fraina, and the rabidly independent and quick-witted editor of a German-language paper, Ludwig Lore.

Foreigners had a decisive effect, initially at least, on the formulation of strategy. A private meeting of twenty revolutionaries (five of them Russians) in Lore's Brooklyn home on January 14, 1917, turned into a debate between Trotsky and another future leader of the Soviet Republic, Nikolai Bukharin. With Fraina, Lore, Louis Boudin (a Left-wing leader who somehow avoided joining the Communist movement), and others listening raptly to the European masters, Bukharin urged an immediate split from the Socialist Party and the formation of a new one. Trotsky, who still had hopes of rehabilitating the defunct Second International, proposed that Fraina, Lore, and the others remain inside the party to consolidate their forces before considering further steps. Instead of severing ties, it was preferable to publish an independent organ and seek converts from within. This was indeed the policy adopted and pursued in the next couple of years. Not long afterward Fraina became editor of the *New International,* a four-page newspaper, and Fraina, Boudin, and Lore jointly edited the *Class Struggle,* a theoretical bimonthly. Only twenty-three, Fraina was now pivot man for the new Left's propaganda.

Ironically, had not the overthrow of the czar occurred, Trotsky might have become one of the leaders, if not *the* leader, of American communism. It was customary for exiled revolutionists those days to work wherever their emigrations took them. Trotsky, in addition to writing for a Russian newspaper printed in New York, worked closely with Fraina in the factional struggle within the Socialist Party. In March 1917, not long before America entered the war, Trotsky and Fraina submitted a minority report to a Manhattan membership meeting which, though antiwar like the majority report, was much sharper and more specific. Since Trotsky could not speak English, Fraina, who had rejoined the party only shortly before, made the speech on both of their behalfs. It received 79 votes to the majority's 101—an impressive showing, considering that the Bolshevik Revolution, which gave the Left its main impetus, was still a half year off.

The foreign flavor to the Left wing was perhaps unavoidable. The influx of thirteen million immigrants to the United States from 1900 to 1914 had the auxiliary effect of altering the composition of the Socialist Party. Old radicals from Italy, Latvia, Russia, and elsewhere, flocked to the movement in America to continue their labors on behalf of the revolution. In 1908 when the party had 40,000 members, 71 percent were American born. But as thousands of new arrivals joined it in ensuing years, the demand grew to establish semiautonomous "language federations." By 1912 there were fourteen such federations—Lettish (Latvian), Finnish, Russian, Italian, Jewish, Scandinavian, and so on—each conducting its affairs in its own language, under its own leadership. Their membership then comprised only 16,000 of the 118,000 in the party, but they kept increasing in numbers and weight so that by 1915 the non-English-speaking groups already totaled one third and by 1919 more than half the party ranks. At one rally in 1917 the audience was treated to a remarkable display of multilinguism when speakers addressed them in seven different languages.

A veneer of native born and Americanized men became leaders of the Left wing. There was Charles Emil Ruthenberg of Cleveland, thirty-eight at the time of the schism with the Socialist Party, whose father was a devout Lutheran, and who once himself considered becoming a minister. Ruthenberg, tall and bald, had a moderately good education behind him, with two years at a business college, and had been employed in white-collar capacities for a book company and then a roofing firm. Joining the Socialist Party in 1909, he became its leading figure in Ohio and a constant candidate for office—state treasurer, mayor, governor, United States senator. Though Fraina's influence was meteoric, and perhaps more important in the first year or two, Ruthenberg's was sustained until his death in March 1927. There was also John Reed, the journalist whose chronicle of the Soviet revolution, *Ten Days That Shook the World*, did more to stir pro-Soviet sentiments than any other document. There was William Bross Lloyd, the millionaire Socialist, who chaired the Left-wing conference in 1919. There was Jay Lovestone, just twenty-one, who came from Russia as a child and graduated from City College in New York, where he was a student leader before becoming a prominent Communist official. There was Benjamin Gitlow, son of Russian-Jewish immigrants, who headed the Retail

Clerks' Union in New York when he was only eighteen and was one of the ten Socialists elected assemblymen in 1917. There were Bertram D. Wolfe, William W. Weinstone, and, of course, Fraina, among others.

But despite such men it was the language federations—in particular the Lettish and later the Russian—which became the bulwark of the new Left. The feelings of national kinship with those suffering and fighting in the Old World stirred them more directly. The Lettish federation, for instance, had been formed originally, at the turn of the century, as an American branch of a Lettish Socialist Party in Europe. The latter, in turn, was in close contact with Lenin. Thus it was no accident that the Letts in the United States as early as 1915 introduced resolutions for a Third International as well as planks to forbid Socialists from joining the armed services. When their motions were defeated by the Massachusetts conference at which they were put forth, the Letts formed the Socialist Propaganda League to mobilize Left-wing sentiment throughout the party, including its English-speaking sections. It was they who underwrote much of Fraina's work.

Whatever its indigenous roots, therefore, the Left wing was an echo to developments abroad. How it would have fared if the Russian Revolution had not taken place is open to speculation. The little newspaper published by Fraina never sold more than a thousand copies. But the revolution in far-off Petrograd kindled the fire into a roaring blaze. Fraina and Rutgers, speaking on behalf of the Socialist Propaganda League, offered to send five hundred Red Guards to fight with Bolshevism against the counterrevolutionaries. The Russian Federation of the Socialist Party, proud as a peacock and living in reflected glory, grew from 792 members to 3,985 in a single year. Boston dissenters, previously in a minority, seized control of the city committee of the party and commissioned the peripatetic Fraina to edit their triweekly *Revolutionary Age.* Chicago leftists, strongly Slavic in composition, formed themselves into the Communist Propaganda League. Early in 1919, the radical faction in New York united under the imposing name, the Left Wing Section of the Greater New York Locals of the Socialist Party, adopted a manifesto and program, and began publishing its own newspaper, the *New York Communist,* with John Reed as editor. The manifesto, dealing with the immediate tasks ahead, called upon the American people to organize Workmen's Councils as the instrument for the seizure of political power. It urged workers' control of industry, repudiation of all national debts (with provisions, however, to safeguard small investors), expropriation of banks, railroads, and large organizations of capital, and socialization of foreign trade. The new group set up an executive committee which, with the exception of Gitlow and one or two others, was entirely unknown in the Socialist movement. Yet it rapidly became the organizing center for the loose-knit Communist faction.

The use of the word "Communist" both in New York and Chicago indicated how far the leftists had moved in three years. The Communist wing by now had its own membership cards, dues structure, and political platforms. It was a party within a party. In point of fact, by the spring of 1919, it was *the* party, for an overwhelming number of branches—Cleveland, Toledo, Detroit, Boston, Philadelphia, Brooklyn, Bronx, Queens, San Francisco, and elsewhere—as well as for seven language federations that endorsed its program. A referendum to affiliate with Lenin's Third International carried by 10 to 1. In the elections for the National Executive Committee, old guard members like Hillquit and Berger fell like tenpins as the Left wing swept twelve out of fifteen seats. Louis Fraina turned out to be the most popular man on the ballot, followed by Charles Ruthenberg. In the vote for four international delegates, Hillquit ran a poor fifth, behind four members of the opposing faction—Fraina, John Reed, Ruthenberg, and Kate Richards O'Hare.

By any equitable standard the Communists were entitled to the leadership of the Socialist Party. Though one may quarrel with the way they themselves handled political opponents in the future, there is no question that in this instance they were the victims of flagrant measures. The old guard, in control of party machinery, simply shouted "fraud"—because only a minority had voted—and refused, by a vote of 8 to 2, to certify the results.

Overlooked in the Right-wing argument, of course, was the fact only a minority had participated in the previous election as well. But Hillquit, back from a bout with tuberculosis, was more determined to split the party than his Left-wing opponents, who in any case predominated with the rank and file. "Better a hundred times to have two numerically small socialist organizations . . . ," said Hillquit, "than to have one big party torn by dissensions and squabbles, an impotent colossus on feet of clay." In a highly bureaucratic manner the Right wing followed this advice of Hillquit's by throwing the majority out of its ranks. First to be expelled was the Michigan organization with 6,000 members, to be followed by suspension of seven language federations with a membership of more than 20,000. Like military generals in a Latin-American *coup d'état* the Right wing cast adrift two thirds of the party, while claiming it represented a "majority." Within six months the Socialist Party had declined from 110,000 members to less than 40,000, and by 1921 it was down to 13,000—barely more than its strength in 1901. Debs, it is true, polled almost a million votes as the Socialist candidate for President—while in jail in 1920—but this was more a barometer of Debs's personal popularity while in jail than of the Socialist Party.

Political differences which many people found difficult to follow thus sundered the Socialist Party beyond repair. Hillquit, in a book *From Marx to Lenin*, published after the break with the Communists, continued to defend the "dictatorship of the proletariat," and another Right-winger, August Claessens, stated that "there is little real difference between the Socialist Party and the Communists." The party voted to apply for membership in Lenin's Communist International, an application which, ironically enough, was rejected by Soviet leader Zinoviev on the ground that the Socialist Party was "an auxiliary organization of the American bourgeoisie."

Yet the differences were there, and would appear sharply with time. At root, the moderate faction endorsed the statement made by Karl Marx in 1872, that in England, the United States, and probably Holland, "the worker may obtain his object by peaceful means." The Communists, on the other hand, were convinced that, as in Russia, capitalism would never yield power without violence. The two factions differed over the role of the political party, with the Socialists opting for a decentralized movement, permitting a considerable degree of autonomy, and the Communists for a centralized organization, since the final assault against capitalism required coordination and discipline. They differed both in tactics and tone. The Socialists placed emphasis on voluntary cooperative organizations and proposed the retention of private ownership in some of the small industries; the Communists favored the seizure of a much wider sector of the economy. The Socialists were willing in many instances to indemnify previous owners; the Communists were bent on expropriation. There were other points of discord over civil liberties, elections, unionism. Only some of these, however, were immediately apparent; they became manifest only after the split, not before it. Meanwhile the magnetism of the Russian Revolution played its magic. The Left wing surged predominant over the Socialist cadres, the Right wing—despite Hillquit's desperate attempt to save it— never fully recovered.

III

As they moved to consolidate their ranks in the spring and summer of 1919, opportunity beckoned coyly to the supercharged Communists. They numbered, on paper, at least seventy thousand adherents, which considering the internecine strife was a good beginning. If they had no renowned figure to present to the public as their leader, they had some hope of winning Eugene Debs to their cause. Debs, still in prison, had many friends among the Communists and found much of their platform—particularly the endorsement of industrial unionism and the class struggle—highly attractive. He kept repeating: "I heartily support the Russian Revolution without reservation." And he was most critical of the way Socialists were treating the Communists. "I was sorry to read a speech of Berger's the other day," he told a Socialist committee, "attacking the Communists. . . . They are as honest as we are." Another potential recruit, soon to achieve national stature as a result of the steel strike, was William Z. Foster. IWW leaders, like James P. Cannon, were enrolling rapidly. The mood of exuberant expectation is attested to by a leaflet distributed by Communists to striking trolley car workers in 1920: "Get ready for armed revolution to overthrow the Capitalist Government and create a Workers Government—as your brothers did in Russia. Stop asking merely for a little more wages."

Beneath the surface, however, forces were at work that whittled away Communist prospects. It had to contend with its own inner factionalism as well as the government's decision to repress it—both of considerable importance. But above all there was the fact that European capitalism, aided to an extent by America, was able to save itself—the revolutionary momentum that began with the Russian Revolution came to an abrupt stop. Nothing explains the saga of communism in America so poignantly as the circumstance that it was born in expectation of revolutionary upsurge—with strategies and tactics to match—while it survived in an era of decline, so that its strategies and tactics often seemed totally unreal.

The first nationwide conference of Communists was held in New York late in June 1919, with ninety-four delegates from twenty states in attendance. Fraina made the opening address as acting chairman. For three days these men and women, who agreed in fundamentals, discussed and debated but failed to find a common base for living together. The language federations—in particular the Russian—and the Michigan branch proposed cutting umbilical ties with the Socialists immediately and the launching of a Communist Party. Most of the English-speaking Communists, led by John Reed and Benjamin Gitlow, proposed "capturing of the Socialist Party for revolutionary Socialism." One group, impatient for independence, wanted to work outside their former party; the other, eager to assemble as many of the old comrades as possible, wanted to convert the Socialist Party to the purposes of communism. When the let's-split-now group failed to have its way, it angrily stalked out of the meeting, leaving the field to the let's-stay-in forces. A month later this group, too, sundered, a majority reversing itself and deciding to "split now." The remnant determined to go ahead with the original plans to "take over" the Socialist Party.

The rest of the tale reads like an old Mack Sennett comedy, with men running in and out of doors and being pelted with pies. In late August and early September 1919 three radical groups mobilized in Chicago. The Right wing—Hillquit, Berger, and others—held what it called an official Socialist Party convention. The followers of Reed and Gitlow, after being refused admittance to this convention, established the Communist Labor Party. A motion that it unite with the other Communist group was defeated 37 to 31. A day later at the headquarters of the Russian Federation on Blue Island Avenue —nicknamed "Smolny" in honor of the Bolshevik headquarters in Petrograd during the Revolution—the Communist Party of America was formed. It was an exciting meeting, as police invaded the hall to arrest the chairman, Dennis E. Batt, for a "subversive" speech he had made three days before, and tore down the banners and decorations. Yet there was great enthusiasm when Fraina announced that "we now end, once and for all, all factional disputes." A short time later, a motion to send a committee to confer with the Communist Labor Party was defeated 75 to 31.

When the splits and splitlets were over, there were three separate parties where there should logically have been one. The Michigan group veered toward a course of its own. Led by Batt, once a machinist, and John Keracher, a storekeeper, the Michigan people had a distinctly different evolution and a distinctly different outlook. Their views had been shaped more by the small and extreme Socialist Party of Great Britain than by the Communist movement in Russia. Labor power, they pointed out, was a commodity like other commodities. And since wages were only the price for this commodity, they looked on the trade-union struggle for higher pay as merely another facet of capitalism. It was part of the purchase and sale of wares, not a step toward revolution. The radical party, they concluded, ought to concentrate on propaganda and politics, rather than unionism and so-called "mass action." They were also convinced—correctly, as it proved—that American capitalism had come out of World War I stronger than it went in, and that it was capable of sustaining itself for a long period. If the Michigan group converged with the other Communists momentarily it was because of a common antipathy to fighting for "immediate demands," more than other factors. Inevitably then, they went their separate way as a small sect called the Proletarian Party. It survived for decades, but it had virtually no influence either with other leftists or workers generally.

The other two hostile children of Marxism were more substantial. According to estimates made by the Communist Labor Party and the Communist Party of each other, it appeared that the former had between ten and thirty thousand members, the latter between twenty-seven and fifty-eight thousand. More likely, the two together numbered forty thousand, with three quarters from East European language federations, and only one tenth English speaking.

What kept the two parties from uniting? It certainly was not ideology. While the Communist Labor Party program was simpler and couched in American idiom, both agreed on basic points— opposition to united fronts with Socialists, labor partyites, and the Nonpartisan League; espousal of dual unionism and praise for the IWW; hostility to immediate reform programs. Both were irrevoca-

"One big union, one big strike." The most revolutionary force during the Progressive Era and World War I was the Industrial Workers of the World—or "Wobblies"—led by 225-pound "Big Bill" Haywood. Haywood, who fought with his fists as well as his words, knew how to win public support for many IWW actions. His most successful strike was the Lawrence, Massachusetts, textile strike of 1912.

Seidman Photo Service

SOCIALIST PARTY
FOR PRESIDENT

EUGENE VICTOR DEBS

Eugene V. Debs, five times Socialist candidate for President, began his career as a railroad worker in Terre Haute, Indiana. Sentenced for violating the Espionage Act in 1917, he polled nearly a million votes in the 1920 election while campaigning from this jail cell.

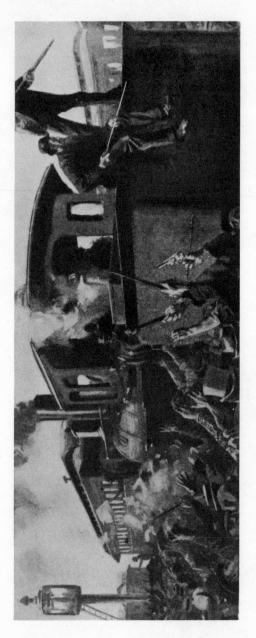

In the Pullman strike of 1894, the American Railway Union was opposed, not only by the well-organized railroad managers, but also by the United States government. The government declared the strike illegal, secured a sweeping court injunction, then deputized officials to fight the union. Above, deputies try to move a train on the Chicago, Rock Island, and Pacific Railroad on July 2, 1894.

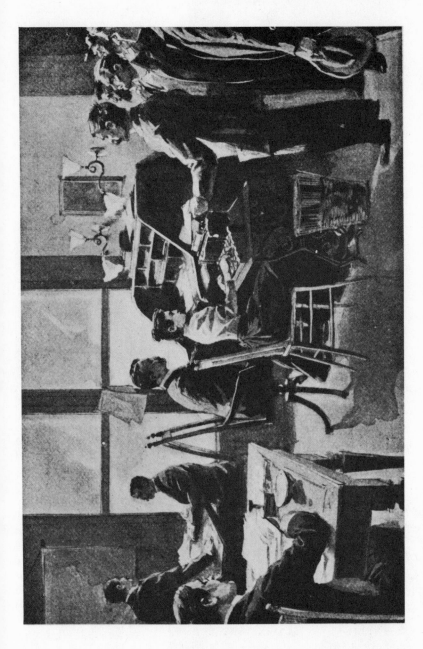

America's most revolutionary strike, the Pullman strike of 1894, was directed from these headquarters on Ashland Avenue, Chicago. But opposition was too great for the ARU to succeed. On August 2, in what amounted to organizational suicide, Debs officially declared the strike over. While his union was suffering defeat, Debs was sentenced to six months in jail for contempt of court.

In 1916 the IWW and the Socialist Party openly opposed entering the war. When a bomb exploded during a Preparedness Day Parade in San Francisco, officials quickly rounded up radical labor leader Tom Mooney. In the trial that followed he was sentenced to death, a sentence later commuted, after world-wide pressures, to life imprisonment. Though innocent, he was not freed until 1939. He is shown here with his wife, Rena.

The Russian Revolution brought radicals a new hope and a new hero—Nikolai Lenin. American Socialists issued a statement of approval, and party leaders wired their congratulations. Many felt that the Revolution was destined to spread to all capitalist countries.

Although they were tried for murder, anarchists Nicola Sacco (right) and Bartolomeo Vanzetti (left) were convicted for their politics. Demonstrators throughout the world protested their execution in 1927. In Boston a quarter of a million people marched silently. The police in Paris fought off an angry crowd before the U.S. embassy.

Socialist leader Eugene Debs identified with and had strong ties with the trade unions. His successor as the image of socialism was Norman Thomas, a minister who appealed to intellectuals and focused on civil liberties. Here Thomas is campaigning for the Presidency in 1928—the first of six elections he ran in.

Leaders of the "Red Decade." Earl R. Browder (right), Communist Party candidate for President, takes time out from the 1940 campaign to confer with William Z. Foster, national party chairman.

Pacifist A. J. Muste preaches nonviolence and civil disobedience in the tradition of Gandhi and Thoreau. His teachings have had major influence on the civil rights, student, and peace movements, which tended to mushroom in the mid-1960's.

Martin Luther King, director of the Southern Christian Leadership Conference, leads nonviolent protests by American Negroes. For his activities he has paid fines, gone to jail, and his home has been bombed. But he cautions his followers to go along the nonviolent path: "Don't go get your weapons," he tells them. "He who lives by the sword will perish by the sword."

Seidman Photo Service

In the largest civil rights demonstration in American history, 150,000 people marched on the nation's capital in the summer of 1963. Above, the crowd gathers in front of the Washington Monument. Below, marchers' placards reveal some of their demands.

The San Francisco - to - Moscow Walk for Peace, 1961. Along the route, demonstrators handed out leaflets, made speeches, and appeared on radio and television. In Moscow, they exchanged views with Soviet students. Here they are shown entering Chicago (above) and Moscow (below).

bly committed to the Third International and the Soviet form of government. Even in structure there was little to choose, since both pledged to continue the language federations. But microscopic and personal items, and above all the question of leadership, kept the warring elements divided.

Even the new wave of government raids that followed a few months later failed to sew together the dismembered parts. Whether it was Communist weakness which made the Communist parties (and the Wobblies) so vulnerable to this second repression, or whether exaggerated fears of Bolshevism caused the Wilson administration to lose all perspective, is not certain. Probably both factors figured in the decision. Some of the statements by government officials were certainly out of focus. Attorney General A. Mitchell Palmer wrote, for instance, that "like a prairie fire the blaze of revolution was sweeping over every American institution of law and order." Prior to May Day 1920, he predicted hundreds of thousands of American Bolsheviks would try to overthrow the government and plant the red flag on Capitol Hill. Though the day passed without incident—not even a bloody nose—the dire predictions of Palmer and others did not cease. The radicals must have prayed their legions would equal what Palmer thought they were.

On November 7, 1919, with the Communists holding meetings to commemorate the second anniversary of the Russian Revolution, Department of Justice agents, aided by local police, raided leftist headquarters in more than a dozen cities. Almost two thousand men fell into the dragnet in New York alone. Two months later, on January 2, 1920, simultaneous assaults were made against the Communists and IWW in thirty-three cities. Seldom has America witnessed such police state methods. Five hundred men and women were arrested in Boston, shackled and driven through the streets. Some 556 aliens with radical background were unceremoniously deported, the peak being reached when 249 Russians, including Alexander Berkman and Emma Goldman, were placed aboard the ship *Buford,* bound for Finland and the Soviet Union. In the next two years so many radicals were indicted and convicted that neither the Communists nor Wobblies could function with anything resembling normalcy. In Chicago twenty Communists received sentences of one to five years. In New York, Gitlow, Ruthenberg, and three others were given terms of five to ten years. In California there were 264 convictions. Though the vast majority never served their terms, winning reversal in the upper courts or being pardoned by liberal governors, such as Alfred E. Smith of New York, the arrests and trials wreaked havoc on the Left. Two labor historians, Selig Perlman and Philip Taft, attribute the decline of the IWW not so much to defections to Bolshevism as to "the systematic removal of its leadership by imprisonment." As for the Communists, they now became "underground" organizations to preserve themselves from police attack. In the process they isolated themselves further, and lost a large share of the members they had taken out of the Socialist Party.

But of greater significance than either the factionalism or the repressions was the ebbing of the revolutionary tide in Europe. The two leftist heroes of Germany, Rosa Luxemburg and Karl Liebknecht, were assassinated in 1919, and though the Germans tried on three or four occasions between 1919 and 1924 to emulate the Soviet Revolution, none succeeded. The Soviet Republic in Hungary, guided by Bela Kun, collapsed, as did the one in Bavaria. Strikes and uprisings in Austria, Finland, and Bulgaria failed to mature into proletarian revolutions. Capitalism stabilized itself in Italy, as Mussolini's Black Shirts took the reins, and in France, Britain, and the Low Countries as the economic machinery began to grind forward. Instead of a shift to the left, much of Europe drifted to the right. The same tendency was evident in the United States, as one major strike after another went down to defeat, and the Republican businessman's regime of Warren G. Harding replaced what Wilson had called the New Freedom. The lustrous hopes of 1918–19 spent themselves, leaving a pall of uncertainty where there was ebullient assurance shortly before.

IV

The first decade of American communism was in a real sense a lost decade—lost not only for radicals but for labor and even liberal segments of society. It began with the short depression of 1921–22, in which five million men lost their jobs, and wages fell by 20 or 25 percent. But, unlike other depression periods, there were no great unemployed demonstrations, and no radical upsurge. The boom that followed the downturn was a lavish one. The number of automobiles on the highways rose from seven million to twenty-four million. A new gadget called radio had fourteen times as many buyers in 1929 as 1922. Washing machines, electric irons, vacuum cleaners, bathtubs invaded middle-class homes by the millions. In a single year, 1925, income from rent, dividends, and interest went up by one third, from $6 billion to $8 billion. Productivity of labor rose by 25 percent and purchasing power of wages by 2 percent annually. Yet, against all previous experience for such booms, the union movement not only did not flourish, but declined. AFL rolls fell by 1,052,000 for the years 1920–23, and another 100,000 in the remaining years of the decade. Whether the loss was due to the AFL's own ineptness, the weakness of the radicals, or the self-confident offensive of management—or all three together—is not entirely clear. All that is known is that contrary to normal experience, there is a labor upsurge in periods of prosperity, there was none this time.

The hated capitalist not only showed no fear of impending doom, but optimism and self-assurance. Judge Gary, whose achievements included the smashing of the 1919 steel strike, told the United States Steel stockholders in 1921 that while labor unions "may have been justified in the long past, for I think the workmen were not always treated justly . . . there is, at present, in the opinion of the large majority of both employers and employees, no necessity for labor unions." This was the façade for a grand offensive. More than five hundred employer organizations embarked on an "open-shop" campaign. One of them, the American Employers' Open-Shop Association, bandied no words: "Should you be threatened with a labor controversy or strike, you can immediately get in touch with us and we will handle it for you. Should you want an undercover man on the inside among your employees, we will also furnish you such a man, and you will receive daily reports on what is going on. In the event of trouble, we will replace any man that may strike against you." The signs of ebb tide were everywhere—in defeated strikes, a rash of company unions, the open-shop campaign, and the legal assault against radicals.

Symptomatic of the times was the Sacco-Vanzetti case which made headlines for most of the decade. Nicola Sacco and Bartolomeo Vanzetti were two Italian immigrants, one a shoe cutter and the other a fish peddler, who lived in the Boston area. Vanzetti had become a fish peddler because he was blacklisted after leading a successful strike of four thousand rope and twine workers. Both men were avowed anarchists and revolutionary agitators. During the Palmer raids in early 1920, one of their friends, a printer named Andrea Salsedo, was arrested in New York, held secretly by the Department of Justice for eight weeks, and either jumped or was pushed out of a fourteenth-floor office to his death. When they heard of it, Vanzetti and Sacco decided to hold a protest meeting in Brockton on May 9. On May 5, however, while distributing circulars announcing the event, they were arrested. The protest meeting was never held. On the day of their arrest the two anarchists were questioned about their radical activities, but on the following day they were accused of murdering a paymaster and a guard during a fifteen-thousand-dollar payroll robbery at South Braintree, Massachusetts, three weeks before. Vanzetti was also charged with an unsuccessful holdup attempt at Bridgewater the previous year.

From the beginning it was obvious that what the men were really in the dock for was their anarchism. Judge Webster Thayer, in instructing the jury during the Bridgewater case, said of Vanzetti: "This man, although he may not have actually committed the crime attributed to him is nevertheless morally culpable, because he is the enemy of our existing institutions." A year and a month after their arrest, the two "Reds" came before the same judge on the murder charge. It was a laborious seven weeks' trial. The prosecution paraded a number of witnesses who said they had seen Sacco and Vanzetti at the scene. But their testimony was crude and confused. One claimed he saw Vanzetti arriving at Braintree the morning of the murder; another, that it was the night before. One placed Vanzetti in the driver's seat of the bandits' car; another put him beside the driver; and a third, in the back seat. On the other hand, nine witnesses swore they had spoken to Sacco in Boston the afternoon of the murder; the clerk of the Italian consulate said that Sacco had been in his office applying for a passport to go to Italy. Six people testified to having spoken with Vanzetti in Plymouth, thirty-five miles from Braintree. But it was to no avail. The judge said of the accused that they were either "conscious of guilt as murderers or as slackers and radicals"—a reference to their views on the late war. He urged the jury to think of "the American soldier boy . . . giving up his life on the battlefield of France." The jury responded by bringing in a verdict of guilty and the men were sentenced to death. "By systematic exploitation of the defendants' alien blood, their imperfect knowledge of English, their unpopular social views and their opposition to the war," wrote Felix Frankfurter, future Supreme Court Justice, "the district attorney invoked against them a riot of political passion and patriotic sentiment; and the trial judge connived at—one had almost written cooperated in—the process." The head of the Department of Justice office in Boston and a special Department agent eventually submitted sworn affidavits that the government knew Sacco and Vanzetti were innocent but prosecuted them exclusively for their political beliefs. Nothing, however, swayed either Judge Thayer or the appellate courts. The decisions were upheld.

For the next six years the Sacco-Vanzetti conviction became a *cause célèbre* throughout the world. Demonstrations and strikes took place in such far-away places as Warsaw, Melbourne, Cairo, Havana, Belgrade, Moscow, Buenos Aires, and many cities of the United States. Hundreds were arrested. Isadora Duncan, the renowned dancer, threatened to dance naked in front of the American embassy in Paris to protest the conviction. When the men were executed in August 1927 a quarter of a million people marched in silent anger in Boston alone and in Paris 150,000 walked before the United States embassy and fought the police.

The final words of the two anarchists had the martyr's ring: "Only two of us will die—our ideal, you, our comrades will live by millions. We have won. We are not vanquished. Just treasure our sufferings, our sorrows, our mistakes, our defeat, our passion, for future battles for the great emancipation. We embrace you all and bid you our extreme good-bye. Now and ever, long life to you all. Long live liberty." Vanzetti's last letter, in halting English, was to become required reading in many colleges: "If it had not been for these things, I might have live out my life talking at street corners to scorning men. I might have die, unmarked, unknown, a failure. This is our career and our triumph. Never in our full life could we hope to do such work for tolerance, for joostice, for man's onderstanding of man as now we do by accident. Our words—our lives—our pains—nothing! The taking of our lives—lives of a good shoemaker and a poor fish-peddler—all! That last moment belongs to us—that agony is our triumph."

V

The Sacco-Vanzetti case was a symbol of the frustration shared by the forces left of center. The Communists went through the decade shifting from one strategical approach to another, grappling with impotence, and emerging in the end with a force much depleted from what it had been at birth.

First item on the agenda, in view of the splintered ranks, was unity. Excluding the Michigan group, there were two separate and quarreling Communist parties, and for one month in 1920 there was a split in one of them, making three. There was also in 1920-21 a newly formed Left wing within the Socialist Party, led by J. Louis Engdahl. This, too, had to be assimilated into a united Communist Party. How it was done and under whose guiding hand is too complicated for this narrative. However, under the prodding of the Communist International, the groups united, divided, reunited in bewildering fashion, becoming a single movement finally only in the fall of 1922.

The achievement of this unity was complicated by the fact that the movement had been driven underground by the government raids. Fearful of legal decapitation, the two parties became conspiratorial organizations with appropriate passwords, codes, pseudonyms, secret meeting places, military discipline, and similar paraphernalia. At one time in 1922 there were four parties, two underground ones, and two "open" parties serving the illegal ones as subordinate appendages. It was a romantic reaction to the repressions, but whether it was necessary is open to question. Engdahl, who thought it was not, criticized his fellow Communists because they "thought and acted as if the Russian Revolution had been bodily transplanted upon American soil." The Bolsheviks, harassed by the czar, had been forced to fashion an illegal apparatus; the American Bolsheviks, harassed by A. Mitchell Palmer, must go through a similar phase. Self-imposed illegality cost the movement many participants who were not ready to risk so much, and made it difficult to conduct serious activity. Nonetheless a majority of the Communist forces, nicknamed the "Geese," insisted underground existence was sound in principle. The "Liquidators," the minority led by Charles Ruthenberg, Jay Lovestone, and James P. Cannon, looked at the issue the other way around. Though they paid obeisance to the need for an underground party, in reality they were sick of the whole business and wanted nothing more but to return to normal—legal—political life. As the postwar hysteria abated, the Liquidators overtook the Geese, and with a representative of the Comintern—Professor H. Valetski—acting as conciliator, umpire, and final authority, the factions were welded together in the fall of 1922 and formally brought above ground early in 1923.

Professor Valetski, a mathematician, was a Pole by birth who looked like an aristocrat but had a long history of factional warfare in the revolutionary movement in Poland. His hooked nose, disheveled mop of hair, and untidy beard belied a certain charm which made most of the Communist leaders like and respect him. In the final analysis, however, it was the authority of the Communist International—formed by Lenin in 1919 as a highly centralized world body of Communist parties—which made his efforts fruitful. He arrived in the United States in July 1922, with two assistants, and was almost immediately made part of the key committees planning the agenda and drafting the documents for the unity convention. Wielding his mandate deftly he was able, by the time proceedings were to begin, to bring the contending forces together.

This final conspiratorial meeting was in itself an ironic climax, for though it yielded to the Liquidators, it seemed to confirm the thesis of the Geese. It was held in Bridgman, Michigan, a village fifteen miles from St. Joseph. To elude detection, delegates were not told their final destination, but were given instructions in various cities en route as to their next port of call. All kinds of measures were taken to make sure that no one was followed. The only trouble with these elaborate precautions was that there was a Department of Justice agent at the convention itself. A man named Francis A. Morrow had insinuated himself into the Communist Party of America as a section organizer from Camden, New Jersey, and had been duly elected a delegate. Just before he took the train to St. Joseph, in the final lap of his journey, he sent off a letter to the federal authorities, giving his destination.

What followed was cops-and-robbers melodrama. After the convention had been in session for a few days, two sleuths arrived from the Department of Justice, but after reconnoitering the woods at Bridgman were unable to find their quarry. Next morning they were on the prowl again. This time they had better luck, but unbeknown to them they had been sighted by William Z. Foster, who sounded the alarm. Before the Justice agents could mobilize their raiding crew on August 22, 1922, all but seventeen of the conventioners had fled, and the others, too, would have been gone had the raid been held off another hour. The roundup netted only a small number of prisoners, and two barrels of documents, including a roster of the delegates. Called to abandon underground activity, the convention tended to prove it was still necessary. Subsequently forty of the participants were picked up in other cities, but only two, Foster and Ruthenberg, were prosecuted. Foster was freed after a three-week trial in which the jury was hung, 6 to 6. Ruthenberg, less fortunate —he had only recently been released from prison—received a three-to-ten-year term. He died during the long period of appeal. The other indictments were dropped; the last one twelve years later. Nonetheless the Bridgman gathering achieved its purpose, the unification of the Communist movement as a legal, aboveground, organization.

In relating to the outside world the Communists found difficulties as imposing as their inner travail. Simultaneous with the problems of unity and disunity, legality and illegality, they had to define an attitude to unions and reform movements such as the farmer-labor parties. The original stand of the two Communist parties formed in 1919 was unequivocally in favor of building dual unions opposed to and separate from the AFL—if the revolution were so close, communism needed its own unions. They differed only as to what kind of dual unionism. John Reed's and Ben Gitlow's Communist Labor Party endorsed the IWW as the union which communism should adopt as its own. Fraina's Communist Party, while it dismissed the AFL out of hand, envisioned a wider spectrum, which included the IWW, as well as other independent unions and those ready to secede from the AFL.

In earlier times the decision of the American parties on such an issue would have needed no further approval. The Socialist Party was an autonomous party within the Second International which had the right to determine its own behavior patterns. But the Communists, recoiling from what they considered the fatal looseness and decentralization of the Second International, thought of themselves as a revolutionary "army." Zinoviev, leader of the Comintern

(Communist International), put the matter succinctly: "In this epoch, the international proletariat must absolutely build a General Staff . . . to centralize the struggle of the proletariat of all countries." Originally this was not as onerous as it sounded, for there was a predisposition to accept proposals made by men who had already led a revolution. The identification with the Bolsheviks was so nearly religious that other Communists eagerly took their advice and deferred to their judgment. With time, however, discipline became mechanistic, depending not on persuasion and prestige but ukase. To some extent that was already visible as the American parties sought the International's seal for their stand on unionism.

One of the first orders of business after American communism took organizational form was to send emissaries to the Soviet Union. The Communist Labor Party dispatched John Reed, who already knew most of the Soviet leaders. The Communist Party ordered its international secretary, Louis Fraina, to the scene. Each, of course, went separately, anxious for some factional advantage by being the first to arrive. One of their immediate disappointments was an incipient shift in Soviet policy. By the time they set foot on Russian soil the leftist mood of Lenin and Trotsky was on the wane. A year earlier the Russian leaders had expected successful Communist revolutions throughout Europe. "The great International Soviet Republic," said a Comintern manifesto, "will be born in the year 1920." But by 1920 it was obvious to these flexible men they had miscalculated. The Bavarian and Hungarian Soviets had been put down. Russia itself was in civil war. The momentum was clearly lost. Lenin, therefore, changed toward a policy of greater compromise. In his brochure *Left-Wing Communism: An Infantile Disorder,* written in 1920, he berated British and German Communists who refused to work inside "reactionary unions" and turned their backs on "bourgeois parliaments." By implication these darts were aimed as well against the two American Communist parties.

Thus when Reed proposed to the higher authorities of the Comintern that they designate the IWW as the only true voice of American unionism, he was firmly overruled. Fraina, though equally hostile to the AFL, was evidently overcome by the awesome atmosphere of Moscow, for he yielded to the arguments of Soviet leaders and partly reversed himself. He accepted, in essence, the triple-pronged position advanced by Karl Radek—to simultaneously work inside the AFL, maintain fraternal relations with the IWW, and establish independent unions where necessary. For Moscow this was a halfway house toward the unequivocal position to be taken the following year which laid the entire emphasis on work in "reactionary" unions such as the AFL. For the time being it sufficed.

As a sidelight, this sad experience virtually marked the end of the Communist careers of both emissaries. Reed, in his early thirties, died suddenly less than three months later and was interred with honors in the Kremlin wall. Some of his friends later claimed he was already on the road to disillusionment. Fraina decided to quit the party in 1922—at the ripe old age of twenty-eight—because of persistent, though unwarranted, charges of financial mishandling, as well as the misgivings he nurtured after the Comintern decision. Under the name of Lewis Corey he eventually became a prominent writer on economic and social issues, and a professor at Antioch College.

As for the "line" on American labor, in due course the Communists changed direction, and with William Z. Foster—an addition to the ranks since 1921—leading the way, they started "boring from within" the AFL, even as the Socialists had done in years past, though with greater purposiveness.

VI

If the new policy were not tailored to accommodate Foster, he was propitiously placed to carry it through. He was indeed the Communists' greatest acquisition in the 1920's, the first nationally known figure they had recruited. Born near Boston forty years before, son of an Irish immigrant and an English-Scottish mother, Foster was as American as apple pie. Brought up in the slums of Philadelphia, he quit school at the age of ten, and for the next twenty-six years roamed the country unable or unwilling to settle down to a single occupation. Tall, wiry, good looking, his labors took him from New York to California, from Florida to Washington, from agriculture to meat packing to building construction and a dozen other industries. Politics became an early passion for this rebellious young man. Foster recalled in later years his elation with the campaign of William Jennings Bryan in 1896. In 1901, barely out of his teens, he joined the Socialist Party, and eight years later the IWW. Though he might have retained membership in both organizations, as did Big Bill Haywood, he quit the Socialist Party because he found it too tepid. As a Wobbly, Foster participated enthusiastically in the free speech fights and was imprisoned, with others, in Spokane. He did not become well known, like Haywood or Elizabeth Gurley Flynn, but he was capable and appreciated. When it came time to send a delegate to an international union conference in Budapest in 1911, Foster was the IWW's choice.

The future Communist leader stayed in Europe a year, studying the various labor movements, and though he remained a convinced syndicalist, he decided that the IWW's separate existence was a disastrous mistake. In an exchange of letters with Big Bill Haywood in the *Industrial Worker*, he pointed out that the IWW was a failure in the United States, and that similar revolutionary unions in England, Germany, and elsewhere were similarly headed nowhere. Syndicalism succeeded, he insisted, only where—as in France—it could capture and revolutionize the existing union movement. This is what he counseled the Wobblies—to enter the AFL and win it from within. Haywood's rebuttal argued that such a strategy was useless, among other reasons because the AFL was not receptive to the unskilled workers whom the IWW was trying to unionize. It imposed on them a "vicious system of apprenticeship, [and] exorbitant fees."

Few Wobblies agreed with Foster. In 1913, therefore, he founded the Syndicalist League of North America to expound the theory of "boring from within," and in 1915 the International Trade Union Educational League, neither one of which enjoyed conspicuous success. Both were, in a sense, satellite organizations to the IWW, attempting to win its members to the Foster strategy.

Meanwhile Foster set about to implement his own thesis. Working as a car inspector in Chicago, he became general organizer of the AFL Railway Carmen and a delegate to the Chicago Federation of Labor. Here, despite his syndicalist views, he was able to ingratiate himself with Sam Gompers and John Fitzpatrick, the Chicago Federation of Labor president. "He was a man of ability," Gompers said later, "a man of good presence, gentle in expression, a commander of good English, and I encouraged him. . . . I was willing to welcome an erring brother into the ranks of constructive labor." The "erring brother" was even better received by Fitzpatrick, who was a radical of sorts himself and saw in Foster a kindred spirit.

[287]

When the Carmen's organizer came up with a plan for unionizing the Chicago-based packinghouse industry, "Fitz" leaped at the proposal.

It was obviously impossible to divide the packinghouse workers into the dozen or more craft unions, since that would make them totally ineffective. Foster got around this obstacle by a formula called "amalgamation": the various AFL unions with an interest in the meat-packing industry established a joint committee and organized the workers into a single unit. The question of their future disposal among contending AFL organizations was left for a later resolution. With Foster as secretary of this improvised industrial structure, two hundred thousand packinghouse workers were enrolled by the AFL. After a strike and preparations for another strike, they won a substantial improvement in their conditions through an arbitration award—large wage increases, the eight-hour day, union recognition. Foster later conceded that there was a trace of opportunism to his wartime activities, for while his former comrades in the IWW were opposing the war and being lynched or jailed, he was—in line with Gompers' policies—helping to sell Liberty Bonds to the packinghouse employees. Yet his campaign was sensational by simple union standards, and with this victory under his belt, Foster was placed in charge of the drive in the steel industry. The national steel strike in 1919, of course, made his name a byword and elevated him to the status of a prominent national figure.

Had he wanted to at this point, Foster could have accepted a soft post with the AFL and perhaps become one of its leaders. But he continued to toy both with the Wobbly notion of organizing the unskilled, and his own hope of making the AFL the vehicle for his task. He therefore formed the Trade Union Educational League in November 1920 to accomplish what he had failed to accomplish a few years before. It was at this juncture in his turbulent career that Foster was contacted by an old associate, Earl Browder, who had once been a member of the Syndicalist League in Kansas City. Browder was now in the Communist movement, assigned to trade-union activity, and it was he who convinced Foster to accompany him to Moscow for an international labor gathering. Foster stayed for three and a half months, after which he was ready to accept a party card.

It is interesting how a man like Foster could make this leap. He still believed, as in his syndicalist days, that the state was man's worst enemy, even if it were a "workers' state." He had some doubts about the outcome of the Russian Revolution since it had taken place in an underdeveloped country. In his thinking socialism could come only in a "highly industrialized" one. He had misgivings about the centralist Communist Party and its suzerainty over the "dictatorship of the proletariat." But there were other factors that outweighed his uncertainties, not the least of which was that Moscow was turning around now to his own views of "boring from within." The Communists were also excellent organizers, and Foster had always felt that if the working class could somehow be totally unionized, the revolution would become inevitable. The Communists, he concluded from what he saw in Moscow, had just the drive to do it. Foster adopted communism; the Communists adopted his Trade Union Educational League (TUEL) as its trade-union arm in the United States. It was a bonanza for the American Communists. They had hoped to recruit Debs, but while the ancient Socialist was friendly, he was ill disposed toward talk of "armed insurrection" and violence. He decided to stand apart. Foster's adherence, while not as valuable, was the next best coup possible.

For some time after Foster was given the mandate, Communist prospects in the labor movement looked very bright. The tide of history was riding in his favor, as AFL ineffectiveness catapulted many unionists to the Left. At the 1920 convention of the AFL the railway unions had forced through a resolution—against Gompers' wishes —for government ownership of the railroads. The vote was better than 3 to 1. At the next convention—with Socialist support—John L. Lewis ran against Gompers for president of the AFL and secured one third of the ballots. The Conference for Progressive Political Action (CPPA), called together in February 1922, listed 124 delegates from 50 national unions, plus the Minnesota Farmer-Labor Party, the Nonpartisan League, and others.

To attract leftward-moving elements, Foster and his team mate, Earl R. Browder, concentrated on two issues: "amalgamation" and a "labor party." Amalgamation was the technique Foster had used in the packinghouse and steel campaigns—a host of craft unions amalgamated into a joint committee to conduct a unionizing drive along industrial lines. Foster now proposed it as a universal method for circumventing craft unionism. It was a slogan with electric appeal endorsed by literally thousands of local unions, seventeen state federations of labor, scores of city federations, and twenty international unions. Left-wingers began to organize their cadres. Four hundred delegates formed the Railroad Workers Amalgamation Committee in December 1923, and two hundred miners from twelve of the thirty mine union districts—including the largest one, Illinois —set up the International Committee of Progressive Miners. Left-wingers gained control of three New York locals of the International Ladies' Garment Workers' Union with thirty thousand members. Pro-TUEL candidates in the miners' union were strong enough in 1924 and 1926 to run George Voyzey and John Brophy for the presidency against John L. Lewis. They lost, but there was always a question as to whether they had been given a fast count. The highest claim for TUEL support was three hundred thousand members, but its sympathizers ran slates in such rock-ribbed organizations as the carpenters' union and the Iron, Steel and Tin Workers, and in Socialist-tinged organizations such as the needle trades and the machinists. One union, the furriers, fell under TUEL sway and remained that way for a quarter of a century.

Foster's efforts were obviously more fruitful than those of the party previously. But there was something too purposive about the Communists. Unlike the Wobblies—dying on the vine by now—the Communists gave the feeling that what they were groping for was not so much a pragmatic objective as a base of power. Where the Wobblies had been free and easy militants whose only enemy was the boss, the Communists had a factional flavor to them, as if union activity were only camouflage for something else. Interspersed between union planks in the TUEL platform, for instance, were such highly political demands as the abolition of the capitalist system, recognition of the Soviet Union, and "affiliation to the militant international trade union movement, known as the Red International of Labor Unions." Such a program, whether intrinsically valid, was not only too much of a pill for American unionists to swallow but too close a replica of the party's own program.

Twenty years later, discussing the "sectarian weaknesses" shown in this period, Foster noted that TUEL had a tendency "to develop its union programs upon a too advanced militant basis and to identify the organizations too closely with the Communist Party." By way of example, one could pick up the TUEL magazine *Workers*

Monthly for May 1925 and read articles about "Communism on the Streets of America," by Earl R. Browder, a story of how the Communists broke up meetings arranged for "Abramovich, the agent of counterrevolution and the Second (Socialist) International"; or the "History of the Russian Communist Party" (Chapter III) by Gregory Zinoviev; or—by the same author—"The Death of Sun Yat-sen." Trade-union articles, such as one about "Coke Miners in Revolt," seemed like an unplanned afterthought.

Whatever the reason, TUEL quickly reached its apogee and just as quickly slumped to near impotence when it failed to rally sufficient support to ward off the inevitable counterattack. In April 1923, Gompers called together a meeting of several hundred AFL officials at which he declared war on the "Reds" and castigated the TUEL as "an organization which attempts to dictate the policy of the trade unions." Communists and TUEL leaders became fair game. A New York bookkeepers' union had its charter revoked when it fell under TUEL leadership. William F. Dunne, a member of the top committee of the Communists, was denied his seat at an AFL convention although he was a duly elected delegate. For the first time measures were taken against bonafide unionists solely for their radical beliefs.

It was a gala circus, a tragicomedy in which brother was arrayed against brother. The Communists were not blameless, for they functioned with the rigid, tight-knit discipline—all voting as a unit—which could only evoke fears that they were interested more in political control than the union's effectiveness. But in this instance the hammer was being wielded by the other side with the machine-like precision the Communists were accused of. Thousands of TUEL members were expelled by AFL affiliates, among them hundreds of Communist Party members. Even the Socialists at the head of the needle trades unions were unsparing. During the 1923 election of delegates in the Ladies' Garment Workers' Union, Left-wingers were arbitrarily removed from the list, and at the convention itself, sixteen were branded as "enemies" and tossed out. John L. Lewis cleaned house of popular figures such as Alex Howat, John Brophy, and Powers Hapgood. William H. Johnstone, president of the machinists, who had beaten out a Left-wing candidate by the razor thin margin of 18,021 to 17,076, ordered locals to divest themselves of "Reds" under penalty of losing their charters. The

Seattle Trade Council, which five years before had sent a delegate to the Red International of Labor Unions, purged six Communists by the narrow vote of 78 to 71. Almost everywhere Foster's legions found doors swinging closed. At the end of the decade the TUEL could record only a single solid bastion, the furriers' union.

The Communists, like the Wobblies, were magnificent strike strategists—at least where political objectives did not inhibit them. Like the Wobblies, too, their sense of dedication bordered on the religious. They bared their heads to policemen's clubs and went to jail singing, convinced they were striking a blow for the emancipation of humanity. For sheer determination and willingness to tread where the staid labor officials shied away, they were unparalleled. The Passaic textile strike in 1927, led by a Communist who had graduated from Harvard Law School, Albert Weisbord, lasted thirteen grueling months. Police rode roughshod through mass picket lines of women and children, turning fire hoses on them in zero weather. Mass meetings were prohibited and broken up, many were arrested. It was an ordeal that would have tested saints, and it attracted more national attention in the press than any strike of the Coolidge era.

Another strike in which the TUEL and the party showed its mettle was the one in Gastonia, North Carolina, two years later. All the tragedy of the little "wars" at Ludlow or Telluride was reenacted here in miniature form—masked mobs attacking strike headquarters, imprisonment of a hundred strikers and conviction of seven for second-degree murder, the killing of organizer Ella May Wiggin.

Whatever criticism may be leveled against the TUEL in its overall strategy, it was clearly a movement of the unskilled, the shirtless, the desperate. There was seldom an issue of its publications without some reference to the plight of Negroes, or a convention without a resolution on the "Negro question." Yet its failure was even more monumental than that of the Socialists. Where Max Hayes and the Socialist factions of previous years sometimes garnered a fourth or a third of the AFL votes for specific Socialist resolutions, the TUEL did not fare even remotely so well. Nor did it ever come close to achieving the glamorous victories of the IWW. Despite its best-laid plans and despite the leadership of so experienced a unionist as William Z. Foster, the TUEL expired without glory. The policy of

"boring from within" was finally abandoned in 1929—again following trade winds from Moscow—for still another escapade in dual
unionism. Communism's first attempt to win a trade-union base was
an abysmal failure.

VII

The same shifts and gyrations which characterized communism's
relations with the unions also marked its relations with reform and
labor parties. Originally "laborism" was sternly eschewed by the national Left wing in the Socialist Party and the two Communist parties that emerged in 1919. One of these, the Communist Party, specifically forbade any type of collaboration with the Socialist Party,
Labor Party, Nonpartisan League, and similar reform movements.
So rigid was this determination that it would not endorse the
candidacy of so close a friend as Eugene Debs because he was running on the Socialist ticket.

But after the Comintern had adopted the slogan "To the masses"
and the policy of "united front," the shunned labor partyites were
wooed with unashamed passion. Collaborating with reformists became the fixed star of revolutionary navigation. Foster and his
TUEL put it on an equal plane with "amalgamation" and "recognition of the Soviet Union." In September 1923 a leading Communist,
John Pepper, went so far as to call the farmer-labor movement "the
third American revolution."

At this juncture in American history various forces were coa-
lescing into a third-party movement that in 1924 would nominate
Senator Robert M. La Follette for President and Senator Burton K.
Wheeler as his running mate. The most important of these was the
Conference for Progressive Political Action (CPPA), formed in the
troubled year 1922 on the initiative of the railroad unions. The injunctions issued in the coal miners' strike of 1919 and the railroad
strike in 1922 dramatized the issue of legal rights and had awakened
these unions to the need for political redress. Other disenchanted
forces, reflecting a burgeoning malaise, decided to join hands with
the railroaders. Present at the meeting were not only such expected
delegates as those from the miners, the Socialist-oriented Ladies'
Garment Workers, and the leftist Amalgamated Clothing Workers,
but from the Nonpartisan League, the Committee of Forty-

eight—a group of Teddy Roosevelt Republicans who had walked out of the party with their leader in 1912, the Methodist Federation of Social Service, the National Catholic Welfare Council, single taxers, agrarians. There were also representatives of the Farmer-Labor Party, in which John Fitzpatrick was the key figure, and the Socialist Party.

For the latter, the CPPA offered a grand opportunity to break out of the isolation imposed by the split with communism. The Socialist Party designated its most eminent figures to speak for it in CPPA councils, including Hillquit, Berger, James Oneal, Daniel Hoan. They hoped that out of the Conference would evolve a permanent Labor Party in which the Socialists would be a constituent part. A motion to that effect, made in December 1922, lost by the close margin of 64 to 52. Nonetheless the Socialists threw themselves into the ensuing campaign with more vigor than they had displayed for some time. They did the lion's share of work in organizing meetings for La Follette in the larger cities, such as the one held in Madison Square Garden in New York. Hillquit, as a member of the CPPA national commitee, played an important role in its deliberations, though he could not convince it to continue as an independent force.

As for the Communists, aligned as they were with so influential a figure as John Fitzpatrick, they rightfully expected to reap a banner harvest out of the third-party movement. The slogan "To the masses" was about to take on meat and marrow. But as events transpired, they were caught in a political meat grinder which was being turned in Moscow. In that far-off city Stalin and Trotsky were debating such abstruse questions as the "bloc of four classes" and whether it was permissible for Communists to align themselves with farmers and other nonproletarians. As one of the concessions to Trotsky, the Comintern withdrew support from La Follette, who, it was assumed, was essentially a farmers' candidate.

What followed was even more bewildering than the trade-union twists. By agreement between the Communists—then called the Workers Party—and Fitzpatrick's Farmer-Labor Party, a call was issued for a convention in July 1923 of "all economic and political organizations favoring the organization of a Farmer-Labor Party." According to Foster, the 650 delegates who gathered in Chicago that day represented 600,000 people, but Fitzpatrick, increasingly alarmed over the mechanistic way in which Communists packed such meetings, proposed the Workers Party be excluded from the movement. To the roaring vote of about 500 to 40, Fitzpatrick was repudiated—and he withdrew. Thus ended the alliance between Foster and Fitzpatrick, which had endured for a decade. The Communists found themselves with their own Federated Farmer Labor Party, which soon proved to have considerably fewer adherents than they had believed. It was virtually a case of capturing themselves. A year later the finishing touches were put on the tragic episode. The Federated Farmer Labor Party, together with allies in Minnesota, called a conclave at St. Paul, ostensibly to nominate La Follette, the overwhelming choice of all progressives at the time. But in a surprising move the Communist faction instead, reflecting the turn of events in Moscow, imposed a ticket made up of two relatively unknown figures, Duncan McDonald, a former mine union leader in Illinois, and William Bouck, chief of a farmer's league in the state of Washington. A few weeks later, after the McDonald-Bouck campaign had already begun and its sterility was apparent, the Communists decided to drop the "opportunist" campaign entirely and run their own ticket—Foster for President, Benjamin Gitlow for Vice President. It received 33,316 votes in the thirteen states where it was on the ballot. La Follette, who did worse than expected and carried only his own state, Wisconsin, nevertheless garnered 5 million votes.

In this whole confusing decade, as they lost one battle after another, the Communists displayed an almost phobic attitude against permitting others any latitude in their joint activities. Thus, when the TUEL held its first conference in August 1922, every facet of power was placed in Communist hands. The five members of the editorial committee were all party members. The individual reporters on various trades—building trades, metal trades, needle trades, and so on—were all Communists. When the first Farmer-Labor Party conference was held, together with Fitzpatrick, it was jam-packed with members and close sympathizers of the Workers Party, functioning as a caucus with military discipline. The conference the following year, held jointly with Minnesota Farmer-Laborites, was similarly manipulated. It was no wonder that William Mahoney, editor of the *Minnesota Union Advocate* and the leading non-Communist present, wrote in anger: "The organized activity of the communists has become a source of fear and irritation to a great many earnest supporters of the new movement."

Inside the party, too, there was the same tautness, the same disposition to factionalize over minor issues. The labor party question brought forth a new spate of faction fights with Foster, James P. Cannon, and Alexander Bittelman forming one group; Ruthenberg, John Pepper, Jay Lovestone, another. Their differences were more theoretic than actual, but the recriminations were boundless. Though Foster could not drive Ruthenberg out of the general secretary's post, he was able to seize the party executive committee by a 2 to 1 margin. It did him little good, because in the meantime the American dispute blended with and became subordinate to the three-way fight between Stalin, Trotsky, and Bukharin in Russia. Each of the American leaders was attached to and protected by leaders in the Soviet Union. Telegrams between them were so frequent that a conundrum making the rounds went like this: *Question:* Why is the Communist Party of the United States like the Brooklyn Bridge? *Answer:* Because it is suspended on cables.

Foster's political star was short lived. Though he won a majority of the delegates to the party convention in August 1925, he submitted to a demand by the head of the Comintern, Zinoviev, to turn the leadership over to Ruthenberg, Pepper, and Lovestone.

Against this weird background of strife and ineffectiveness, the Communist Party came to the end of the decade, 1929, with only 9,642 members, less than a seventh of its claimed forces at birth. The rest of the radical movement was in similar disarray. The IWW, having lost some of its stalwarts to the Communists and others to the Palmer raids, was now a sect with a glorious past but a hopeless future. The Socialist Party in 1928 showed only 7,793 members on the roster, almost half in foreign-language federations. If it were not for the $500 a month subsidy that it received from the *Jewish Daily Forward*, it might have been forced to close its headquarters.

The decade that began with lustrous hopes that the revolution was only a matter of months or at worst a few years off, ended in glum despair.

CHAPTER XV

THE RED DECADE

RADICALISM's "lost decade"—the Golden Twenties—was followed by what Eugene Lyons, a former Moscow correspondent, called the "Red Decade." It was not Red in the sense that councils of workers and peasants took over the government, or that, as rightists argued after 1933, a socialist upstart was ensconced in the White House. But it was Red in the sense that the center of political gravity swung sharply to the Left, and millions of jobless, war veterans, and mass industry workers took to the streets in demonstrations or "seized" factories in sit-down strikes. It was Red in tone, mood, flavor as thousands of artists, intellectuals, movie stars, and literary figures found an emotional haven with various radical parties. As suddenly as the prosperity of the Golden Twenties turned into the stock market collapse of Black Thursday, the fortunes of the American Left began to soar, until by the mid-1930's, it reached new peaks comparable to 1912.

Where the 1920's had been an era of vulgar prosperity and wild speculation, which undercut insurgency, the next decade was one of enervating depression, hunger, unemployment, and the most extensive face lifting capitalism has ever known. President Herbert Hoover, a few months after taking office in March 1929, told the nation in lyric optimism: "We in America today are nearer to the final triumph over poverty than ever before in the history of our land. The poorhouse is vanishing from among us." But on October 24—Black Thursday as it became known in history—the bottom fell out of the stock market. In a frenzy of selling, denoting a decline in confidence, share prices plunged precipitously downward. Five days later, after J. P. Morgan & Company and other bankers had assured the public that the economy was "sound," the disaster became worse. As reported by the New York *Times*, "stock prices virtually collapsed yesterday, swept downward with gigantic losses in the most disastrous trading in the stock market's history."

The effect of the crash was cumulative. Speculators, who had been playing the market on margin, were wiped out when they could not cover their losses. Some of them jumped from stockbrokers' windows. Banks began to call in loans; fear and anixety slowed new investment as well as production. By March 1930 there were four million out of work; by March 1931, eight million; and a year later, twelve and a half million. Before it was checked—it did not really end until World War II—the Great Depression resulted in 5,761 bank failures, a decline in farm and industrial income by half, and a fearsome reduction in wages. Factory earnings in Ohio, typically, fell from an average of thirty dollars a week to nineteen dollars in just three years. By 1934 there were two and a half million proletarians who had not worked for at least two years, and six million whose last job was more than a year past. When a Chicago department store held a liquidation sale, ten thousand unemployed stormed the premises looking for work. Twice they had to be physically dispersed by the police. Desperate family men, with no means of support, took to selling apples on street corners, shining shoes (seven thousand new shoeshine "boys" appeared in New York alone), and hawking newspapers.

In four years a million farmers lost their farms. Hundreds of thousands of city apartment dwellers were served dispossess notices, and many actually evicted to the streets. On the outskirts of most urban centers shacktowns of tin and cardboard began to appear, appropriately called "Hoovervilles"—a dubious honor for the President. It was, in scope and numbers involved, the worst crisis in American history.

In this turbulence the Socialists regained a degree of influence, and a purged Communist movement became for the first time a substantial factor in American life.

II

The two men who dominated the leftist scene in the Red Decade —one for the Socialists, the other for the Communists—were a former minister, Norman Thomas, and a onetime accountant, Earl R. Browder. Thomas, a tall, handsome man with an impressive baritone voice, became a Socialist by a slow process of self-persuasion. Unlike Debs or Bill Haywood, whose ideology evolved from deprived circumstance and turgid experience, Thomas endured only minor hardship either as a young man or an adult. He was the eldest of six children born to a Presbyterian minister in Marion, Ohio—the same town which produced Warren G. Harding. The father's salary was inadequate for the large family, so young Norman worked at delivering newspapers after school. With the aid of a wealthy uncle, who gave him four hundred dollars, and his earnings as a summer worker in a chair factory, he received a college education at Princeton. Later he made a trip around the world, enrolled at Union Theological Seminary, and in 1911 was ordained a minister. So far, except for a sympathetic relationship with the slum dwellers of East Harlem who lived near his church, there was nothing in this saga to suggest his future career as a Socialist. In 1912, as a matter of fact, Thomas endorsed Teddy Roosevelt's Progressives, and in 1916, voted for one of his former professors at Princeton, Woodrow Wilson.

What drew Thomas to socialism finally—at the age of thirty-three—was a devout and ingrained pacifism. Prior to the war he had served as secretary of a pacifist group to which many ministers belonged, the Fellowship of Reconciliation. Thus when Morris Hillquit ran for mayor of New York in 1917, his antiwar program won a fervid supporter in the minister from East Harlem. Thomas became active in the campaign and not long thereafter in the Socialist Party. Like other Socialists, he had to make up his mind about the Russian Revolution, and he decided strongly in its favor. On one occasion, when two representatives of the Bolshevik government were unable to find a meeting hall, Thomas turned over his East 17th Street home to them. He was severely critical of Hillquit's high-handed methods in expelling the Communists. But Thomas neither then nor subsequently was much of a factionalist. Though he sympathized with the Third International generally, he found its centralist controls alien, and he was much taken aback by the bombastic methods of Left-wingers in his branch, notably Jay Lovestone.

Thomas remained inside the Socialist Party, and in 1928, at one of its lowest ebbs, was nominated for President of the United States— the first of six such nominations. The honor, let it be said, came to him by default. Debs had died in 1926. Hillquit and Berger, both more prominent, were ineligible because they had been born overseas. Dan Hoan, Socialist mayor of Milwaukee, was unwilling to trade a substantive post—which he might have to resign—for the flimsy luxury of a Presidential campaign. The task therefore went to Thomas, who had already run for office in New York on four occasions. To everyone's surprise, he did quite well. Despite the party's impotence and its near bankruptcy, he amassed 267,420 votes in the approximately twenty states where he was on the ballot. It was small compared to Debs's showing in 1920, the last such Socialist campaign, but it was weighty in light of the fact that there was virtually no party to back him up. His success can be measured against the 48,228 votes that Foster and Gitlow polled the same year.

Thomas gave the Socialist Party a different image from that of Debs. It was not merely that so much water had flowed over the dam since the Russian Revolution. Thomas and Debs were different kinds of personalities. Debs was at heart the unionist with whom rank-and-file labor men could exchange pleasantries over a shot of whisky; Thomas, though he walked scores of picket lines, never became the symbol of militant unionism. He and his party won friends easily among intellectuals like Stuart Chase, Paul H. Douglas, Floyd Dell, Morris Ernst, Oswald Garrison Villard. A few younger Socialists led important strikes—Walter Reuther, for instance. Thomas himself showed courage in various civil liberties fights. On May Day 1938, for instance, he held a meeting in Jersey City in defiance of Mayor Frank "Boss" Hague's ban and won national headlines when he was duly thrown in jail. But Norman Thomas' party no longer had the trade-union roots which characterized it in the years it was challenging Gompers. It was more of a people's party than a "labor" party.

By contrast, the Communist Party during the Red Decade was to enjoy a far greater success in wooing the proletariat. Its leader, Earl Russell Browder, was born in Wichita, Kansas, in 1891, seven years after Norman Thomas. He was, if anything, even more pure-bred American, for his ancestors traced back to a hundred years before the Revolution. His grandfather had been a preacher in Illinois; his father, a struggling prairie farmer who had staked out a quarter section in Kansas during the 1870's. Young Earl had to go to work before the age of ten when his father became an invalid. He moved

along the economic ladder smoothly—from errand boy to accountant and credit manager of a drug company. For a while he went into
business for himself, and in 1914—like so many other radicals—
finished a correspondence course in law.

But simultaneous with his business career, Browder became active in the Left-wing movement. It was almost an automatic reflex.
The Browder father had been a Unitarian, a Populist and a Socialist.
Of the seven Browder children who lived to maturity (three others
died), four were to become Communists. Young Earl was selling the
Socialist *Appeal to Reason* on the streets of Wichita long before he
was out of knee pants. It was not surprising, therefore, that at the
age of sixteen—in 1907—he joined the Socialist Party. He quit five
years later in protest over the ouster of Big Bill Haywood from the
party's executive committee. Instead of joining the IWW, however,
he linked his fate with William Z. Foster's Syndicalist League of
North America. It was the beginning of three decades of collaboration. Another associate was James P. Cannon, future leader of the
Trotskyist movement, with whom Browder published an esoteric little sheet, the *Toiler*.

When the wartime repression broke out, Earl Browder was one
of its first victims. In 1917 he was sent to prison on the charge of
conspiring to hamper the draft law. While in jail he learned with
elation of the Russian Revolution and on his release rejoined the Socialist Party to become, with Cannon, leader of the Kansas City Left
wing. His freedom, however, was short lived. In June 1919 Browder
was returned to jail, together with his brothers William and Ralph,
for having advised striking coal miners to defy a court injunction.
Whatever the physical hardships, prison raised Browder's stature in
the Communist movement—which he formally joined not long after
his release in January 1921. Here was a native American, living in
the mysterious Midwest, a mass worker, and a class war prisoner.
When he was released a second time, the United Communist Party
(in which both warring wings were temporarily fused) arranged for
Browder to be a delegate to the first congress of the Red International of Labor Unions. To this congress he took William Z. Foster
and secretly inducted him into the party. For the next seven or eight
years he and Foster were politically inseparable. They worked together in the Trade Union Educational League and in the factional
fights, Browder always serving under Foster. But by 1930 it was ob-

vious Moscow preferred to deal with Browder rather than his mentor. Browder's elevation to the key post was therefore not a choice of the party's rank and file, but that of Stalin's Comintern. The exact reason why Foster was bypassed was not made clear, though educated speculation attributed it to the fact that Stalin was sick of the factionalism and insubordination of the American party, and that he was repaying Foster for a brief friendship with the Trotskyists. At any rate, for the next decade and a half Browder was communism's top spokesman in America.

His enemies called Browder a "hack" and a "mediocrity." The *New Yorker* magazine once described him as "a haggard little man with grizzling hair and a stubbly mustache who looks as though he's just eaten something that didn't agree with him." As a speaker and a writer he was not exceptional, his voice was too thin, his pen lackluster. Yet he showed far more talent than his critics gave him credit for. He was a keen strategist who, despite the zigzags in Moscow policy, finally made the united front policy work. He was also the architect—at least behind the scenes—of scores of organizations subsidiary to the Communist Party, which would take a few pages to list. In a period of severe control by Moscow, Browder, a man capable of blending into the background, was probably just what the Communists needed.

III

The Communist Party which Earl Browder inherited at the beginning of the Red Decade was a drastically remodeled version. It bore little resemblance to the early Communist movement because there was no longer any inner life to the party. By this time the three-cornered fight in Moscow between Stalin, Trotsky, and Bukharin had been resolved in Stalin's favor. And, as a backlash here, James P. Cannon, the Trotskyite, was expelled in 1928 and Jay Lovestone, the Bukharinist, in mid-1929. Before his expulsion, Lovestone—who succeeded Charles Ruthenberg to the party leadership after the latter's death in 1927—enjoyed the support of 85 percent of the membership. But the American party was now so servile to Moscow it meekly accepted Stalin's ukase to replace Lovestone with Foster and Browder. All factions and factionalism were henceforth prohibited; open discussion and polemics no longer tolerated. Like its sister parties elsewhere, the American Communist Party became a full-scale monolith.

Politically, too, the 1929–30 party was oriented in a different direction from the one in the mid-1920's. Like the internal realignment, this was similarly decreed by Moscow. According to Stalin, the world was at the threshold of a "third period." The first, from 1918 to 1923, had been one of revolutionary upsurge; the second, from 1923 to 1928, had been one of democratic pacifism and the relative stabilization of capitalism. From 1928 onward Stalin foresaw another outbreak of proletarian revolt—even in the United States. "I think," said the Soviet leader on May 6, 1929, "the moment is not far off when a revolutionary crisis will develop in America."

In preparation for this "revolutionary crisis," the Communists, a few months later, embalmed the Trade Union Educational League and unveiled the Trade Union Unity League (TUUL). Six hundred and ninety delegates from eighteen states—half of them from recently formed industrial unions in textile, the needle trades, and mining—cut the cord with the AFL and returned once more to the policy of rival unionism. Where the TUEL had functioned within the AFL, the TUUL, despite its mischievous use of the word "unity," was to function outside. The TUUL program and tone were virtually a carbon of the Communist Party's. It denounced the United States government as the "instrument of the American ruling class to maintain this system of capitalist exploitation." It condemned the AFL and the Socialist Party for betraying the working class, and called on American labor to "follow the path beaten out by the Russian workers." With such a near-complete revolutionary program, it was not entirely clear why the Communists did not recruit shopworkers directly into their party rather than the intermediate unions of the TUUL.

Actually the TUUL was a stillborn baby. It was to lead a few strikes and at its peak it claimed 125,000 members, but it was never a viable force. If it made any important contribution, it was only in producing some of the future secondary leaders of the CIO. It was disbanded in stages from 1933 to 1935, when world politics—again according to Stalin—entered the "fourth period."

Concomitant with isolationism on the trade-union front, the Communists pursued a harsh and embittered course toward political rivals. From 1929 to 1935—throughout the third period, that is—the

Socialists were classed not as brothers in the struggle for socialism, but as "social fascists." They were in fact the "twin" of fascism. "During the war and since the war," wrote Earl Browder in one of his pamphlets, "the capitalist class has placed its main reliance for holding the masses in support of its class dictatorship upon the parties of the Second International. . . . Today the social fascists are the main prop of capitalism among the working class masses." Naked fascism would be used, according to Browder, only when "the declining capitalist class sensed the approach of a revolutionary crisis." At other times they relied on the Socialists to keep the working class quiescent. There was thus a division of labor between Socialists and Fascists, each served the same capitalist masters, except they were designed for different periods.

It was an unbelievable thesis, but typical of many advanced by the Communists in the "third period." Since Socialists and Fascists were of the same breed, it was permissible to break up Socialist (and Trotskyist and Lovestoneite) meetings. Indeed it was sometimes a revolutionary duty. When Norman Thomas held a rally at Madison Square Garden in February 1934 to protest the murder of Socialists by the semi-Fascist Dollfuss regime in Vienna, Stalinist strong-arm men made a shambles of it with catcalls, shrieks, knives, and physical force until it was adjourned. It was not unusual for Communists to break into a meeting of another leftist group, armed with lead pipes, brass knuckles, sticks, and knives to force it to suspend. Every now and then a brick was thrown at an outdoor meeting of the Trotskyites. It became so bad that rivals had to form "defense squads" to protect their gatherings.

Despite a cataclysmic depression which strongly favored radical activity, the Communists added only eight thousand new members from 1929 to 1933. With the dual union and social-fascist millstones around its neck, it was not able to expand beyond that.

Other leftist forces also made modest gains in the first few years of the depression, but none was able to overtake the Communist Party—small as it was—in size or influence. Norman Thomas' Socialists showed a surge of vitality. Under the guidance of a new secretary, Clarence Senior, the ranks padded out, money began to fill depleted coffers, and thirteen organizers were hired to revive old branches and build new ones. By 1930 the Milwaukee Socialists had increased their representation in the Wisconsin lower house from three to nine; two Socialists were elected to the Pennsylvania legislature; novelist Upton Sinclair received 50,000 votes for governor of California; and Louis Waldman, running against Franklin D. Roosevelt, 120,000 votes for governor of New York. Two years later Norman Thomas was able to muster 900,000 ballots running for the Presidency, a highly impressive showing considering the relative weakness of his organization. The Socialist Party itself was back to 17,000 members—only slightly smaller than the Communist Party. Yet at the grass roots, among the poorest workers, the Negroes and the jobless, the Socialist Party was not nearly as effective as its rival.

A new leftist group emerged in May 1929, the Conference for Progressive Labor Action (CPLA), that showed promise of unifying the many radicals who felt the Socialist Party too timid, the Communist Party too closely controlled by Moscow. Under the aegis of A. J. Muste, the pacifist minister who had led the Lawrence strike and initiated the independent textile union after World War I, the 151 Left-wing Socialists, intellectuals, and unionists who met at the Presbyterian Labor Temple in New York were primarily concerned, at first, with reforming the AFL from within. Their program called for industrial—as against craft—unionism, the formation of a Labor Party, recognition of the Soviet Union, a five-day week, unemployment benefits. The CPLA enjoyed a certain success in a Southern organizing campaign, in fighting corruption in AFL unions, and among the unemployed. When it found its limited role as a prodding iron to the AFL too confining, the CPLA converted to a full-fledged political party, the American Workers Party. It forged a good-sized unemployed movement and led some significant strikes, but it failed to become a true rallying point.

As for the two groups expelled from Communist ranks—the Trotskyists and Lovestoneites—neither was able to expand into a viable force. At first they operated on the theory that their exclusion from the party was only temporary; some of their zealots entertained hopes that Bukharin or Trotsky might torpedo Stalin from power and return Lovestone or Cannon—as the case might be—to his rightful place in the American hierarchy. When it became clear that Stalin was firmly entrenched, both the Lovestone "Right opposition" and the Cannon "Left opposition" embarked on an independent course. Each gained a degree of influence in the trade-union movement. Lovestone at one time was the key adviser to Homer Martin,

[305]

president of the strategically placed United Auto Workers, and some of his followers played important roles in David Dubinsky's Ladies' Garment Workers' Union. The Trotskyists, by merging with Muste's American Workers Party in 1934, secured a base among the unemployed and to some extent in the auto union. They led a sensational strike of truck drivers in Minneapolis, which was a major factor in the evolution of the Teamsters' Union.

But neither group commanded more than one thousand or fifteen hundred followers at its height. Lovestone's party, under a variety of names, was liquidated in 1941, and Lovestone himself eventually became one of the most bitter anti-Communists in America. The Trotskyists, after merging with Muste, entered the Socialist Party in 1935, left it a few years later, and became embroiled in continuous factionalism leading to a dozen interesting but—from the point of view of influence—irrelevant splits.

IV

The America Left, then, did not score a sudden triumph in the Red Decade. But it laid roots for the future and appreciably widened its popular following from the very beginning.

While President Hoover repeated saccharine assurances that the nation was basically healthy and was turning the corner, the Communists responded to the depression with exemplary speed. Four months after Black Thursday, on March 6, 1930, they held demonstrations in more than a dozen cities, demanding relief and unemployment insurance—two reforms which were not yet on the books in America. Under the makeshift banner of the Trade Union Unity League they led almost a million jobless in protest—a hundred thousand each in New York and Detroit alone. "Work or Wages!" "Don't Starve—Fight!" read their slogans. For good measure there were placards against war, fascism, Jim Crow, and wage cuts. In New York, after William Z. Foster announced there would be a march down Broadway to present a petition to the mayor, police charged the crowd with billy clubs flying. As a New York *World* reporter described it, "women [were] struck in the face with blackjacks, boys beaten by gangs of seven and eight policemen, and an old man backed into a doorway and knocked down time after time, only to be dragged to his feet and struck with fist and club. . . ."

Hundreds were arrested, including Foster and three other leading Communists.

On May Day, less than two months later, the Communists held another national protest, this time drawing only a third as many people. Even so, for a party that had less than ten thousand members, three quarters of them only a year or two in the ranks, this was no small undertaking. Following these initial sallies, the Communists mustered 1,320 delegates in Chicago on Independence Day to form the National Unemployed Council. In much the same way the Socialists established the Workers Alliance, and A. J. Muste's Conference for Progressive Labor Action set up the National Unemployed Leagues.

Newspapers of the time are filled with hundreds of little incidents in which the Councils, the Leagues, or the Alliance guided the unemployed to some act of resistance. Typically, an Associated Press dispatch of January 20, 1931, from Oklahoma City read: "A crowd of men and women, shouting that they were hungry and jobless, raided a grocery store near the City Hall today. Twenty-six of the men were arrested. . . ." Later in the day police accused Francis Owens of the Oklahoma City Unemployed Council "of instigating the raid." Unemployed despair was so great that it was no problem for a single radical to enroll fifty or a hundred men in a League or a Council almost overnight.

Throughout the 1930's the unemployed were the backbone of social protest. When tenants were evicted from their homes, jobless groups often moved them back, clashing with police and constables in the process. A. J. Muste's paper dated May 1, 1934, records an instance in which "the eviction was stopped by a mass demonstration. When leaving the house, 'an accident' occurred to the constable and landlord. They went to the hospital. 'Who threw the bricks?' Shrugged shoulders was the reply. No more evictions for six months." The Unemployed Councils of New York boasted that in a four-year period they moved seventy-seven thousand evicted families back to their apartments. If it were an exaggeration, it nonetheless reflected the frequency with which the unemployed took direct, and extralegal, action.

Hungry men demonstrated in front of relief stations or sat inside until arrested, demanding coal, bread, rent money. Twice, in December 1931 and again in December 1932, Communists led small unemployed detachments to Washington—reminiscent of Coxey's Army forty years before. Men who had no work often came to the aid of those who did. For instance, in 1934 when a judge issued an injunction against strikers at the Auto-Lite plant in Toledo, the Unemployed League mobilized ten thousand to defy the ban. The jobless and strikers resisted the National Guard for six days—two men were killed and twenty-five wounded—until the plant was closed and the Guard withdrawn. The Auto-Lite victory played an important part in the evolution of the CIO auto workers' union.

With the unemployed as the base for their activity, radical groups were able to fan out into other milieus—with veterans, Negroes, unionists. A peak of protest in the pre-New Deal days was that of twenty thousand veterans encamped in Washington. Assembled by the Communist-dominated Workers Ex-Servicemen's League— "weasels" as they were called—the former soldiers demanded immediate payment of $50 and $100 bonuses promised them under a 1923 act but not due until 1945. Their slogans were pitiful reminders of man's changing fortunes: "Heroes in 1917—Bums in 1932." "We Fought for Democracy—What Did We Get?" They came from all sections of the country, improvising various techniques—both ingenious and obvious—to get transport and food. Four hundred seized a Baltimore & Ohio freight train in East St. Louis. Others persuaded local officials to give them automobiles and trucks just to get rid of them. Wherever they went they held meetings, collected funds, solicited recruits. They streamed into Washington steadily, sometimes with wives and shrieking children by their side, and set up a makeshift colony across the Potomac at a place called Anacostia Flats. By June 15 they had reached their peak, twenty thousand.

Here was something more threatening than a simple unemployed demonstration. The veterans had military training. They knew something about guns and if their appeals to police and the Regular Army were effective, Washington might find itself in difficulties. President Hoover decided both to tread warily and prepare for any contingency. When the "Bonus Expeditionary Force" arrived in town, the government put up some of its members in unused buildings and loaned them army rolling kitchens. The Regular Army, however, was alerted for an "emergency." On July 20, 1932, after being in town about two months, two hundred members of the expedition marched to the White House, where they were dispersed with tear gas. Congress offered $100,000 to pay the veterans' way home, but it was refused because, among other things, the sum would be deducted from future bonus payments. Not a few of the men were counseling violent action. Walter W. Waters, their thirty-four-year-old leader, who had been out of work himself for one and a half years, acted as a restraining force on the extremists, but their mood was far from relaxed. On July 21 the government issued an ultimatum for the veterans to clear their quarters by August 4. A week later when they refused to evacuate a building at Third Street and Pennsylvania Avenue, the police chief ordered his men to seize it. The ex-soldiers resisted; two of them were killed. Soon thereafter President Hoover called on Army Chief of Staff Douglas MacArthur (one of whose aides was Dwight D. Eisenhower) to drive the veterans, some of whom had wives and children along, out of Anacostia Flats. In the words of the New York *Times:* "Amidst scenes reminiscent of the mopping up of a town in the World War, Federal troops . . . drove the army of bonus seekers from the shanty village. . . ." General MacArthur noted, in justification of his act, that "the mob was a bad-looking one. It was marked by signs of revolution."

It is not clear what the Communists expected from the weasels, whether they hoped it would be an economic pressure group or something more. Slogans such as "workers defense squads" were common in the 1930's so that a Left-wing veterans group might have served as an armed adjunct to unions or unemployed organizations. But the weasels were not durable; they made little long-run impact.

Of greater permanent significance was the Negro movement. Here was an insurgent reservoir that was still untapped. The depression affected the Negro more than anyone else, since he was the first to lose his job or his farm. It served to emphasize how small had been his gains since the Civil War. As of 1915, half of America's Negroes were still illiterate, and three quarters lived as impoverished sharecroppers or tenants. They had exchanged *de jure* for *de facto* bondage. There were actually fewer Negro craftsmen in 1915 than there had been at the time of the Emancipation Proclamation. One third of all employed Negroes were domestic servants. In the forty-five years from 1885 to 1930, 3,256 Negroes had been lynched with impunity. Race riots, every so often, such as those after World War

I, resulted in death and injury for hundreds. Yet the Negro was not organized to alter his status.

At the turn of the century a Socialist, William English Walling, brought together sixty-five men and women to form the National Association for the Advancement of Colored People, but most of the founders were white. During the 1920's Marcus Garvey's "Back to Africa" movement won thousands of converts in Harlem and on Chicago's South Side, but it did little to ameliorate conditions in America. Thus the Negro made no appreciable gains until the 1930's when the radicals, particularly the Communists, and later the CIO, took up cudgels on his behalf.

During the third period the Communists proposed a unique, if impractical, strategy for winning the Negro's freedom. It was summed up in the slogan "self-determination for the Black Belt." They argued that Negroes had the same right to establish an independent republic in the South, as, say, India had to free itself from British rule. Assuming that the United States were ever willing to grant such a demand, it was never spelled out how Negro and white economies would be disentangled, or how the populations would be shifted. "Self-determination" was solely a slogan, tailored to third-period extravagance. As such, it was not as alluring to the average Negro as anticipated.

But on the practical plane the Communists trod firmly where others shied away. One of their major preoccupations in the Red Decade was the Scottsboro case. On March 25, 1931, nine Negro boys, the youngest only thirteen, were hauled off a freight train at Paint Rock, Alabama, and put in the county jail at Scottsboro. The boys had been hoboing from Chattanooga to Huntsville. On the same train were some white youngsters, with whom the Negroes had had a minor altercation, and two teen-age white girls, dressed in overalls. The Negroes were charged with raping them. The only evidence of rape that came out at the trial a few days after the arrest was the testimony of the alleged victims, neither of whom was of impeccable virtue. At a subsequent trial one of the girls repudiated her claims and toured the country urging the Scottsboro boys' freedom. But at the original proceeding, in a hostile Southern town, nine Negroes had little chance of asserting their innocence. The trial was routine—the usual all-white jury, whispers of impending lynchings, hostile crowds, an unsympathetic judge, an unsympathetic defense attorney appointed by the judge. The sentence matched the harshness of the surroundings—all but the thirteen-year-old were sentenced to death in the electric chair.

The incident received no national headlines until a Communist organizer in Alabama wired the details to his paper the *Daily Worker*. Thus began a long and bitter battle, conducted both in the courts and on the streets, that was not finally concluded until seventeen years later. The Scottsboro case, unlike the Mooney-Billings, Sacco-Vanzetti, or Haywood-Moyer-Pettibone cases, did not center on the "Red" issue. No one was being punished for leading a strike or preparing a revolution. But it was a dramatic reminder of the second-class status of the Negro. The Communists, through their International Labor Defense, which provided the lawyers for the case, and through innumerable meetings and demonstrations, made this point over and over again. Though they eventually relinquished their legal role to two nationally known attorneys, Samuel Leibowitz and Osmond K. Fraenkel, they remained the major organizers of mass rallies.

Once the Communists entered the case, and with the glare of publicity stirring passions in Negro communities, the first convictions were set aside by the United States Supreme Court on the ground that the defendants had been inadequately represented. The condemned men were retried, convicted again, and again there were reversals in the higher courts—usually on the plea that no Negroes had served on the juries. But the state would not surrender; after each legal setback it modified its strategy and proceeded anew. One man, Haywood Patterson, was convicted four times, another three times. As execution dates drew close, protest meetings were held throughout the United States and in Europe. Once Scottsboro sympathizers marched on Washington to present to the President a petition with two hundred thousand signatures. Under the pressures of persistent agitation, the case against four defendants was finally dropped in 1936—more than five years after the alleged rape. Three were released on parole in 1944, one escaped from prison in 1948. The ninth Negro, involved in an act of violence while in prison, was convicted for assault with intent to kill and given twenty years.

There were other Negro civil liberties cases in the 1930's, such as the one of Angelo Herndon, a member of the Young Communist League, tried in Atlanta on an 1861 law for "incitement to insurrection." He received a sentence of eighteen to twenty years, but was freed by the Supreme Court in 1937. Simultaneously the Communists, Socialists, and Trotskyists organized tens of thousands of Negroes into unemployed organizations, and subsequently into the mass production unions, where they gained wage standards, seniority rights, and status never enjoyed before. For the first time the Negro issue received high priority in radical ranks. Of the 233 delegates to the 1934 Communist Party convention, 39 were Negroes. The party structure included a special Negro Department. The party was also responsible for the formation of the American Negro Labor Congress, which changed its name in 1930 to the League for Struggle for Negro Rights.

Wherever one looked in the 1930's there was ferment—not merely among Negroes, veterans, or unemployed. Farmers in Nebraska or Iowa or New York were stopping trucks and dumping thousands of gallons of milk rather than permit it to be moved to market and depress prices further. The New York *Times* carried this news item from Sioux City, Iowa, on August 16, 1932: "Scores of trucks loaded with milk, farm products and livestock headed for Sioux City have been turned back today on nearly every highway after the drivers have been warned in no uncertain terms. . . . A few trucks crashed through a steel cable which was stretched across a bridge, but were blocked a second time when railroad ties were thrown under the wheels." Farmers often stood with guns or pitchforks at an auction to prevent foreclosure sales. Anyone who seriously bid for a repossessed farm did so at the peril of his life. When the farm had been "sold" to an agreed-on rebel for a few dollars, it was turned back to its owner.

Before the decade ended, millions had been in and out of a host of reform and panacea movements. There was Dr. Francis Townsend's National Recovery Plan, which promised $200 a month for the aged, to be financed by a $20 billion transaction tax. There was Howard Scott's Technocracy, and Upton Sinclair's EPIC—End Poverty in California. There was L. W. Allen's "Ham and Eggs" movement, which promised $30 every Thursday for every unemployed or retired resident over fifty. There was E. J. Reed's Utopian Society, which spoke of the "Brotherhood of Man" and proposed to solve the social problems of the day through government ownership of the means of production. There were also rightists catering to the poor, such as Father Charles E. Coughlin, who had ten million radio listeners each week, and Senator Huey P. Long, whose "Share the Wealth" program proposed a capital levy of $165 billion to be allocated so that everyone would have a minimum of $2,500 a year. "Every man a king" was Huey's slogan. In a world whose moorings were lost, all ideas, no matter how bizarre—or for that matter, how sensible—received a hearing.

V

The drama of the 1930's was enacted on three levels, each feeding the other: the streets, the radical groups, the New Deal. The picket lines and demonstrations measured the discontent. The radical groups fanned the discontent and gave it organizational form. The New Deal allayed it by a series of alphabetical innovations which transformed America from a laissez-faire capitalism to a state-controlled capitalism—from "rugged individualism" to a semiwelfare state. "The 'New Deal,'" wrote Ferdinand Lundberg in his *America's Sixty Families,* "is not revolutionary nor radical in any sense. . . . Its mild, tentative reformist coloration is but a necessary concession in the face of widespread unrest."

What might have happened to America if Roosevelt had not given it a face lifting is not certain. Many people, not necessarily leftists, were convinced that revolution was in the offing. "Fear of a revolution," writes David A. Shannon, a historian of the depression, "was very widespread during the last several months of President Hoover's administration, and much of the politics of the period can be understood fully only by viewing political events against the background of anxiety about violent revolt. The vigor with which the army dispersed the Bonus Expeditionary Force from Washington in the summer of 1932, for example, had it roots in revolutionary fear." Roosevelt and his "brain trust" mitigated that fear. Though they did not fully solve the problems of the depression—unemployment still hovered at eight million, or 15 percent of the work force, as late as 1940—they did proceed with vigor.

Three and a third billion dollars were appropriated for public works to make jobs. A federal emergency relief program granted large sums to the states for direct relief to the hungry. The National Recovery Administration, under General Hugh Johnson, set codes for fair-trade practices and established a stable price level to buttress business. Section 7(a), though grudgingly included in the National Recovery Act, guaranteed labor the right to organize. Armed with Section 7(a), John L. Lewis gambled his organization's treasury to rebuild the miners' union from 150,000 to 500,000 members in a few months. The New Deal's Agricultural Adjustment Act sought to raise farm prices by granting subsidies to those who curbed production. Its Works Progress Administration spent $10.5 billion on a wide variety of projects and created three million synthetic jobs. Its Tennessee Valley Authority built dams, powerhouses, hydroelectric plants under direct government ownership and control, and helped regenerate a large area in the South. The New Deal passed the Wagner Act, for the first time spelling out labor's right to unionize. It introduced laws to insure bank deposits and laws to control the stock market. It provided unemployment compensation for the jobless and social security for the aged.

Implicit in all this was the recognition that laissez-faire capitalism was dead and that the market was not, as old-line economists insisted, an automatic regulating mechanism that kept the economy in running order. Roosevelt, by all accounts, understood little of economics, but his advisers, while they did not embrace Marxism, operated along the lines expounded by Maynard Keynes of a state controlled capitalism. They also plagiarized much of Norman Thomas' social program. In the 1928 campaign the Socialist standard-bearer had urged a public works program "at hours and wages fixed by bona-fide labor unions," old-age pensions, unemployment insurance, shortening of the work week, joining of the League of Nations, and diplomatic recognition of the Soviet Union (which had been withheld since 1917). All of these—some in modified form—became official policy under Roosevelt.

Yet notwithstanding such reforms, the radicals—except for the Right wing of the Socialist Party—were vociferously opposed to Franklin D. Roosevelt. They were not interested in patching up a decaying corpse. They wanted to bury it. Capitalism was hopeless, with or without the patches, and the only way to assure the good society was to overthrow it. In this respect the Communists were as intransigent as the others. Had they remained so, the 1930's might have been written, for better or for worse, in other terms. But they made as complete a reversal in their attitude toward Roosevelt as was humanly possible. At first, under the prevailing dogma of the third period, Communists castigated the Roosevelt reformers, like the Socialists, as "twins" of fascism. The New Deal, Browder wrote, "is a policy of brutal oppression at home and of imperialism abroad." Roosevelt, far from being a saint, was "carrying out more thoroughly, more brutally than Hoover, the capitalist attack against the living standards of the masses." The National Recovery Administration was called reactionary and its symbol, the Blue Eagle, which employers and store owners posted on their premises as a sign of compliance, was referred to as the "fascist Blue Eagle." As late as February 1935 a party manifesto carried the caption: "Against the 'New Deal' of Hunger, Fascism and War!"

In July of that year, however, the Communist International held its Seventh Congress and confirmed a policy already in operation for many months. The third period and its ultraleftist baggage were jettisoned, a fourth period proclaimed. By this time Hitler and the Nazis were ensconced in Germany and Stalin was looking for friends in the international arena anywhere he could find them. In May 1935 he and Pierre Laval signed the Franco-Soviet Pact, pledging mutual assistance between Russia and France. Communists in France, Spain, Austria, and elsewhere were urged to form permanent blocs—popular fronts—with Socialist and Left-wing capitalist parties. Yesterday's social-fascists became today's betrothed as Maurice Thorez for the Communists and Leon Blum for the Socialists joined in a *Front populaire* in France. The implementation of this soft line in the United States required, among other things, a changed approach toward Franklin Roosevelt. Browder, who had been calling Roosevelt a reactionary, now cried that "when Wall Street hates anyone as it does President Roosevelt, then that man is not our enemy."

In the fourth period Roosevelt was referred to as a "middle of the roader," who merited support, though with some qualification. "President Roosevelt's re-election," said Browder in 1936, "will be a rebuke to the worst reactionaries but is no guarantee against the further progress of fascism in America." The Communists always left themselves a little leeway. They did not associate completely with Roosevelt, but they made sure to identify him as part of the "camp of democracy" against fascism.

It was a clever, if not entirely consistent, policy. Under the popular front theme, Browder again unfurled the Farmer-Labor Party banner and pleaded with the "confused" Norman Thomas for joint activity. The American Labor Party and the Washington and Oregon Commonwealth Federations, which a year before would have been pilloried as bastions of reaction, were hailed as members in good standing of the progressive camp. The platform on which Browder made a lackadaisical campaign for the Presidency in 1936—a considerable majority of party followers voted for Roosevelt—was as mild as any the "reformist" Socialists had ever put forth. It called for a sharply graduated income tax, enforcement of the Thirteenth, Fourteenth, and Fifteenth Amendments, unemployment insurance and old-age pensions, education opportunities, jobs and a living wage, guarantees to farmers and Negroes, endorsement of the Kellogg Peace Pact. There was little in it that either Norman Thomas or Franklin Roosevelt could not accept. In a major redefinition of communism at about this time, Browder stated that "Communism is twentieth-century Americanism." References to force and violence, so prominent before, were deleted from programmatic statements and speeches.

The transition from third to fourth period was so melodramatic it inspired young Socialists and young Trotskyists to compose songs of derision:

Kaleidoscopic what I mean
Our line's been changed again.
Now we're red and now we're green,
Our line's been changed again.

I knows it, Browder. I knows it, Browder,
Our line's been changed again.

We must appear to be sedate,
Our line's been changed again—
The revolution? That can wait,
Our line's been changed again.

Imperialist wars we once attacked,
Our line's been changed again—
But since the Franco-Soviet pact,
Our line's been changed again.

If the 180-degree turn in Communist strategy, however, brought snickers from rivals and a few defections inside the party, it nonetheless opened wide many new doors. While the Socialist Party became embroiled in factional disputes and splits which cut its membership to a low of 6,488 by February 1937, the Communists grew to 70,000 by 1939. "Americanization" made the Communist Party acceptable to many who had shunned it before. By tying itself, if only tenuously, to New Deal coattails the party gained an aura of respectability which made recruitment much simpler. To make communism "American," the names of many "front" groups were modified. The League Against War and Fascism was changed to League for Peace and Democracy. The League of Struggle for Negro Rights was superseded by the National Negro Congress. Negative words like "against" and aggressive ones like "struggle" were offensive to the new image and therefore taboo. The party's periphery enlarged greatly, penetrating dozens of milieus. There was the American Student Union (result of a merger with a Socialist student group but controlled by the Communists) to enroll young people, the National Negro Congress for Negroes, the Friends of the Abraham Lincoln Brigade for sympathizers of the Republicans in the Spanish Civil War, the League of American Writers for literary figures, and many others. Only a handful in each organization were Communist Party members, but they exerted enough influence and held down enough key jobs to commit it to party policy.

Unlike satellite groups in previous periods of Communist history, the newly named ones included men of reputation and substance—professors, actors, lawyers, writers, many internationally known. In April 1938 one hundred and fifty people issued a statement endorsing one of the Soviet Union's purge trials. The list read like a who's who of the arts and sciences, betokening the wide support Browder could expect in the community. Exclusive of unions, Earl Browder's party could depend on at least a million friends in front groups, probably more. For the beleaguered and isolated party of 1928–29, this was no negligible achievement.

V I

The door that the radicals wanted most to pry open during the Red Decade was the labor door. For more than a half century the

American Left had been trying with might and main to achieve what Socialists and anarchists had won elsewhere, namely, a decisive role in the union movement. In the 1930's the Communists came closer than ever before. Though they did not capture the CIO—and certainly not the AFL—they were the spark plugs of the organizing drives and strikes, winding up with hundreds of local unions and approximately a dozen national unions under their guiding hand. The Socialists, with young men such as Walter Reuther and his brothers Victor and Roy in the forefront, gained important bastions in the auto union and elsewhere. Older—and more moderate—Socialists in the needle trades were also active in the organizing drives. Indeed, from one end of the radical rainbow to the other—Trotskyists, Musteites, Lovestoneites, even a few regenerated ex-Wobblies and ex-De Leonists—the leftists were caught up in the crusade to enroll the unorganized.

It was an exciting time for young radicals. Standing on improvised soapboxes at factory gates or on platforms in meeting halls, they made thousands of impassioned speeches condemning the moguls of industry. In urging a worker to join a union to end speedup or win a nickel an hour raise, they also reminded him how evil was the capitalist system, how it led to poverty amidst plenty, how it spent "millions for war" but little for the working class. They appealed to the insurgent impulse, not just the desire for "more." They passed out leaflets, held organizing meetings, led strikes with a zeal that no one else could muster. And they were willing to make personal sacrifices in a way that the staid leadership of labor was not. Whatever one may think of Communist political foibles, individual members faced hardships, beatings, and the threat of jail with considerable courage. During a New York restaurant strike the courts issued 110 injunctions against a Communist-led union in a vain attempt to dampen its ardor. From late 1929 to 1932 twenty-three men and women were shot down in strikes and unemployed demonstrations led by Communists. It is doubtful whether American labor would have experienced so forceful a resurgence without them or the other radicals.

By 1934 it was no longer a question as to whether the millions of unorganized workers would form unions—but under whose auspices they would do it. Hundreds of important strikes broke out in the first two years of the New Deal, most of them spontaneously. Typically, a group of factory workers, enraged over some grievance or low wages, would discuss what they could do about it. Invariably a Communist, a Socialist, Trotskyite, Lovestoneite, or ex-Wobbly employed at the plant would assume leadership in sponsoring a union. Sometimes an unemployed group in the area would direct the campaign.

From July 1933 to July 1934 the AFL, then led by William Green, issued thirteen hundred federal local charters—unions directly affiliated with the AFL itself rather than a national union. This was five times as many as in the previous five years. In 1933, 1.2 million workers went on strike and 1.5 million in 1934—five times the number two years before. There were so many federal locals being formed and so many independent unions that Charles P. Howard, a founder of the CIO, was constrained to say at the 1935 AFL convention: "I don't know, there is no one in this convention who knows . . . how many workers have been organized into independent unions, company unions and associations that may have some affiliation with subversive influences during the past few years." The number, he said, was "'far greater than any one of us would grant."

Four pivotal strikes in 1934 indicated the trend. The national textile walkout in September involved 475,000 operatives in twenty states from Massachusetts to Alabama. Eleven thousand National Guardsmen were mobilized in sixteen of these states. Ten strikers were killed, hundreds wounded, and fifteen thousand workers were blacklisted when the strike was lost. Though it was led by AFL "labor skates," many a radical who had participated in the Lawrence, Marion, Passaic, and other campaigns was on hand to form flying squads to keep out strikebreakers.

The walkout at the Toledo Auto-Lite plant, as already mentioned, was led by A. J. Muste and members of his American Workers Party. In Minneapolis, Farrell Dobbs and the three Dunne brothers—Vincent, Grant, and Miles—all Trotskyists, introduced techniques which were responsible for the growth of the national teamsters' union. During a city-wide truck drivers' strike, they divided the city into sections, with roving automobiles—flying squads—touring each one. When they came upon a scab truck, they curbed it and used whatever force was necessary to make the driver reconsider. It was so effective a technique that the police began to tap telephone lines in the strikers' garage to find out where the flying squads were going. The game became elaborate as the Trotskyists set up dummy garages to fool the police, and police chased cars all over the city, not knowing which were the real flying squads, which were not. At one point there was a pitched battle between police and strikers at the city market, which went on intermittently for two days. The police were forced to flee. One striker drove a truck with twenty-five pickets directly into police lines, sending them scurrying for cover. On the second day of this engagement, the authorities mobilized two thousand special deputies, but again were unable to move the trucks. Two people were killed. The strikers won their major demand—recognition of their union.

Another major industrial battle in 1934 was the one of West Coast longshoremen and maritime workers led by Harry Bridges. Though not a Communist Party member, Bridges was not unfriendly; around him were men of similar bent, some inside, some outside the party. The walkout, initiated by Bridges' longshoremen in San Francisco, spread to the AFL maritime unions, so that by the end of May there were 35,000 on strike from Vancouver in the north to San Diego in the south. One day in early July—"Bloody Thursday," the strikers called it—police tried to open the docks but were met with the furious resistance of thousands of determined pickets. Two strikers were killed, hundreds wounded. The incident so outraged San Francisco unionists that for three days 127,000 of them—defying an order of AFL President William Green—struck in sympathy with the beleaguered longshoremen. After three months the strike ended in arbitration and a moderate victory for the maritime men. But Bridges emerged with a reputation of militancy that made him the key West Coast figure in the future CIO.

The strikes of 1933 and 1934 were only a prelude. The road was now clear to storm industrial fortresses like United States Steel, which had resisted unionization for decades. This was the indicated next step.

For the institutionalized bureaucracy of the AFL, however, such a step posed the danger of being swamped by a new generation of militants. Green and his friends reacted with utter confusion, obviously incapable of handling the problem—except to close their eyes to it. But middle-of-the-road leaders, like John L. Lewis of the miners and Sidney Hillman of the Amalgamated Clothing Workers, decided the way to checkmate the radicals was to assume leadership of the movement themselves. "I stand here," said Lewis at the 1935 AFL convention, "and plead for a policy . . . that will protect our form of government against the isms and the philosophies of foreign lands that now seem to be rampant in high and low places throughout the country." What he wanted the AFL to do was to charter vertical unions in mass production industries such as auto, rubber, packinghouse, steel, so that control would rest with the moderates rather than the far Left. If the AFL itself took the initiative, the radicals would be relegated to secondary positions. When Lewis' advice went unheeded—it was turned down by a vote of 2 to 1—eight national unions, with approximately one million members, formed into a caucus, the Committee for Industrial Organization— soon to become the Congress of Industrial Organizations (CIO).

The break came at a favorable time. Two circumstances assured the CIO quick and sensational success. One was the shift in Communist policy. In 1932, William Z. Foster had referred to Lewis and other AFL leaders as "practically open fascists." This was, of course, justification for a dual union policy. Had the Communists remained outside CIO ranks, Lewis' organizational efforts might have been reduced in scale, perhaps aborted. As Max Kampelman, a writer on Communist labor tactics, points out, "the Stalinists knew how to make speeches, write reports, run mimeograph machines, prepare leaflets, set up a picket line, hold the chair in turbulent meetings, and manipulate parliamentary procedure." They were also, of course, militant, ready to resist police, vigilantes, and troops. Their role in the CIO is indisputable. Though the CIO at the top was run by old-time officials like Lewis, Hillman, and Philip Murray, one notch below was an assortment of leftists—with the Communists predominating—who were not only visible but decisive. In a book published years later, Foster claimed that of the staff of two hundred hired by the CIO Steel Workers Organizing Committee, sixty were Communist Party members—including Gus Hall, who was to become the Communist Party chieftain in the 1960's. Though the Reuther brothers, Socialists, played an important role in the sitdown strike at General Motors—the strike which most observers believe made the CIO—the main strategists were Communists. There was also a sizable body of men who were not in the party, some of whom have become bitter enemies since, but who collaborated with it in the 1930's. Among them were Harry Bridges, Michael Quill of the transport union, Joseph Curran of the maritime union, and James B. Carey of the electrical workers. According to Edward Levinson, one-time educational director of the auto union, the Communists controlled national unions with one fifth the CIO membership. They were also ensconced in scores of local unions. Their abandonment of the policy of dual unionism, therefore, was not only a precondition for their own improved fortunes but for that of the CIO. When John L. Lewis was once asked why he hired so many Communists and other radicals he quipped back: "Who gets the bird, the hunter or the dog?"

A second fortunate circumstance for the CIO was the adoption of the sit-down strike technique. Mass picket lines outside a plant were vulnerable to attacks by police or troops. But by seizing the plant—sitting in—strikers gained a degree of immunity. Corporations were loath to have police battle workers near expensive machinery. Furthermore, the odds would be with the unionists because they knew the terrain so well. The sit-down was an old technique that had been used by the Wobblies as far back as the 1906 strike at General Electric in Schenectady. In 1919 Italian workers used the sit-in, or sit-down, as a revolutionary weapon. Miners in Pécs, Hungary, in 1934 seized the pits and threatened mass suicide unless their demands were granted. The outburst of sit-downs in the United States was, therefore, not new, but it was widespread and unusually effective. In the nine months from September 1936 to June 1937 almost a half-million American workers seized their factories. There were 150 "quickie" sit-downs in the rubber plants alone, lasting from half an hour to four days. All told, from 1935 to 1937, there were at least 900 sit-downs, the major ones led by radicals of various brands.

The one sit-down which captured the imagination of millions of American workers and lent a dynamic quality to the letters in the abbreviation CIO was in the General Motors plants of Flint, Michigan. This was the citadel of the General Motors empire, and General Motors was one of the citadels of the mass production industry. To force General Motors to recognize the union was a breakthrough for the American proletariat comparable to the defeat of Cornwallis in the American Revolution.

The conflict with General Motors began mildly in November 1936 when the company discharged four employees at its Atlanta plant for wearing union buttons. The men went out on strike, but they realized it was useless to close a single plant of so large a company. The cry went out to "spread the strike"—a popular slogan in the 1930's—and within a month and a half operations were shut down in Kansas City and more than a dozen other units, as well as the heartland of General Motors, Flint. Of the fifty thousand strikers at Flint, thousands sat inside the factories. Others formed flying squads to patrol the area. Under the on-the-spot leadership of Left-wingers Robert Travis and Wyndham Mortimer, as well as others, unionists showed considerable ingenuity. They formed squads to keep order, they "manufactured" billy clubs of wood and leatherette for possible defense, set up kitchens to feed the sit-ins, even arranged for recreation to mitigate the boredom.

Management and the city government, of course, responded with time-honored methods—court injunction, a vigilante group, police, and the National Guard. There was no means, however, of ejecting the sit-downers without considerable damage to property. The only feasible prospect was to starve and freeze them out. General Motors had been heating the Fisher 2 plant to protect its equipment and water pipes. On January 11 management decided to throw caution to the winds; it shut off the heat. A few hours later police surrounded the entrance to prevent any food being sent in. This turned out to be a key incident in American labor history. A young Socialist, Victor Reuther, stood at the microphone exhorting the unionists not to yield. Women alternately argued and pleaded with police to let food into the plant. Early in the morning pickets temporarily broke through police lines, but were soon met with tear gas and buckshot. "We wanted peace," shouted a strike leader. "General Motors chose war. Give it to them." The war went on for three hours, with the strikers inside turning a water hose against their tormentors and throwing door hinges at them. The "Battle of the Running Bulls," as it became known, ended in a victory for the unionists; a defeat for the bulls.

The CIO did not win its objectives immediately—there was mediation by the governor and more quickie sit-downs—but industrial unionism was now firmly established. What the Wobblies had failed to do in the first quarter of the century and the William Z. Foster-John Fitzpatrick team in the 1919 steel strike, the CIO accomplished in a few months in 1937.

After Flint there was a sit-down at the Chrysler plants, involving another fifty-nine thousand workers. By this time many large corporations—notably United States Steel—decided accommodation with the CIO would be the best thing. Rather than face the kind of turmoil visited on General Motors and Chrysler, the steel men came to terms peaceably with John L. Lewis. Here and there, there were holdouts, such as the Ford Company or the "Little Steel" corporations, where a strike in 1937 led to seventeen deaths. But the auto union grew from thirty thousand to four hundred thousand in a single year, and within a few years the CIO as a whole quadrupled from one million to four million members.

VII

The triumph of the CIO also marked the high-water mark for American radicalism. Not all segments of the Left benefited—the Socialists, indeed, declined again to a minuscule force. A new and enervating series of faction fights consumed its energies. The majority faction, the militants, to which Norman Thomas adhered, was composed in the main of Marxists who were attracted anew— though not uncritically—to the Bolshevik experiment in Russia. At the 1932 convention of the Socialist Party the militants, though urging Soviet Russia to release political prisoners and restore civil liberties, carried their resolution endorsing "the effort being made in Russia to create the economic foundations of a socialist society." The old guard faction demurred sharply. On this and on the trade-union issue old guards and militants polemicized with unrestrained vigor.

Two years later, in 1934, with the rise of fascism in Europe and the fear of possible Fascist trends in the United States, a declaration of principles was formulated in strong leftist tones: "Capitalism is doomed," it said. "If it can be superseded by majority vote, the Socialist Party will rejoice. If the crisis comes through the denial of majority rights after the electorate has given us a mandate we shall not hesitate to crush by our labor solidarity the reckless forces of reaction and to consolidate the Socialist state. If the capitalist system should collapse in a general chaos and confusion . . . the Socialist Party, whether or not in such a case it is a majority, will not shrink from the responsibility of organizing and maintaining a government under the workers' rule." Though the words "force and violence" were not used, some of the concepts came close to it. Even this, however, did not satisfy the extreme Left wing, the Revolutionary Policy Committee, which proclaimed that "the aim of socialism is to . . . transform capitalist society by means of the dictatorship of the proletariat." The Socialist Party shifted with the times, leftward, but it was destined for fragmentation and inertia. Until 1934, according to Norman Thomas, "it looked as if we were going to go places. . . ." Afterward it was obvious that it was not. Socialist Party rolls fell to 11,922 by 1936, and a mere 6,488 by 1937 as both old guard and extreme Left members broke away.

But while the Socialists lost ground precipitously, the Communists gained appreciably. They not only had the largest trade-union base any radical group in America had ever forged—national and local unions with perhaps a million and a half members—but were strongly entrenched in the CIO national office. The CIO newspaper and legal staff were manned by people very close to the Communist party. In addition, of course, there was the Workers Alliance—the unified unemployed movement—also in the Communist roster, as well as a plethora of satellite organizations. The tenth convention of the Communist Party in May 1938 claimed seventy-five thousand members—an increase of thirty-five thousand in just two years. The Young Communist League in the same time doubled from ten to twenty thousand. Optimism abounded as the Communists launched two more daily newspapers, the *People's World* and the *Midwest Daily Record,* to supplement the *Daily Worker.*

The revolution that Communists had envisioned in the third period was far more remote than it appeared in 1929, but Earl Browder did succeed in converting the Communist Party from a sect to a movement.

CHAPTER XVI

EPILOGUE AND PROLOGUE

THE QUARTER of a century that followed the Red Decade was an epilogue—and perhaps a prologue. An old Left played out a role to which it was already committed. But there were no signs of impending revolution and few people believed it was either inevitable or necessary. The expected preconditions for one—such as depression, unemployment, and slashed wage levels—had failed to appear. The cadres of radicalism, therefore, contracted, expanded, contracted again, and then all but disappeared. It was like the final spasms of a terminal patient.

There were almost no points of similarity with the previous twenty-five years. Except for a handful of Trotskyists and the tiny band of Wobblies that still remained, there was no opposition to United States participation in World War II. The government did not resort to repressions during hostilities, and those that followed during the cold war period, while of much longer duration than those after World War I, were milder. There were new splitlets in the various parties, including the Communist Party, but nothing remotely approaching in significance the 1919 split between Communists and Socialists. Even the revolutions overseas, except to some extent the Cuban Revolution, did not arouse American leftists in the same way as the Russian Revolution or the assassination of Liebknecht and Luxemburg in Germany. There were no grand meetings in Madison Square Garden to hail the Chinese Revolution, or the Ghanaian Revolution when Nkrumah took the reins from British imperialism.

Radical influence in the trade unions, the best barometer of leftist status, waned so seriously after 1948 that within a decade there was hardly a trace left. A few leaders in the unions expelled from the CIO remained insurgents at heart but there was no organized faction of any kind at the disposal either of the Communist or Socialist Parties. Ex-Socialists and ex-Communists and ex-Trotskyists were prominent in many unions, and worked with diligence for higher wages, social insurance, housing, civil rights. They were by now, however, frank devotees of the free enterprise system—mild reformers rather than revolutionaries. Not since the days before Fanny Wright were the radicals so impotent in the house of labor. By 1957, after many thousands of defections resulting from the Khrushchev speech at the 20th Congress of the Soviet Communist Party and the Soviet offensive against the Hungarian Revolution, the American Communist Party was again a sect, weaker than at any time in its history.

For all practical purposes the old Left was gone. An amorphous new Left began to appear simultaneously, but it had few of the characteristics of the old one, and its destiny was far from clear even after a decade of activity.

II

Toward the end of August 1939 American Communists picked up their newspapers to learn that Soviet Russia and Nazi Germany had signed a "nonaggression" pact. It was unbelievable. An arrangement with the Nazi butcher Hitler? Impossible. Six weeks earlier Browder had stated at an institute in Virginia that "there is about as much chance of such an agreement [between Germany and Russia] as of Earl Browder being elected president of the American Chamber of Commerce." For one day the *Daily Worker* did not report the Hitler-Stalin pact. It was obvious that even the party leaders did not understand its significance, for in an interview with the press, Browder insisted there would be an "escape clause" giving Stalin the right to repudiate it if Hitler invaded Poland or Rumania. Another party official went further, predicting if Poland were attacked by Germany, the Soviet Union would come to its aid. Instead of representing the pact as a release for Hitler from any worry on the eastern front, the Communist Party, when it recovered its poise, claimed it was actually a contribution to peace. In September World War II began. Hitler overran Poland from the west; Russia, though not a belligerent, seized the eastern two thirds of the country.

The shock and confusion of these events, though costly for the Communist Party, were not devastating. Many dependable allies, such as David Lasser of the Workers Alliance and Joseph P. Lash of the American Student Union, deserted the ship. A number of front groups declined to impotence or simply closed shop. Among pro-Communist workers in the needle trades' unions the political mortality rate was high because a large portion of them were Jews who considered any *rapprochement* with Hitler an act of treachery. All told, it is estimated that from ten to fifteen thousand party members tore up their cards and many times that number of sympathizers stopped coming to meetings of front groups.

The main body of communism, however, survived. The blow was hard but not a knockout. Soon the party evolved a rationale. Russia, it said, had to buy time since the Western powers, by appeasing Hitler when he seized Austria and Czechoslovakia, were only prodding him to attack the Soviet Union. Furthermore, the aggressor in this war was not Germany. Foster recorded his agreement with Stalin that "it was not Germany who attacked France and England, but France and England which attacked Germany, assuming responsibility for the present war." The Allies, he said, "assumed further responsibility by rejecting the peace proposals of Germany, the Netherlands and the Soviet Union."

By clever sleight of hand, the Communists turned the issue of the pact and Russia's culpability in seizing parts of Poland into an anti-war stance. At a meeting of the National Committee on September 19, 1939, the party called the conflict "a war between rival imperialisms for world domination." It further declared: "Keep America out of the imperialist war. Support the peace policy of the Soviet Union —the land of Socialist democracy, progress, peace and national liberation." For those who had made the survival of the Soviet Union—the only "socialist state" in the world—the kernel of their world outlook, this argument was reassuring. At any rate, it served to hold intact most of the Communist bastions in the unions— though weakened—as well as 85 percent of the party membership itself.

To cover their flanks the Communists once more adopted a hard line. Roosevelt, who was aiding the Allies, again became the subject

[329]

of rebuke. During the 1940 Presidential campaign, candidate Earl Browder caustically noted that "Mr. Roosevelt has studied well the Hitlerian art and bids fair to outdo the record of his teacher." Communists challenged Roosevelt on his conscription bill, lend-lease aid to the Allies, and the giving of fifty destroyers to Britain. A pro-Communist union official described the conscription law as "a death sentence on the trade union and all democratic institutions." Wherever they could, Communists called strikes in plants closely associated with military preparations, such as Vultee Aircraft, North American Aircraft, Milwaukee's Allis-Chalmers. The favorite party slogan in the period from September 1939 to June 1941 read: "The Yanks are not coming."

All in all, it was a shrewd strategy devised to capitalize on widespread sentiments for neutrality. In October 1939 the AFL declared: "As for our country, we demand that it stay out of the European conflict, maintaining neutrality in spirit and act." The CIO seconded this theme: "Labor wants no war nor any part of war." The auto union distributed a hundred thousand copies of an antiwar pamphlet called *Soldiers Get Free Graves*. Even the candidates for President of the United States, while not neutral, nevertheless spoke against becoming belligerents. "I am for keeping out of war," said Republican Wendell Willkie. "I have said this before, but I shall say it again and again and again," said Franklin D. Roosevelt. "Your boys are not going to be sent into any foreign wars." Though the Communists were unpopular, therefore, for their dramatic about-face, they were not entirely isolated. They remained on good terms with former CIO President John L. Lewis (who resigned because the CIO would not endorse Willkie) and moderately so with Philip Murray, his successor.

Communist activity in that interlude between the Stalin-Hitler pact and the next reversal in policy less than two years later, did not bring forth that frenzy of arrests, jailings, and lynchings that punctuated the World War I period.

A month or two after hostilities began in Europe, Browder was indicted for a passport irregularity. It was a flimsy charge. Back in the 1920's, when he had traveled to such places as China on assignment for the Communist International, he had used a pseudonym in applying for passports. In 1934, when he applied legally, under his own name, he committed the technical infraction of not mentioning the previous applications. The Department of Justice, of course, had been aware of all this for some time and could have prosecuted five years before. That it chose to do so now was clearly because Browder was out of step with United States policy. He was convicted and given the unusually harsh sentence of four years in prison and a two-thousand-dollar fine. He entered jail in Atlanta in March 1941, but was released by Roosevelt a year later, after the Communists had become fervid supporters of government policy. The only other important reprisal against the Communists was the revocation of the citizenship of William Schneiderman, party secretary in California, who had been naturalized in the 1920's. Schneiderman was charged with having withheld the information of previous membership in the party. His defense was taken by no less a figure than the Republican standard-bearer, Wendell Willkie, who secured a reversal from the United States Supreme Court.

The only radicals seriously penalized during the war were members and friends of the Socialist Workers Party—Trotskyists. In October 1941 twenty-nine of them, including James P. Cannon, their leader, went on trial on two counts. The first charged them, under an 1861 statute, with conspiring to overthrow the government by force and violence. The second, under the Smith Act passed in 1940, accused them of conspiring to *advocate* such overthrow. After a five-week trial in which the government quoted long and laboriously from Trotskyist writings, eighteen of the defendants were adjudged guilty on the second count and given prison terms of twelve to sixteen months. Since the Trotskyists did not recant their antiwar position, they served the full terms, with the usual time off for good behavior.

Even the Trotskyists might have avoided prison if they had not been involved in a dispute with Daniel Tobin, national president of the teamsters' union. Local 544 in Minneapolis, led by the Trotskyist Dunne brothers, had been a thorn in Tobin's side for years—and a menace to his power. After a continuing rift in which the Dunnes challenged Tobin's attempt to centralize power, the latter decided to discipline them, and Local 544, in turn, seceded from the AFL to join the CIO. It was at this point that Tobin, an influential Democrat, appealed to Roosevelt for help. The American Civil Liberties Union accused the government of injecting "itself into an inter-union controversy" and the CIO charged that "Dan Tobin has

[*331*]

persuaded Roosevelt to carry out this action in payment of his political debt to Tobin." Left of center, only the Communists, who were themselves to be victimized by the Smith Act seven or eight years later, applauded the efforts "to exterminate the Trotskyite Fifth Column from the life of our nation."

The Trotskyist trials ended just a few days before Pearl Harbor. It was, interestingly enough, the last instance of repression against radicals in the war period. Since there was no antiwar movement anyway, there was no reason for it. The labor movement, both AFL and CIO, was by now fully committed to the war effort. Except for John L. Lewis of the independent miners' union, the house of labor gave Roosevelt an unconditional pledge not to strike for the duration of hostilities. Even Lewis' refusal was not based on any antiwar precepts but on the purely tactical ground that he did not want to give management any advantage. Nowhere on the horizon was there a revolutionary union like the IWW to challenge national unity or "class peace." What remained of the radical battalions—except for the Communists—was divided, immobilized, and impotent. In the 1940 elections Norman Thomas centered his campaign on keeping the United States out of war. Still pacifistic at heart, he was willing to preach the gospel from any podium—including one which was a cause of embarrassment, the conservative and isolationist America First Committee. But his vote, 117,000, was only two thirds of what it had been four years before, and only a fraction of the 900,000 in 1932. The Socialist Party, now barely a few thousand members, saw one faction after another desert to join the prowar legions. Jack Altman, a union leader, withdrew a group of supporters to align himself with William Allen White's Committee to Defend America by Aiding the Allies. Another group, including James Loeb, future ambassador to Peru, resigned to form the Union for Democratic Action, which later metamorphosed into the liberal Americans for Democratic Action. When the United States actually joined the fray, even Norman Thomas' opposition gave out. At the 1942 convention of his party he proposed "critical support" of the war effort—which meant that he reserved the right to criticize the government for such transgressions on civil liberties as the incarceration of Japanese-Americans on the West Coast or mistreatment of conscientious objectors, while endorsing the main war aims. About half the delegates accepted Thomas' position, most of the others took the harder line of "political nonsupport." But it was of little consequence because by now the party was an enervated shell.

As for the splinter group dissidents, their voices were only a whisper. The Lovestoneites had disbanded early in 1941. The few Trotskyist organizations and what was left of the IWW could cause hardly a ripple. From one end of the social spectrum to the other— that is, from the Communists to the Chicago *Tribune* on the Right— national unity was assured. Repression would only draw attention to an antiwar movement that was less than a shadow.

Whatever danger the government confronted from the Left disappeared entirely in June 1941 when Hitler turned on his erstwhile ally, Stalin, and sent German troops headlong into Russia. With as little fanfare as it takes to change a shirt, the Communists overnight emerged the most zealous supporters of Roosevelt and the war effort in the United States. The sharp turn, just as the one in September 1939, caused minor embarrassment here and there. The July issue of the *Communist*, for instance, was just being locked up with a dissertation by William Z. Foster, noting that "the present war constitutes a violent division of the world among the great imperialist powers," when news of the attack on Russia reached the editors. It was too late to pull it out. All they could do was add an editorial supporting the Soviet Union "in its struggle against Hitlerism." Two diametrically opposite positions appeared in the same issue, lending enchantment to diversity but hardly improving the Communist image for consistency. For critics on the Left and Right such incidents were proof of the subservience of the American Communist Party to a foreign power, its willingness to shift and twist to the needs of Soviet policy. Yet the individual Communist was so convinced— emotionally as well as intellectually—that the interests of the Soviet Union, the only "workers' state," were paramount to all others, he could live at peace with this kind of inconsistency. He was, in fact, somewhat relieved because the "new line" placed him again in the popular Roosevelt camp.

Six days after the invasion of the Soviet Union the Communist Party here issued a statement calling for "full and unlimited collaboration of the United States, Great Britain, and the Soviet Union, to bring about the military defeat of Hitler." After Pearl Harbor the party pledged "its loyalty, its devoted labor and the last drop of its blood in support of our country in this greatest of all crises that ever threatened its existence." The "Yanks are not coming" slogan was replaced by "All out for the war effort." The "imperialist war" was transformed into the "people's war."

According to Foster, 15,000 Communists joined or were drafted to the colors, many distinguishing themselves for bravery. Gathering for a meeting in 1947, 414 Communist veterans listed 1,353 decorations between them, ranging from 1,019 battle stars to one Distinguished Service Cross. In the "Battle for Production" Communist trade unionists went further than anyone else, not only endorsing the no-strike pledge but urging piecework rates and incentive plans —both of which labor had usually considered anathema. The one strike that the CIO and most of the AFL supported—against the Montgomery Ward company in Chicago, after it refused to abide by an order of President Roosevelt—was boycotted and condemned by the Communists. Old militants in the party who had been decrying the speed-up for ages were now urging their fellow workers to work faster. Earl Browder defending himself against a charge of strikebreaking had this to say: "As regards the fomenting of the strike movements that threaten America at this time, I consider it the greatest honor to be a breaker of this movement." Harry Bridges in May 1944 went further. "The strike weapon," he said, "is overboard, not only for the duration of the war, but after the war too."

There was an idyllic mood to Earl Browder's communism in the war years. He wanted to be friends with everyone—except, of course, the Trotskyites. In his book *Victory—and After* he spoke of "uniting the entire nation, including the biggest capitalists, for a complete and all-out drive for victory." After the Teheran Conference between Roosevelt, Churchill, and Stalin, in November-December 1943, Browder noted with what, in hindsight, was premature effusiveness, that "capitalism and socialism have begun to find the way to peaceful coexistence and collaboration in the same world." Presumably there was no longer anything in capitalism that required its overthrow. "We frankly declare," said Browder before the 1944 elections, "that we are ready to cooperate in making Capitalism work effectively in the post-war period with the least possible burden upon the people."

In June 1943, like Communists elsewhere, Browder applauded Stalin's order dissolving the Communist International. A year later the American Communist Party too was dissolved and replaced by the Communist Political Association. Browder explained that the Association was solely an "educational" society, rather than a political party seeking state power. In the 1944 Presidential elections the Communists endorsed Roosevelt without qualifications and, for the first time since 1920, had no candidate of their own. Browder even suggested—tentatively—that the Republicans and Democrats ought to nominate a single "win-the-war" ticket.

Philosophically, of course, this was a good many leagues removed from the orthodox radicalism which holds that the "power elite," or "establishment" or "capitalist class"—call it what you will—is the main enemy of humanity. But whatever its philosophical demerits, the softer pose made the party acceptable to a considerably wider circle. Peter V. Cacchione, a Communist, was elected a New York City councilman in 1941 and re-elected two years later by a 40 percent larger margin. Benjamin Davis, Jr., became the first Negro Communist to hold public office when he, too, was elected to the council in 1943. The Communists gained an important political base when they won away the American Labor Party in New York from the former Socialists of the needle trades' unions. Through Vito Marcantonio, the single American Labor Party member in the House of Representatives, representing the impoverished Puerto Ricans of East Harlem, they had an ally in Congress who saw eye to eye with them on almost everything. Numerically, the Communist Party in early 1944 reached an all-time peak of eighty thousand members. Thirty-three thousand had been recruited in the previous year alone, indicating at one and the same time how rapid was the turnover in party membership and how successful it was in drawing in new blood. Equally impressive, in a single year—1943—the number of Communist workers in the auto industry doubled, those in steel went up by 50 percent, and so on. Compared to prewar Communist parties in Europe, the one in the United States was weak. But it seemed to be moving ahead rapidly. How much farther it would go was anyone's guess.

In April 1945, however, less than a month before the surrender of Nazi Germany, it became clear that Browder's best-laid plans had gone awry. Somewhere in the maze of world communism a decision had been taken to make some changes. The blow was delivered obliquely. Jacques Duclos, secretary of the French Communist Party, after a meeting with Stalin, published an article in the

French journal *Cahiers du Communisme,* which obviously placed the skids under his American counterpart. In it he condemned Browder for "transforming the Teheran declaration of the Allied governments . . . into a political platform of class peace in the postwar world." Browder, it seems, had been under the illusion that Europe, west of the Soviet Union, would "be reconstituted on a bourgeois-democratic basis and not on a fascist-capitalist or Soviet basis." In other words, instead of a placid continuation of the present order of things, as Browder prognosticated, the Western world must expect a turbulent and violent struggle, at the end of which either fascism or communism would prevail. Duclos' article carried implied endorsement of William Z. Foster, who had been opposing Browder behind the scenes. In a private letter to the National Committee of the party in 1944, Foster had—as he himself paraphrases it in one of his books—"attacked Browder's underestimation of the general crisis of capitalism, his illusions about the liquidation of imperialism." Foster, in his own words, "foresaw a post-war perspective of class struggle instead of class peace, opposed Browder's acceptance of the two-party system, attacked the post-war no-strike policy, condemned the discarding of socialism, and warned the Party of the danger of falling into the right Social-Democratic error of tailing after the bourgeoisie."

The fact that a Frenchman was making observations about the policies of the American party was unique enough in itself. But the fact that it immediately plunged the Americans into a vendetta against "Browderism" was even more revealing. At the meeting of the party's National Committee in June, two thirds of the members repudiated Browder's "class peace" policies. The man who had been called "the beloved leader of our movement" only shortly before soon became the single voice defending Browderism. Browder was removed as general secretary of the party. A secretariat of three, with Foster in the key role, took his place. In February 1946 Browder was unanimously expelled by the National Committee, a doleful climax to a political career that had begun thirty-nine years before. "A mere handful," writes Foster, "his wife, his brother, his financial 'angel' and a few others—departed with him as his following." Why Moscow had become disenchanted with Browder was not immediately obvious. Perhaps it can be gleaned from a sentence in President Roosevelt's speech to Congress on January 6, 1945: "The nearer we came to vanquishing our enemies the more we inevitably became conscious of differences among victors." With friction growing, Stalin probably concluded that capitalism and communism were not as predestined to coexist as had been originally believed. Even if it did not lead to a full break immediately, sterner hands were needed at the tiller. Browder was sacrificed to the very "objective changes" which he had referred to so frequently in explaining the lightning shifts from one period to another.

III

Wars, traditionally, leave a backwash of discontent. Wages fall behind prices. Many people are killed and wounded. The postwar cutback in production results in severe unemployment and depression—sometimes a revolution. All of this had happened after World War I. As Germany and Japan surrendered in 1945, American radicals wondered whether it would happen again. Would there be a depression on the order of 1921? Or 1929? Would there be a strike wave as in 1919? Would it be led by radicals like William Z. Foster or the Wobblies? Would there be a second series of revolutions in Europe to capture and inflame American imaginations?

Earl Browder had concluded that history would not repeat itself. Whether this was his own view or shared by Moscow is not clear, but one of his supporters, Robert Minor, stated categorically that "events duplicating those that occurred in Russia in 1917 . . . are not expected to occur; the orientation of the communists is definitely that history will take a different course." Specifically, he predicted that new governments will come into being in Europe— supported by the Communists—in which "all classes" would participate. This would be possible because "for the first time in history there has come an assurance of orderly, democratic and peaceful progress. . . ." The postwar world, in this vignette, would evidently be one in which rival nations on the one hand, and rival classes on the other, would coexist in moderate harmony. With Russia and the United States working together, old-style revolutions were not necessary; collaboration between "all classes" would make it possible to avoid depressions. The practical conclusion from such a thesis was of course a Communist Party considerably to the Right of Norman Thomas' Socialists. It would result, as Harry Bridges was saying, in continuing the union no-strike pledge into the distant future, support of the Democratic Party in elections, toning down criticism of "American imperialism" in Latin America, and an over-all moderation.

Foster and Eugene Dennis, who became general secretary of the party after Browder's removal, took a more orthodox line. At the very convention which gave Browder the *coup de grâce*, the party prophesied the "growth of reaction and fascism" if monopoly capital were not checkmated. In 1946 Dennis talked of "the next cyclical economic crisis," as if it were predestined. He predicted it would "enormously accentuate the dangers of fascism in the United States." A year later, another party leader, Henry Winston, argued that the country was succumbing to a "state of affairs that existed in Japan and Hitler Germany . . . thought control, gestapo groups, the extension of the spy system within the labor movement." The implication was, faced with these twin specters, economic collapse and fascism, the American masses would soon be caught in a torrent of militancy and radicalism.

First postwar developments lent a mite of credence to this analysis. Hostilities were hardly over when there was an outburst of strikes that outstripped all previous records. Four and a half million workers paced the picket lines in 1946, a half million more than in 1919, and stayed out of the factories for a total of 113 million days, four times as many as in the "sit-down year" 1937. General Motors workers, led by Walter Reuther, then a vice-president of the auto union, stayed out for four months. Walkouts closed operations in the steel mills, the coalpits, the oil refineries. City-wide stoppages immobilized a half dozen cities from Stamford, Connecticut, to Oakland, California. There was certainly a blaze of action, but as *Fortune* magazine summarized it: "The strikes and strike threats of 1945-6 generated violent emotions, but it was an impressive fact that for the first time a great wave of strikes stirred up almost no physical violence. The strikers of 1945-6 were not desperate men. On the public platform their leaders sounded off with booming phrases directed at the enemy Capital; but privately they, like the strikers, were calm, cool, even friendly warriors."

For a variety of reasons big business preferred to come to terms rather than try to smash the mass production unions. It had long since adjusted to the ogre of unionism. Some industries, such as steel, had been privately assured by the government that it could pass on the costs of wage increases to the consumer. Others were enjoying a boom in demand because of accumulated wartime wants. At a certain point therefore—after a period in which the lid was raised to let off workers' steam—an accommodation was reached. In the first round of negotiations union men generally romped off with raises of 18½ ¢ an hour, and many fringe benefits. The "packages" for the second, third, and fourth years were slightly smaller, but not negligible.

In this circumstance, whatever misgivings rank-and-file unionists might have about middle-of-the-road leaders in the CIO or conservative ones in the AFL, they were not searching avidly for new ones. Often they found former radicals like Reuther as aggressive in pressing their demands as the Communists might be, or more so. As *Fortune* noted, they were not desperate. The Communists, thus, were reduced to playing second string in someone else's orchestra. The first-round pattern of settlement was set by Philip Murray, president of the steelworkers', and was then followed, more or less tamely, by most others, including those unions, like the United Electrical Workers, under Communist aegis.

Had there been a depression, the Communists might have been called on to do the leading. But contrary to expectations, none took place in the postwar period. The four economic slumps in the next two decades, painful as they were, could not be compared in severity to the cataclysm of 1929, or even 1921. Unemployment ranged from 4 to 7 percent—as against 25 percent in the 1929 downturn. To indicate the dimensions of the change, a new term was coined— recession—to distinguish the new phenomenon from the tempests of other times. So that, while the Communists repeated their dire predictions periodically, history bedeviled them by not repeating itself. There were no unemployed to organize and increasingly fewer workers searching for more radical horizons.

For a while it appeared as if the Communists might record a sensational success consummating a *rapprochement* with liberals. Despite Foster's tough granitelike phrases about "class struggle," the winning of "bourgeois liberals" to a parallel strategy was a major preoccupation of the Communist Party.

As things stood in 1946–47, the liberal movement was divided over issues that presaged the cold war. A Win-the-War Conference

[*339*]

to discuss peace issues, early in 1946, was chaired by the pro-Communist singer Paul Robeson. It adopted a resolution for unrestricted aid to the Soviet Union, while opposing a loan to Britain "until sufficient guarantees have been made that these materials and funds will not be used for the exploitation and oppression of the colonial people." As a follow-up a few months later, the CIO and two other organizations called a Conference of Progressives. The Communists again were major figures, directing the conference's darts primarily against "British imperialism," while urging a *modus vivendi* with the Soviets. The array of liberals who supported this affair was impressive: two former members of Roosevelt's cabinet, Harold Ickes and Henry Morgenthau, Jr., former Vice-President Henry A. Wallace, as well as James Patton, president of the National Farmers Union, A. F. Whitney, president of the Brotherhood of Railway Trainmen, and Walter White, secretary of the National Association for the Advancement of Colored People.

The rival of the progressives, its ranks also studded with prominent names—Eleanor Roosevelt, Walter Reuther, Chester Bowles, and others—was the Americans for Democratic Action (ADA). This group began by damning both the Soviets and British imperialism with equal fervor, but in the end yielded to the cold war thesis of the United States that the main enemy was the Soviets. It considered communism and liberalism incompatible, and while it did not impose a loyalty test, it openly declared that Communists were not welcome in its fold. Had the relationship of forces between the progressives and the ADA remained the same, the Communists would have operated from a favorable vantage point, since the progressives were twice as large as the ADA and considerably more influential. Aligned with the CIO and counting on so many prominent liberal Democrats, the Communists appeared on the verge of another breakthrough, similar to the one in the 1930's.

In less than two years, however, Foster and Dennis—now quarreling a little among themselves over just how hard the line should be—were deprived of their capital both in liberal circles and the unions. In the growing anti-Communist temper of the nation, the Communists began to lose friends and allies at a rapid pace. Joseph Curran, of the National Maritime Union, severed his links by 1947, in the process cutting to shreds a party faction in his union that had numbered almost a thousand at one time. Michael Quill, of the

Transport Workers' Union, similarly turned against an alliance he had maintained for fourteen years. In the auto union, the most dynamic in America, Walter Reuther scored an upset in 1946 against president R. J. Thomas, who had the support of the large Communist faction. Relations of the Communist Party faction in the CIO with Philip Murray cooled to the frigid point.

The stigma which the Communists could not erase was that they were agents of a foreign power. The adjustment and readjustment of policy to synchronize with Soviet needs was so patent it needed little documentation. "The one question I couldn't answer to my satisfaction, no matter how good my answer sounded to others," writes John Gates, a former editor of the *Daily Worker*, "was the familiar old one: 'Name one example in which the American Party ever differed from Soviet policy?'" He could not think of any. This was the point being made in hundreds of newspapers and by every anti-Communist force in the country from the ADA to the extreme Right. "You just can't run a labor union," cried Willard Townsend, a Negro member of the CIO executive board, "when certain members follow the policies of the Soviet Union." Walter Reuther reminded the Communists, who were now urging President Truman to return to the "peaceful policies" of President Roosevelt, that they had called Roosevelt a "warmonger" in 1940. In the white heat of anti-Sovietism which accompanied the Truman Doctrine and cold war, there was no bypassing the charge that the Communist Party had consistently meshed gears with Soviet foreign policy.

The Communists tried to appease Philip Murray. On at least two occasions they voted against a position held by the Soviet Union, to conjure an image of independence. At a New York CIO meeting Communist delegates criticized Russia for exercising a veto at the United Nations. At the 1947 CIO national convention the Communist faction voted to endorse the Marshall Plan—which Stalin was castigating. But it was in vain; the die was cast. "If communism is an issue in any of your unions," Murray told an executive board meeting of the CIO in July 1947, "throw it to hell out . . . and throw its advocates out along with it."

Communism, of course, had become *the* issue, not only for the unions but for the United States. Murray therefore was bound to take his own advice—"throw its advocates out along with it"—seriously.

[*341*]

Three major points of friction were the ostensible causes for ouster of the Left-wing unions from the CIO. One was over the Taft-Hartley Act passed by a conservative Congress in June 1947. Everyone in the labor movement opposed this law, among other things for the provision requiring union officials to sign affidavits that they were not members of the Communist Party. The penalty for refusing was for their unions to lose the facilities of the National Labor Relations Board, making it difficult to unionize new shops, and impossible to conclude union shop contracts. After expressing their opposition to the "slave" bill, all union leaders except John L. Lewis filed the required affidavits. To the Communists, very directly involved, this was a serious blow, and, in a sense, a desertion by old associates. They had hoped that Murray would support them by refusing to comply, thereby forcing the government's hand. When he did not, they accused him of a sellout, and made their peace with the affidavit as best they could—usually by *pro forma* resignation from the party or by changing their status from elected to appointed officials.

A second dispute hinged on an issue directly related to the American-Soviet conflict. In mid-1947 Secretary of State George C. Marshall proclaimed the Marshall Plan program for economic aid to Europe. It was offered to all countries but turned down by the Soviet bloc on the ground that it was an effort to weld the Continent into an alliance—and eventually a war—against Russia. For William Z. Foster, and of course Communists in the CIO, the Marshall Plan was "a policy that could lead to world fascism and war." To Philip Murray this position was still another, and flagrant, proof that the Communists were agents of a foreign power.

The last straw was the formation of the Progressive Party, and Henry Wallace's Presidential campaign in 1948. The former Vice-President of the United States was feuding with President Truman over foreign policy and was willing to run against him "if it is apparent that the Democratic Party is a war party." For the Communists, seeking some means of breaking out of a bind, and hoping to mobilize sentiment against the cold war, this was manna from heaven. They threw themselves into the campaign with the vigor and determination that was their hallmark. In the process they elbowed into the background all non-Communist elements, giving the Progressive Party a distinctly Communist aura, which turned out to be its main handicap in the election. They also cut whatever tenuous ties still remained with the CIO leadership, losing any hopes of forging a true labor party. By a vote of 33 to 11 the CIO executive board in January 1948 decried the Wallace candidacy as "politically unwise." Emil Mazey, newly elected secretary-treasurer of the auto union, who favored a third party, refused to have anything to do with this one. Party members too expressed misgivings about running a candidate without endorsement of one of the other labor federations. But Dennis and Foster were determined. The founding convention of the Progressive Party was held in Philadelphia in July 1948.

Thirty-two hundred delegates and alternates gathered to nominate Wallace and former Senator Glenn Taylor of Idaho on a program of "peace, freedom, and abundance." With the bands playing, delegates singing "Friendly Henry Wallace," and sundry speakers detailing the glowing prospects for the new party, the convention seemed to confirm exaggerated hopes. "The Wallace movement," said a Communist Party statement, "already has a broader working class base than had the La Follette movement in 1924." It convinced itself, further, that "the emergence of this new anti-monopoly, anti-fascist people's party has deepened the crisis in the Democratic Party and is leading to its disintegration." According to Foster, twelve national unions with about a million and a half members were "active supporters" of Wallace and Taylor. But when the ballots were counted in November, the former Vice-President polled only 1,158,000 votes—slightly less than the States Rights' candidate, Right-winger J. Strom Thurmond of South Carolina, whose campaign was confined to the South. It was a shattering setback, a virtual death warrant. In 1949 the CIO expelled eleven national unions charged with being Communist-dominated. From then on the road for the Communist Party was steadily downhill.

IV

Concomitant with its decline, the Communist Party now had to face a period of repression that was much longer, though considerably milder, than the one after World War I. There were no Palmer raids this time, but many new means were found to harass the isolated Left. One of the favorites was the use of a Congressional committee as an agency for prosecution. The penalty was usually the loss of a job, and sometimes a prison term, for contempt of Congress. In June 1947 leaders of the Joint Anti-Fascist Refugee Committee were convicted for failing to turn over their records to the House Committee on Un-American Activities (HUAC). They were given sentences up to six months and fined five hundred dollars. A few months later ten well-known Hollywood figures—the Hollywood Ten—were indicted when they refused to discuss their political beliefs or their former associates in the Communist milieu. They received up to a year in jail and fines of one thousand dollars each. More important, they lost their jobs—though some were able to sell scripts under pen names. Eugene Dennis, a former seaman and teamster who was then general secretary of the Communist Party, defied HUAC by claiming it was illegally constituted. He went to jail for a year and was fined one thousand dollars. Many similar cases caught the headlines, each one catering to latent fears and building up a mood for continued reprisals. No one has ever tabulated the number of people discharged because they were named as Communists, fellow travelers, or "Fifth-Amendment" Communists in unsubstantiated testimony before HUAC or, later, the Senate Internal Security Committee. Many victims preferred to remain in obscurity in the hope of finding other work. But the figure is estimated by civil libertarians at many thousands. After Russia had exploded its first atom bomb in 1949, and with the Korean War, the anti-Communist crusade was picked up by Senator Joseph McCarthy of Wisconsin and "McCarthyism" became a synonym all around the world for wild charges and flagrant transgressions on freedom.

In addition to Congressional harassment, the Communists had to contend with three pieces of legislation designed, in part or in whole, to force them out of business. The party was not declared illegal—though outlawing it was once considered by Secretary of Labor Lewis K. Schwellenbach—but it was so handicapped in its operations that it could not function as a normal organization. The Taft-Hartley provision on non-Communist affidavits was intended to force Communists to disclose their identity to union members, whereupon, it was assumed, they would be made to resign. It was not as effective as expected because ways were found to get around it. Nonetheless a group of unionists in Cleveland were sent to jail for "conspiring" to evade the affidavit requirement, and leaders of the Mine, Mill and Smelters Union were put on trial at various times covering a span of more than a decade and a half on similar, though not identical, charges.

A second law, the McCarran Act, passed during the Korean crisis, required Communist, "Communist-front," and "Communist-infiltrated" organizations to turn over their membership lists to the government and to label their publications as "Communist." Members of such vaguely defined groups were prohibited from applying for passports or holding jobs in unions or defense industry. If they were noncitizens they could be deported, and if recently naturalized, denaturalized. The penalty for nonregistration was a ten-thousand-dollar fine and five years in prison for *each day* of noncompliance. As of this writing, not a single organization has registered and no provisions of the act have been enforceable under Supreme Court rulings. Yet the many court cases and the litigation have drained Communist energies and depleted its coffers—to that extent adding to its load.

The one law that did considerable injury to the Communists was the Smith Act, passed in 1940—the same one under which eighteen Trotskyists went to jail during the war. On July 20, 1948, twelve leaders of the Communist Party, including Foster and Dennis, were arrested and accused of conspiring to "teach and advocate the overthrow and destruction of the Government of the United States by force and violence." Eleven were convicted in a prolonged nine-month trial (Foster was too sick to be prosecuted) and sent to jail for three to five years. One hundred and eighteen secondary leaders were also convicted under the Smith Act. They were more fortunate, however, on appeal all but one of the convictions being reversed by the higher courts. Only Junius Scales, who, ironically, had completely broken with communism, was forced to serve part of his term. He was freed by President John F. Kennedy at the urging of liberals who recommended his release.

The persistent harassment of the Communist Party in the decade after World War II adversely affected it in two ways. First, it was driven into a twilight zone where it was not outlawed, yet could not function as an open, legal party. It had to take elaborate precautions to guard its members from informers. Its sympathizers were loath to attend rallies for fear of being photographed and identified by FBI agents. So heated were the passions that there were incidents in which factory workers beat up fellow workers simply because they had been subpoenaed before HUAC or named by McCarthy. Second, McCarthyism cast a pall of orthodoxy over the nation which harmed not only the Communists but everyone left of center, even liberals. Landlords refused to rent halls to Left-wingers. Readers of radical publications canceled subscriptions to avoid being listed in FBI or HUAC files. Men shied away from joining civil liberties or civil rights groups out of fear that in so doing they might compromise their future.

It would be false to say that all this was the *cause* of Communist decimation; the repression, added to the setbacks in the CIO and in the Progressive Party campaign, only accelerated disintegration. But it coincided with the party's decline and punctuated it. Within a few years after the eleven national unions had been expelled from the CIO, most had either shed Communist leadership or gone out of business. Three or four continued independent existence—such as the United Electrical Workers or Harry Bridges' longshoremen—but though their leaders remained leftist in a broad sense, they no longer related to the party or accepted its discipline in any way.

The Communists continued their activity, trying desperately to regain a base. They solicited two and a half million signatures for a petition of the pro-Soviet World Peace Congress. They held a peace demonstration attended by fifteen thousand at Peekskill, New York, at which Paul Robeson sang—and which rightists attacked. They published newspapers and pamphlets. But these were the sputterings of decline rather than the omens of growth. The Korean War in 1950 doomed the party to further estrangement, since its support of North Korea clashed sharply with American sympathies for South Korea and for the United Nations armies fighting with the South. By 1950–51 the party's membership was less than forty thousand. In just six years the ranks had thinned by more than a half, and its influence in labor and the community by far more.

For a brief moment in 1956–57 liberal winds pierced the façade. Stalin was dead by now. Khrushchev had made his famous speech at a closed session of the Twentieth Congress of the Russian Communist Party, February 24–25, 1956. It revealed many of Stalin's crimes and confirmed what other radicals had said of Stalinism for years. The speech was not published by the Soviet Union, but the U.S.

State Department secured a text somehow and released it in June 1956. The effect was traumatic. For years, even decades, the rank-and-file party member had brushed such charges aside as "capitalist propaganda" and "red-baiting." Now the words of authentication came from the apex of the Soviet pyramid itself. Innumerable party members and leaders, who had been subduing their reservations for years, burst the bounds of monolithicism. They began to write letters to the editor of the *Daily Worker*, rebuking their leaders for hiding the sins of Stalin and for undemocratic and sectarian practices. Open and free debate was heard for the first time in a quarter of a century. John Gates, editor of the *Daily Worker*, poured fuel on the flames by publishing the text of Khrushchev's speech. He was soon the leader of a vague and unorganized "liberal" wing in the party.

While Khrushchev's revelations were still on everyone's mind, two events of historic magnitude added further to the malaise. In Poland, after a strike of factory workers in Poznań and student demonstrations in Warsaw, an alarmed Marxist leadership turned over the reins of government to Wladyslaw Gomulka. In Stalin's day Gomulka had been imprisoned as a "Titoist"—liberal Communist—and therefore enjoyed more popularity with the Polish masses than any other official. When Khrushchev flew in from Moscow with some of his aides, to dissuade the Poles from appointing Gomulka, there was a tense moment in which violence seemed inevitable. Khrushchev threatened to use troops to enforce his "suggestion," while workers sat in their factories, armed and ready to defend Gomulka if Khrushchev carried out his threat. In the face of this prospect the Soviet leader retreated; Gomulka and the young "revisionist" Communists carried the day. They referred to this event in the future as the "Polish October." Poland remained a Communist society, of course, but a far more liberal one. It evoked enthusiasm from the youth of Warsaw and a spate of free criticism that had not been seen for a long time.

A few days after the Polish October similar stirrings occurred in Hungary. After demonstrations of young people, intellectuals, and workers in front of the statue of Josef Bem and at the radio station, secret police fired on the crowds and thus initiated a period of turmoil that became known as the Hungarian Revolution. The regime of Erno Gero, which had only recently inherited power from

[347]

the brutal one of Matyas Rakosi, was replaced by a liberal Communist government under Imre Nagy. This time, however, events went farther than the Russians would tolerate. Nagy threatened to withdraw Hungary from the Soviet military alliance, the Warsaw Pact, and to steer his nation along a neutralist path. Russian troops and tanks thereupon struck at the population in a bloodletting that shocked not only foes of communism but many party members everywhere. Estimates in Budapest put the number of civilians killed at forty-seven thousand. At a time when many believed that Stalinism was buried for good and that far-reaching changes impended, the Hungarian events were a cause of deep consternation.

The American Communist Party, too, was caught in the swirl. In November 1956 its National Committee condemned Janos Kadar, Soviet-imposed premier, and the Russians for their suppression of the revolution: "Instead of meeting the legitimate grievances of the Hungarian working class and people, they again resorted to repression. Their calling in the Soviet troops stationed in Hungary to put down the popular demonstrations was a tragic error. . . . This dramatized the bankruptcy of a policy which was not based securely upon national needs. . . ." Gates in the *Daily Worker* was even sterner: "The action of the Soviet troops in Hungary does not advance but retards the development of socialism because socialism cannot be imposed on a country by force." To appease dissenters, strong words of self-criticism began to appear in party resolutions. The party, said one, had "viewed uncritically developments in the Soviet Union." It had "suffered from an oversimplified approach to and an uncritical acceptance of many views and ideas of Marxists in other countries."

But even while the discussions and re-evaluations were going on, the Foster faction was demanding a return to "unity," while Gates and men of similar bent, discouraged and disillusioned, were simply leaving the party. The liberals undoubtedly commanded a majority for a while, but they did not choose to organize their faction. When enough of them had left, so that the balance was again tipped toward the hard elements, schematic centralism was reasserted.

After nearly four decades the Communist Party, too, had been transformed, like the Socialist Labor Party, the Industrial Workers of the World, and the Socialists, into a sect. Its claimed membership soon fell to ten thousand; its actual membership probably less, much of it middle-aged and tired. Jack Levine, a former FBI agent, could report in the *Nation* of October 20, 1962, that there were nearly fifteen hundred FBI informants in the Communist Party—a ratio, he said, of one informant for every 5.7 members. The figures indicated not only how harsh was the surveillance, but how deathly weak the party had become.

V

Was this, then, the death of American radicalism?

Certainly there was little of it still visible. Some critics would argue that it had died a long time back, that the Communists were not a genuine leftist force but an agency of Moscow. Others would insist radicalism was buried only because the Communists had tainted it, that otherwise it would have survived and flourished. It is only a matter of time, they say, until people forget the treacherous conduct of "Moscow's henchmen" and rejoin the "cause." But say what one will of the Communist Party and the world Communist movement as such, the average party member, in the United States as elsewhere, did not consider himself part of any "conspiracy." He received nothing of value for his subservience to Moscow. He served it only because in doing so he felt he was truly serving humanity, including his fellow Americans. He was not an "agent" in the sense of being paid—and he made sacrifices that were often exemplary. If he was naïve or misguided, that is another matter.

Under any circumstances the old Left did not disappear either because the Communists were duplicitous or because they had misjudged the course of events. Other leftist forces too, it should be remembered, failed. Norman Thomas' Socialists were native American and quite moderate by Leninist standards. Yet their failure was as monumental as that of the Communists. The Trotskyists, on the other side, were ideologically to the left of the Communists and unblemished by any "agent" charges; yet they, too, could gain no momentum.

The fact is that insofar as the old radical movement is concerned, history had passed it by. The preconditions for its success no longer existed—in fact, they were already disappearing during World War II. If the Communists and Socialists grew strong in Europe immediately after hostilities, it was only because they capitalized on a short

[*349*]

period of devastation and hunger. Once entrenched, they remained so, with some slight gains or losses. But in the United States, there was no devastation, no general hunger. On the contrary, the war marked the end of a long era in which catastrophic depressions had caused untold hardship once or more—usually—every decade.

The goal of the radical has always been—since the days of the prophets Amos and Hosea—to abolish privilege, to win for the underprivileged equality. Until now underprivilege has been essentially an economic matter, measured in terms of poverty, and that was what radicals sought to rectify. Nathaniel Bacon fought for his rural tobacco growers because they were being impoverished by cruel and discriminatory officials. Sam Adams' revolution was meant to achieve independence, but in the word "independence" were embodied such goals as free land, unhampered enterprise, greater economic opportunity for the mechanic. Fanny Wright's "Free Enquirer" movement sought to establish equality between rich and poor by sending the children of both to the same boarding schools. Robert Owen's and Albert Brisbane's utopian communities were meant to elevate the common man from his universal poverty. The crusades of William Lloyd Garrison and John Brown were designed to free the slave from his shackles. William Sylvis, Daniel De Leon, Eugene Debs, Big Bill Haywood, Norman Thomas, yes, Earl Browder and William Z. Foster, all proposed to liberate the propertyless proletarian from "wage slavery," either through the ballot box, the revolutionary union, or some other form of revolutionary action. In each case the radical cause was based on specific grievances that in the vast majority of instances were economic.

But after World War II a new factor was added to the equation. As already noted, there were no depressions, just periodic and—by the standards of the past—relatively mild "recessions." Some leftists argued that the stability was bought at the expense of a permanently militarized economy, that, in other words, it was the $800 billion spent for armaments in the two decades after the war which staved off depressions. This unhealthy situation, they claimed, cannot last indefinitely. Whatever the cause, however, the alarmist predictions by Communists and others of sharp economic downturns after the war did not come to pass. There were still, by the estimate of Michael Harrington, forty to fifty million people at the poverty level. The plight of these unfortunates, living in city slums or in rural shacks, was a stigma against a nation as rich United States. But the poor, as Harrington also notes, were now visible." They were isolated in certain areas, certain minorities, certain occupations, rather than spread through the whole population as in the 1930's. And they were, by and large, quiescent.

These forty or fifty million, numerous as they were, were not forming revolutionary organizations, and except in the case of the Negro poor, not forming any organizations at all. Poverty per se, it was quite clear, was no longer the main lever for building a radical movement. Negroes might recognize that at the end of the civil rights rainbow was economic equality and the extirpation of their poverty, but it was the race issue—discrimination—which drew them to the "civil rights revolution." If an insurgent impulse, as C. Wright Mills called it, was to revive radicalism anew, it would come from other causes than poverty. It would come from such social diseases as racial discrimination, militarism, war, alienation. And it would awaken first not in the working classes or their spokesmen, but among Negroes, students, radical pacifists, intellectuals, middle-class women.

The United States of the 1950's and 1960's was as far removed from that of the 1930's as modern industry is from that of the seventeenth century. The sickness of the 1930's could be tabulated in economic statistics—so many million unemployed, so many business bankruptcies, so much of a reduction in the gross national product. The sicknesses of the latter period were more subtle.

For almost a century the promise of racial equality, unequivocably written into the Constitution after the Civil War, was a dead letter. Ten percent of the population were second-class citizens in fact, if not in law. But with the postwar period the ingredients of revolt were coming to a boil in this segment of America. A social revolution was under way in most of Asia and Africa, in which hundreds of millions of colored peoples were liberating themselves from colonialism. An African, Kwame Nkrumah, had become prime minister of Ghana. Two dozen other African leaders were soon taking the helm in their newly independent countries. Hundreds of thousands of American Negroes, who had been soldiers in World War II and had been told they were fighting for freedom, were back home in the un-freedom of the South or the squalor of the slums in the North. This young generation, better educated than its forebears, more impatient for change, conscious of world developments, became the raw material of a civil rights revolution.

Another difference was the increasing dehumanization of the average man as society became ever more complex, and the individual ever less significant. Psychoanalyst Erich Fromm had drawn attention in a number of best-selling books to the alienation of man both in the capitalist and Communist worlds. Not only bigness, but its corollary, escapism, had resulted, he said, in the individual being alienated from himself. The average man had little opportunity or desire to express his creativity. Sociologist Daniel Bell discussed this phenomenon insofar as it applied to laborers in his book *Work and Its Discontents*. Students at gigantic universities—multiversities, they were called—with tens of thousands of students, complained that their education was being "manufactured." Fromm listed a mass of statistics to show that while the United States was richer than any other nation, it also led the world in homicides per capita, mental sickness, alcoholism, and similar symptoms of emotional insecurity.

Most important, however, were the changes wrought by militarism. For the first time in American history the nation maintained a large armed force—up to three million men—in peacetime. A conservative estimate put the property at the disposal of the Army, Navy, and Air Force at more than $200 billion, three times the combined holdings of the five largest corporations. They owned more land than the seven smallest states together. They spent $25 billion a year for procurement, operated 3,553 military installations around the world, and had so strong an impact on society that President Dwight D. Eisenhower warned in his farewell address on January 17, 1961, against "this conjunction of an immense military establishment and a large armaments industry"—something "new in the American experience."

Newer still was the weaponry at the disposal of the military. The atomic bomb that fell on Hiroshima, Japan, in 1945, with its appalling devastation, failed to spur the nations of the world to disarmament. Instead a "cold war" drove them to an arms race which cost the world $120 billion a year, and the United States alone some $800 billion in the first two decades after 1945. To gauge its dimensions one need only consider these facts: weapons used in World War II by both sides in six years of war were equivalent to 6 million tons of

[352]

dynamite, but one single hydrogen bomb tested by the Soviets was equivalent to almost ten times that much—58 million tons. The nuclear bombs at the disposal of the United States in the early 1960's were judged to be 40,000 megatons—40 billion tons of dynamite, enough to kill every Russian or every American many times over. In addition, the United States had stockpiles of chemical, radiological, and biological weapons seldom referred to by the press or administration. President Kennedy advised the nation shortly after the Cuban crisis in October 1962, that if the confrontation with Russia had escalated into a total war, there would have been 300 million people dead almost immediately—100 million each in Europe, the Soviet Union, and the United States. In such a war, he said, no matter how it started or by whom, "all we have built up, all we have worked for, would be destroyed in the first twenty-four hours."

These were the issues—peace, freedom, participation in decision making—which occupied the attention of an increasing number of people after World War II, and required answers. No radical force emerged with a rounded theory to explain either the problems or the cure—as had Albert Brisbane, for instance, in another day. The old Left avoided a basic re-examination of its doctrine. A new radicalism emerged finally which was less philosophical, more activist, less concerned with final blueprints, more with means.

A prime architect of the new radicalism, though not by any means its only or leading practitioner, was the pacifist minister A. J. Muste. Tall, spare, with a decidedly long nose and thin lips, Muste could melt into any crowd without being noticed. At meetings or in private conversation he seldom spoke until everyone else was finished. But it was precisely this capacity to let other people unwind, without jarring their egos, which was his strongest leadership asset. No one ever felt "threatened" by Muste, no matter how much he disagreed with him. When Muste did speak, it was in a low voice; his thoughts were always well organized. As an orator he was neither bombastic nor flowery, and as a writer he seldom turned a clever phrase, but he had the quality of digging to the root of a problem that held the unflagging interest both of an audience or a reader.

By 1953, when he was sixty-eight and had retired as executive secretary of the Fellowship of Reconciliation (FOR), Muste's career had spanned a wide variety of fields. He had been a minister, an active pacifist, a union leader, union educator, official of a national group of unemployed. In the middle of the 1930's he had merged his American Workers Party with the Trotskyists for a short interlude that lasted two years. After his disenchantment, Muste returned to pacifism and the church, not to turn his back on his revolutionary past but to find a new road. He found it in Gandhi's and Thoreau's theories of nonviolence and civil disobedience.

Civil disobedience, as Muste saw it, meant conscious violation of those laws and governmental actions which were unjust—and a willingness to pay the penalty for it. The nonviolent lawbreaker does not ask for mercy. He is prepared to go to jail for his beliefs, in the hopes that his act of sacrifice will stir the conscience of many others.

Though it seems like a simple strategy, it has wide ramifications. The nonviolent radical not only will not strike back when hit, but will not insult his detractors. He informs the police of all his planned actions, disdaining to proceed in secret. Unlike the passive resister, who turns the other cheek, he believes that evil must be resisted *actively*. And while he himself will not use or advocate violence, he makes a distinction between the violence used by a Negro, say, to stop someone from burning his home and that of the arsonists; or between a revolutionary fighting for the independence of his country and the colonialist power. He believes that all men must love each other—in the sense of understanding the deep human motivations which drive them to their deeds, either good or bad. Muste once said, "If I can't love Hitler, I can't love at all." To most people this would appear blissfully naïve, but for the radical pacifist there is a distinction between a man and his deeds. The man must be "loved"—understood—for what he is; the deeds must be resisted by all nonviolent means, even if it results in death for those resisting.

Muste did not personally convert the leaders of the civil rights, peace, and student movements to nonviolence, but his impulse fanned outward. The carriers of the message were radical pacifists who had worked with Muste during his FOR tenure—most of them former conscientious objectors who had served a prison term or had been in conscientious objectors' camps during World War II. There were also such men as Bayard Rustin and James Farmer, who had served as assistants to Muste. Rustin was to become a key aide to the Baptist minister, Martin Luther King, and to AFL-CIO Vice-

President, A. Philip Randolph. He trained King's followers in non-violence, helped form the Southern Christian Leadership Conference (SCLC), and personally organized the largest civil rights demonstration in American history, the one in Washington in the summer of 1963 in which 150,000 people participated. Farmer was an assistant to Muste in charge of race relations when the FOR launched the Congress of Racial Equality (CORE). Subsequently, as it was spun off on its own independent path, Farmer became its national director and one of the three or four most prominent figures in the civil rights movement.

Such were the men who, obliquely or directly, gave the new radicalism its original impetus in the mid-1950's.

VI

On December 1, 1955, a Negro woman, Mrs. Rosa Parks, took a seat on the Cleveland Avenue bus in Montgomery, Alabama, and refused to give it up to a white man when the bus driver demanded she do so. Mrs. Parks, long active in the NAACP, was arrested, starting a chain of events as consequential as William Lloyd Garrison's decision to publish the *Liberator* in 1831. Within twenty-four hours the Negro leaders of the city had gathered and proclaimed a boycott of the city buses. Seventeen thousand colored citizens organized car pools or walked back and forth to work, in rain as well as sunshine, for 381 days, rather than accept second-class status.

Among the men who launched and soon led this movement was the twenty-six-year-old minister of the Dexter Avenue Baptist Church. Born in Atlanta of religious parents—his father and maternal grandfather were also ministers—Martin Luther King's life had been inauspicious until this moment. He had attended the small but integrated Crozer Theological Seminary in Chester, Pennsylvania, had been ordained, and had served from 1947 to 1954 in his father's church until assigned the one in Montgomery. Studious and exceedingly well read, King had formed a social and political action committee within his church and urged his members to join the NAACP and register to vote. Beyond this there was as yet little to distinguish him. But his leadership of the Montgomery bus boycott made him famous the world over. Here was a minority group abused for decades, accepting arrest and violence without striking back in the same manner. King's home was bombed on January 30, 1956 (as were many others), but he implored his followers not to use violence. "Don't go get your weapons. He who lives by the sword will perish by the sword." The nobility of his words captured the imagination of most Americans. In February 1956 twenty-four ministers, including King, were arrested and two months later convicted for sponsoring the boycott. King was sentenced to 140 days in jail and fined $500, but the boycott continued while the cases were being appealed. In June that year, with the national and international spotlight on Montgomery, a three-judge federal court issued an injunction against segregation and in December, more than a year after Rosa Parks had started it all, the first desegregated buses began to move in Montgomery.

This was the first time that American Negroes had developed a viable leadership of their own, capable of winning substantive reforms. These leaders were not radicals like the Socialists or Wobblies who proposed to uproot the capitalist system—though a few were—but they were certainly radical in their methods. In the following years the civil rights movement involved large numbers of people; there had been nothing like it since the CIO was formed in the 1930's. James Farmer organized "freedom rides" of Negroes and whites on Southern buses. There were demonstrations in scores of cities for jobs, voter registration rights, equal use of city facilities. Hardly a day passed beginning with 1960 without some civil rights headline in the newspapers. Police brutality against demonstrators in Selma, Alabama, shocked the nation to the point where President Lyndon B. Johnson introduced a far-reaching new voting law. Like other revolts, the Negro revolt buried many martyrs—including Medgar Evers of the NAACP, three young people shot in Neshoba, Mississippi, in 1965, a minister killed in Selma, the bombings of many Negro churches and homes.

In the course of the revolt there emerged a plethora of groups, ranging from King's SCLC (and the older Urban League and NAACP), to some that believed in violence, such as the Deacons for Defense and Justice and Malcolm X's black nationalists. Leaving aside those committed to violence—who played only a minor role anyway—the most radical of the civil rights forces was the Student Nonviolent Coordinating Committee (SNCC). Led by Robert Moses, John Lewis, and James Foreman—to the extent that it can

[356]

be led, since it does not believe in centralized leadership—SNCC claimed a staff of two hundred men and women in their teens and twenties working throughout the South—usually at ten to twenty dollars a week. These zealots, often risking their lives, registered Negroes for voting and organized them for marches, demonstrations, strikes, and a dozen other activities. Though not professing any explicit ideology, SNCC was certainly leftist in its mood, and men like Moses, in particular, saw a clear relationship between the campaign for civil rights and those against poverty and war. If they did not define their philosophy further, they believed that at the end of their triple crusade a new type of society would emerge.

VII

In the final analysis there are only three ways of effecting social change: through persuasion of the men who hold power in the existing system, through a conspiratorial *coup d'état,* or through the open mobilization of the people against the prevailing order. The first is the technique of liberals, the second of one type of anarchist, the third of most other radicals.

The civil rights movement beginning with Montgomery was fortunate in that there were hundreds of thousands of Negroes ready to be mobilized. After the first nonviolent activities many whites— churchmen, pacifists, liberals, reformers—were also ready to participate. But the peace movement, slowly coming to life in the mid-1950's, had no such ready constituency. The idea of bombs killing hundreds of thousands of human beings was unreal. Too many people refused even to think about it. And the thought of children dying from leukemia as a result of nuclear tests hundreds or thousands of miles away either seemed like science fiction or was too gory to contemplate.

What Muste and similar men did, therefore, was to devise imaginative projects to rouse the American conscience. While only small numbers of people participated, large numbers—sometimes the whole nation—were informed of it. In a sense there was a parallel with Robert Owen's communities or Albert Brisbane's phalanxes, which included only a few thousand participants but were likewise discussed by a vastly larger number.

On the twelfth anniversary of Hiroshima, August 7, 1957, thirty-five religious and nonreligious pacifists, led by a minister, Lawrence Scott, congregated in front of the Mercury Project, seventy miles northwest of Las Vegas. This was a testing ground used by the Atomic Energy Commission for its nuclear program. In advance of the gathering, Muste met with the state highway police and told them what the demonstrators proposed to do and where. He hoped, he said, that the police would cooperate, but he advised them that the pacifists would go through with their plans anyway, whatever the result. At the appointed time, the thirty-five men and women conducted a twenty-four-hour vigil and prayer at the front entrance, standing silently for the most part except for an occasional circular walk to stretch their legs. After talking with the guards and trying to convince them that the work done at the project was immoral, eleven of the pacifists illegally walked into the site and were arrested for trespassing, and later given suspended sentences. "The tone of the whole proceeding," said the New York *Times*, "was almost amiable." The demonstrators had insulted no one, had initiated no riots. They were simply determined to dramatize the message that nuclear war is an evil. Among them were Albert Bigelow, a former lieutenant commander in the Navy, who had turned pacifist, and Jim Peck, of a well-to-do family, who was a regular participant in freedom rides and peace actions which resulted in not a few jailings and beatings.

The Las Vegas demonstration was followed by many similar ones. Typical was the one in Nebraska in the summer of 1959, conducted by the Committee for Nonviolent Action (CNVA), of which Muste was the chairman. The CNVA concentrated on a missile base in Mead, Nebraska—thirty miles from Omaha. Before the main demonstrations, CNVA members held meetings, distributed pamphlets, and conducted peace walks to inform the community of their aims and get publicity. They also hoped to win additional recruits. For a month the small band of young men and women kept a vigil in front of the Mead base. On July 1 they "invaded" it. While police, newsmen, friends, and some hostile bystanders watched, Muste climbed over a four-and-a-half-foot fence, followed by fourteen others. The commander of the base, according to regulations, first gave the actionists a letter asking them to leave and then conducted them back through the gate. A few moments later the fifteen climbed the fence again, were duly arrested, and lodged in jail.

Two of the most dramatic projects of the radical pacifists were the voyage of the *Golden Rule* and the San Francisco-to-Moscow Walk. In 1958 four members of the CNVA, including the former Navy lieutenant commander, Bigelow, sailed a sloop, the *Golden Rule*, from San Pedro, California, to Honolulu. This was to be the first lap of a 4,500-mile journey into an area of the Pacific Ocean where the United States was conducting nuclear bomb tests. Five days after the pacifist sailors arrived in Honolulu, the United States Attorney secured a federal court order restraining them from taking their boat from port. A few days later the crew set sail anyway, only to be arrested by the Coast Guard two miles offshore. Out on bail, while awaiting trial, they again tried to take their ship to the prohibited area. Bigelow was arrested ten minutes prior to departure time on a charge of "criminal conspiracy"; the others were picked up six miles out by two Coast Guard cutters.

While the *Golden Rule* was thus immobilized, however, another small ship, the *Phoenix*, manned by Professor Earl Reynolds, with his wife and two children, coming from Japan, did enter the forbidden area. They were duly escorted out by the Navy and forced to port. But for the pacifists this was a welcome and unexpected climax. Their effort had gained them international publicity and had undoubtedly drawn many people toward the peace movement. There was something noble about four men willing to enter a test area and, if need be, submit to radiation and possible death to dramatize their concern.

The San Francisco-to-Moscow Walk began on December 1, 1961, and ended in Moscow ten months and a week later. The small band of walkers, members of the CNVA, marched along the highways from town to town, giving out circulars in opposition to the military preparations both of the United States and Russia. Everywhere they held meetings, appeared on radio, spoke at churches. (A young model who worked for an auto company was so moved by the walkers she convinced her boss to loan them a Mercedes. She also joined the walk and eventually married one of the march leaders.)

After extended activities in the United States, including two weeks of picketing in front of the Pentagon, fifteen of the marchers were flown to Europe to continue their walk for peace. There they were joined by European pacifists and continued onward just as in the United States—distributing leaflets in the native language, holding meetings, appearing on radio and television. France refused them passage; East Germany imposed so many conditions that the marchers bypassed it. The high point of the trip was the distribution of leaflets in Moscow criticizing the Soviet as well as the American governments, and a two-and-a-half-hour meeting with students at Moscow University in which there was an exchange of views. Such things had not happened in Moscow for decades; it strengthened the mood for an international thaw.

In the following years there were many similar actions, some involving a few dozen people, others as many as a thousand or more. In New England, Musteites conducted an ongoing campaign against the United States submarine base in New London, Connecticut, where work was being completed to outfit submarines with Polaris missiles. During the Viet Nam crisis, after 1964, two or three hundred radical pacifists "invaded" the Pentagon, distributed thirty thousand leaflets to the employees and officers, and held meetings on the premises. No arrests were made, the Secretary of Defense agreeing to the conditions put forth by the CNVA, rather than cause an "incident." A few weeks later three hundred participants in an *ad hoc* demonstration of "unrepresented people" were arrested as they walked toward the Capitol in Washington. On another occasion, to show their international character, Muste, Bayard Rustin, and others flew to Tanganyika, ready to conduct a nonviolent march into Northern Rhodesia to win independence for that country. When Britain came to terms with Kenneth Kaunda, the nationalist leader in Northern Rhodesia, the demonstration was called off.

More than anything else, the radical pacifists set a tone for the rest of the peace movement. They also rescued it from possible control by the Communists, and a one-sided approach. "It's true," said John Gates, former Communist leader and editor of the *Daily Worker*, "that if it hadn't been for Muste, there might well have been a vacuum in the peace movement into which we could have moved." Until the mid-1950's the only peace activity, other than that of old, traditional pacifist organizations such as the American Friends Service Committee and the Fellowship of Reconciliation, was conducted by a Communist peace group affiliated with the World Peace Council in Stockholm. Its propaganda was unusually weighted in one direction, criticizing all the American military preparations, but explaining away Soviet bomb tests and rearmament on the thesis that it was necessary to counteract the Americans. What the new peace movement did was to inject a note of consistency—it opposed both "war camps."

By the mid-1960's the peace movement was a rainbow of organizations stretching from moderate groups like the Committee for a Sane Nuclear Policy (SANE) to the CNVA. SANE, organized by one of Muste's followers, a personable young man named Robert Gilmore, was the largest of the organized peace groups—fifteen or twenty thousand members—with a special appeal to the nonradical element in the population. Women Strike for Peace, launched in 1961 by a Washington book illustrator, Dagmar Wilson, called itself a "non-organization." In a couple of years it had become not only national but international in scope, with counterparts as far off as New Zealand. Though it did not espouse civil disobedience, Women Strike for Peace was exclusively an "action" organization, capable of mobilizing a few thousand women in such cities as New York and Washington when the occasion demanded.

Wherever one turned in the 1960's new peace groups were emerging to supplement the old. Under the initiative of Gilmore, a Council of Correspondence was formed, composed of intellectuals in the academic field. The Student Peace Union concentrated on college students. PAX in Boston and Voters for Peace in Chicago, along with a variety of *ad hoc* groups, ran or supported thirty-two "peace" candidates for Congress in 1962. Bob Pickus in Berkeley formed Acts for Peace, an alliance of peace groups in the area, and later Turn Toward Peace, a national movement aimed at winning voluntary organizations and unions to the cause. Under the leadership of a Michigan professor, Otto Feinstein, an interuniversity committee was set up during the Viet Nam war to conduct "teach-ins." In April 1965 the Students for a Democratic Society (SDS)—youth affiliate of the pro-Socialist League for Industrial Democracy, but more leftist—mobilized twenty-five thousand students and adults in Washington to protest the Vietnamese war. It was the largest peace demonstration of the period—to be exceeded later that year.

SDS was more than a peace organization; in a sense it was an embryo political party, except that it concentrated on people under twenty-five. Its activities centered not only in the area of peace, but civil rights and jobs. SDS projects undertaken in slum areas of Newark, Chicago, Cleveland, and a few other cities sought to mobilize the poor in the war against poverty. SDS was the most dramatic youth group since World War II, with uniquely different methods from others. It adhered to the principles of a "participatory" democracy, so that most of its decisions were made not by a formal vote but by consensus. Like the civil rights group, the Student Nonviolent Coordinating Committee, with whom it has excellent relations, SDS had a low opinion of the hierarchal structure.

A contemporary of SDS, also growing rapidly, but leaning toward a vague Marxism, was the W. E. B. Dubois Clubs. Originating on the West Coast, with broad aims paralleling SDS but with more traditional methods, it spread eastward. If there were no political party viable enough to lead a crusade, semispontaneously all kinds of groups were springing up in America—especially among the youth —to hold student demonstrations against the administration of the University of California for curbing their liberties, to set up picket lines against the House Committee on Un-American Activities in Chicago, to conduct innumerable teach-ins at which they listened to opposing views on the Viet Nam war.

In this amorphous polyglot of organizations and activities were the cadres groping for something which they themselves could not yet define. If they had a single common characteristic, it was only in their refusal to be reconciled to the establishment.

Does this new radicalism have a future? Will it unite? Will it play a role in American affairs? Will it build a political party to challenge for state power? Will it remain essentially nonviolent?

There was no immediate answer. All that was clear was that if there were to be a new Left, it would have to be tailored to the measure of new problems. These problems were more ominous than those of the 1930's, but far less visible. That was the new Left's greatest handicap. The concerns of the depression era were hunger, unemployment. Those of the postwar period were nuclear incineration, civil rights, alienation, cybernation. The new radicals were convinced that these were more portentous than those of the past. But while a hungry man in 1933 was corporeally identifiable, the "menace of nuclear war" was abstract, something that could only be conjured up in the mind's eye. The unemployed of the 1930's could be marched to a relief station to demand a sack of coal, but how did one mobilize the "alienated" and "dehumanized?" How did one raise the specter of automation to union workers who lived increasingly on middle-class standards?

This was the kind of dilemma that faced the new radicals. They had not yet found the levers to prod the populace toward their banners. It was not yet clear therefore where they were going, except that they were intent on seeking radical solutions and using radical methods.

Perhaps the new radicalism is doomed. Perhaps it is not, and a new generation will mold a new kind of movement of sizable dimensions.

Who knows? All that is certain is that the radicals have in the past given America what Henri Bergson called *l'élan vital*—and may do so again.

SELECTED BIBLIOGRAPHY

This bibliography has been restricted to books. Pamphlets, articles, and newspaper clippings have been omitted because of space considerations, though in many instances they are more valuable as source material than books. Books useful as source material for a number of chapters have been referred to only in the earliest one, e.g., the Perlam-Taft *History of Labor* . . . , though listed in Chapter XII, also has relevance for Chapters XIII and XIV.

Chapter I. The Radical as History

Adamic, Louis. *Dynamite: The Story of Class Violence in America.* Viking. 1934.

Beard, Charles A. and Mary B. *The Rise of American Civilization.* Macmillan. 1927.

Bimba, Anthony. *The History of the American Working Class.* International Publishers. 1927.

Boyer, Richard O., and Morais, Herbert M. *Labor's Untold Story.* Cameron. 1955.

Commons, John R., *et al. History of Labour in the United States.* 4 vols. Macmillan. 1918–1940.

Faulkner, Harold Underwood. *Economic History of the United States.* Macmillan. 1928.

Fine, Nathan. *Labor and Farmer Parties in the United States, 1828–1928.* Rand Book Store. 1928.

Foner, Philip S. *History of the Labor Movement in the United States.* Vols. 1, 2, 3. International Publishers. 1947, 1955, 1964.

Hacker, Louis M. *The Triumph of American Capitalism.* Simon and Schuster, 1940.

Hale, William Harlan. *The March of Freedom.* Harper. 1947.

Hillquit, Morris. *History of Socialism in the United States.* Funk & Wagnalls. 1903.

Huberman, Leo. *We, the People.* Harper. 1947.

Laidler, Harry W. *A History of Socialist Thought.* Thomas Y. Crowell. 1927.

——. *Social-Economic Movements.* Thomas Y. Crowell. 1944.

Lens, Sidney. *Left, Right and Center.* Regnery. 1949.

Lorwin, Lewis I. *Labor and Internationalism.* Macmillan. 1929.

McMaster, J. B. *History of the People of the United States.* 8 vols. Appleton-Century. 1914–1934.

Madison, Charles A. *Critics & Crusaders: A Century of American Protest.* Holt. 1947.

Nomad, Max. *Rebels and Renegades.* Macmillan. 1932.

Simons, A. M. *Social Forces in American History.* Macmillan. 1913.

Symes, Lillian, and Clement, Travers. *Rebel America: The Story of Social Revolt in the United States.* Harper. 1934.

Yellen, Samuel. *American Labor Struggles.* Harcourt, Brace. 1956.

Chapter II. Colonial Rebels

Aptheker, Herbert. *The Colonial Era.* International Publishers. 1959.

——. *Negro Slave Revolts in the United States.* International Publishers. 1939.

Barck, Oscar Theodore, Jr., and Lefler, Hugh Talmage. *Colonial America.* Macmillan. 1958.

Binkely, Wilfred E. *American Political Parties.* Knopf. 1943.

Calverton, V. F. *The Awakening of America.* John Day. 1939.

Douglass, Elisha P. *Rebels and Democrats.* University of North Carolina. 1955.

Jernagan, Marcus W. *Laboring and Dependent Classes in Colonial America.* University of Chicago. 1931.

Mark, Irving. *Agrarian Conflicts in Colonial New York, 1711–1775.* Columbia University. 1940.

Morris, Richard B. *Government and Labor in Early America.* Columbia University. 1946.

Myers, Gustavus. *History of the Great American Fortunes.* Modern Library. 1936.

Nettels, Curtis P. *The Roots of American Civilization.* Crofts. 1938.

Reich, Jerome R. *Leisler's Rebellion.* University of Chicago. 1953.

Washburn, Wilcomb E. *The Governor and the Rebel: A History of*

Bacon's Rebellion in Virginia. University of North Carolina. 1958.

Winslow, O. E. *Master Roger Williams.* Macmillan. 1957.

Chapter III. The Revolution

Allen, Herbert S. *John Hancock.* Macmillan. 1948.

Axelrad, Jacob. *Patrick Henry: The Voice of Freedom.* Random House. 1947.

Dyer, Walter A. *Sons of Liberty.* Holt. 1920.

Hardy, Jack. *The First American Revolution.* International Publishers. 1937.

Harlow, Ralph Volney. *Samuel Adams.* Holt. 1923.

Heffner, Richard. *Documentary History of the United States.* New American Library. 1952.

Jameson, J. Franklin. *The American Revolution Considered as a Social Event.* Princeton University. 1926.

Kimball, Marie. *Jefferson: The Road to Glory, 1743–1776.* Coward, McCann. 1943.

Knollenberg, Bernhard. *Washington and the Revolution.* Macmillan. 1940.

Miller, John C. *Sam Adams.* Little, Brown. 1936.

———. *The Origins of the American Revolution.* Little, Brown. 1943.

Montross, Lynn. *Rag, Tail and Bobtail: The Story of the Continental Army.* Harper. 1952.

Morris, R. B., ed. *The Era of the American Revolution.* Columbia University. 1939.

Nevins, Allan. *The American States During and After the Revolution, 1775–1789.* Macmillan. 1924.

Oneal, James. *The Workers in American History.* Rand Book Store. 1921.

Pearson, Hesketh. *Tom Paine: Friend of Mankind.* Harper. 1937.

Schlesinger, Arthur. *Colonial Merchants and the American Revolution.* Frederick Ungar. 1918.

Taylor, Emerson. *Paul Revere.* Dodd, Mead. 1930.

Van Doren, Carl. *Secret History of the American Revolution.* Viking. 1941.

Van Tyne, Claude H. *The Loyalists in the American Revolution.* Macmillan. 1902.

Chapter IV. End of the Beginning

Allan, Herbert S. *John Hancock.* Macmillan. 1948.

Beard, Charles A. *An Economic Interpretation of the Constitution of the United States.* Macmillan. 1952.

Boorstin, Daniel J. *The Lost World of Thomas Jefferson.* Holt. 1948.

Bowers, Claude G. *Jefferson and Hamilton: The Struggle for Democracy in America.* Houghton, Mifflin. 1925.

Coleman, McAlister. *Pioneers of Freedom.* Vanguard. 1929.

Daver, Manning J. *The Adams Federalists.* Johns Hopkins. 1953.

Dunbar, Louise B. *A Study of Monarchical Tendencies in the United States, from 1776 to 1801.* University of Illinois. 1923.

Greene, Evarts B. *The Revolutionary Generation.* Macmillan. 1943.

Link, Eugene P. *Democratic-Republican Societies.* Columbia University. 1942.

Nevins, Allan, and Commager, Henry Steele. *America, the Story of a Free People.* Little, Brown. 1942.

Nock, Albert Jay. *Jefferson.* Harcourt, Brace. 1926.

Padover, Saul K. *A Jefferson Profile.* John Day. 1956.

Prescott, Arthur T. *Drafting the Federal Constitution.* University of Louisiana. 1941.

Rochester, Anna. *American Capitalism, 1607–1800.* International Publishers. 1949.

Schachner, Nathan. *Alexander Hamilton.* Appleton-Century. 1946.

Chapter V. Utopias and Workies

Bestor, Arthur, Jr. *Backwoods Utopias.* University of Pennsylvania. 1950.

Cole, G. D. H. *Robert Owen.* Ernest Benn (London). 1925.

Cole, Margaret. *Robert Owen of New Lanark.* Oxford. 1953.

Engels, Frederick. *Socialism: Utopian and Scientific.* International Publishers. 1935.

Harris, Herbert. *American Labor.* Yale University. 1938.

James, Marquis. *Andrew Jackson: Portrait of a President.* Bobbs-Merrill. 1937.

Lockwood, George B. *The New Harmony Movement.* Appleton. 1905.

Mumford, Lewis. *The Story of Utopias*. Harrap (London). 1923.

Nordhoff, Charles. *The Communistic Societies in the United States*. Hillary House. 1875.

Noyes, John Humphrey. *History of American Socialisms*. Lippincott. 1870.

Owen, Robert Dale. *Threading My Way*. G. W. Carleton. 1874.

Perkins, A. J. G., and Wolfson, Theresa. *Frances Wright, Free Enquirer*. Harper. 1939.

Podmore, Frank. *Robert Owen: A Biography*. Appleton. 1924.

Schlesinger, Arthur, Jr. *The Age of Jackson*. Little, Brown. 1949.

Waterman, William Randall. *Frances Wright*. Columbia University. 1924.

Wright, Frances. Edited by Paul R. Baker. *Views of Society and Manners in America*. Harvard University. 1963.

Chapter VI. The Dreams of Midpassage

Brisbane, Albert. *Association; or a Concise Exposition of the Practical Part of Fourier's Social Science*. Greeley & McElrath. 1843.
———. *Social Destiny of Man*. Stollmeyer. 1840.

Calverton, V. F. *Where Angels Dared to Tread*. Bobbs-Merrill. 1941.

Codman, John Thomas. *Brook Farm: Historic and Personal Memoirs*. Arena. 1894.

Ely, Richard T. *French and German Socialism*. Harper. 1883.

Greeley, Horace. *Recollections of a Busy Life*. J. B. Ford. 1868.

Hinds, W. A. *American Communities*. Kerr. 1902.

Holbrook, Stewart H. *Dreamers of the American Dream*. Doubleday. 1957.

Mowry, Arthur M. *The Dorr's War*. Providence. 1901.

Noyes, Pierrepont. *My Father's House: An Oneida Boyhood*. Farrar and Rinehart. 1937.

Sotheran, Charles. *Horace Greeley and Other Pioneers of American Socialism*. Mitchell Kennerley. 1915.

Swift, Lindsay. *Brook Farm: Its Members, Scholars, and Visitors*. Macmillan. 1900.

Wagner, Donald O. *Social Reformers*. Macmillan. 1934.

Ware, Norman J. *Industrial Worker, 1840–60*. P. Smith. 1924.

Wilson, Edmund. *To the Finland Station*. Doubleday. 1953.

Chapter VII. The Outside Agitators

Bartlett, Irving H. *Wendell Phillips, Brahmin Radical.* Beacon. 1961.

DuBois, William E. B. *John Brown.* International Publishers. 1962.

Foner, Philip S. *Business and Slavery.* University of North Carolina. 1941.

Garrison, W. P., and Garrison, F. J. *William Lloyd Garrison: Story of His Life Told by His Children.* 4 Vols. Unwin (London). 1885–89.

Korngold, Ralph. *Two Friends of Man.* Little, Brown. 1950.

Mandel, Bernard. *Labor: Free and Slave.* Associated Authors. 1955.

Marx, Karl, and Engels, Frederick. *The Civil War in the United States.* International Publishers. 1961.

Phillips, Ulrich B. *American Negro Slavery.* Appleton. 1918.

Schlueter, Hermann. *Lincoln, Labor, and Slavery.* Socialist Literature Co. 1913.

Sherwin, Oscar. *Prophet of Liberty: The Life and Times of Wendell Phillips.* Bookman Associates. 1958.

Siebert, Wilbur H. *The Mysteries of Ohio's Underground Railroads.* Long's College Book Co. (Columbus, Ohio). 1951.

Thomas, John L. *The Liberator, William Lloyd Garrison.* Little, Brown. 1963.

Villard, O. G. *John Brown 1800–1859.* Knopf. 1943.

Chapter VIII. The Gilded Age

Allen, James S. *Reconstruction: The Battle for Democracy.* International Publishers. 1937.

Bimba, Anthony. *The Molly Maguires.* International Publishers. 1932.

Coleman, James W. *The Molly Maguire Riots: Industrial Conflict in the Pennsylvania Coal Region.* Garrett (Richmond, Va.). 1937.

Dacus, Joseph A. *Annals of the Great Strikes.* L. T. Palmer (Philadelphia). 1877.

Destler, Chester M. *American Radicalism 1865–1901.* Connecticut College. 1946.

Dewees, Francis P. *The Molly Maguires.* Lippincott. 1877.

Dulles, Foster Rhea. *Labor in America.* Thomas Y. Crowell. 1949.

Friedman, Morris. *The Pinkerton Labor Spy*. Wilshire Book Co. 1907.

Grossman, Jonathan. *William Sylvis, Pioneer of American Labor*. Columbia University. 1945.

Hacker, L. M., and Kendrick, B. B. *United States Since 1865*. Appleton-Century. 1949.

Josephson, M. *The Robber Barons: The Great American Capitalists, 1861–1901*. Harcourt, Brace. 1934.

Martin, Edward Winslow. *The History of the Great Riots*. National Publishing Co. 1877.

Nevins, Allan. *Emergence of Modern America, 1865–1878*. Macmillan. 1954.

Pinkerton, Allan. *The Molly Maguires and the Detectives*. G. W. Dillingham. 1905.

Rayback, Joseph G. *A History of American Labor*. Macmillan. 1959.

Sandburg, Carl. *Abraham Lincoln: The Prairie Years and The War Years*. Harcourt, Brace. 1954.

Sylvis, J. C. *The Life, Speeches, Labors and Essays of William H. Sylvis*. Claxton, Remse & Haffelfinger (Philadelphia). 1872.

Todes, Charlotte. *William H. Sylvis and The National Labor Union*. International Publishers. 1942.

Chapter IX. Enter Karl Marx

Bakunin, Mikhail A. *The Political Philosophy of Bakunin*. Free Press. 1953.

Beer, M. *The Life and Teaching of Karl Marx*. Small, Maynard (Boston). 1924.

Boudin, Louis B. *Socialism and War*. New Review Publishing Association. 1916.

———. *The Theoretical System of Karl Marx*. Kerr. 1907.

Brandes, George. *Ferdinand Lassalle*. Bernard G. Richards. 1925.

David, Henry. *The History of the Haymarket Affair*. Farrar & Rinehart. 1936.

Founding of the First International: A Documentary Record. (Sept.–Nov. 1864.) International Publishers. 1937.

Fried, Albert, and Sanders, Ronald, eds. *Socialist Thought: A Documentary History*. Doubleday. 1964.

George, Charles H., ed. *Revolution: Five Centuries of Europe in Conflict.* Dell. 1962.

Handbook of Marxism. International Publishers. 1935.

Holbrook, Stewart H. *Dreamers of the American Dream.* Doubleday. 1957.

Hook, Sidney. *Towards the Understanding of Karl Marx.* John Day. 1933.

Horowitz, Irving L., ed. *The Anarchists.* Dell. 1964.

Markham, S. F. *A History of Socialism.* Macmillan. 1930.

Marx, Karl. *Capital: The Communist Manifesto and Other Writings.* Introduction by Max Eastman. Modern Library. 1932.

Mayer, Gustav. *Friedrich Engels.* Knopf. 1936.

Mehring, Franz. *Karl Marx.* Covici, Friede. 1935.

Obermann, Karl. *Joseph Weydemeyer, Pioneer of American Socialism.* International Publishers. 1947.

Parsons, Lucy E. *Life of Albert R. Parsons with a Brief History of the Labor Movement in America.* L. E. Parsons (Chicago). 1889.

Postgate, Raymond W. *Revolution from 1789 to 1906.* G. Richards (London). 1920.

Rosenberg, Arthur. *Democracy and Socialism.* Knopf. 1939.

Ruhle, Otto. *Karl Marx: His Life and Work.* Viking. 1929.

Schaack, Michael J. *Anarchy and Anarchists.* F. J. Schulte (Chicago). 1877.

Vizetelly, Ernest Alfred. *The Anarchists: Their Faith and Their Record.* John Lane. 1911.

Chapter X. The Unconsummated Marriage

Aveling, Edward, and Marx, Eleanor. *The Working Class Movement in America.* Sonnenschein (London). 1891.

Bellamy, Edward. *Looking Backward, 2000–1887.* Houghton, Mifflin. 1898.

Coxey, Jacob S. *The Coxey Plan.* J. S. Coxey (Massillon, Ohio). 1914.

Daniel De Leon: The Man and His Work. (A Symposium.) New York Labor News Co. 1926.

De Leon, Daniel. *The Burning Question of Trade Unionism.* New York Labor News. 1947.

————. *Socialist Reconstruction of Society.* New York Labor News. 1920.

George, Henry. *Progress and Poverty.* Vanguard. 1926.

Gompers, Samuel. *Seventy Years of Life and Labor.* Dutton. 1925.

Groat, George G. *Organized Labor in America.* Macmillan. 1916.

Haynes, Fred E. *Third Party Movements Since the Civil War.* State Historical Society of Iowa. 1916.

Lloyd, Henry Demarest. *Wealth Against Commonwealth.* Harpers. 1894.

Lorwin, Lewis L. *The American Federation of Labor: History, Policies and Prospects.* Brookings Institution. 1933.

McMurry, Donald L. *Coxey's Army.* Little, Brown. 1929.

Peterson, Arnold. *Daniel De Leon.* New York Labor News. 1941.

Powderly, Terence V. *Thirty Years of Labor.* Excelsior Publishing House (Columbus, Ohio). 1889.

Rochester, Anna. *The Populist Movement in the United States.* International Publishers. 1943.

Taft, Philip. *The A.F. of L. in the Time of Gompers.* Harper. 1957.

Tarbell, Ida. *The Nationalizing of Business, 1878–1898.* Macmillan. 1936.

Vincent, Henry. *The Story of the Commonweal.* W. B. Conkey Co. (Chicago). 1894.

Young, Arthur N. *The Single Tax Movement in the United States.* Princeton University. 1916.

Chapter XI. The Man from Terre Haute

Berger, Victor L. *Voice and Pen of Victor L. Berger.* Socialist Party (Milwaukee). 1929.

Coleman, McAlister. *The Man Unafraid: Eugene V. Debs.* Greenberg. 1930.

Darrow, Clarence S. *The Story of My Life.* Scribner's. 1934.

Debs, Eugene V. *Walls and Bars.* Socialist Party (Chicago). 1927.

————. *Writings and Speeches of Eugene Victor Debs.* Hermitage. 1948.

Faulkner, Harold U. *The Quest for Social Justice.* Macmillan. 1931.

Ginger, Ray. *The Bending Cross: A Biography of Eugene V. Debs.* Rutgers University. 1949.

Hillquit, Morris. *Loose Leaves from a Busy Life.* Macmillan. 1934.

Hughan, Jessie W. *American Socialism of the Present Day*. Lane. 1911.

Kelly, Edmond. *Twentieth Century Socialism*. Longmans (London). 1910.

Kipnis, Ira. *The American Socialist Movement, 1897–1912*. Columbia University. 1952.

Laidler, Harry W. *Socialism in Thought and Action*. Macmillan. 1920.

Lindsey, Almont. *The Pullman Strike*. University of Chicago. 1942.

London, Jack. *Revolution and Other Essays*. Macmillan. 1910.

MacKaye, James. *Americanized Socialism*. Doubleday, Page. 1916.

Nevins, Allan. *Grover Cleveland*. Dodd, Mead. 1948.

Quint, Howard H. *The Forging of American Socialism*. University of South Carolina. 1953.

Rogoff, H. *An East Side Epic—Meyer London*. Vanguard. 1930.

Shannon, David A. *The Socialist Party of America*. Macmillan. 1955.

Chapter XII. One Big Union

Brissenden, Paul F. *The I.W.W.* Columbia University. 1919.

Brooks, J. G. *American Syndicalism, The I.W.W.* Macmillan. 1913.

Chaplin, Ralph. *Wobbly: The Rough and Tumble Story of An American Radical*. University of Chicago. 1948.

Ebert, Justus. *The Trial of a New Society*. I.W.W. Publishing Bureau (Cleveland). 1913.

Gambs, John S. *The Decline of the I.W.W.* Columbia University. 1932.

Haywood, William D. *Bill Haywood's Book*. International Publishers. 1929.

Jensen, Vernon H. *Heritage of Conflict*. Cornell University. 1950.

Jones, Mrs. Mary (Harris). *Autobiography of Mother Jones*. Introduction by Clarence Darrow. Kerr. 1925.

Perlman, Selig, and Taft, Philip. *History of Labor in the United States, 1896–1932*. Macmillan. 1935.

Saposs, David J. *Left-Wing Unionism*. International Publishers. 1926.

Savage, Marion D. *Industrial Unionism in America*. Ronald. 1922.

Thompson, Fred. *The I.W.W.: Its First Fifty Years*. I.W.W. (Chicago). 1955.

Tridon, André. *The New Unionism*. Huebsch. 1917.

Ward, Harry F. *The Labor Movement*. Sturgis and Walton. 1917.

Chapter XIII. Ides of War and Revolution

Bing, Alexander M. *War Time Strikes and Their Adjustment.* Dutton. 1921.

Boudin, Louis B. *Socialism and War.* New Review Publishing Co. 1916.

Burns, William J. *The Masked War.* George H. Doran Co. 1913.

Chaplin, Ralph. *The Centralia Conspiracy.* I.W.W. (Chicago). 1924.

Dowell, Eldridge F. *A History of Criminal Syndicalism Legislation in the United States.* Johns Hopkins University. 1939.

Draper, Theodore. *The Roots of American Communism.* Viking. 1957.

Foster, William Z. *The Great Steel Strike.* Huebsch. 1920.

————. *Pages From a Worker's Life.* International Publishers. 1939.

Goldman, Emma. *Living My Life.* Knopf. 1931.

Hunt, Henry T. *The Case of Thomas J. Mooney and Warren K. Billings.* National Mooney-Billings Committee. 1929.

Murray, Robert K. *Red Scare: A Study in National Hysteria, 1919–1920.* University of Minnesota. 1955.

O'Connor, Harvey. *Revolution in Seattle.* Monthly Review Press. 1964.

Oneal, James. *American Communism.* Rand Book Store. 1927.

Peterson, H. C., and Fite, Gilbert C. *Opponents of War.* University of Wisconsin. 1957.

Preston, William, Jr. *Aliens and Dissenters.* Harvard University. 1963.

Reed, John. *Ten Days That Shook the World.* Boni & Liveright. 1919.

Revolutionary Radicalism. (Report of the Joint Legislative Committee Investigating Seditious Activities, Lusk Report.) J. B. Lyon Co. 1920.

Steffens, Lincoln. *The Autobiography of Lincoln Steffens.* Harcourt, Brace. 1931.

Wolfe, Bertram. *Three Who Made A Revolution.* Dial Press. 1948.

Chapter XIV. The Lost Decade

Borkenau, Franz. *World Communism: A History of the Communist International.* Norton. 1939.

Cannon, James P. *The History of American Trotskyism*. Pioneer Publishers. 1944.

Davis, Jerome. *Contemporary Social Movements*. Century. 1930.

Dunn, Robert W. *The Palmer Raids*. International Publishers. 1948.

Foster, William Z. *History of the Communist Party of the United States*. International Publishers. 1952.

———. *Misleaders of Labor*. International Publishers. 1929.

Flynn, E. G. *Debs, Haywood and Ruthenberg*. International Publishers. 1939.

Fraina, Louis C. *Revolutionary Socialism*. The Communist Press. 1918.

Frankfurter, Felix. *The Case of Sacco and Vanzetti*. Little, Brown. 1927.

Gitlow, Benjamin. *I Confess*. Dutton. 1939.

———. *The Whole of Their Lives*. Scribner's. 1948.

Hardman, J. B. S., ed. *American Labor Dynamics*. Harcourt. 1928.

Hicks, Granville. *John Reed: The Making of a Revolutionary*. Macmillan. 1936.

Howe, Irving, and Coser, Lewis. *The American Communist Party*. Praeger. 1962.

Karson, Marc. *American Labor Unions and Politics*. Southern Illinois University. 1958.

Laski, Harold J. *Communism*. Holt. 1927.

Lenin, V. I. *The Letters of Lenin*. Harcourt, Brace. 1937.

Le Rossignol, James E. *From Marx to Stalin*. Thomas Y. Crowell. 1940.

Lyons, Eugene. *The Life and Death of Sacco and Vanzetti*. International Publishers. 1927.

Nomad, Max. *Rebels and Renegades*. Macmillan. 1932.

Schneider, David M. *The Workers' (Communist) Party and American Trade Unions*. Johns Hopkins University. 1928.

Seldes, George. *World Panorama 1918–33*. Little, Brown. 1933.

Souvarine, Boris. *Stalin*. Longmans (London). 1929.

Trotsky, Leon. *The First Five Years of the Communist International*. Pioneer Publishers. 1945.

Chapter XV. The Red Decade

Alinsky, Saul. *John L. Lewis: An Unauthorized Biography*. Putnam's. 1949.

Browder, Earl. *Communism in the United States*. International Publishers. 1935.

———. *The People's Front*. International Publishers. 1938.

Coleman, McAlister. *Men and Coal*. Farrar and Rinehart. 1943.

Corey, Louis. *The Decline of American Capitalism*. Covici, Friede. 1934.

Fleischman, Harry. *Norman Thomas*. Norton. 1964.

Harris, Herbert. *Labor's Civil War*. Knopf. 1940.

Hill, Herbert, and Greenberg, Jack. *Citizen's Guide to Desegregation*. Beacon. 1955.

Hoover, J. Edgar. *Masters of Deceit*. Holt. 1958.

Howe, Irving, and Widick, B. J. *The UAW and Walter Reuther*. Random House. 1949.

Kampelman, Max. *The Communist Party vs. the C.I.O.* Praeger. 1957.

Kraus, Herbert. *The Many and the Few*. Plantin Press. 1947.

Levinson, Edward. *Labor on the March*. Harper. 1938.

Lindley, Ernest K. *The Roosevelt Revolution, First Phase*. Viking. 1933.

Lyons, Eugene. *The Red Decade: The Stalinist Penetration of America*. Bobbs-Merrill. 1941.

Mitchell, Broadus. *Depression Decade*. Rinehart. 1947.

Patterson, Haywood, and Conrad, Earl. *Scottsboro Boy*. Doubleday. 1950.

Preis, Art. *Labor's Giant Step: Twenty Years of the CIO*. Pioneer Publishers. 1964.

Rossi, A. *A Communist Party in Action*. Yale University. 1949.

Seldes, G. V. *The Years of the Locust, America, 1929–32*. Little, Brown. 1933.

Shannon, David A. *The Great Depression*. Prentice-Hall. 1960.

Stolberg, Benjamin. *Story of the C.I.O.* Viking. 1938.

Vorse, Mary Heaton. *Labor's New Millions*. Modern Age Books. 1938.

Wechsler, James A. *Labor Baron, a Portrait of John L. Lewis*. Morrow. 1944.

Chapter XVI. Epilogue and Prologue

Anderson, Jackson, and May, Ronald W. *McCarthy: The Man, the Senator, the Ism*. Beacon. 1952.

Brock, Clifton. *Americans for Democratic Action.* Public Affairs Press. 1962.

Browder, Earl. *The Second Imperialist War.* International Publishers. 1940.

———. *Teheran and America.* Workers Library Publishers. 1944.

Draper, Hal. *Berkeley: The New Student Revolt.* Grove Press. 1965.

Fryer, Peter. *Hungarian Tragedy.* Dennis Dobson (London). 1957.

Gates, John. *The Story of an American Communist.* Thomas Nelson. 1958.

Goodman, Paul, ed. *Seeds of Liberation.* George Braziller. 1964.

Harrington, Michael. *The Other America. Poverty in the United States.* Macmillan. 1962.

Hentoff, Nat. *Peace Agitator: The Story of A. J. Muste.* Macmillan. 1963.

Kempton, Murray. *Part of Our Time.* Simon and Schuster. 1955.

King, Martin Luther, Jr. *Stride Toward Freedom.* Harper. 1958.

Lens, Sidney. *The Crisis of American Labor.* Sagamore Press. 1959.

———. *The Futile Crusade.* Quadrangle. 1964.

Lomax, Louis. *Negro Revolt.* Harper. 1962.

Macdonald, Dwight. *Henry Wallace, The Man and the Myth.* Vanguard. 1948.

Macdougall, Curtis D. *Gideon's Army.* Marzani & Munsell. 1965.

Mills, C. Wright. *New Men of Power.* Harcourt, Brace. 1948.

INDEX

[379]